Nineteenth-Century French Poetry

Twayne's Critical History of Poetry Series
FRENCH LITERATURE

David O'Connell, Editor
Georgia State University

NINETEENTH-CENTURY FRENCH POETRY

MICHAEL BISHOP
Dalhousie University

Twayne Publishers • New York
Maxwell Macmillan Canada • Toronto
Maxwell Macmillan International • New York Oxford Singapore Sydney

Twayne's Critical History of Poetry Series

Nineteeth-century French Poetry
Michael Bishop

Copyright © 1993 by Twayne Publishers

Twayne Publishers
Macmillan Publishing Company
866 Third Avenue
New York, New York 10022

Maxwell Macmillan Canada, Inc.
1200 Eglinton Avenue East
Suite 200
Don Mills, Ontario M3C 3N1

Library of Congress Cataloging-in-Publication Data

Bishop, Michael, 1938-
    Nineteenth-century French poetry/Michael Bishop.
       p.   cm. —(Twayne's critical history of poetry series.
    French literature)
    Includes bibliographical references and index.
    ISBN 0-8057-8453-5
    1. French poetry—19th century—History and criticism. I. Title.
II. Title: 19th century French poetry. III. Series.
PQ431.B57   1993
841'.709—dc20

93-27520
CIP

The paper used in this publication meets the minimum requirements of American National Standard for Information Sciences—Permanence of Paper for Printed Library Materials. ANSI Z3948-1984.∞™

10 9 8 7 6 5 4 3 2 1

Printed in the United States of America

· Contents ·

· *Underpinnings, Windows, Choices:* ·
An Introduction

To speak of the great poets of nineteenth-century France is, wittingly or implicitly, with or without an intertextual reading of them, to found a discourse upon a poetic tradition still fresh with the refined, even precious, but straining, yearning lyricism of Chénier and Florian, a tradition arching back—over the charm and personal power of Bertran de Born, Chrétien de Troyes, and Jaufré Rudel—to the orality and anonymity of *La Chanson de Roland.* Just as the major poets of our own age—from Reverdy, Apollinaire, and Eluard to Ponge and Char, Bonnefoy and Deguy—have known and often defined themselves in various degrees of counterdistinction to the poets who concern us in this book, so do the latter pastiche and challenge, rethink and develop, the great and diverse mosaic upon which French poetry itself stands in the crucial period of 1820 to 1880. Thus Marceline Desbordes-Valmore, with whose work I open this study—the choice is at once chronological and emblematic—does not only stand in special, historic relation to those women poets that long precede her: Marie de France, Pernette du Guillet, and Louise Labé. Beyond feminine spirituality and culture in general, there are the bonds of rhythm, rhetoric, and poetic process that tie her to factors arguably beyond gender, to the vast, teeming heritage of French poiesis. Although I have little occasion, for lack of space, to demonstrate both the specific and the broad poetic rootings of Lamartine and Vigny, Rimbaud and Laforgue, and have, if anything, preferred to look on to the contemporary impact and legacy of their work, I do wish to stress here the crucial technical, aesthetic, tonal, and psycho-philosophical underpinnings that literally make possible an enormous *Jocelyn* by Lamartine, a "last sonnet" by Mallarmé, the antipoems of Lautréamont's *Poésies.* Thus is it that, like faded palimpsests below the surface of much of the nineteenth-century poetry I shall discuss, there lie the sure marks of Guillaume de Lorris's and Jean de

Underpinnings, Windows, Choices: An Introduction

Meung's *Roman de la Rose,* with the former's insistence upon courtly love, dream, socio-psycho-mystical allegory, the latter's rather clashing predilection for rationalism and irony and the resultant tensions between art and didacticism. Thus is it that, between the lines of a Vigny poem or many a text by Hugo or Lamartine, we may read, spectrally, the quizzical realism of Rutebeuf's fabliaux, the pulling between his earthiness and his impersonalness, or else a Charles d'Orléans's delicately elegiac melancholy and apolitical lyricism. Reading Baudelaire or Rimbaud or Lautréamont, does the mind not slip through the chimera of time to the sheer individual power of Villon's poetic voice, with its extensive range of tone and inspiration, its linguistic vigor, its blatant confessional impact? Does not Marot, with the ingenious intricacies of his rondeaux, his ballades and his chansons, and does not Scève, with the powerful factors of concentration, limitation, and enshrinement that guide his *Délie,* join hands across the ages not only with Mallarmé and Verlaine but with Hugo in certain modes and, again, Desbordes-Valmore, Lamartine, and Vigny? And how can the great poetic surges of this postrevolutionary century be adequately envisaged without at least a parenthetic acknowledgment of the *Pléiade* poets? Does not Du Bellay, while linking contemporary culture to the Greek and Latin traditions and to the exquisite advances of Italian poetry, claim for the French language that power of articulation Hugo and others will varyingly renew; do not his formal innovativeness and his fusing of the lyrical and the humanistic pave the way for those otherwise barely conceivable advances in technique and treatment that prime the liberation of romantic and postromantic poets alike? And Ronsard, rediscovered almost 250 years after his death in 1585, does he not emblematize for all who admire him the ultra-delicate problematics of the interpenetration of art and existence, the eternal slippages from sensuality and sentimentality to spirituality and aesthetics, within what one might call the culture, the cultivation, of our experience of the earth? And so on, through the tragic somberness and spiritual ethics of D'Aubigné, the purism and rhetorical stiffness of Malherbe, the persiflage of Saint-Amant, the pastoral yet socially alert verse of Racan, to the philosophical classicalness of La Fontaine, the practical clarification and the isolating, anti-instinctual perfectionism of Boileau, the darkly beautiful, swirling passions of Racine.

Underpinnings, Windows, Choices: An Introduction

To speak of Vigny, Rimbaud, and Laforgue in 1993 is also, of course, to come to terms with a modern criticism, sprawling but interconnected—*les différences d'un même* ("differences of sameness"), Deguy might say—which largely emerged during the self-conscious "periods" of romanticism, realism and symbolism, fired as it so frequently was by the existential-cum-aesthetic interrogations and theories of the major poets themselves. Indeed, modern literary theory not only coincides with this secondary flowering but remains fascinated with its origins, returning implacably to Baudelaire or Mallarmé or even to the bare, self-reflexive scribblings of Rimbaud, to anchor and justify its own elucubrations. My own approach has not sought to attach itself to the prestige, but also the limitations, of a particular contemporary methodology. I speak of form without acceding to the more radical temptations of Propp or the more supple options of Todorov or Genette. I inevitably structure and shape a discourse, while remaining alert to contradiction, paradox, tension, and yet seeking to prevent my perception of textual polysemia, *indécidabilité* ("undecidability"), or overall intrinsic self-deconstruction, from allowing broad and determining lines of force to articulate themselves. My foci are often multiple, and in that merely reflect the teeming fascinations and functional modes of the poets themselves. Thus will there be elements of Bachelard, flashes of Jean-Pierre Richard, shades of Blanchot, touches à la Barthes or à la Sartre. But I invoke no specific critical gods, while recognizing in the broadest terms possible the impacts of persons as widely divergent as Starobinski, Poulet, Proust, Camus, Jakobson, Goldmann, Cohen, Derrida, Lacan, Lawler, Bowie, Caws, Knapp, and Riffaterre. And here I speak of a general critical optic, where debts are at times difficult to weigh. Needless to say, my debts to the very many major critics who have thrown so much light upon the poetry of the nineteenth century are considerable, and I have gone some way at least in acknowledgment of them in the selected bibliography given at the end of this study. The windows, in short, that I have endeavored to keep open upon the poetry at hand are numerous, though the source of the light flooding through them is obscured by time's multiple crisscrossings. This said, the detail and coherence of perceptions are mine, and they are based upon intimate rereadings of the entire poetic oeuvre of each poet.

Underpinnings, Windows, Choices: An Introduction

A few final remarks are in order. First, I have elected to speak of only ten central poetic figures of the century: Desbordes-Valmore, Lamartine, Vigny, Baudelaire, Hugo, Mallarmé, Verlaine, Rimbaud, Laforgue, and Lautréamont. My primary task I have thus felt to be that of offering a compact but personally probing and textually alert critical analysis of the principal parameters and the complex integrity of these ten poetic oeuvres, deemed to be intrinsically powerful and historically determining. Secondly, omissions have been difficult but, I hope, compensated by both the increased intensity of analysis thus permitted and the parentheses opened at times upon the poets thus sidelined: Musset, Gautier, Nerval, and Leconte de Lisle principally, but also Nouveau, Corbière, Cros, Banville, and others. There will be some who will be particularly sorry to see no specific account of Nerval. I share their sentiments. I have, however, chosen to remain within certain rough generic limits in my discussion of poetry—for the nineteenth century this means versified texts and prose forms consciously designated as poems: Baudelaire's *Le Spleen de Paris*, Lautréamont's *Poésies*, and so on. To have gone beyond the eight beautiful poems of Nerval's *Les Chimères* and the handful of *autres chimères* to *Les Filles du feu* and other *récits* would have also obliged me to plunge into *Les Misérables*, and much else. Let me add that if I deem the seminal power of the ten poetic oeuvres to be beyond dispute, my liking remains undiminished for the now jaunty, now sentimental, always somewhat unpredictable work of Musset, the sculpted, restrained Parnassian lyricism of Gautier, or the exquisite gravity and discretion of Leconte de Lisle. Thirdly, my decision to give preference to the coherence, the tensions, and the essential individual integrity of a given oeuvre has meant that I have refused the temptations of neat historical compartmentalizations, schools, overly reductive isms. This does not mean, as will be readily seen, that I have ignored factors of evolution in sensibility, in consciousness, and in form, but I have sought to remain alert also to elements of continuity beyond strict historical evolution. It is for this reason that my own discourse is intimately immersed in the specificity of poetic textuality; and it is for this reason, too, that I endeavor to remain sensitive to the originality of each poet's self-perception rather than shroud the poet in a lacework of preconceptions or sweeping generalizations for the sake of a history quickly parceled into myth.

· ONE ·

Desbordes-Valmore

Actress, mother of five—two dying in infancy—Marceline Desbordes-Valmore came relatively late to poetry, a lateness that did
not, however, prevent her from becoming the focus of a profound
and wide admiration shared by contemporaries such as Lamartine,
Hugo, Baudelaire, Sainte-Beuve, and Mallarmé. Verlaine and
Rimbaud were to fall under the charm and the power of her most
unrhetorical rhetoric of love, and the surrealists were unambiguous in their praise of her unaltered passion: Breton claims her for
the cause in his 1924 *Manifeste du surréalisme* (*Manifesto of Surrealism*), and Aragon deems her "one of the greatest poets, not just of
the nineteenth century, but of all time." The "queen" of lived emotions rather than of theory, of sweeping ideas, in Hugo's assessment, Marceline Desbordes-Valmore pushes to an extreme limit
what Verlaine was rightly to perceive as a natural poetics of self-
giving, of gift beyond recall. It is no doubt in this perspective that
this "extraordinary poet," as Verlaine calls her, may be characterized by Baudelaire—beyond misogyny, I believe. The context is
clear: Baudelaire knows that a deeply alternative, feminine discourse has been founded for a modernity perhaps still to be born—
as "woman, . . . always woman, . . . absolutely only woman."
   Born on 20 June 1786, in Douai, Desbordes-Valmore may be slow
to articulate publicly her nascent sensibility, but to her go both the
shared glory of romantic fervor, unhesitant self-discovery, and vigorous yet discreet self-confession, and the unpretentious yet radical affirmation of a newly spun femininity. Her deeply marked and
maturing youthful consciousness returns from the painful loss of
her mother in the Guadeloupe adventure of 1801–1802, to wrestle
with the dilemmas of vulnerability and protection in a postrevolutionary France still dominated by masculine psychology and sociology. Her determining liaison at the age of twenty with Henri de
Latouche was to soar and sputter for a number of years, her child

by him dying in 1810. This period sees the publication of her first poems (1807), but it is not until 1819–1820, after her marriage to the actor Prosper Valmore (1817), that her first poetic collections appear: *Elégies et Poésies* (*Elegies and Poems*), along with certain prose *récits* of a quasi-autobiographical nature.

Residing largely either in Lyon—in the oddly great French feminine literary tradition—or Paris, Desbordes-Valmore lived a life of individual and collective upheaval, of increasing practical, material difficulty, yet a life whose chagrins are shot through with the shimmering light of love, adoration, and faith. Three volumes of her *Poésies* (*Poems*), appeared in 1830, and the decade or so that followed confirmed her exquisite and uncluttered poetic genius: *Les Pleurs* (*Tears*, 1833), *Pauvres Fleurs* (*Poor Flowers*, 1839), *Bouquets et prières* (*Bouquets and Prayers*, 1843). Her death on 23 July 1859 followed that of her much-loved children, Ondine and Inès.

Critical attention has been sluggish despite the proclamations of other great poets, but the efforts of Lucien Descaves, Jacques Boulenger, Jeanine Moulin, Eliane Jasenas, Marc Bertrand, and Yves Bonnefoy have finally told. Her role in the creation of modern French poetry is seminal and definitive. The essential judgment behind Bonnefoy's asssessment of her "Rêve intermittent d'une nuit triste" ("Broken Dream one sad night") carries into her oeuvre at large: "an extraordinary poem, at the almost outer limits of Western poetry" (*P*, 24).

Love

Love is the mistress power driving the entire work and, if we are to believe this work, the entire existence of Marceline Desbordes-Valmore. It is the "muse" and the "breaker" of that same muse, as she declares in one of her earliest and greatest poems, "La Nuit d'hiver" ("Winter's Night"), published in 1819 and taken up again in the 1830 edition of *Poésies* (*P*, 39). Love always is sensed by Desbordes-Valmore to be a force of totality and absoluteness, and as such it embodies contradiction and paradox that render its experience full, complete, profound. "Son Image" ("Her Image"), from the same early period, speaks of the blissful oblivion wrought by love (*P*, 37) and "Elégie" clarifies that it is a matter of "Supreme felicity,/Complete self-oblivion,/The need to love for love's sake" (*P*, 45), while at the same time arguing the centrality of that self-revelation that love surprisingly performs: "I knew myself not at all, I had not loved./Love! if you could not, who could teach me?" Not dissimilarly, "Je ne sais plus, je ne veux plus" ("I don't know, I don't want any more"), also from this early collection, evokes like a Scève or a Louise Labé, the emotional intricacies of even the most constant and transparent of loves (*P*, 56). Many poems, and from all periods, speak not just of the possible painful corollaries of what Marceline Desbordes-Valmore terms, in an 1853 poem reproduced by Verlaine in *Les Poètes maudits*, "the cross of love" (*P*, 225), but also of love as an act, Christlike but rationally hazardous; of martyrdom, of self-sacrificial giving (cf. *P*, 142)—an act of the deepest, the most precarious, delicacy, linked to one's greatest vulnerability because to one's greatest availability. "On pleure dès qu'on aime" ("One weeps from the moment one loves"), we read in this moving "Jours d'été" ("Summer Days") of *Bouquets et prières* (*P*, 150), love occasioning an immediate and exquisite flowering of this sensibility, understood here as the site of a complex awakening to our inner spiritual wealth. Thus, if love is self-exposure, it remains "ma force" (*P*, 156), the ultimate locus and logic of existence: "Ah! for a day of lovers' life," Desbordes-Valmore affirms in an 1830 poem, "Qui ne mourrait? la vie est dans l'amour" ("Who would not die? Life is in love"; *P*, 67).

For love is felt to involve a confusion of being, an intertwining of form and spirit, inevitably disturbing but powerfully transmuting, that, for Desbordes-Valmore, as she suggests in one of her numerous early *élégies*, would root itself in ontological designs beyond our immanence yet available to our intuition and to our capacity for recognition:

> "I belonged to you perhaps before seeing you.
> My life, emerging, was promised to yours:
> Your name warned me with unforeseen emotion,
> Your soul hid within to awaken mine
> ("Elégie": "J'étais à toi . . ." ["I was yours . . . "], *P*, 43).

Not surprisingly, as the same poem from the *Poésies* will conclude, love is the alpha and omega of (her) existence; the relationship with Henri de Latouche is conjured here, but finally love is a much vaster, cosmic project, beyond even the tight affinities evoked.

Love also reveals itself in plurivalent signs and emblems of vision, sound, sentiment:

> Nom chéri! nom charmant! oracle de mon sort!
> Hélas! que tu me plais, que ta grâce me touche!
> Tu m'annonças la vie, et, mêlé dans la mort,
> Comme un dernier baiser tu fermeras ma bouche.

> Charming, beloved name! oracle of my fate!
> Ah! how you delight me, how your grace touches me!
> You told me of life, and, mingled in death,
> You will seal my lips with a final kiss.

(*P*, 44)

The plurivalency of love is, indeed, evident: "il veut dire à la fois bonheur, éternité,/... puissance ... divine" ("it means at once happiness, eternity,/divine power"; "Elégie": "Je m'ignorais..." ["I knew myself not..."], *P*, 45). Love's meaning is of here and now, but also divinely transcendent, like the brilliance of that "love of a day," shining through the "nights" of years, illuminating the "soul" with the fresh eternalness of the lived instant. Plurivalency could, of course, be said to imply ambivalence—"Often death is in love," we read in "L'Amour" from the *Poésies* (*P*, 68)—but, with Desbordes-Valmore, no real disintegration occurs: the depth of her love always remains undefinable, beyond quantification, limit, nameableness (cf. "Avant toi" ("Before you"), *P*, 115); its thirst is constant, infinitely welling up, quite beyond reciprocity. The logic of love is thus plunged, always, implicitly, into a nostalgia of completeness and entirety, a remembrance of that time, beyond time, "quand j'aimais sans savoir ce que j'aimais, quand l'âme/Me palpitait heureuse, et de quoi? Je ne sais" ("when I loved not knowing what I loved, when my soul/Quivered in happiness, for what? I know not"), as Desbordes-Valmore expresses it in "L'Impossible" from *Les Pleurs* (*P*, 98).

Such a nostalgia, perhaps inevitably, stems from the privileged sense of love's pure equilibrium, of love's rustic symphoniousness, experienced in the all too brief, but determining contact with the adored and adoring mother before the fateful journey to Guadeloupe: "her dreamy voice/... lilted with harmonious love,/That my heart drank in playing in the yard!", Desbordes-Valmore recalls in the intense yet simple "La Maison de ma mère" ("My

Mother's House") from *Pauvres fleurs* (*Poor Flowers*, *P*, 109). It is steeped, too, in an overriding sense of love's purity, a "belief" in love's divineness, in the divine slow birth and death of all that is. "At the hour falling slow and sacred,/As one listens to God, so I listened to love" ("Avant toi," *P*, 115). The wisdom of love is, far from the "wisdom" of the world, not anchored in caution and calculation. Its "care," as Deguy might say, and not unlike Heidegger, is impetuous, of deeply ontic, not simply worldly, pertinence; its reason is intrinsic, self-justifying, nonutilitarian, yet linked to the only practice worthy of humanity. ("Ne sachant bien *qu'aimer* je priais Dieu pour vous" ("Knowing *only to love*, I prayed for you to God"), Desbordes-Valmore cries out in the late "Ondine à l'école" ("Ondine at school," 1848, Bonnefoy suggests). Love is the very genius, the exquisite savoir-faire, of Marceline Desbordes-Valmore. No wonder, in her deep (un)earthly wisdom, she will recommend it, in "Les Prisons et les prières" ("Prisons and Prayers") of the same period (and posthumously published in the 1860 *Poésies inédites* [*Unpublished Poems*], as an exclusive guide for her troubled compatriots:

> Ô France! il faut aimer, il faut rompre les chaînes,
> Ton Dieu, le Dieu du peuple, a tant besoin d'amour!

> Oh France, Love must reign, the chains must be broken,
> Your God, the people's God, needs love so much
>
> (*P*, 231)

If, as "La Nuit d'hiver" already hints (*P*, 39), there is a profound distinction to be made between living love and "saying" love, such a distinction removes nothing of the urgency and beauty of love's ontic, livable meaning.

Divineness

In Desbordes-Valmore's work, as with every other major poet of the century, down to Rimbaud and even Laforgue and Lautréamont, the notion of "God" retains a certain centrality. Divineness in general remains, however, beyond ideology and the niceties of refined theological definition. It is a given barely nameable yet indisputable, absolute—a given in which we participate, as does the humble glow-worm, like some "étincelle échappée à la source divine,/[qui] n'appar[aît] que pour briller" ("some spark broke loose from divine origin,/appearing but to shine forth"; "Le Ver luisant" ["The Glow-worm"], *P*, 63), in a spectacular flash of presence as sufficient unto itself as Jaccottet's gleaming catkins caught in the light of being before their fall to dust. It is true that Desbordes-Valmore's sense of God may be said to be bound to more traditional patterns and expression. God is "personal," has voice, can be listened and prayed to (see "Le Dernier Rendez-vous," *P*, 70); and churches have a high relevance. Yet all of this accomplishes itself in a perspective, as she so straightforwardly puts it in "Tristesse" ("Sadness"), from *Les Pleurs*, "sans pompe, sans culte et sans prêtre" ("without pomp, cult, or priest) (*P*, 85). Divineness is not as overtly pagan or majestically cosmic as in Hugo; nor is it occult, ritualized, or simply intellectualized as, explicitly or implicitly, in Nerval. But it does penetrate all, via both her instinct and her will, a received and a desired sense of the world. Not only can her father, in all the simplicity of his proffered hand, assume the proportions of God (cf. "Tristesse," *P*, 87); not only can she herself understand herself to be, "Lord! . . . a little of yourself/Fallen from your diadem" ("Au Christ" ["To Christ"], *P*, 140); but, as the beautiful poem "Départ de Lyon" ("Leaving Lyon") from *Bouquets et prières* makes clear, the very life of the most anonymous and humble of phenomena, that of barely glimpsed, "unknown" flowers in the topmost gutter of some untraceable Lyon tenement, constitutes for her "un divin moment" (*P*, 153), a splendid instance of divineness made available to s/he who remains available to its passage.

Certainly, as "Au Christ" demonstrates, the sense of the divine can spell awe and quick fright, but the "angelicism" of Marceline Desbordes-Valmore is neither Mallarméan, elitist-aesthetic, nor fondly, absently transcendent: it manifests itself always, first, as a mode, curiously, of immanence. "J'aimais tant les anges" ("I so loved angels"), Desbordes-Valmore tells us in the 1843 "Jours d'été", "Gliding in the sunlight!/A pure flowing,/Of unparalleled love" (*Bouquets et prières*, *P*, 147). It is the angelicism of presence, human or other, a divineness linked to the light, the fire, the dancing movement of life. "Jour d'Orient" ("Eastern Day"), another of the poems quoted by Verlaine in *Les poètes maudits* and taken up by Revilliod in the posthumous *Poésies inédites* (Geneva, 1860), speaks of "a day of divine charity/When eternity moves forth in the blue air" (*P*, 173). Divineness, here as elsewhere, not only is linked to feelings of love, togetherness, harmony, and an interlocked being in which timelessness and temporality fuse seamlessly, but becomes synonymous with the very fact of being, breathing, doing, thinking, and unthinking. "Rêve intermittent d'une nuit triste" ("Broken Dream One Sad Night," *P*, 206–210), which Bonnefoy describes as "one of the most beautiful poems of our language, [a poem] which would suffice in itself to place its author alongside the greatest of those 'masters' she was afraid to be compared with" (cf. *P*, 263), evokes similarly the divineness of all actuality, of all upsurging being: the birth of Desbordes-Valmore's third child, Inès, the "divine source" from which rises the milk that is to feed this "frail water nymph" (*P*, 208), the pure angelicalness of Inès' newborn fragility: "En la soulevant par ses blanches aisselles/J'ai cru bien souvent que j'y sentais des ailes!" ("Raising her by her white underarms/I often thought that I could feel wings!"; *P*, 208). Such sentiments are not to be construed as merely rhetorical: they constitute, rather, the expression of an innocence, a brilliant spiritual simplicity that *sees* and *feels* the deep grace of presence, that knows all to be a gift of astonishing proportion and significance. In this optic, all phenomena may be read as "divine books like leaves from the heavens" (*Poésies inédites, P*, 227), and all experience becomes extraordinary, whether it be the sight and touch of Ondine's hair ("more divine veil . . ./Never has shaded child's face" ["Ondine à l'école", *P*, 212]) or that remarkable evocation of "L'Ame errante" ("Wandering Soul," *P*, 215), also from the *Poésies inédites,* where, again, consciousness melds the ephemeral and the "godly," matter and soul, with uncluttered ease:

> Je suis la prière qui passe
> Sur la terre où rien n'est à moi;
> Je suis le ramier dans l'espace,
> Amour, où je cherche après toi.
> Effleurant la route féconde,
> Glanant la vie à chaque lieu,
> J'ai touché les deux flancs du monde,
> Suspendue au souffle de Dieu.

> I am the passing prayer
> Upon the earth where nothing is mine;
> I am the woodpigeon in space,
> Love, seeking after you.

Skimming the fecund way,
Gleaning life in every place,
I have touched both sides of the world,
Hanging upon the breath of God.

Earth

Marceline Desbordes-Valmore's sense of the divine is thus rooted in the most intense traversal of the quotidian, of what Bonnefoy calls *présence*. "Révélation," one of the greatest poems of this 1833 collection *Les Pleurs*, describes eloquently this traversal, which is one of sensory contact, love, belonging—but an intimacy beyond possession—and emotional, psychic illumination:

L'été, le monde ému frémit comme une fête;
La terre en fleurs palpite et parfume sa tête;
Les cailloux plus cléments, loin d'offenser nos pas,
Nous font un doux chemin; on vole, on dit tout bas:
"Voyez! tout m'obéit, tout m'appartient, tout m'aime!
Que j'ai bien fait de naître!"

In summer, the moved world trembles as in celebration;
The flowered earth quivers and scents its head;
The gentle pebbles, far from offending our steps,
Offer a sweet pathway; we fly along, whispering:
"Look! all obeys me, belongs to me, loves me!
How my birth was well chosen!"

(*P*, 77)

The deep but instinctive, unprepared wisdom of presence, of terrestrial lesson, is very much a mark of Marceline Desbordes-Valmore's poetics. Her death, she hopes, will confirm her, and those she loves, as "amants de la terre" ("Lovers of the earth"), as "Révélation" also tells us. The day-fly, living sign of *l'éphémère*, of our terrestrial passingness, is the vibrant (and symbolic) joining of our apparent "nothingness" or what Deguy would call *insignifiance* and our capacity to incarnate happiness, energy, or spirit as meaning, as self-sufficient mystery. "Happy nothingness! your career dwells in these flowers./Drink in your life from the soul, and may your swift breath/Savor all the scents that quench the meadow" ("L'Ephémère," *P*, 102). "Départ de Lyon" offers a delicate yet vigorous appraisal of the poet's immersion in the bounty and splen-

· 8 ·

dor of what Bonnefoy calls "les choses du simple" ("the things of the simple"):

> Charmes des blés mouvants! fleurs des grandes prairies!
> Tumulte harmonieux élevé des champs verts!
> Bruits des nids! flots courants! chantantes rêveries!
> N'êtes-vous qu'une voix parcourant l'univers?

> Magic of swaying wheatfields! flowers of open meadows!
> Harmonious uproar risen from green pastures!
> Nesting sounds! running waters! singing revery!
> Are you but a voice traversing the universe?

> > (*P*, 154)

Here, as commonly elsewhere, the world falls upon the poet as a nearly ineffable (witness the exclamations) but gentle magic. All is movement, at once tumultuous, almost chaotic, and yet symphonic, finally orchestrated—sung tellurism, the exquisitely dreamed melody of some universality rendered present, audible, visible, tangible, mortal. "Jour d'Orient," from *Poésies inédites*, similarly links dream to ephemeralness, intense passage through the "hour of birds, scents and sun" (*P*, 173) to a total and curious "oubli de tout" ("total oblivion") that we have seen before and that would tend to evoke that experience of the earth of which Bonnefoy speaks at the close of *Dans le leurre du seuil* (*In the Lure of the Threshold*):

> . . . the sky
> Today,
> something gathering, dispersing.
> . . . the sky,
> Infinite
> Yet suddenly surging entire in the brief pool

This is an experience in which ontic origin is stunningly understood as ever of the *hic et nunc*, when, as Desbordes-Valmore so inconspicuously puts it, "the earth plays and becomes a child once more" (*P*, 173). The moving "Rêve intermittent d'une nuit triste"— the poem was "received" at the time of Marceline's long watch beside her dying daughter, Inès—opens with an intense apostrophizing of her native earth, with its gentle fields and yoke elms, its waves of innocent young children, its cool, clear waters nourishing goats and reeds. If the evocation is specific, it is equally, and typically, at the limits of articulation: "Oh land of my birth! to your beloved name/My soul goes off in utter ecstasy" (*P*, 206): the experience of the earth, and especially of privileged, lived loci, can often lead to that "unsayableness" to which Desbordes-Valmore quite frequently alludes in her most personal of poems, yet which never prevents her from conveying a sense of that simple yet richly affecting meaning of traversed presence. The 1836 poem from *Pauvres fleurs*, "A Monsieur A. L." ("To Mr. A. L."), centered upon the terrible massacres of starving men, women and children in Lyon in 1834, insistently focuses upon the fact of "being-there" (cf. *P*, 124): its tone is exclamatory because earthly experience is poignantly unrepeatable, its meaning nearly unspeakable. No doubt this explains Desbordes-Valmore's proclivity for designating specific place and time in her poetry. The Lyon poems are good examples (*P*, 125, 129, 133, 139). But so, too, are those that evoke Douai, "notre Flandre verte" ("Our green Flanders," (*P*, 135), her "native soil" (*P*, 134), or "Rouen, rue Ancrière." Desbordes-Valmore's experience of the earth, however, no matter how plunged into the specificity of sensoriness, topography, or lived history, remains available to a sacredness, an emblematicalness of mortality that, without diminishing its urgency, situates it within some emotionally, spiritually heightening context. Her "native soil" cannot but be a "gentle dot in the Universe" ("Rêve intermittent d'une nuit triste," *P*, 210).

Dream and Project

If the earth can anchor, attach, and charm, then dream, in the poetics of Desbordes-Valmore, as with poets from the romantic and the surrealist period and beyond into formalist idealism, can offer the appealing counter-logic of pure irreality, the temptation of suspended, ethereal life: "ma vie . . . dans ce rêve où tu ne fuis jamais" ("Elégie": "Toi qui m'as . . ."/"You who have . . .," *P*, 41). With Desbordes-Valmore this can become manifest in certain poems upon childhood (see *P*, 94) or in others devoted to the intricacies of projected, "dreamed" continuity of love, where dream hovers between a lived past and a wanting present, between a determining experience of body and soul and the unearthliness, yet lived sentimentality, of soul-hope, of trust in the power of "dreams":

Go, my soul, above the passing crowds,
Like bird bathing in space.
Go and see! To return only having touched
Dream . . . my beautiful dream hidden from the earth
("Le Nid solitaire," *P*, 193)

It must not, however, be overlooked that Desbordes-Valmore's poetics of the dream always entails a belief both in the real "enchantability" of existence and in the idea that a (senti)mental project is not only possible but essential. Life, in this optic, is no longer a submission, a passive exposure; it can become, rather, the object of our creation, a place in which our self-project, the project of all otherness, all being, may unfold with meaning and a sense of deep pertinence. "Credulousness" (see "Tristesse," *P*, 87), far from being a refusal of clarity of vision, looks upon the world with confidence, trust, and love. Only to the extent that "lucidity" is equated with skepticism and fear may the projection of "credulousness" upon what is, be said to be a refusal of lucidity. "Le monde est en nous" ("The world is within"), she affirms in "Ma Fille" ("My Daughter"), and, in consequence, she urges us to "remain within ourselves" (*P*, 96)—in our only true locus of being, wherein our self-project and our entire ontological project can be lived, felt— willed into being, Bonnefoy suggests in *La Présence et l'image*. "I invented via the world a path to you" ("Avant toi," *P*, 113) is thus no idle trope, no mere decorative *fioriture;* rather is it the sign of a belief in our invention of all being, doing, even dying (see *P*, 124), an assumption of existence less à la Vigny or Sartre, altogether less stoical than joyous—a penetration of the meaning of love, of its very possibility. "Ennemi de lui seul!" she says of Leopardi, "aimer, et ne pas croire!" ("His own enemy! Loving, and not believing")—love being the firmly knowable proof of a confident project buoying us up, but easily denied within us, easily transformed—equally by will and project—into chance, into something totally unassumed as meaning within us ("Au livre de Léopardi" ["To Leopardi's Book], *Poésies inédites*, *P*, 189–90).

It is here that we can see the degree to which Desbordes-Valmore does not participate in that "former movement of hope," as Bonnefoy calls it, of modern Mallarméan, aestheticizing poetry, and can realize the extent of her poetry's final reliance upon an experience of the real borne up by the further "hope" of her trust in love, birth, childhood, and what I have termed her awareness of the possibility of the ontological (self-) project. Memory and thought, as we shall see, are part of this project; but, more importantly, feeling—love, hope—can, beyond all illusion, determine the *quality* of what is, of the "world . . . within us" (see *P*, 96). Such a hope can, at times, give the clear impression of detaching itself from the fleeting shadowiness of immediacy—"Put your hands over my eyes," the poet cries out in "Ma Fille," "Show me hope and hide away the earth" (*P*, 95)—but this poem is also the site of her total assumption of the world as self-project. Rather Desbordes-Valmore's poetics of hope should be seen as assimilated to the logic of love, of *confiance* ("confidence") as Bonnefoy perceives it. It offers a sense of the co-extensiveness of the upswelling of being, ontic breath, and our possible affective buoyancy in "the air in which hope swims" ("Cantique des bannis" ["Canticle of the Outlawed,"] *P*, 133). Desbordes-Valmore's father's injunction, "singing for all: 'Hope! hope! hope!'" ("Rêve intermittent," *P*, 208), echoes through the entire work of the poet, allowing the temptations of elegy and *plainte* (see *P*, 61) to be transmuted into an act of hope willfully projected upon existence. If she can say, already, in "If He had known" from *Poésies*, "Ma vie était un doux espoir déçu" ("My life was a gentle hope deceived," *P*, 54), it is nonetheless true that love, hope, and that Rimbaldian trust in some "future Vigor" direct and inspire ceaselessly her poetic practice and her entire existential project.

Memory and Death

Memory, like hope, is, in Desbordes-Valmore's poetics, a mechanism of creation, of ontic saving. If it is inevitably remembrance, commemoration, celebration, these are never, as often with Lamartine, Vigny, or Hugo, centered upon conspicuous history or a fetishistic sense of heroic, epic grandeur. Rather do they dip into inner events, the "history" of emotion, that "memory upon which love feeds" ("Elégie: Toi qui m'as . . .," *P*, 41) or where, uncharacteristically, "the mocking torch of bitter remembrance" may flare up ("Tristesse," *P*, 85). Memory, of course, occasions a measuring of the slippage between present and past ("Quand mes deux bras s'ouvraient devant ces jours . . . passés ["When my arms opened before those past days"]; "L'Impossible," *P*, 98), but it remains, most importantly, as a deep reservoir of existential enigma and yet certainty, as these beautiful quasi-Rimbaldian lines from "Sol natal" ("Native Soil") suggest:

> Mémoire! étang profond couvert de fleurs légères;
> Lac aux poissons dormeurs tapis dans les fougères,
> Quand la pitié du temps, quand son pied calme et sûr
> Enfoncent le passé dans ton flot teint d'azur,
> Mémoire! au moindre éclair, au moindre goût d'orage,
> Tu montres tes secrets, tes débris, tes naufrages.

> Memory! deep pond covered with slight flowers;
> Lake with sleepy fish crouched in the ferns,
> When the pity of time, when its calm, sure foot
> Thrust the past down into your azure-tinged waters,
> Memory! at the first flash, at the least taste of storm,
> You show your secrets, your debris, your wreckage.
>
> (*P*, 134–35)

Memory, indeed, might be deemed here to be one of the privileged, and improbable, loci of presence itself—not unlike the "affective" memory Georges Poulet attributes to Lamartine, or the Proustian event, hovering similarly between loss and recovery, death and presence, vibration now. The celebrated "Les Roses de Saadi" ("The Roses of Saadi") from *Poésies inédites* evokes such a possibility of the suppression of time ("Respires-en sur moi l'odorant souvenir" ["Breathe in upon me their fragrant memory"], *P*, 181) and, even when—as in "Un ruisseau de la Scarpe" ("A Stream off the Scarpe") from the same collection—"dear memory is but a cry of suffering!" (*P*, 198), one remains sensitive to the fact that the cry and the suffering are both *actual*, real, streaming with the only reality available, present as voice *now*: "Là voilà qui me parle, ô mémoire sonore!" ("There it is, speaking to me, oh sonorous memory!"; *P*, 199). Not only is memory faithful to what was and is (see *P*, 200), but it remains a "guarantee" of both presence and future: "Living bouquet of sparks / . . . If it is not to return, / Why recall it?" she asks in "La Mère qui pleure" ("Weeping Mother," *Poésies inédites, P*, 213): memory, thus, as implicit retrieval, as a meaningful symbol of continuing pertinence and, indeed, nonlinearity. "Mon seul avoir, le souvenir" ("My only possession, memory"), Desbordes-Valmore says in "L'Ame errante" (*P*, 215), a declaration that, typically, succeeds in giving equal stress to the beauty of sheer nonpossession, of quasi-Taoist flow, and the affective, spiritual centering of existence, the positioning of being within an atemporal, unlocatable framework, that of the memory, now, for our self-project via time and space, yet outside of any quantifiable parameters.

Death, in this optic, perhaps not surprisingly, is lived doubly, upon a knife-edge. "No! nothing dies," Desbordes-Valmore will not hesitate to affirm in "Révélation" (*P*, 79): death is seen as mere "absence" or "veiling" (*P*, 91), and, in parallel fashion, birth and childhood are seen as pure presence, pure accession to bliss from nothingness (see *P*, 110), pure creation, poiesis (see *P*, 148), dripping with the implicit exquisiteness of what underlies all of being, of what "death" renders occult yet also sensible via "presence." If, too, ultimate truth can only be expected via, and beyond, death— "Et le vrai, c'est la mort!" ("Truth is death!"), Desbordes-Valmore exclaims at the end of "L'Ephémère" at the end of *Les Pleurs*, "and I await its secret"—revelation, as we have already seen in the poem of the title ("Révélation," *P*, 77–79), occurs equally in the vulnerability of physical incarnation, of which death is a critical experience. Poems such as "A Monsieur A. L." and "Dans la rue" ("On the street"), both from *Pauvres fleurs* (*P*, 123–25, 143–44), demonstrate the degree to which the traversal of death was, for Desbordes-Valmore, no minor event, but rather completely available to her consciousness as a profound physiological, emotional, sociopolitical trauma. Yet, just as "Rêve intermittent" shows that death, for her, as for any child, constitutes the known end of birth, and of the self-project (see *P*, 209: "Children know they are born to fly away"), so death can be seen to be "the true reawakening from day-dream" ("Au livre de Léopardi," *P*, 190), a critical slippage, or transposition, from one dream-project to another, more enlightened. And love, as with other apparent, and *real*, obstacles, "breaks open the tomb" (see *P*, 229), gives to the temporal its *other* dimensionality, that of all *otherness*.

Poetry and Voice

"La Nuit d'hiver," first published in 1819, reveals the significantly self-reflexive nature of Marceline's poetry from its inception. Comparable to the texts of the poets of antiquity or of a Michel Deguy of our own time, "La Nuit d'hiver" (*P*, 38–40) addresses itself to her poetic muse, which the self sees as synonymous with "fantasy," imagination, and gentle feminine voice, delicate, vulnerable—because exposed to emotion and thought—yet curiously independent in its movements, and this for reasons we can understand as partly having to do with Desbordes-Valmore's sense of all as a divine given within which the self-project occurs, but by which it is upheld. "Je suis seule sans votre voix" ("I am alone without your voice"), she will thus say in "Au Christ" (*P*, 140); and, in "Ma Fille", she will recommend to her daughter that she allow her voice to be buoyed up by the voice of divineness (see *P*, 96). Poetry, in this way, is at once part of the self's function and yet embedded in a collective, planetary, even cosmic poiesis that Desbordes-Valmore will commonly evoke. The other, the loved other—this means both affinitary and anonymous figures—can thus be the locus of poetry, as in "Avant toi" (*P*, 115); poetry can be communication, contact, a "farewell" intimacy (see *P*, 171): "Afin que dans mon coeur tu puisses lire/Comme en partant" ("So that in my heart you may read/As if departing"); it can be, literally, love, an act of love (see "Allez en paix" ["Go in Peace"], *P*, 175) in which naming can be an alchemical, symbolic *acte de présence*, as Bonnefoy might say, or, in Reverdyan terms, a gesture of ontological substitution: "Votre nom vous remplacera bien" ("Your name will well replace you," (*P*, 174).

But poetic voice, as primordially, pretextually other, can flow from any and all phenomena into the voice that is Desbordes-Valmore's. All is osmosis, free deployment of voice, whether it be the streams that speak to her ("Rêve intermittent," *P*, 209); the "rhymes and prose" of the countryside entering our consciousness, "poeticising our being" (see "Une ruelle de Flandre" ["An Alleyway in Flanders"], *P*, 203); or "A prayer/Rising up from everywhere;/A moaning of the earth,/From the creeping moss/To the oaks of the ramparts" ("Sol natal," *P*, 137)—a passage reminiscent in essence of many pages of Francis Ponge, even though his optic begins with the *muettes instances* ("mute beckonings") of those endless things of the earth to which he brings his particular *rage de l'expression*. The language of being, in short, "traversing the universe" (*P*, 154), dovetails with that, embryonic, nascent in the self, allowing something ineffable, yet simple and unpretentious, to well up as poetic text.

What, further, is of great interest in Desbordes-Valmore's poetics, is her refusal to privilege the text per se, to regard its gesture as transcendent, its form as a locus of closed, high aesthetic function. "All the books in the world/Were not worth a song of the distant round," she declares unambiguously in "Jours d'été" (*Bouquets et prières, P*, 147), giving back to the earth, to pulsations of our simple existentiality, the primacy of which all art, all literature, falsely perceived, would rob them. The ideal exchange, for Desbordes-Valmore, would bypass not only the written word but all verbality, offering in their place a *parole* of the soul, beyond the complexities of voice, grammar, and form. "Parle-moi doucement! sans voix, parle à mon âme," ("Speak to me gently! voicelessly, speak to my soul"), she asks in "Révélation" (*P*, 78). Perhaps such a plea is linked to her occasional allusions to an (un)sayable beyond the *feuillets noirs* ("the black endpapers"; "Tristesse," *P*, 86) of her poetry, to those "words begun that I cannot write,/Bursting with innocence and magical to reread" (*P*, 86; see *P*, 198)—words almost certainly formulated but never "written" for Henri de Latouche, but revealing a nostalgia for a nonverbal communion beyond the clutter and congealment of our linguistic limitations. And, as Lucien Descaves suggested, this exceptional, throwaway poem, untitled, unpublished during her lifetime, could be appropriately "engraved upon Marceline's tomb" (see *P*, 264):

> Que mon nom ne soit rien qu'une ombre douce et vaine,
> Qu'il ne cause jamais ni l'effroi ni la peine!
> Qu'un indigent l'emporte après m'avoir parlé
> Et le garde longtemps dans son coeur consolé!

> Let my name be no more than a soft, vain shadow,
> Let it cause never fright nor pain!
> May some poor soul bear it off, having spoken with me,
> To keep it long within the heart consoled!
>
> (*P*, 234)

Such a "fragment"—for it is possible that it is part of an unfinished piece and it is important to recognize the relative nature of Desbordes-Valmore's aesthetic concern—reveals well a poetics of the minimal, of the self-effacing, quite distinct from but nevertheless related to the *poétique du peu* (poetics of the minimum) of Henri Michaux. The overriding factors determining poetic voice remain, however, less that self-exploration emerging from the surrealist ambition than love, care for the other, a *consolatio* addressed, rather than to the self, to that *passant/e* ("passer-by") dear to poets from Baudelaire to Char, but in his or her full indigence, the glory of a facelessness.

Action

Lest it be thought that the above might conceivably imply a degree of retreat from raw contact with the world and a stressing of "shadowy," anonymous sociopoetic function, it is essential to realize that, even as for Pierre Reverdy, all poetic commitment of the self is for Marceline Desbordes-Valmore what Sartre would have called an *engagement*—but beyond any quasi-ideological specificity. In her work there is no manifest tension between action and "dream," as with the surrealists, but her poetic interventions of a sociopolitical nature, while arguably discreet, should not be thought of as less critical, less courageous, less telling. The 1830 Revolution and its aftermath produced from Desbordes-Valmore's pen many of the powerful and extended poems of *Pauvres Fleurs,* "A Monsieur A. L.", "Cantiques des mères" ("Canticles of Mothers"), "Cantique des bannis," "Dans la rue"—politically explosive, dangerous poems that made quiet but sure demands and claims; poems of great sensitivity and intelligence; feminist poems that reveal simply all that needs radical revision in a male-dominated economy and, if the term remains meaningful, spirituality. "Kings for a time; God forever," she will affirm in that "wild and tender hymn" that is "Cantique des bannis" (*Pauvres Fleurs, P,* 131). At such moments, her poetry rises up serenely yet urgently *against:* against political or ideological murder, suppression, religious kowtowing and corruption, all flagrant manifestation of power or "heroism." But, of course, with a poet so irresistibly drawn to a positive expression of her being-in-the-world, expression-against quickly yields to *expression-for:* for spiritual militancy, discreet, personal, beyond all dogmatism, all formalism; for feminine claim and clamor (see "Une lettre de femme" ["A Woman's Letter,"] *Poésies inédites, P,* 171); for love and compassion—and what greater *engagement* could there possibly be?; for what the 1789 Revolution stood for beyond its inevitable contradictions:

> la liberté toute riante et mûre
> . . . . . comme aux cieux, sans glaive, sans armure,
>
> Sans peur, sans audace et sans austérité,
> Disant: "Aimez-moi, je suis la liberté!["]

> freedom laughing and ripe
> . . . . . as in the heavens, without sword or armor,
>
> Without fear, without audacity and austereness,
> Saying: "Love me, I am freedom!["]

Once again, it is the extraordinary "Rêve intermittent" that cries out to us its delicate nuances (*P*, 207).

Form

The poetry of Marceline Desbordes-Valmore is not underpinned by any elaborate theoretical or aesthetic writing, as to some extent with her contemporaries, Lamartine, Vigny, and Hugo, and increasingly with Baudelaire and Mallarmé and poets who will write, consciously, in their twentieth-century wake. Desbordes-Valmore's poetry implies three attitudes to form: first, a recognition and acceptance of tradition from the Renaissance to Chénier; secondly, an alertness to new tonality, freer metric options, and metric variation (here, she is arguably as instrumental, initially, as Lamartine or Hugo, without, subsequently, that systematic endeavor to explore the treasures of technicality that marks Hugo's fervor); and thirdly, a certain happy indifference to aesthetic adherence that will lead Bonnefoy to regard her work as a place—rather than of closure, interior orchestration, and narcissistic chiseling—of "imperfection," of poetic simplicity, rough and tumble—but a *chant de grillon* ("cricket's song") as essential to poetry, and our sense of *présence*, as any caressed and cultured Baudelairean or Mallarméan pearl (see *Préface, P*, 24–26).

In fundamental terms Desbordes-Valmore's work can be said to present a stable grammar and a stable lexicon, beyond all esotericism and beyond the temptations of either inconsistent or radically visionary metaphoricalness, as of purely decorative or contrived figuration (whether the intention be momentary or part of a vaster aesthetic project). Similarly, her metric and strophic practice remains firmly within the bounds of convention, while pushing, in accordance perhaps with the demands of a pressured creative process, as Bonnefoy rightly emphasizes (see *P*, 26), in the direction of a looseness and a certain *désinvolture* that Verlaine, Rimbaud, and Laforgue will pursue, along with Hugo, in radically differing perspectives. The use of the *vers impair*, especially the eleven-syllable line, brings about a particular formal—but, implicitly, ex-istential—destabilization to which Bonnefoy is most sensitive, and the tendency to multiply, within the same poems, strophic and metric variations, gives Desbordes-Valmore's work an aeration, a freedom from closure and aesthetic primness, that, when com-pared with the implacable drive of the couplet in Vigny or even the elegant harmonies of Lamartine, can be most refreshing.

If, as Bakhtin has somewhat impulsively proposed, poetry may be said to be monological in its mode, it is equally true that the monologue in Desbordes-Valmore, as so often in Lamartine or Baudelaire, is centered upon the at least implicit presence/ab-sence of the other: her poetic mode is indeed in accordance with the main element of her poetics—love—profoundly dialogical in character. Her imperatives address and exhort. Her exclamations ring with the problematics of communication. Her "descriptions" or affective "topologies" bristle with the urge to rejoin, to contact, to reintegrate. And, in all of this, we should not neglect that cru-cial poetic tone that belongs, above all, to Desbordes-Valmore, a tone hovering between high seriousness and delight, simple en-thusiasm; between the intensities of joy or sorrow and the *décon-traction*, the ease of ballad or soft melody, between what Barbey d'Aurevilly called *cri* ("crying out"; (see *P*, 249), and mere chan-son; between an omnipresent and warming spirituality and that down-to-earth, aconceptual urge that never leaves her. In such marriages Desbordes-Valmore cannot but bring to mind the tonal-ity of Apollinaire, but nor is she immeasurably removed from that haunting the work of Eluard or, nearer to us, Guillevic—*toutes pro-portions gardées*.

Flowers

This is certainly not the occasion for a detailed, speculative analy-sis of any relationships linking Baudelaire's *Fleurs du Mal* (*Flowers of Evil*) and what are, in effect, a whole series of titles and passages in Desbordes-Valmore's work centered upon the motif of the flower: *Pauvres Fleurs, Bouquets et prières,* "Bouquet sous la croix" ("Bouquet beneath the Cross"), "La Fleur d'eau" ("Water Flowers"), "Fleur d'enfance" ("Childhood Flower"), "Les Roses de Saadi," "La Rose flamande" ("The Flemish Rose"). But to bear in mind the implications of Baudelaire's title, remembering too his great admiration for her poetry expressed in *Les Poètes français,* is to restore to Desbordes-Valmore's symbol all its freshness, its uncomplicatedness, its direct evocativeness. For, if in Baudelaire notions of blossoming and beauty undoubtedly exist, they are riveted to those of aesthetic, poetic transformation and transcendence; they speak of a journey away from the earth, from the real, dew-laden frailty of daisies or fuchsia—from what he held to be the giddying stage of "evil"—toward the rarefied and ambivalent hot-house atmosphere within which the flowers of a newly imagined sensibility might grow and flourish.

For Desbordes-Valmore, flowers certainly possess broad symbolic value—after all, in her poetry, all flowers inescapably become verbalized, and, in that sense, Baudelairean. A number of poems are quite explicit: "Fleur naine et bleue, et triste, où se cache un emblème,/Où l'absence a souvent respiré le mot: J'aime!" ("Dwarf, blue, and sad flower, wherein hides an emblem,/Where absence has often breathed the words: I am in love!"), we read in "La Fleur d'eau" from *Pauvres Fleurs* (*P,* 111), a poem redolent of that thick but primitive emblematicalness haunting the poems of Louise Labé or Maurice Scève; or again, in "Fleur d'enfance" from the same 1839 collection, the power of transference and simple association emerges, clear, magical, yet as accepted as the flower itself:

> Flower given my childhood,
> I love you! like his mirror.
> Our days are now unmoved.
> But you recall to me his eyes
> (*P,* 121)

The "flowers" of Desbordes-Valmore's poetry, however, are largely "wild," as in the latter poem, rather than finely bred, mentally sophisticated. They are often anonymous, flowers of field or mere, occasionally town-flowers, but lodged in beneath the tiles of the attic room of Lyon, "humble" (see "Départ de Lyon," *P,* 153). Such flowers, caught in the temporal drift of existence, nevertheless participate in a divineness that only attaches itself by proud metaphoricalness to the "flowers of evil" Baudelaire creates. If Desbordes-Valmore can go as far toward Baudelairean or Mallarméan thinking as to declare, "A tout exil sa fleur!" ("To each exile its flower!"; "Départ de Lyon," *P*, 154), once more her point of anchorage is lived, "non-poetic" experience—although, as we have seen, she understands fully the rich poeticalness of primacy, as, seemingly, her symbolist admirers never quite did. "Départ de Lyon" (*P*, 153–56) and "Une halte sur le Simplon" ("A Stop upon the Simplon") from *Bouquets et prières* (*P*, 159–64) render manifest that the flowers which linger in Desbordes-Valmore's imagination are essentially the free, ephemeral blooms of the open meadows, emblems of universal love, of innocence, of joy:

> Et les fleurs se parlaient: le bruit de leurs haleines,
> Dans l'herbe, ressemblait à des baisers d'enfants
> Qui s'embrassent entre eux, rieurs et triomphants.

> And flowers conversed: the sound of their breathing
> In the grass, was like kisses between children
> Embracing one another, laughing and triumphant.
> (*P*, 160)

Valmorian flowers are thus beyond exoticism and effeteness, or, indeed, any need to transmute them into rarefied concoctions. They are natural, raw emblems of a beauty and a delicate refinement already in being, a richness within poverty, an exquisite reminder of "eternity" within precariousness and death (see "Refuge," *P*, 218). And it is not uncommon, perhaps out of sheer grammatical surrender, to associate them with femininity (see "Ondine á l'école," *P*, 212).

Fear and Sorrow

If love is the single most significant element in Desbordes-Valmore's poetics, it is perhaps not surprising that its psychic opposite, fear, can persist in playing a noticeable role in an opus where, in the final analysis, the reality of sorrow translates itself into a forceful imaginative "structure." "Le Mal du pays" ("Homesickness"), from *Les Pleurs*, offers a vivid picture of a psyche crying out for "sleep," for "evasion" beyond the realm of "fright" (see

P, 89)—here, precisely, of lovelessness—yet it is fundamental to note that the entire poem, despite its outburst of deep emotion and, perhaps, anguish, remains the occasion for a reversal of fear, for a singing of dreamed possibility as real as that lived and lost. Elsewhere, fear can be the fear of excessive, cried-out expression ("Sol natal," *P*, 136), a fear of giving herself to all that she ever was, poetically, affectively—a fear, as in "Un ruisseau de la Scarpe," of living "à poitrine pleine," of breathing in "all the air my breathing needs" (*P*, 198). And, in not dissimilar fashion, other poems can reveal a fear of the fullness of Christ ("Au Christ," *P*, 140), an old, channeled concern perhaps, a misgiving as to one's individual participation in the plenitude sensed beyond physical reduction to nothingness ("Les Sanglots" ("Sobbing"), *P*, 225). Oddly, the clearest recognition of the deeper meaning of fear, namely its adjacency to love, comes in the same "Les Sanglots," where Desbordes-Valmore exclaims: "Ah! j'ai peur d'avoir peur, d'avoir froid; je me cache/Comme un oiseau tombé qui tremble qu'on l'attache" ("Ah! I am afraid of being afraid, of being cold; I hide/Like a fallen bird trembling lest it be found," (*P*, 226). Here, we can see the poet's lucid comprehension of the absolute need for risk, self-exposure, what the surrealists, in a different context, called "availability."

For, if, as we have seen in the 1832 "Tristesse" (*P*, 84–88), rendering oneself available both to primary experience and the process of memory and commemoration is painful, it also permits a recuperation otherwise quite beyond us: a traversal of ephemerality and its possibly concomitant sorrow, and an accession, even, to joy. The "mortality" of existence, as poets such as Jaccottet, Frénaud, and Bonnefoy demonstrate today, may be accompanied by a sense of our utter fragility and a harshly leveling futility—"From so much wrong, so much right,/Nothing will remain to me," Desbordes-Valmore discouragedly affirms in "Dernière entrevue" ("Last Interview") from *Poésie inédites* (*P*, 187)—yet it is certain that for her, as for them, only a risky traversal of our flickering but oddly sure *présence* can give the latter any deep meaning, can allow love to survive its own "shipwreck"—as the end of the same poem suggests (*P*, 188). Sorrow, then, a recurrent theme in this poet of the *élégiaque*, must be read not as an absolute, or an end-state, but as one of various elements in flux both within the deployment of their intrinsic meaning and within the shifting network of imaginative/affective "structures" of her oeuvre. The *élégie* itself implies restraint and nostalgia, just as Jules Laforgue's *complaintes* will imply irony: in both cases, resistance and recuperation enter into play, beyond upset or grief. The poetry of Bernard Noël today operates in both "elegiacal" and "grating" modes, but, again, the first mode in itself is plurivocal, not merely in plain opposition to what he terms *le grinçant* (gratingness)—of books like *Bruits de langues*, for instance. Thus, for Desbordes-Valmore, sorrow may stem from apparent separation or the "unfinishedness" of love, but then, for her, such terms are relative, as are the states they would evoke. If the posthumous "Les Cloches et les larmes" ("Bells and Tears," (*P,* 176–77) can begin with a seemingly incontrovertible affirmation, "Upon the earth where the hour rings forth,/All weeps, oh, my God, all weeps," it should not astonish us that Desbordes-Valmore, beyond all trace of irony, can cry out in reaffirmation of the moving mystery of life, in the last *faux quatrain:*

> Sonnez, cloches ruisselantes!
> Ruisselez, larmes brûlantes!
> Cloches qui pleurez le jour!
> Beaux yeux qui pleurez l'amour!
>
> Ring forth, streaming bells!
> Stream away, burning tears!
> Bells that weep the day!
> Fair eyes that weep love!

Can a more touching expression of a certain adherence in Marceline Desbordes-Valmore to a Taoist principle of sheer ontological "streamingness" be found? It is a principle tending to annul all equations, other than that of oneness, or general equivalence—what Char can call *équité.*

From Origin to Forgiveness

Of course, such an adherence undermines in no way a natural human tendency to question the nature and logic of being. Fear and sorrow well up, seemingly instinctual, but not outside of being itself, and when, in "Tristesse" (*P,* 84), Desbordes-Valmore cries out over the very origin of the ontic/affective impulse: "How is it that of fine years memory is bitter?/How is it we love so much a fleeting joy?/How is it that speaking of it my voice melts to tears?" her questioning should not be held to query the fact or ground of being, but rather its blinding mystery. Origin's beauteous enigma often fascinates this poet par excellence of maternity, of birth, of childhood.

"La Maison de ma mère" (*P*, 109–10) characteristically questions the origins of maternal voice, gentle, mellifluous, as "angelic," as divine as some intuited original music distilled at birth; and "Avant toi" points to the power of life to manifest itself, physicality to become physicality, feeling to assume its mystery, "comme on voit au soleil/Se dresser une fleur sans que rien la soutienne" ("as we see in the sun/Rise up a flower beyond all support," *P*, 115). In all of this, the soul's reality remains certain, as in contemporaries as different as Stendhal and Hugo. The soul exudes a natural propensity to love (*P*, 83), to flow through physicality, "like a limpid water/. . . racing,/Loving and dying" ("La Sincère" ["The Sincere One"], *P*, 93), a "wandering soul" ("L'Ame errante," *P*, 215) among other wandering souls. Few poets have as sublime a sense of the soul's need to traverse different experiences, to complete individual trajectories before unificatory plenitude ("La Fleur d'eau," *P*, 112).

Once more, such a privileging vision of things does not render desire and will irrelevant, afunctional: on the contrary, it recognizes the divine nature of the individual self-project everywhere, and an essential equilibrium—in a *certain* sense, equivalence—between what is (origin, being, soul, physicality, affective life) and what can be via the assumption of being's fullness. In this perspective, it is essential to give proper weight to a feature of Desbordes-Valmore's poetics that, again, remains sublimely exceptional: the necessity, the beauty of forgiveness. This is forgiveness that is total, complete; a forgiveness that gives to love its freedom, its fullness, its most exquisite feasibility. Rare are those who can write: "yes, I believe all is possible;/I forgive you all, be happy, all is well" (Elégie: Toi qui m'as . . . ," *P*, 42). "Amour! amour! pardon! pardon!" ("Love! love! forgiveness! forgiveness!") are the guiding thoughts Desbordes-Valmore expresses in the deeply compassionate "Cantique des mères" (*P*, 129). For-give-ness, *par-don*, is the logic of love pushed to the fullness of its gift, freeing giver and receiver from the cloying fixities of will not assumed. "L'on *veut* donner quand on aime" ("One wants to give when one loves"), Desbordes-Valmore says, with the utter simplicity of that *voyance* that Rimbaud will come to know in partially different terms (*P*, 183).

Sisterhood and Sameness

"A mes soeurs" ("To My Sisters") from *Poésies* (*P*, 60–62) is not a poem about Marceline Desbordes-Valmore's sisters, but rather a poem reminiscent of those improbable but terribly real days when her mother, accompanied by fifteen-year-old Marceline alone, set sail for Guadeloupe in the hope of reestablishing the severely diminished post-Revolution family fortunes under the protection of an unfortunately deceased relative, only to die herself of yellow fever, leaving the youthful Marceline Desbordes to return, via Dunkirk, to her father and sisters in Douai. But it is a poem, that, like so many others, falls under the spell of close feminine relationship, a poem of sororal dedication and giving, beyond all possession, a poem of togetherness despite separation and individual identity. Various other poems, offered to Desbordes-Valmore's childhood friend, Albertine Gantier, who, like her own two daughters, Inès and Ondine, will die very young, demonstrate that her conception of sisterhood is broad, collective, based on close feminine ties rather than strict blood relations, even though poems on the theme, or rather the experience, of daughterhood and motherhood are abundant. The dominant features of all such relations are innocence and purity ("Rêve d'une femme" ["A Woman's Dream"], *P*, 119), and, as "Sol natal" makes eloquently clear, deep sensitivity and affective and spiritual "quickness," compassion and generosity in the midst of vulnerability (*P*, 137). "Dans la rue," with its subtitles *La Femme* and *Des femmes* (*P*, 143–44), emphasizes like certain other texts both the single and collective experience of women, their quiet but sure taking up of voice, poetic and other; and "Une lettre de femme" from *Poésies inédites* (*P*, 171–72) places stress upon, less the abstract and the purely conceptual—again one can readily understand Bonnefoy's affinity for her work—but rather the urgently felt, the spiritually pertinent.

The Proustian—there is no doubt about the influence—"Blonds essaims de jeunes Albertines" ("Fair swarms of young Albertines"; "Une ruelle de Flandre," *P*, 201) that people the imagination and the heart of Desbordes-Valmore, are, then, the simple but eloquent sign of that lived and loved gentle sisterhood—which did not exclude the paternal figure, as various poems testify ("Rêve d'une femme," *P*, 119–20, or "Rêve intermittent," *P*, 206–210)—a "sisterhood" in the broadest sense as we have seen, but always blessed with at once real and ideal feminine presences, soft, sharing, bent on communion. Lest we feel that this sororal or feminizing proclivity may constitute a determining imaginative "structure" in Desbordes-Valmore's poetry, I stress two points: first, as I have earlier stated, it is not my intention to argue, nor is it my belief, that any absolute fixity of thought, sentiment, or imagination lies at the center of this work—or, indeed, any other—hence both my focusing upon multiple features and motifs, and an effort to "deconstruct" at the same time the latter's function and meaning. Secondly, there can be little doubt that sisterhood, daughterhood, motherhood, and other important elements of Desbordes-Valmore's acute feminine consciousness, are subsumed within the overall ontological strategy her poetry both reflects and, in itself, represents: love, and the poet's recurrent privileging, in her own discreet manner, of a notion dear to the contemporary poet and philosopher Michel Deguy, namely sameness.

Sameness, in a sense, is a sign of love taken to its most idyllic expression. It involves a merging, a con-fusion—no wonder the image of the storm often associates itself with love ("Orages de l'amour, nobles et hauts orages" ["Love's storms, high and noble storms"], "Les Eclairs" ["Lightning"]—of being, in love, in friendship, in pain as in bliss. Desbordes-Valmore's consciousness of sameness, however, goes further. "You see: the same sky loves and guides us," she says in the 1830 *Poésies*, in "A mes soeurs" (*P*, 61), where what is privileged is the degree to which all existence remains buoyed up and governed by what we might think of as ecological and spiritual factors already giving oneness and unification. The same ontic flow or way belongs to all of us, all of our ways. Sameness, though, commonly enough betrays a desire for original identity and simplicity ("Je veux un même lit près du même ruisseau" ["I want a same bed next to the same stream"], "Le Mal du pays," *P*, 89), or else for constancy-within-storminess ("Go and find love again, the same!/Stormy lamp, light up!" *P*, 120), a desire that, as we can see from the second poem quoted, "Rêve d'une femme" (*P*, 119–20), in no way restricts the concept/experience of sameness to some pale and improbable ideality. In its most exquisite expression, Valmorian sameness reveals a sensitivity to the *original identity* of circumstance and, implicitly, ecologico-spiritual purpose or project of all people: if affinitary, exclusive relations, and perhaps especially the gentle "sisterhoods" evoked, provide model experiential "structures" in which sameness and love may be explored, the latter are clearly sensed to be universal phenomena, phenomena wherein "uni-versality"—the "pouring out" of oneness into its differences.

· TWO ·

Lamartine

Born in Mâcon on 21 October 1790, and brought up in his nearby beloved Milly in a relatively impecunious but nevertheless advantaged aristocratic family, Alphonse de Lamartine was able to enjoy the privilege of youthful study in idyllic circumstances that he was sensitive and wise enough to recognize as exceptional and determining. His travels to Italy led him to meet Julie Charles, whose premature death in 1817 gave us the celebrated "Le Lac." The ten or so years that followed saw the great creative thrust of his early work, with the publication of the admired and tonally new *Méditations poétiques* (*Poetic Meditations*, 1820), *Nouvelles méditations poétiques* (*New Poetic Meditations*, 1823), and, ultimately, his delicate though vigorous *Harmonies poétiques et religieuses* (*Poetic and Religious Harmonies*, 1830). This period is also one of great transformation and exploration in other domains: his entry into the diplomatic service; his 1820 marriage to the Englishwoman Marianne Elisa Birch, met in Naples during his stint there as *attaché d'ambassade;* his contemplation of great future personal and literary projects. The latter were both to flower and to fade in the decade to come: on the one hand, the birth and childhood of his beloved daughter, Julia, the family's spiritual pilgrimage in 1832–1833 via Greece to the holy places of Lebanon and the Near East, the immense success of *Jocelyn* (1836), the great project of *Les Visions* (*The Visions*), never completed as such; on the other hand, the stunning death of the young Julia in 1833 in mid-pilgrimage and the cool reception given to the massive *La Chute d'un ange* (1838), which was only marginally compensated by the publication of the *Recueillements poétiques* (*Poetic Recollections*, 1839). Having left the diplomatic service in 1830 with the advent to power of Louis-Philippe, Lamartine gave himself to politics in a continuous way from the early 1830s to 1851. A great orator, tending to the Left and the ethics of liberalism though imbued with traditional principles of

conservative order, Lamartine's immense popularity raised him to
the very helm of the 1848 provisional government prior to the same
little-Napoleonic coup d'état that was to lead to Victor Hugo's exile and Lamartine's eclipsed and soured return to private life and
the pressing problem of his family debts.

Writing, thinking, and politically acting in that critical space between Voltaireanism and Rousseauism, classical order and Romantic idealism, a need for moderation and earthy contemplation
and a revolutionary spirit that made him cry out against slavery—
read his superb play, *Toussaint Louverture*—and embrace republi-
canism, Lamartine is very much a poet of self-interrogation,
(self-)search, yet within the bounds of a residual, intuitive
confidence or faith. His later years plunge him into hackish,
though very motivated writing of a largely historic or autobiographical nature, though his famous monthly *Cours familier de littérature* (*Private Lesson in Literature*) with its poetic gems like "La
Vigne et la Maison" ("The Vine and the House") show his delicate
grittiness in the face of adversity.

Semiconscious for well over a year, Lamartine was to die on
28 February 1869. Jules Laforgue may have regarded his poetic
oeuvre as "raphaélesque" and given to facileness, and Lautréamont may have gone further in accusing him of uncombative sentimentality, despite recognizing an "intelligence of the first order."
Neither, clearly, understood, nor perhaps fully read, his great
works of metaphysical questioning and immense intuitive penetration of the boundless small marvels of human experience. But
Hugo knew intimately the innovative creativity of his esteemed
contemporary, and Rimbaud himself was to recognize in Lamartine a power of seeing restricted only by the bonds of form. And
Baudelaire, too, protested at the absurdity of interpretations that
would make of this great, supple liberator of poetic mode and inspiration a merely "religious author." But it was left to the reserved
Vigny to weep tears of impotence and admiration upon his reading
of *Jocelyn*, where "everything is beautiful and great."

Time

The "negative" effects of what we call time form part of the fabric
of all literature, though in French Romantic poetry, and arguably

in that of Lamartine in particular—Vigny has other foci, Hugo is simply too vast, too finally cosmic in his orientation, and Desbordes-Valmore always operates a psychological and spiritual compensation that inhabits much of Lamartine's work—its expression reaches sublimely moving heights. Poems such as "Le Lac" ("The Lake") or "La Vigne et la maison" readily testify to a consciousness steeped in time's erasure and erosion, in a sense of impermanence and what Bonnefoy would call "imperfection," which would exile us—via the death of the loved, the cherished—rather than reinsert us into an exquisite, if painful, immediacy of being. Temporality in Lamartine, as in Jaccottet (v. *Requiem*), is thus first, and indeed to some extent continuingly, experienced as loss, separation, even, remarkably, nonbeing: "What is no longer, has it ever been?" he goes as far as to suggest in "Consolation," from the *Nouvelles Méditations poétiques* (*OPC*, 154), just as in the 1823 "Le Passé" ("The Past"), from the same collection, "our rapid summers" are seemingly ever immersed in disillusionment and, "Here, tired hope/That folded its azure wings" (*OPC*, 132). Even a poem such as the beautiful and diversely inspired "La Poésie sacrée ("Sacred Poetry"), from Lamartine's first volume, while seeking to transcend finality and all temporal schism—"Ô tombeau! vous êtes mon père!/Et je dis aux vers de la terre:/Vous êtes ma mère et mes soeurs!" ("Oh tomb! you are my father!/And I say to the worms of the earth:/You are my mother and my sisters!")—cannot but remain profoundly attached to a truly traversed experience of the "melting" of self's time and the severe abridgment of hope that "flees like water from my hand" (*OPC*, 78–79).

Lamartine's perspective upon time—and we see here a broad dialectical pattern I shall later explore specifically—while sensitized singularly to passingness as problem, as grief, as lament, is finely equilibrated by various other factors, not the least of which is that capacity for the sympathetic penetration of problem in order to reveal its latent meaning, rather than wallow in its evident burdensomeness. Ephemerality can thus be lived as an incentive to delve into the intensity and uniqueness of time ("Elégie," *OPC*, 193); abandonment to all experience becomes "wisdom" ("La Sagesse," *OPC*, 178). And elsewhere Lamartine will insist, significantly, upon the coincidence, the simultaneity, of eternity and actuality, finiteness and infinity. "Yes, the hour of your adoration is your eternal hour," he will declare in one of his lovely "hymns" of the *Harmonies poétiques et religieuses*, "Hymne au matin" (*OPC*, 303); and in the tellingly titled "Eternité de la nature, brièveté de l'homme" ("Eternity of Nature, Briefness of Man"), we are told to what extent "in the passing minute/The infinite of time and space/In my gaze has been repeated" (*OPC*, 467)—in an experience of leveling symbiosis conveying the interdependence, even the equivalence, of the fleeting and all that permits it. Other poems, such as "Pensée des morts" ("Thought of the Dead"), also from the 1830 *Harmonies*, stress the essential inseparability of time, of what is humanly traversed as chronology: "And never do you separate/Past from future;/You are alive, alive!" Lamartine exclaims (*OPC*, 341) in a Derrida-like dismissal of simple category and an insistence upon the "dissemination" of origin within a "nowness" at once experiential and verbal. "La vie et la mort . . . sont . . . même, hélas!/Deux mots créés par l'homme et que Dieu n'entend pas," ("Life and death . . . are . . . even, alas!/Two words created by man and that God does not understand"), he muses in "Novissima verba" (*OPC*, 474), with an element of regret understandable given the "deconstruction" of our conceptions thus implied.

This does not mean that the fusing of eternity and ephemeralness in Lamartine's poetics is now suddenly plunged into emotional confusion. Far from it; but it does show not only how aware he is of the vulnerability of our classifications, but also, and perhaps more importantly, how much he himself is attached both to the bittersweetness of irreplaceable passingness and to the intuition of a transcendence that will ceaselessly haunt his mind. For, in "eternity," all temporal experience is recuperable: "Come! where eternity resides,/where the past is recovered" (*OPC*, 133), Lamartine urges in "Le Passé," and does not "Le Lac" express similarly the most touching faith in the ability of all that is—"Eternity, nothingness, past, dark abysses/. . . lake! mute rocks! caves! somber forest" (*OPC*, 39)—to offer permanent affective incarnation, deep spiritual continuity to the seeming vicissitudes of fugitive life? Such echoes, via both what Georges Poulet calls the Lamartine *mémoire affective* that, as Proust demonstrates later, belongs to us all, and the carrying and caring power of all things and beings—what Lamartine tends to term *Nature*—such echoes become (a)temporally guaranteed via a poetics that, from the outset, as the closing lines of the beautiful 1814 "A Elvire" ("To Elvire") show, remains anchored in a sense of available and complete cosmic consciousness annulling the harsh cynicism of finality:

> Le tombeau qui l'attend l'engloutit tout entière,
> Un silence éternel succède à ses amours;
> Mais les siècles auront passé sur ta poussière,
> Elvire, et tu vivras toujours!

> The tomb awaiting her swallows her complete,
> An eternal silence follows her loving;
> But the centuries will have passed over your dust,
> Elvire, and you will still be living!

(OPC, 13)

Here, we rejoin that emotionally ambivalent expression—in "La Poésie sacrée" (*OPC*, 79), as we have seen above—of the deep circular truth of death-(re)birth-life, a truth deeply sensed by many nineteenth-century thinkers, such as Lamennais and Michelet, and not just its major poets. Once again what is involved, most fundamentally, is a transgression of conceptual category—not foreign, it should be emphasized, to contemporary poets such as André Frénaud, Philippe Jaccottet, or Yves Bonnefoy, or women as different as Anne Teyssiéras, Heather Dohollau, or Marie Etienne—that will demand a rethinking, and by no means in traditional religious terms (even though Lamartinian poetics, like Valmorian poetics, may be deemed largely Christian) of the basic possibility of expressing, verbally, linguistically, via a human logos, what we are. Despite Lamartine's ability to give himself to a sense of time that will see lived events, as he says in "Ressouvenir du Lac Léman" ("Reremembrance of Lake Léman"), and like a Bonnefidian "foam," or a clump of catkins surging into life in Jaccottet, "monter, briller et fondre, ainsi que font nos jours" ("rising up, shining and melting away, like our days," *OPC*, 1183); despite his being able to give himself to a perception of life as "a step in the ladder of worlds/That we must take to arrive elsewhere," as he says in "Epître à M. de Sainte-Beuve" ("Epistle to Sainte-Beuve," *OPC*, 418) in a passage that would appear to hierarchize time as well as render it osmotically one, interlocked—despite these two principal modes of "positive" temporal knowledge, Lamartine's placing in question of the validity of all reductive, categorizing perception—a part of the latter perception, of course—can be seen as a singularly modern gesture, even though his doubt, unlike that of, say, Ponge or Michaux or Frénaud, refounds a hope, a unity, a deep possibility.

Exoticism and Familiarity

Lamartine is frequently thought of as the poet of the intimate, the closely rural, the delicately interior; and there is much to this thesis, more intrinsically complicated as it is, as we shall shortly see. His affection is, however, much broader than such a critical portrayal would have us believe: poems such as "Le Golfe de Baya" ("The Gulf of Baya," *OPC*, 60–62), "Sapho" (*OPC*, 113–19), "Bonaparte" (*OPC*, 118–23), "A une jeune Arabe" ("To a Young Arab Woman," *OPC*, 550–52), or "Sultan, le cheval arabe" ("Sultan, the Arabian Horse," *OPC*, 1204–1205) testify to an early and enduring sensitivity to the beauty, the mystery, the sheer fascination of that which lies beyond the quotidian, the homely or the broadly native experience. And this is not to exclude what we might think of as a certain exoticism of mind or thought, as displayed, for example, as early as in the long poems *La Mort de Socrate* (*The Death of Socrates*, *OPC*, 87–108) and *Le Dernier Chant du pèlerinage d'Harold* (*The Last Song of Harold's Pilgrimage*, *OPC*, 193–245), where intellectual and poetico-spiritual intrigue along with distant codes and patterns are quickly, if for some laboriously, blatant. "Le Golfe de Baya," however, is characteristic in that the scents, the freshness, even the scene of the returning fisherman, while no doubt personally vibrant and meaningful, surrender the evocative specificity of a Leconte de Lisle or a Flaubert to the meditations so dear to Lamartine, here upon freedom, the passage of time, the traceless "presences"—in the poet's mind and heart—of Horace, Propertius, Tibullus, Tasso. "Sapho," similarly, offers little local color—Lamartine is, perhaps, closer to Ingres than Delacroix in his contemplative, idealizing mode, but Ingres inevitably outstrips him in sheer physical evocativeness—and stresses, rather, inner "description" or emotional states, as well as an "exoticism" allowing a fuller deployment of his fascination with themes such as poetic capacity,

the problematics and yet overall transcendent logic of love, a real
despair that, far from being merely rhetorical—a common contemporary tactical error in reading the intense work of poets as disparate as Lamartine and Laforgue (although the latter is usually
"forgiven" because of a "redeeming" irony)—is powerfully articulated by the "exotic" (but symbolic and validating) voice of Sapho:

> Que ne puis-je de même engloutir dans ces mers
> Et ma fatale gloire, et mes chants, et mes vers!
>
> Why can I not, too, plunge into the seas
> My fatal glory, my songs and my poems!
>
> (*OPC*, 117)

If "Bonaparte" is a pretext for reflection upon "action"—as the
surrealists might say—upon a "glory" far more modern than Cor-
nelian, upon history and presence, upon genius and tyranny, we
have here a foretaste of the fine twist of the otherwise "official" and
ultra 1825 *Chant du sacre* (*Song of Consecration;* "Come then, come! it
is time, sluggish FREEDOM," *OPC*, 271) and, better, of that "modern tragedy" that is the 1850 *Toussaint Louverture*, with its incarnation of what Lamartine calls the "angel of victory and freedom"
(*OPC*, 1400). The poems "A une jeune Arabe" and "Sultan, le cheval
arabe," while divergent in tone and emotion, demonstrate a Lamartinian sensitivity to the Baudelairean exotic propensity that should
not surprise us in a poet so finely attuned to sight, sound, and, indeed, the gamut of the sensual, despite his greater refinement,
pudeur, and more overtly aphysical spirituality.

Again, in pictorial terms, we might be tempted to think of a most
discreet canvas by Ingres, or, here, even Delacroix, without the
raw, fiery edges. The subtitle alone ("smoking the narghile in an
Aleppo garden") is enough to evoke something of Baudelaire, as is
this beautiful stanza that, exceeding sensual evocation, plunges us
back into a deeply reflective mode that knows to what degree such
an *inconnu* is a profound challenge both to our sensibility and our
concept of poeticity:

> Il n'est rien dans les sons que la langue murmure,
> Rien dans le front rêveur des bardes comme moi,
> Rien dans les doux soupirs d'une âme fraîche et pure,
> Rien d'aussi poétique et d'aussi frais que toi!

Lamartine

There is nothing in the sounds that language whispers,
Nothing in the dreaming mind of bards such as I,
Nothing in the soft sighing of a pure and fresh soul,
Nothing as poetical, as fresh as you!

(OPC, 551)

"Sultan" is not without bringing to mind certain poems of Vigny or Hugo, yet its insistence upon the significance of that interstitial zone between sensuality and dream, death and ideality, is not only Baudelairean, but highly modern—one thinks of the poetics of Rimbaud, Reverdy, Bonnefoy, in their varying but pertinent forms. The nostalgic imaginative power of "Sultan"—commemorative of the crushing death of Lamartine's beloved ten-year-old daughter, Julia, during their travels to the Middle East—lifts the poem from any temptation of pure aesthetic exoticism and reimplants it firmly on that soil of intimate meditation that is his essential terrain. I shall not go into that other mode of Lamartinian "exoticism" that is equally Hugolian and even Rimbaldian, and thus less specifically his—though, with Hugo, Lamartine will undoubtedly innovate its radical exploration: an exoticism that delves into the swirling *unknowns* of the butterfly, of godliness, of stars, of visionary experience, of the microscopic, of the cosmic, with an equal and, indeed, fused fascination.

Suffice it to say that such an exploration of the senses and of consciousness, merging objective perception and psychic subjectiveness, reveals an awareness of the exotic far from banal and, in fact, extravagantly, though simply, modern in both the respect for the mystery of all otherness and the intuition that the self is the locus of all discovery and truth, the (senti)mental womb of all that, seemingly, we are not.

It should not, therefore, surprise us to find that Lamartine is also the poet of the familiar, the long known, the intimately felt, and I shall not dwell upon this feature of his poetics—given that the next section will deal with its corollary—except to make two points. The first, and perhaps the more important, is that "familiarity" is a notion, as we have now seen, interlocked with that of the unknown or the exotic, redefining the latter to some degree, even interchangeable with it. For Lamartine's explorations always turn out to be deeply affective, spiritual, meditative: there is no contentment with pure externality, a geometry à la Robbe-Grillet or even an exotic psychicalness à la Breton, automatically registered and pondered only extratextually. All of Lamartine's poetry is intense personal meditation, whether it centers itself upon an almond tree branch, an Arabian horse, the teeming stars of the night sky, the "idea of God," Sappho, autumnal landscapes or the mill of his native village, Milly. The second point is that typical poems in the mode of "familiarity," such as "L'Automne" ("Autumn," *OPC*, 75–76), "La Cloche" (*OPC*, 799), or "La Fenêtre de la maison paternelle" ("The Window of my Father's House," *OPC*, 1205–1206), are neither facilely exploitative (any more than of the "exotic") nor simply acquiescent, complacent. Rather are they discreetly, but insistently, probing, moving beyond their tender gesture of welcome. They remain filled with desire, even restlessness, despite their affection. They are centered, in short, upon discourse, dialogue, and exceed, in this, mere anecdotality or narration, for all presence is, for Lamartine, symbolic, full of various latencies, becoming, living rather than stagnant in its meaning, caught in a moving interpenetration of self and others.

Special Places

Like so many other writers and, of course, companion Romantic poets, Lamartine's sensibility is often drawn compulsively to certain loci of intense affective pertinence. We shall look at two "series"—the word is already misleading, because there is no endeavor to systematize, orchestrate, or inflate the meaning of an "inspiration" that is very much spontaneous, steeped in the urgency of *présence*, memory, and desire: first, some of the Naples poems, "Le Golfe de Baya" (*OPC*, 60–62) from the *Méditations poétiques* and, from the *Nouvelles méditations poétiques*, "Adieux à la mer" ("Farewell to the Sea," *OPC*, 171–74), "Ischia" (*OPC*, 138–41), "Chant d'amour" ("Love-song," *OPC*, 180–87); and, secondly, some of the Milly poems, "Milly ou la terre natale" ("Milly or Homeland," *OPC*, 392–99), from the 1830 *Harmonies*, "Le Moulin de Milly" ("The Mill in Milly," (*OPC*, 1227–29), later added to the *Harmonies*, and "La Vigne et la maison," *OPC*, 1484–94), composed in October 1856, from the *Cours familier de littérature*. Specialness, in the case of all these, and other, poems is, certainly, born of an affective, psychic meaning attaching to places, but for the other, another, and not just for the self. Specialness stems, thus, from a sense of union, joining, indelible spiritual and visceral marking-together.

Lamartinian specialness leaps beyond all aesthetic nicety. It is, therefore, paradoxically, already beyond the specificity, whether "exotic" or "familiar," that, equally, founds it, volatilizing a concreteness far from inessential into what Marius-François Guyard calls "atmosphere, ambiance, mood" (*OPC*, xvii). There is, however, nothing pure, definitively idealizing, hygienically Mallarméan about these poems. Place, presence, is a sine qua non through which deep emotion and spiritual meaning are experienced and verbally explored and recorded. All of the Naples poems mentioned above center "specialness" upon certain qualities or phenomena unleashing the poetic impulse: 1. an affinitary love: Antonia Iacomina—whom Lamartine met during his 1811–1812 stay in Naples, and who inspires not only "Le Golfe de Baya," but other early (1813) poems such as "Adieu à Graziella" ("Farewell to Graziella," *OPC*, 361) as well as, with *Jocelyn*, the most widely read of all of Lamartine's works, "Graziella"—Antonia was to die in 1815, as suddenly as his other celebrated love (see "Le Lac"), Julie Charles, met in 1815 and dead in 1817; and the 1820–1822 poems singing the enchantments of body and soul during the honeymoon (1820–1821) of Lamartine and his English wife, Marianne-Elisa (Birch), the *Elyse* of "Ischia" (*OPC*, 141), the woman to whom he can address the characteristically passionate lines of "Chant d'amour":

> Pourquoi de tes regards percer ainsi mon âme?
> Baisse, oh! baisse tes yeux pleins d'une chaste flamme:
> Baisse-les, ou je meurs.
> Viens plutôt, lève-toi! Mets ta main dans la mienne,
> Que mon bras arrondi t'entoure et te soutienne
> Sur ce tapis de fleurs.

> Why with your gaze pierce thus my soul?
> Turn away the full flame of its purity:
> Look away or I die.
> Come, rather, arise! Put your hand in mine,
> Let my arm wrap you round, hold you firm,
> Upon this carpet of flowers.

> (*OPC*, 184)

2. the sweetness of scented days and nights and the gentleness of what, again in "Chant d'amour," Lamartine will refer to as the convergence of "innocence and love" (*OPC*, 186); 3. a tranquillity that will not by any means exclude the sensuous nor even the blatantly sensual; 4. the fascination of light—whether filtered light, sunlight, moonlight, crepuscular chiaroscuro—in both its physical and symbolic significance; 5. the coming together of water and soft breeze, with its potential for (again) real or metaphoric dynamism and change, and the gentle, elegant movements of sail or drift (one thinks of Rousseau lost in summer reverie); 6. the unspeakable intensity of emotion figured in the grammaticality of repeated exclamations; 7. the sense of the mystery of the special, often caught in the (serious) rhetoric of questioning; 8. an aural sensitivity that is often linked to the feeling that place and poetry are—Michel Deguy will often come back to this, taking Baudelaire as his point of departure—inextricably linked in the rhythm of their sounds and silence, the equally poetic ebb and flow of their "breath" or their watery movement; 9. the need for memories beyond violence, beyond death (this will change focus somewhat with the Milly poems); 10. that wonderful Lamartinian melding of the simplicity of passing experience, the alert, even skeptical memory of past greatness, and the sense of the truly possible divinity of human "knowledge" ("He who, suspending fugitive hours," Lamartine writes in "Ischia," "Fixing his soul with love in this lovely place,/Forgets that time still flows upon these banks,/Is he mortal, or is he a god?" *OPC*, 141); 11. the feeling of vulnerability, within confidence, that can suddenly sweep over Lamartine's poetry of special places; 12. the coincidence of notions of permanence and passingness, remembrance and farewell, in such places: the feeling that, despite the assault of time and disillusionment, these loci offer "un asile, une patrie,/Et des débris de [m]on bonheur" ("an asylum, a homeland,/And fragments of [my] bliss," *OPC*, 174), full as they are of the power of dream and, above all, the intense movingness of the real, "the torrents of life," as Lamartine writes in "Ischia" (*OPC*, 139).

The Milly poems, while conforming largely to these deployed factors of "specialness," stress certain of them in particular and introduce somewhat new though related criteria. Let us look briefly at the three poems in turn. "Milly ou la terre natale" (*OPC*, 392–99), one of Lamartine's most celebrated poems with "Le Lac" and "La

Vigne et la maison," which we shall shortly turn to, considers the particularity of loved and lived place as intimately connected at once to body and to soul. Such place is once more *patrie*, in this case a homeland in the truest sense, of course, a place residing not only in its exteriority but also in the deep recesses of the "heart," a place of manifest ruggedness yet a place wherein what, in speaking of Marceline Desbordes-Valmore, I termed the self-project, the self's dreamed and projected being, may unfold, unhindered, ideal but astonishingly real—a place where intimacy is at its height and where reciprocity is, too, paramount:

> Tout m'y parle une langue aux intimes accents
> Dont les mots, entendus dans l'âme et dans les sens,
> Sont des bruits, des parfums, des foudres, des orages,
> Des rochers, des torrents, et ces douces images,
> Et ces vieux souvenirs dormant au fond de nous,
> Qu'un site nous conserve et qu'il nous rend plus doux.

> All to me speaks a language of intimate tone
> Whose words, heard in soul and senses,
> Are sounds, scents, storms and bolts,
> Rocks, torrents and the sweet images,
> The old memories sleeping within,
> That place keeps for us, and sweetens.
>
> (*OPC*, 395)

Such a place, as we have seen for the Naples poems, continues also to be a meeting point for "greatness," utterly redefined, and simplicity; a space within which love, here maternal and sororal essentially, can flourish, within which the ephemeral may be intuited in its full divineness, death even "greeted" as a place of gathering. Milly gives, further, particular emphasis to the worked-in, lived-in nature of such specialness: seeing is not enough, nor thought, "intelligence"; the soul is the "measure" of all, and the *all* experienced is, like the natural tomb Lamartine conjures in his mind's eye, both beyond idle aestheticism, personal pretention, and time itself. "No century or name upon this rustic page," he will finally declare (*OPC*, 399): specialness is ultimately and astonishingly impersonal—but only because all livedness is recuperated by a logic of divine transcendence and unity.

The delicate and lovely "Le Moulin de Milly" (*OPC*, 1227–29) cannot absorb too much of our attention here, but it is important to stress that, as the subtitle hints ("Strophes à chanter" ["Stanzas to be sung"]), any place faintly special—and this would be true for Desbordes-Valmore and Hugo, somewhat less for the more remote and conceptual Vigny—leads to poetry: the Romantic link is strong with the telluric and its particular lived configurations. Moreover, this short, gentle poem, where again the sororal attachment is privileged, gives special voice both to the simple, inevitable tensions dwelling within "special places" ("My sister, oh what delights . . ./And before it all/You have but tears?/Ah! if he were there," *OPC*, 1229) and to the recurring theme of the intertwinement of a veritably deluging sensuous wealth and that "divine dream" ("like") which all things are (see *OPC*, 1228).

The very beautiful "La Vigne et la maison" (*OPC*, 1484–94) has received much commentary. What I should like to stress in the present context is how special place becomes a place of dialogue—with the other, as in the Naples poems, yes, but also, more pointedly here, with the self's other(s). Once again, tension and dialectic reign; the poem becomes *psalmodies* ("intonings"), a plurality, a music or gently rocking cadence of musics between, dialogically, "mon âme et moi" ("My soul and me"). Between, too, sorrow and fond remembrance, refusal and spiritual acquiescence; between a sense of emptiness and recognition, the apparently divergent *prestiges* of past and living presence. In addition, "La Vigne et la maison" draws out the idea that the meaning of Milly—although unnamed here—is that of a specialness wherein the whole of life can be perceived: birth, growth, fructification, death. The question of origin thus resurfaces, and the "return" to origin, Milly serving as a living symbol of the enigma of all questions of continuity and finality: "Oh family! oh mystery! oh heart of nature!" (*OPC*, 1491). The revelation available via such special symbolism is channeled through the heart, Lamartine stresses: seeing is not flatly rational (*OPC*, 1492). Milly, or more properly, "La Vigne et la maison," is an exclamatory apostrophe plunged into the ineffable ("Ô famille!"); its answers to the questions and tensions raised in this special place are, like the notion of origin itself, fundamentally *indécidables* ("undecidable"); if they seem to exist, and they do, they reside in emotion, in the *feeling* we have— and Lamartine has—of all that being/origin/threshold/death might conceivably mean for a heart and soul in a given and intensely special place of being.

Hymn

Lamartine's fascination with things, with the "things" of nature, manifests itself, as with Hugo and Desbordes-Valmore, from the earliest creative moments. It is a fascination, in contemporary terms, less Pongean than that commonly surging forth in the work of Jaccottet, Bonnefoy, or Char—as can be seen from poems such as "L'Isolement" ("Isolation"), "Le Vallon ("The Vale"), "Le Lac", from the *Méditations poétiques* (*OPC,* 3–4, 19–20, 38–40), "Le Papillon" ("The Butterfly") and "La Branche d'amandier" ("The Almond Branch"), from the *Nouvelles Méditations poétiques* (OPC, 128, 141–42), or "A une jeune fille poète" ("To a Young Girl Poet"), from the *Recueillements poétiques* (*OPC,* 1117–21), one lovely stanza of which I shall not resist quoting:

> Des vents sur les guérets, ces immenses coups d'ailes,
> Qui donnent aux épis leurs sonores frissons,
> L'aubépine neigeant sur les nids des buissons,
> Les verts étangs rasés du vol des hirondelles;
> Les vergers allongeant leur grande ombre du soir,
> Les foyers des hameaux ravivant leurs lumières,
> Les arbres morts couchés près du seuil des chaumières
> Où les couples viennent s'asseoir

> Winds upon the fields, great flappings of wings,
> Giving the wheat its shivering sounds,
> Hawthorn snowing on the bushes' nests,
> Green ponds clipped by the flight of swallows;
> Orchards lengthening their great evening shadow,
> Hearths in hamlets reviving their lights,
> Dead trees lying by cottage thresholds
> Where couples come and sit

All such poems reveal a poet immensely alert to the teeming presence of natural phenomena, their separate beauties and unpretentious appeal, their fragility and yet the firmness of their impact, the implacable relationships they establish with humanity, relationships at once physical and symbolic, viscerally present and psychically essential. The poems of *Méditations poétiques* already regard the "choses du simple" ("things of the simple"), as Bonnefoy terms them, as "loving" and "inviting" (see *OPC*, 20); together the latter form an "admirable palace" (*OPC*, 49), a kind of Baudelairean *temple*, where death and immortality converge in an experience of the divine (*OPC*, 17), where the creator is intrinsically worshipped by his own creations, "in his brilliant language" (*OPC*, 45). No wonder that, in "Le Golfe de Baya" of the same first volume, nature—always, inevitably, specific elements of it—may be termed "poetic." It is, indeed, the language of pure, primary poiesis (*OPC*, 62), "this sublime language," as Lamartine will put it in "L'Abbaye de Vallombreuse" ("Vallombreuse Abbey") from the *Harmonies*, "That nature speaks to the heart of the wretched" (*OPC*, 333). No wonder that human love of nature is regarded as "the first hymn to the Creator" (*OPC*, 355). "Cantique sur un rayon de soleil" ("Canticle on sunlight," *OPC*, 1121–26) already, via its title, speaks the full and reciprocal trajectory of the natural to the divine, wherein the quotidian experience, available nearly to all, of sun, trees, wind, water, flies, engages emotion, revelation, ecstasy. Another poem from the *Recueillements*, appropriately titled "Utopie" (*OPC*, 1149–57), hints moreover at the degree to which such penetration of the multiple, of the streamingness of all experience and involvement, is a self-multiplication permitting a greater sense of the infinity of the divine (*OPC*, 1156).

The *Harmonies poétiques et religieuses*, of 1830, give us no doubt the fullest and most intense reading of Lamartine's undying desire, and natural inclination, to make of his poetic act and text what he himself will repeatedly call a *hymn* to the manifold elements and experiences of the earth. "L'Hymne de la nuit" ("Hymn to Night") will be followed by "Hymne au matin" ("Hymn to Morning"); "Hymne de l'enfant à son réveil" ("Hymn to the Waking Child") by "Hymne du soir dans les temples" ("Evening Hymn in the Temples"); the second book will offer the "Hymne à la douleur" ("Hymn to Pain"); the third, "Encore un hymne ("One More Hymn") and "Hymne au Christ"; the fourth, "Hymne de la mort" ("Hymn to Death") and "Hymne de l'ange de la terre après la destruction du globe" ("Hymn of the Angel of Earth after the Planet's Destruction"). If the Lamartinian hymn still anchors itself relentlessly in the consciousness and adoration of the entire gamut of "things" (all is animate in this optic), "from the humble ant in its sandy cities/To the eagle of the sky sleeping on the wind" ("Hymne de l'ange," *OPC*, 461), it is equally clear that the concept of hymn, involving initially a singing of the glory of nature's mystery and abundance, expands in an important though comprehensible manner.

Hymn, for Lamartine, always remains celebration, worship, and, in consequence, acceptance and love, confidence and gratitude. We are not far, here, moreover, from essential components of the poetics of writers as far apart as Perse (*Eloges* [*Eulogies*]), Bonnefoy ("Dévotion"), and Deguy (his poems on/of "recognition"). But in many of the "hymns" of the *Harmonies* the song of worship and love embraces absolutely all that is, conceptually, abstractly, psychically, and not only in purely materially based terms. Hymn can become a song of intense dialogue: within acceptance and submissive adoration, but involving, too, exploration and inquiry—a profound sense, that is, of the profound multiplicity, infinity even, of those paradoxical, contradictory-complementary forces that constitute our collective and our individual unity. Once more, "Hymne de l'ange de la terre" (*OPC*, 457–63) gives an exquisitely delicate sense of such factors. Moreover, seen in this perspective, the poetics of the hymn, of buoyant enthusiasm and glorification of all that is, ceases to appear in conflict with sentiments of exile and solitariness upon the earth, with the "things" of nature: loneliness and being-with, chaos and meaning, refusal and belief, these are the very (il)limits of our consciousness—and thus, as "Hymne de l'ange de la terre" suggests, of what can be sung, celebrated, within us and without, of our terrestrial mystery and, as with the poem itself, *unfinished* meaning and obscurely brilliant glory.

God and Godliness: Transcendence and Assumption

Innumerable are the attributions and qualifications applied to God throughout the poetry of Lamartine, though there are three poems, in particular, that give to the notions of God and godliness especial attention: "Dieu" ("God"), from the *Méditations poétiques* (*OPC*, 71–75), "L'Esprit de Dieu" ("The Spirit of God," *OPC*, 111–113), from the *Nouvelles Méditations poétiques* and "Jéhova ou l'idée de Dieu" ("Jehova or the Idea of God"), a suite of four poems, from the *Harmonies poétiques et religieuses* (*OPC*, 361–77). In global terms, we may initially say that God(liness) is perceived by Lamartine—who will convert in 1820—as a transcendence, as a force available and speaking to humanity (*OPC*, 20), magnanimous (*OPC*, 35), the locus of all actuality and potentiality (*OPC*, 49), "The other, eternal, sublime, universal, immense," as he will put it in "Dieu" (*OPC*, 71). God is thus a manifest given, the source of "truth" (*OPC*, 85), infinite creation (*OPC*, 370), all that is realized or realizable, beyond specification or articulable comprehension. God(liness) in this sense is what we cannot but recognize, despite our humble humanity, as in being, all being, all that accounts for and bears up what is. The relatively early "Dieu" (*OPC*, 71–75), written in 1819—after all Lamartine was twenty-eight, almost twenty-nine—reveals something of both his deep sensitivity to the divine and the sense of urgency he no doubt felt upon the eve of his conversion and in contact with his wife-to-be: God is pure spirituality, that "inconceivable essence" his own "spirit" seeks nevertheless to penetrate—for God is available via the "language" of love, prayer, and "enthusiasm," all of which, like godliness itself, remain atemporal and aspatial. God, in effect, is constant origin-ation, via the force of a will for being, "cette volonté, sans ombre et sans faiblesse,/ . . . à la fois puissance, ordre, équité, sagesse" ("that will, without shadow or weakness,/ . . . at once power, order, equity, wisdom," *OPC*, 72), which is a gift—and, like all gifts, out of "nothingness"—as endless as it is misstated by the whims of clericalness, as prodigious as is our fear or ill-perception thereof.

"L'Esprit de Dieu" (*OPC*, 111–13) is an altogether less elaborate poem dating from the 1821–1822 post-honeymoon period, and it presses home that desire articulated at the end of "Dieu" for a second coming of sorts, for a blowing of the now assumed, but intrinsically transcendent "Divine Breath"—upon all, but also upon himself. The poem emphasizes the need for availability, openness, "poetic silence" one might say, in order to receive and feel such a breath: ironically, our very struggle, uncertainty, and doubt are modes of (divine) being closing themselves to the very mystery of their (divine) being.

"Jéhova ou l'idée de Dieu," a long four-part poem completed in 1829 (*OPC*, 361–77) traces some of the world's varying but sure forms of adoration of God and God's symbols: the divineness of light's diurnal ebb and flow; God as the pure mystery of the Other; God as implacably necessary human "invention"—and symbolic multiplication/representation of the enigmas/splendors of what is; God as ubiquitous, infinite and simultaneous materialization; and so on. Lamartine proceeds finally to invite our participation in the godly, via the senses and the soul ("Listen in your senses, listen within your soul"), in a revelatory penetration of the earth's natural, but symbolic, signs,

> when the earth breathing out its balsamic soul
> With its vital scent will intoxicate your senses,
> And the very insect, intoning its canticle
> Will hum with love upon the dawning buds!
> *(OPC, 366)*

The second part ("Le Chêne" ["The Oak"]) sings the remarkable mystery of growth and, in consequence, of all (forms of) creation/Creation. One might profitably compare it with Valéry's "Palme," and especially the lines that speak of

> Cette intelligence divine
> Qui pressent, calcule, devine
> Et s'organise pour sa fin,
> Et cette force qui renferme
> Dans un gland le germe du germe
> D'êtres sans nombres et sans fin.

> That divine intelligence,
> Intuitive, calculating, anticipating
> And organizing for its end,
> And that force enclosing
> Within an acorn the germ of the germ
> Of beings countless and endless.
> *(OPC, 370)*

The third part ("L'Humanité" ["Humanity"]) dwells in different but always movingly fundamental terms upon the fact and inherent significance of birth and maternity, and the astonishing rising up within the created individual of (implicitly) all that is possible via the senses, thought, language. "It gazes," Lamartine says of the newborn,

and daylight is painted upon its eye;
It thinks, and the universe within its soul appears!
It speaks, and its voice, like another light,
Flies painting itself in others' souls, line for line!

(*OPC*, 374)

The final section ("L'Idée de Dieu" ["The Idea of God"]) emphasizes the dialectics of seeing and blindness, and urges a reading of
the natural signs of the universe such that the latter's intrinsic
meaning, namely its godliness, may move from latency to actuality, transcendence to assumption. The closing stanzas, while stressing both the "consolation" thus available to humankind—for an
ethics of suffering persists as a firm and typical Romantic vestige of
Christian heritage (not that it is not manifest in "areligious" form
in writers as diverse as Proust and Beckett, Char and Frénaud)—
and the extent to which a sense of the divine is essential to all reasoning, do not hesitate to demonstrate how the human mind shifts
between the negative and positive poles of what it can assume and
project.

In large measure, then, Lamartine's poetry is inclined to give
weight to the notion of transcendent godliness, preexistent, unwavering, original, inexplicably present and eternal at the same time.
A good number of poems, however—and we shall return to this in
more general terms in our next section—as the close of "Jéhova"
itself reveals, underline the specific role of the individual in the
perception, and, in a sense, the reality—the full realization—of
godliness. For Lamartine never ceases to work at the idea of the
necessary assumption, the taking upon, within, oneself of the (divine) profundity and simplicity of being. Human incomprehension
is rife and Lamartine shares in it ("I have sought in vain the words
of the universe./... But the world to pride is a closed book!" he
will say in the early 1819 "L'Homme" ("Man"), from *Méditations*
(*OPC*, 7); and it can lead to doubt (*OPC*, 74, 429), fear (*OPC*, 363),
"blasphemy" (*OPC*, 7). Beyond such real "perils"—to which will
testify, often with great ambivalence and tension, much of the poetry from Vigny, through Baudelaire and Rimbaud, to Laforgue
and Lautréamont, and beyond to our days—Lamartine will never
lose sight of the potential, and already the intrinsic meaning, of
love, recognition, and desire (*OPC*, 73). As, again in "L'Homme,"
he argues, "Man is a fallen god remembering the heavens" (*OPC*,

6), "a child slipped from some divine race" (*OPC*, 11). The enthusiasms, poetic or other, lasting or short-lived, that traverse men and
women, are in themselves, he can say in an ecstatic moment of intimacy with the divine, "an echo of your own greatness" ("Le Cri de
l'âme," *OPC*, 401). But assumption is essential: individual action,
consciousness, choosing, intervention. "Oui, mon âme se plaît," we
read in "Dieu," "à secouer ses chaînes/. . . Je plane en liberté dans
les champs du possible"/"Yes, my soul delights in shaking off its
chains/. . . I hover in freedom in the fields of possibility" (*OPC*, 71):
we, as individuals, are the site of the possible, the only locus of any
freedom available to us. Godliness, "transcendent" as it may be,
depends upon personal creation. There are, indeed, gods of fear
and gods of desire, as he himself points out ("Jéhova," *OPC*, 364):
the "gods" are everywhere, as poets like Char or Jaccottet will suggest in contemplation of the simple things of the earth. "Homeland
is where the gods are," he will write, speaking of the Amerindian
(*OPC*, 365): but, as we have already seen, all "homeland" is within
the heart, awaiting our attention, our openness, our embrace—our
giving of intrinsic meaning to form, sign, being.

Question and Truth

Perhaps contrary to expectancy, the act of questioning remains of
central pertinence in the poetry of Lamartine, as to some important degree it will in that of Vigny and, in a mode altogether distinct, that of Hugo. Lamartine's interrogation is at once multiple,
varied in its focus, and general, even all-embracing. A poem such
as "L'Immortalité" ("Immortality"), from *Méditations* (*OPC*, 15–
18), can generate the most basic questioning of identity and existential purpose, worthy of a Bernard Noël were it not for a sense
of separation from an ever-intuited universal divineness. And
"Philosophie," from the same collection (*OPC*, 56–59), faced with
the "doubt" and "vanity" of the worldly actions around Lamartine, addresses to his "friend" the Marquis de la Maisonfort a plea
for guidance—in his frequent "tell me if" manner—which, for all
its conceivable undercurrents of intention, reveals a poet far from
basking in the complacency, or the simple joy, of certainty, calm,
utter confidence. The very worthiness of the self, the appropriate-
ness of the poet's endeavors, may even be queried, in the midst of
hymn ("L'Hymne de la nuit," *OPC*, 297: "Et moi, pour te louer,

Dieu des soleils, qui suis-je?" ["And who am I to praise you, God of suns"]). Such questioning should not be held to be mere posturing: Lamartine is capable, like any individual, of moments of anguish and despair, despite the power of his fervor, and beautiful and moving poems such as "Pourquoi mon âme est-elle triste" ("Why is my Soul Sad?" *OPC*, 424–30) or "Novissima verba" (*OPC*, 472–88) offer eloquent testimony to the depths beneath the latency. Ironically, even, the very rhetorical questions to which Lamartine can resort—in, for example, "Pourquoi mon âme est-elle triste?"—questions asking for the definition of the earth, life, glory, accomplishment, or love, offer confirmation of the emotionally and spiritually unstable states not uncommonly sweeping over the poet. The "answers" to such questions are sharply soured or cynical: earth is "a floating prison," life "the awakening of a moment," glory "a derision of our vainness," love itself, so magnificent and symbolically exquisite, "would be all, if it were not to end" (*OPC*, 424–25). And because we know that such answers can only be partial, fragmentary, tilted with the bias of the moment, they ultimately return us to the original questioning, the secret agenda of all (rhetorical) questioning: what does it mean to feel, to enthuse over, to doubt, for a comprehension of our being?

Similar questioning can occur outside all apparent rhetoricalness, as in "Invocation pour les Grecs" ("Invocation for the Greeks," *OPC*, 446–47), for example, where the silence of God that Vigny will bemoan is invoked; or in "Novissima verba" (*OPC*, 472–88), where questioning is seen to stem from human incapacity, "the sterile power/To embrace the infinite within my intelligence" (*OPC*, 481). Such questioning of the very root purpose of every existential trace—"Je demande à tout: Pourquoi? pourquoi? pourquoi?" ("I ask everything: Why? Why? Why?" Lamartine declares in the same poem (*OPC*, 481)—reveals the full ontic restlessness that, perhaps surprisingly, can inhabit this poetics of hymn, divine intuition, and harmony. Even a poem like "A Laurence" ("To Laurence"), from *Edition des souscripteurs* (*Subscribers' Edition*), where the repeated questioning seems initially fanciful ("Are you of Europe? are you of Asia?/Are you dream? are you poetry?" *OPC*, 1206), can generate rapidly an intensity of emotional quavering that, in turn, will translate itself into questions, perhaps rhetorically suspended, but in consequence all the more acute in their frustration, perhaps their deeper anguish ("Why are you come so late/... Oh God! who will give back my life?" *OPC*, 1206), and, above all, blatant signs that questioning is real, not contrived, for Lamartine, that his nobler strengths and high enthusiasms can be riddled with foible, uncertainty, and a sentimental fluttering metonymically symbolic of profound anguish or deep philosophical inquiry.

Of course, all questioning ultimately is synonymous with that thirst for knowledge, that awareness of the symphonic structure of being and dis/incarnation constantly underpinning Lamartine's poetico-ontological quest. "Je te cherche partout, j'aspire à toi, je t'aime" ("I seek you everywhere, I aspire to you, I love you"), he will write in "La Prière ("Prayer") of *Méditations* (*OPC*, 47); and of course, there are frequent moments of powerful intuition of cosmic truth, as in "L'Hymne de la nuit," where he will declare of the stars and the "oceans of azure," "I understand them, lord! all sings, all informs me" (*OPC*, 296); and of course questioning can be implicitly ecstatic, as in the delightful poem following from the *Harmonies*, "Hymne du matin":

> Pourquoi bondissez-vous sur la plage écumante,
> Vagues dont aucun vent n'a creusé les sillons?
>
> . . . .
>
> Pourquoi balancez-vous vos fronts que l'aube essuie,
> Forêts, qui tressaillez avant l'heure du bruit?
>
> . . . .
>
> Pourquoi relevez-vous, ô fleurs, vos pleins calices,
> Comme un front incliné que relève l'amour?
>
> Why do you leap upon the foaming beach,
> Waves furrowed by no wind?
>
> . . . .
>
> Why swing your brows wiped by dawn,
> Forests, quivering before sound's hour?
>
> . . . .
>
> Why, oh flowers, raise your full chalices,
> Like a head hung low raised by love?
>
> (*OPC*, 298)

For a sense of truth, like godliness, at once present and transcendent, is by no means exclusive in Lamartine of a questioning that may even be grating. In effect truth and questioning are but the two sides of the same phenomenon; in a sense they are equivalent, inseparable, unable to exist without each other notionally. For truth is answer, beyond question only inasmuch as it has (provisionally) absorbed it, recovered their oneness. As such it is perceived in its human form as those (consequently plural) "dazzling truths" available to genius, truth(s) nevertheless firmly set upon the "immovable base of eternal truth" and, as it were, participating in the latter ("Le Génie" ["Genius"], *OPC*, 53–54).

Let me stress once more that truth, like godliness, thus requires our assumption, a responsible, self-determining taking upon ourselves of answer—this despite all temporal setbacks and despite our inability to locate, quantify, and specify truth. The essential equation, and all the factoring involved, in "establishing" truth, is that employed in the perception and measurement of the divine, and, indeed, in the epigraph to *La Mort de Socrate,* Lamartine will go so far as to declare: "Truth is God!" (*OPC*, 85). A passage of the 1828 poem "Souvenir d'enfance ou la vie cachée" ("Childhood Memory or Hidden Life"), from *Harmonies,* makes clear his view that truth, despite our noblest efforts, remains atextual, unspeakable, though decidedly intuitable for all that (*OPC*, 380) via the *already, intrinsically illuminated* passage of being and a confidence, even, as Bonnefoy would say, a will in the depth of enigma—that very enigma that is synonymous, simultaneous, with truth and revelation. For, improbably—again one might think of the poetics of Bonnefoy—truth is finally always "palpable and practical," as Lamartine puts it in "Hymne au Christ": it is available, assumable; it circulates constantly, offering itself to the senses and to the emotions, if we give credence to their depth, their purpose, their meaning. And though Lamartine bemoans the loose and swarming multiplicity of human, mundane truth (in "Novissima verba," *OPC*, 478–79), one might argue, far from entirely against him, that such deformation of truth is nevertheless truth working itself out—in the abortive differences of the oneness that, ultimately, Lamartine feels, reigns supreme. The "mille vérités où Dieu n'en a mis qu'une" ("thousand truths where God has put only one," *OPC*, 478–79) are the finite gropings back towards divine truth's inconceivable infinity—beyond time, origin, separation—in what we might think of as pure Derridean—but self-knowing, omniscient—*différance.*

Dialectics and Harmony

We have already seen something of the extent to which Lamartine's mind tends to favor—beyond willful and contrived structuring, though the longer poems in particular would be necessarily conscious of a rhythmic orchestration of preoccupation—oppositions, paradoxes, firm or seeming distinctions. The present section presses this tendency further, while showing that, as such, difference and division are far from being at the heart of Lamartine's ideal poetics. To some degree, a dialectical conception and expression of the universe, as Derrida has shown, is essential to the structure of Western thought and language as a whole, and it is certainly of especial pertinence to the poetry of nineteenth-century France. Further, one must not overlook the simple fact that the articulation of *this* phenomenon, then *that* phenomenon, in time and in space, via a language syntagmatically and paradigmatically inspired (or at least currently conceived) and a poetic form privileging rhyme, fixed meter, and so on—such an articulation is intrinsically dialectical from the outset.

Lamartinian dialectics *is* the difference of being, the variation of emotion, the revision of thought, the doubting of affirmation, a sensitive respect for that ceaseless conversation within the self that the text gleans, moment by moment, day by day. It is a dialectics that conveys a sense of Lamartine's own infinity, but in inevitably finite terms. Such a dialectics can convey itself—without, moreover, any absolute synthesis, although Lamartine generally seeks conciliation and recuperation: we shall return to this—in the complex comings and goings of idea and sentiment of longer poems such as "L'Homme" (*OPC,* 4–11) or "Novissima verba" (*OPC,* 472–88), not to forget the vast *Jocelyn* (*OPC,* 567–757) or *La Chute d'un ange* (*The Fall of an Angel, OPC,* 803–1081). Or it may become manifest dialogue, as in *La Mort de Socrate* (*OPC,* 85–109) or "La Vigne et la maison" (*OPC,* 1484–94). Or one poem may offer symphonic counterpoise to that preceding, as does "La Providence à l'homme" ("Providence to Man," *OPC,* 24–27) to "Le Désespoir" ("Despair," *OPC,* 21–24), in *Méditations.* Or, again, Lamartinian dialectics may express itself in substantial mosaic poems, such as "La Poésie sacrée" from *Méditations* (OPC, 76–83) or "Les Préludes" ("The Preludes") from *Nouvelles méditations* (*OPC*, 156–66), where the poem is composed of a number of poems, in themselves sometimes fragmented and elliptical, setting up a multiple play of explicit or implicit oppositions and interpenetrations destabilizing simple thematic or notional structures and often resisting synthesis of a reductive nature. And, inevitably, other dialectical forms exist, often more subtle, with individual poems; inconceivably complex if we take the entire oeuvre as our "corpus."

In all of the above frameworks, moreover, one is struck by the modern and contemporary pertinence of Lamartine's poetic debate—by, in short, the degree to which Lamartinian dialectics is both fundamental and ever available to reassessment, new efforts of resolution, synthesis, or absorption. For Lamartine's struggles and analyses, his refusals and his insights, his propositions and re-propositions, are very much with us now: the tensions of exile and aspiration, or, equally, of exile and the bliss of presence, of being-there; the dialectics of *hasard* and will, or of *dérive*, existential or psychic drift, and desire, choice; the conceptual and emotional niceties interlocking atheism or agnosticism and what Bonnefoy will call *le sentiment religieux*—a feeling, of course, beyond formal religion; the temptation, for many, of *mauvaise foi* ("bad faith"), of a world ever imposed, and, as we have seen, the assumption of being; language viewable as empty, swirling sign, as opposed to language as deep symbol, as meaning's moving trace; the dialectics of despair and hope, or even what André Frénaud will call *non-espoir* (non-hope); knowledge and lesson as programmable, readable, dependent upon the high initiates of intellectualism or some other ism, and knowledge and lesson as located and growing within the self. The list could be considerably extended, yet would not lose any of its endless relevance.

The very inherent rhythms of any dialectical "structure" are, arguably, already related to the concept of harmony, both in the latter's partial synonymy with the notion of synthesis and, paradoxically, its own oppositional relationship with the ideas of difference, tension, discordance. One might say, too, that Lamartine's pluralization of "harmony" in *Harmonies poétiques et religieuses* is also significant for it speaks at once of a necessarily repeated effort of harmonization; a sense of sameness or equivalent symphony within different phenomena and circumstances; and, of course, both a distinction between, and a rendering parallel, osmotically related, of the poetic and the religious. As "L'Humanité" affirms, Lamartinian "harmony" involves a concordance of the diverse, a sym-pathy, a grace, a beauty, a genial music (*OPC*, 371)—in which the poetic act endeavors to participate in a metric cadencing ("Souvenir d'enfance," *OPC*, 378–85) symbolic of that mystery that gives language, as from a hidden but certain source: "How is it," asks Lamartine in the same poem,

> that, beyond my knowledge, wedded to my voice,
> Harmonious words link up at my fingertips?
> And that in brilliant meter my cadenced verve
> Like a limpid current carries off my thought?
>
> (*OPC*, 379)

An answer to this question of profound significance—how *is* it that song is possible, or the simple balance of speech, or exquisite "given" musical composition such as Mozart's?—seems to be forthcoming in the following poem from *Harmonies:*

> Loi sainte et mystérieuse!
> Une âme mélodieuse
> Anime tout l'univers;
> Chaque être a son harmonie,
> Chaque étoile son génie,
> Chaque élément ses concerts.
>
> Mysterious and holy law!
> A melodious soul
> Animates the entire universe;
> Each being has its harmony,
> Each star its genius,
> Each element its symphony.
>
> (*OPC*, 386)

Harmony, in this optic, is both cosmic, universal, all-penetrating, and yet also individualized, within each element, each *difference*, constituting and permitting it, rendering already symphonic the "simple," the "single"—harmonizing, better, the unthinkable complexities of the elemental, the microcosmic, as the macrocosm harmonizing the totality of its differences, its parts, in a one-souled melody whose presence we can intuit, but whose psychic-material mystery we cannot analytically fathom. In this optic, again, all is sym-phony and a sym-pathy; all individual "harmonies" are super-orchestrated by, subsumed within, the "original" "soul-melody" of all that is-was-will be. "Harmony is the soul of the heavens," Lamartine will announce—metaphorically, but also metonymically; the expression is, can be no more than, partial, synecdochic—at the outset of "La Voix humaine" ("The Human Voice"), in *Harmonies* (*OPC*, 446), yet harmony, for him, is clearly traversable, experienceable, in *any* of its (in)finite modes: here, the human voice; there, the song of the nightingale ("Au rossignol" ["To the Nightingale"]):

> Tu ne sais pas que mon oreille,
> Suspendue à ta douce voix,
> De l'harmonieuse merveille
> S'enivre longtemps sous les bois!

> You know not that my ear,
> Hung upon your sweet voice,
> Has long drunk in beneath the woods
> Its harmonious wonder!
>
> (*OPC*, 4 55).

The "harmonies" of *Harmonies,* as indeed of other works of Lamartine, are "poetic" and "religious," of self and Other; they seek to symphonize personal and cosmic rhythms, finite, different musics and the universal music, the infinite muse, of all that bears up difference and dialectics. As such, they join, in the oneness of their col-lection, their col-lation, hymn and lament, "cry" and elegy, remembrance and the imagination of pure spirit, the telluric and the interstellar. As such Lamartinian harmonies evoke *equally*— and in every sense of the word—the logic of difference, separation, inalienable specificity or "exile," and the logic of *différance*, the dissemination and deployment of oneness, both as opposition, dissociation, and as nondifference, recuperation, reciprocal absorption, indistinction, mystery, an *in-connu* intuitable and poeticizable, symbolizable: as Michel Deguy would say, "thrown together" (*sum-ballein*) into an improbable oneness.

From Meter to Tone

Lamartine's poetic form is often celebrated, and rightly, less for its metric innovation per se, than for an exceptional rhythmic delicacy within traditionally available metric patterns. There is no doubt that the alexandrine remains his principal prosodic strategy, and, as for Vigny, Hugo, and others, even Rimbaud, this will be particularly so in the narrative or discursive poems, even though common in other modes, as with almost all other poets of the century. Despite this embrace of convention, in the hands of Lamartine the alexandrine becomes a supple, elegant, yet intimate expressive tool, via enjambment, subtle displacements of the caesura, delicate, gentle *coupes,* and the widespread use of extended rhythmic groups, the more occasional, but equally effective mixing of the alexandrine with single lines or whole sub-poems of different meter (*pair* or, even, *impair*), the frequent unfixing of the implacable rhyming couplet and the consequent "development" of rhyming patterns of greater unpredictability. In this distinct effort of prosodic liberation, it is interesting to find that Lamartine almost never resorts to the ten-syllable line—one sees it very occasionally, as in "Pensée des morts" ("Thought of the Dead," in *Harmonies, OPC,* 335–41)—though he dips into a wide arsenal of other meters, used either separately or in conjunction, commonly, with the alexandrine. Here, although the semi-alexandrine can be employed (as in "Le Lac," *OPC,* 38–40), he favors the line of eight syllables ("Adieu", from *Méditations, OPC,* 65–67; "La Sagesse" ["Wisdom"], from *Nouvelles méditations, OPC,* 177–79; "Amitié de femme" ["Woman's Friendship"], from *Recueillements, OPC,* 1107–1108), but he can quite often opt for the *impair,* especially the seven-syllable line, again for exclusive use with individual poems ("Désir" ["Desire"], in *Harmonies, OPC,* 385–88) or for combinatory effects (12/5 as in "Jéhova," *OPC,* 361–66, 12/7 as in "Pourquoi mon âme est-elle triste," *OPC,* 424–30; these are Lamartine's distinctly preferred modulations, though often, as here, with eight-syllable stanzas intercollated).

Stanzaic form in Lamartine's work amply repays examination and contributes substantially to that musical, compositional genius which is specifically his. Rooted in solid tradition, yet emerging from it with beautiful flexibility and surprising unpredictability, such form is at once largely stable within the oeuvre as a whole, yet varied, delicately and vigorously, from poem to poem as well as within many individual poems. The first few poems of *Méditations* are already reasonably indicative of what will come: "L'Isolement" (*OPC*, 4–11) has thirteen stanzas whose line-count is as follows: 20-22-16-32-12-40-6-38-12-40-14-10-20; "A Elvire" (*OPC*, 12–13) three-stanzaic groups of 26-20-8; "Le Soir" ("Evening, *OPC*, 13–15) thirteen *faux quatrains*; "L'Immortalité" (*OPC*, 15–18) is all of a piece, but set in eleven "paragraphs"; "Le Vallon" (*OPC*, 19–20) has sixteen *faux quatrains*; "Le Désespoir" twenty-one stanzas of six lines each; "La Providence à l'homme" (*OPC*, 24–27) six quatrains, four ten-line stanzas, two of five lines, three of seven, and, finally, two more of ten. Apart from the variation in stanzaic length, there is, of course, here as elsewhere, varying meter and rhyme scheme. Longer poems, such as "La Providence à l'homme," "L'Homme," or "L'Immortalité" opt either for interior groupings of short poem or stanza forms (as with the former), or for loose, but still con-sciously composed, structures, where, arguably, the notion of stanza tends to fade (as with "L'Homme"), or, again, for massive monolithic blocks, where, once more, stanzaic pertinence is re-duced.

The overall impact, however, conveys great sensitivity to and flexibility toward such issues. The *Nouvelles méditations* continue and expand, as do the *Harmonies*, this policy of discreet but sure freeing up of stanzaic composition. A few illustrations will suf-fice, first from the *Nouvelles méditations*, where "Le Papillon" (*OPC*, 128) offers us a single ten-line stanza; "Elégie" (*OPC*, 143–44) a quatrain, followed by two stanzas of eight lines, two of five, and delightfully, an unusual closing eleven-line stanza; "Les Préludes" (*OPC*, 156–66) provides the following astonishing com-plex of sub-poems and stanzaic structure (given in line count): 16/4/5×13/12/4/52/5/20+61+18+16/20/5/4×18/14; and "Adieux à la poésie" ("Farewell to Poetry," *OPC*, 189–92) gives twenty-four five-line stanzas. As for the *Harmonies*, two examples will do: "L'Hymne de la nuit" (*OPC*, 295–98), where we see: 5-4×2-5-16-10×2-6-10-14-6-10-8; and "Hymne au Christ" (*OPC*, 405–15), where the stanzaic configuration is again unexpectedly complex and varied and this time without formal division into "sub-po-ems" as above (once more, in line count per stanza): 10-4-17-5-40-7×12-15-10×10-20-12×2-10 × 4-25.

The great poems *Jocelyn* and *La Chute d'un ange* have their own particular compositional logics, which, different one from the other, also differ from the stanzaic configurations already examined. Both show that, while the strict notion of stanza is superseded by the vast narrative thrust, relatively stable groupings and limits persist, with pauses, or, more strikingly, with poetic "black holes," marked by *points de suspension,* as in Bonnefoy's *Dans le leurre du seuil (In the Lure of the Threshold),* and, despite differences of perspective, the effect is far from dissimilar: there is a deaestheticizing result and a consequent recentering upon *présence* or "combative" thought, as Denis Roche would say. It might be noted, too, that the compositional/stanzaic rhythm represents in all likelihood the intermittent creative rhythms of these poems' actual writing. The *Recueillements poétiques* reveal stanzaic patterning broadly similar to that of the 1820, 1823, and 1830 collections, although the eight-line stanza assumes a role of distinctly privileged usage, and, within given poems, much greater stanzaic stability is to be found. "Utopie" (*OPC,* 1149–57) is in many ways characteristic to the extent that it offers variation within an overall elegance of composition: ten stanzas of seven lines, followed by thirteen of ten, terminated by eleven, once more, of seven.

Before moving, finally, in this brief assessment of major stylistic features in Lamartine's poetry, to the matter of tone, I should like to cast an eye upon a few other important factors whose more detailed analysis is not feasible here—first of all, rhyme. Lamartinian rhyme-schemes are traditional but as supple as his use of meter and stanzaic form, indeed, in part, stemming from the shifting option his use of the latter permits. The *rime plate,* especially in the longer poems, remains a staple diet, but great delicacy prevails in many of the poems from *Méditations* to *Recueillements: rimes croisées, rimes embrassées,* of course, but all kinds of resultant combinations: *abaab,* as in "Adieux à la mer" (*OPC,* 172–74); *abbacc,* as in "La Retraite" ("Retirement," *OPC,* 36–38); *aabccb,* as in "Bonaparte" (*OPC,* 118–23); *aabcccb,* as in "Utopie" (*OPC,* 1149–57). And others can be found. Secondly, the continuity of Lamartine's poems, not to mention that of the oeuvre as a whole, a continuity, moreover, already buoyed up by the interlocking intricacies of meter, stanza, and rhyme—such a continuity is a most perceptible and impressive feature, and one that will be admired by contemporaries and successors alike.

Here, a careful study of the length of Lamartine's poems, and of the many other mechanisms permitting their complex articulation, would prove fruitful. Interesting contrasts with modern poetics of the brief, the fragmentary, the elliptic, from Mallarmé to Reverdy, Char and Dupin, and with the art of poets of the extended such as Perse, Bonnefoy, and Guillevic, would be richly available. But continuity clearly can be exquisitely delicate even in the (rather rare) short poems of Lamartine: "Le Papillon" of *Nouvelles méditations* (*OPC*, 128), "Raphaël," of *Edition des souscripteurs* (*OPC*, 1250–51), or the posthumous "Le Réveil" ("Reawakening," *OPC*, 1722–23); although the poems of medium length, such as "Le Lac" (*OPC*, 38–40) or "Encore un hymne" (*OPC*, 388–91), and, perhaps surprisingly, longer poems from the main collections, can offer great rolling swaths of verse carried forward by anaphora, complex but clear subordinate clauses, hyperbaton, crescendo, and so on. "Philosophie" or "Dieu," from *Méditations*, give ample evidence of this. But then, so do the great poetic masses of *Jocelyn*, *La Chute d'un ange*, and *Les Visions*, any page of which will provide sweeping Hugolian passages of ten to thirty lines. Lamartinian continuity can, as we have already seen, take different forms, as in "Les Préludes" (*OPC*, 156–66) and "Chant d'amour" (*OPC*, 180–87), where, to some extent as in the work as a whole, and in a manner surprisingly modern (one thinks of Apollinaire and Frénaud), sub-poems are elaborated in close but also discontinuous juxtaposition, whose interpenetration derives in part from form, in part from theme.

Thirdly, Lamartine's use of apostrophe and general strategy of intimacy is a constantly recurrent element contributing greatly to tonal quality, as we shall see, and enmeshing the poetics of writing and reading in a way perhaps not sufficiently acknowledged. The entire Lamartinian opus, like much Romantic and, in effect, post-Romantic and even contemporary poetry, is centered upon the elaboration of subjective experience (indeed, one might ask, is there any other?)—the *je*, in the literary mode, and indeed implicitly via its inclusion within the paradigm *je-tu-il-elle*, always implying exchange, conversation, as well as openness, self-revelation, a natural bent for engagement with the *tu*, the other/Other, the silent, unspeaking non-self. Apostrophe evidently goes further in this engagement, which may, perhaps always implicitly, seek to contact the other *of* the self, in a quest for oneness and universality we have seen to be central to Lamartine's poetics. "Toi, dont le monde ignore le vrai nom" ("You, whose true name the world ignores"), begins "L'Homme" (*OPC*, 4); "Doux reflet d'un globe de flamme,/Charmant rayon, que me veux-tu?" ("Sweet reflection of a flaming globe,/Ray of delights, what do you want with me?") Lamartine asks in "Le Soir" (*OPC*, 14); "Je te salue, ô mort! Libérateur céleste" ("I greet you, oh death! Celestial liberator"), we read in "L'Immortalité" (*OPC*, 15); and so the poems of *Méditations* continue: apostrophe; dialogue; *dédoublement;* tender whispering; merging intimacy of *je* and *tu* in the *nous* and *ils* of poems like "Le Lac" (OPC, 38–40); blatant, bold address; quiet, humble, but firm, colloquy.

Fourthly, Lamartine's metaphoric and other figurative modes, underestimated in their range and delicate complexity, perhaps owing largely to the effect upon some of exclamatory, circumlocutionary, or slightly sententious effects ("Oh lake! the year barely has completed its circle," "Le Lac," *OPC*, 38; "Happy those who, stepping from the paths here below," *OPC*, 135, the opening line of "La Solitude"). Let me quote, more or less at random, one of the sub-poems from "Les Préludes" (*OPC*, 159):

> J'entends, j'entends de loin comme une voix qui gronde;
> Un souffle impétueux fait frissonner les airs,
>   Comme l'on voit frissonner l'onde
> Quand l'aigle, au vol pesant, rase le sein des mers.

> I hear, I hear from afar as a voice rumbling;
> An impetuous breath makes the air to shiver,
>   As we see shiver the water
> When the heavy-flighted eagle brushes the sea's bosom.

One will stress, initially, what Reverdy will call that *marge de silence* framing the poem, out of which it emerges into, precisely, its poemness or what he calls its *antinature,* a process Lamartine would seem to be dramatically figuring, moreover, via this poem, which in the final analysis evades our reductive grasp, being without title and evident linkage to the preceding and following poems. Repetition, and yet repetition with elaboration, marks the first line, with the simile that is also a *fausse comparaison*—or better, a figure that is Lamartine's only way of evoking the reality he perceives, or else a simile without completion. Already the mechanisms of what Reverdy terms *cette émotion appelée poésie* ("the emotion called poetry")—the multiple aesthetic or figurative transmutations, small as they may be—are mounting up. The uncertainty of the latter trope and that of the overall semantic optic should not, either, be over-looked. The second line offers personification, continuing ambiguity (this "impetuous breath" could be many things: wind, brewing storm, poetic muse, consciousness, the rise of emotion, especially love), the slightly unusual pluralization of *airs,* and a phonetic, allit-erative consonantal play, different from the nasal insistence of the first line. The third line returns to comparison, but in a modified grammatical mode, and sets up echoes not just with the preceding line but also with the first (the rhyme and *voit/voix*)—and there is also the internal echo (*l'on/l'onde*).

The cumulative aesthetic/tropological effect is by now quite considerable; the final line of this *faux quatrain* poem-within-a-poem brings a good deal more: first, the delicate metaphor (*vol pe-sant*), which locks, in thoroughly appropriate but unexpected tension, motions of flight and weight/gravity; secondly, the beau-tiful metaphor of *le sein des mers,* which gives sensual and possibly affective symbolic depth to the text: is it, indeed, a most subtle of love poems? (I discount the would-be metaphoricity of *rase,* "brushes," "skims," although, as Michel Deguy has aptly argued, all language is symbolic and, strictly, metaphoric: *comme-si* ["as-if"], the *être-comme* ["being-as"] of our being); thirdly, the matching pluralization of *mers,* with *airs;* fourthly, the continuing alliterative and somewhat onomatopoeic play: *pesant, rase, sein,* after *souffle* and *frissonner;* finally, the reabsorption of the poem by its framing "margin of silence," its plunging of the reader back into the basic questions of its meaning, its mystery, its multiple semanticity. Many other poems could be adduced and similarly displayed in the fullness of their discreet but rich figurativeness.

Let me, in conclusion, draw very brief attention to the great tonal range, and yet curiously the tonal constancy of this poetry. Much could be developed here, in accordance both with the above and with the rich thematics essentially outlined. Elegy abounds, with its admixture of nostalgia, melancholy, and yet alertness to both the beauty of ephemeralness and the mystery of all creation. Lyri-cism, too, penetrates everywhere, into the evocations and "impres-sionistic" portrayals of the things of nature and country life, the great love poems, the "hymns," the occasional simple "songs," even the philosophically oriented poems, and, again, the immense imaginings of *Jocelyn, La Chute d'un ange,* and *Les Visions.* Philosophy, or what Lamartine will properly call *méditation,* a mixture of *rêverie,* rigorous thought, and intuitive postulation, plays a significant role in moulding his poetic tone. Religious inspiration, usually in the broadest sense of the term, clearly has its effect also, as do in their various ways, the epics, the personal homages, the occasionally political or sociologically attuned pieces. What is perhaps most striking, however, once this range is acknowledged, is the relative tonal evenness that finally prevails. This constancy, without returning to the above notions, I should describe as combative, restless, and yet never aggressive, always resorting to the relative warmness, intimacy and gentleness of an enthusiasm, a desire, a will that give intentional, explicative, and not just purely passive and contemplative, tonality to Lamartine's work.

Reason and Poetry

For the accomplishment of the poetic, or indeed existential, task before Lamartine, intelligence and reason can, at times, seem inadequate tools. All too often, "our feeble reason muddies over in confusion," as he says in "L'Immortalité" (*OPC,* 17); it is an "[insufficient torch] that pales [and] abandons me to darkness" ("La Foi" ["Faith"], *OPC,* 53), far from the paradoxical strengths of "instinct" (*OPC,* 17) or of love and worship of being (*OPC,* 53). In "La Sagesse," Lamartine can thus go as far as to say—though in distress and removed from all Rimbaldian or surrealist construction we might be tempted to place upon his statement: "Insensé le mortel qui pense!/Toute pensée est une erreur" ("Insane the thinking mortal!/All thought is error," *OPC,* 177). And yet what he himself calls the "hymn of reason" can rise upon within him, and despite feeling at times "the sterile power," as he puts it in "Novissima verba," "of embracing the infinite within my intelligence" (*OPC,* 481), he can appreciate that "the voice of the universe is my intelligence" ("La Prière," *OPC,* 46); that intelligence lies deep within all things, all that is ("Hymne de l'ange," *OPC,* 459); that "reason" has the ability to traverse the darkness of incomprehension (*OPC,* 47); that imagination is the "eye of thought" permitting illuminated seeing (*OPC,* 1103); that—the human participating in the at once transcendent and osmotically available divine—(wo)man may

know, as Lamartine says in "L'Utopie" (*OPC*, 1152), "of intelli-
gence/The multiple prodigies/[That] allow the treading under of
the impossible/Across time and space"; that, amazingly, *all* being
already given via the intrinsic intelligence of (all) being, no expla-
nations are in a sense needed: being is exquisitely self-explanatory,
tautological, one might say: "L'amour m'explique l'amour!"
("Love explains love to me!"), he cries out in "La Semaine sainte à
la Roche-Guyon" ("The Holy Week in Roche-Guyon"), "puis-je
douter encore?" ("can I still doubt?" *OPC*, 69).

Lamartine's conception of poetry allies itself broadly to the latter
interpretations of reason and intelligence. His *méditations, harmonies,* and *recueillements* defy notions of strictly logical creation and
composition, based upon laborious and systematic development.
His poetics may not be that of pure Rimbaldian *dérive* ("drifting")
and *dérèglement* ("disturbance"), but the "poetic delirium" he
evokes explicitly in "Adieux à la poésie" of *Nouvelles méditations*
(*OPC*, 189) clearly lies at a conceptual intersection of recuperative
Rimbaldian reason ("un long, immense et raisonné dérèglement de
tous les sens" ["a long, vast and reasoned disturbance of all
senses"]), a kind of surrealist—or, better, Reverdyan—surrender to
one's "availability" without letting the phantasmagorical dominate, and sheer ecstasy upon finding oneself to be the focus—privileged, genial, but one among others—of, literally, a coming within
the self of the divine, of that voice described in the above-examined
sub-poem from "Les Préludes," "J'entends, j'entends de loin"
(*OPC*, 159). Poetry, in this perspective, is that intelligence or
"thought,/[That,] before seeking its tone,/Rises quick like in-
cense/In rhythmed, divine meter" ("Invocation," *OPC*, 294); it is a
gift beyond learning, an incontrovertible way—of being—for some
individuals (*OPC*, 147), a logic of song beyond specific existential
conditions (*OPC*, 144). No wonder that Lamartine deems it "sacred" (*OPC*, 76), "divine" (*OPC*, 145), and, as "Le Poète mourant"
("The Dying Poet") of *Nouvelles méditations* (*OPC*, 144–49) continues to make clear, synonymous and synchronous with the ac-
tive/passive surging forth within the self of love and prayer, the
result of passions acting sublimely upon the soul.

"Musique intérieure," he will write in the first sub-poem of "Les
Préludes," "ineffable harmonie,/Harpes que j'entendais résonner
dans les airs/Comme un écho lointain des célestes concerts" ("Inner music, ineffable harmony,/Harps heard echoing upon the

air/Like a distant sound of some celestial symphony," *OPC*, 156). Poetry may be enigma, "blindness" as Jacques Dupin would say, but, assumed and "seen," "heard," it may become as sublime as all recognized ontic possibility, all ontic giving/receiving. It is, therefore, not surprising that the poetic act may be felt as a "consolation," as with Marceline Desbordes-Valmore, "to lay pain to sleep" (*OPC*, 190), and although Lamartine may say, in the same poem, "Adieux à la poésie," rather dispiritedly it may seem, that "all that sings repeats/But yearnings or desire" (*OPC*, 190), the greatest "sweetness" is associated with such seeming ambivalence—and, in effect, does Lamartine not recognize, here, what Bernard Noël will call the logic of the *mot-mort*, that all writing is merely absence and repetition? This with the major difference, however, that Lamartine senses more specifically, *at the same time*, the passage of being, the very rising up of being, within an act, *as* an act, whose textual product, rather, will tend to fix the contemporary attention.

The "Invocation" at the beginning of the *Harmonies* (*OPC*, 291–93) will thus stress—and in this sense he meets up again with poets of the body and the senses, from Rimbaud to Michaux, Bataille, and Noël—the linking of the poetic act to the sensorial and the sensual. But in so doing he will tend to re-ground poetry in presence. Moreover, his insistence upon the soul as the twin channel of voice, poiesis, should not be viewed askance by contemporary cynics: the soul is synonymous with ontic actuality, the (senti)mental/spiritual buoyancy of what, strangely, is—as strangely for Lamartine, in many ways, as for all people, ever. The same poem also, with the same intuition, reinserts poetic voice into the conceptual—and real, actual—framework of all voicing, all other voices, the voices of the Other: poiesis is at once oneness, universality, and difference, specificity—the logic pursued above in discussing "dialectics" and "harmony" resurfaces.

"Au Rossignol" (*OPC*, 455–57) offers a simple articulation of this duality/multiplicity of voice/being and the reabsorption into oneness that is perceptible, intuitable. "Oh! mingle your voice with mine!" Lamartine exclaims, "The same ear hears us;/. . . It is the echo of a nature/But love and purity" (*OPC*, 457). And in the pointedly titled "Poésie, ou paysage dans le Golfe de Gênes ("Poetry, or Landscape in the Gulf of Genoa")—where a kind of equivalence is already hinted at between individual poetry and universal self-expression—Lamartine again affirms, despite his feeling that human poetry can be so precariously close to cacophony, mere "noise," "bruits de langues," Noël will call it, that all language is but emblematic of, metonymically and metaphorically participating in, that divine, given language—*poésie* or *paysage*—"[dont] toute creature/Entend [l]es sublimes accents/Ô langue! et, selon sa mesure,/En pénètre plus loin le sens!" ("[whose] sublime tones, oh language!/are heard by every creature, penetrating/Further, to his measure, their fuller sense," *OPC*, 331).

In this optic, Lamartine's conception of poetry remains simultaneously immanent—plunged in the ephemeral, the corporal, the imperfect—and transcendent, because not only conscious of and committed to self's higher aspirations, but also aware of the a priori, in-principle interpenetration of self and all otherness, the unity of all poiesis, all creation, all being in its infinite emergence. "De l'hymne universel," he writes in "A l'esprit saint" ("To the Holy Spirit"), in the last lines of *Harmonies*, "être une voix choisie" ("To be a chosen voice of the universal hymn"): a poetic voice chosen no doubt in the sense of being the locus of an exceptional and enigmatic gift, enabling universal voice to be heard just that much more clearly; but chosen, too, in the way all being and doing remains to be assumed, made a real part of the self's dream-project, a choice lived in its frustrations as in its joyous privilege.

· THREE ·

Vigny

Seven years after the birth of Lamartine, Alfred de Vigny came into the world, on 22 March 1797, in the town of Loches. Moved to Paris, experiencing the powerful and ambivalent influence of his mother during schooldays less than perfect, Vigny perhaps not surprisingly opts early on for an army career that would see him participate in the Hundred Days War yet undergo frustration, disappointment, and disillusion both materially and spiritually. This not-so-grand military adventure, from 1814 to 1827, was also a period of poetic awakening, his earliest poems dating from 1816 and small, but critically developing publications continuing throughout: *Poèmes* in 1822, the first collection of the *Poèmes antiques et modernes* (*Ancient and Modern Poems*) in 1826 and slowly amplified until 1837. Witness in 1822 at Victor Hugo's youthful marriage, Vigny himself was to marry the Englishwoman Lydia Bunbury in 1825. His wife's illness, her subsequent decline and, with the years, worsening condition were to plunge him into the ambiguities of faithfulness and desire that will haunt a good deal of his work.

Prose and the theater were equally to draw his scrupulous attention: important and staged translations of Shakespeare, his own theatrical creations such as *La Maréchale d'Ancre* (1831) and the powerfully austere *Chatterton* (1834), great novelistic or short-prose successes such as *Cinq-Mars* (1826), *Stello* (1832) and *Servitude et grandeur militaires* (*Military Slavery and Greatness*, 1835). A number of women play crucial roles in the evolution of a sensibility at once delicate and troubled: Delphine Gay, the future Mme de Girardin, with whom he had fallen in love before meeting his wife; the young, newly wed Tryphina Holmes, met in Dieppe; the intense actress Marie Dorval with whom he only definitively broke in 1837, the year of his mother's death; Julia Dupré, the young American in Paris; years later, from 1858 on, Augusta Froustey, who would bear him a never-recognized son shortly after his death.

Unsuccessful in his would-be political forays, divided in his allegiances and impulses by both the 1830 and 1848 revolutions, only half-heartedly linked to literary and other groups, Vigny cuts a largely solitary, ill-adapted figure. Elected to the Académie Française only upon his sixth endeavor in 1845, his tenure is immediately soured by the Comte Molé's response to his own less than transcendent *discours de réception*. It is no surprise to see him withdraw, despite friendships with artists such as Berlioz, Liszt, and Chopin, to the calm entrenchedness of his property of the Maine-Giraud in the Angoumois. For years—since 1839, in effect—Vigny had been preparing, planning, theorizing, symbolically orchestrating the texts of that great poetic collection he never was to publish in his own lifetime, due largely to greatly failing health in his last years: *Les Destinées* (*The Destinies*). To his friend, Louis Ratisbonne, goes this honour, in the year following Vigny's difficult passing on 17 September 1863. "Chaste et fataliste," is the youthful Laforgue's cryptic designation over twenty years later, but Baudelaire is more ample in his conviction that it was Vigny, who, with one or two other great creative voices, "brought French poetry back to life": a proper and weighed judgment by a poet who understood what his own transformation owed to those, heroic and crucial, immediately preceding his own.

Episode and Essence

Vigny's 1837 preface to *Poèmes antiques et modernes* (*Ancient and Modern Poems*) argues that the volume's originality stems from the fact that "a philosophical thought is enacted in Epic or Dramatic form" (*OC*, I, 5), that there is in effect convergence and balancing of modes, without any effort to give priority to one or the other. Vigny's double predilection for the *récit* and the theatrical is, of course, easy to demonstrate: translations of Shakespeare's *Roméo et Juliette* (1827–1828), *Le More de Venise* (*The Moor of Venice*, 1829), and *Le Marchand de Venise* (*The Merchant of Venice*, 1830); the creation of his own theater, crowned by the staging of *Chatterton* (1835); the publication of novels and *récits* rendering him the seeming and provisional French equivalent of Walter Scott: *Cinq-Mars* (1826), *Stello* (1832), *Servitude et grandeur militaires* (*Military Slavery and Greatness*, 1835)—all of this teeming activity being intimately intertwined with the development of the various editions of the

Vigny

Poèmes antiques et modernes, from 1822 to 1837. And to the very end of his life his posthumously published and perhaps most celebrated of books, *Les Destinées* (*The Destinies*, 1864) was to engage Vigny in the same dialectics and synthesis of the dramatic, the episodic or the epic and the whole aesthetic and intellectual dynamics of what the collection's subtitle simply calls *poèmes philosophiques*.

Vigny's dramatized epic—one thinks of modern poets such as Saint-John Perse, with *Anabase* (*Anabasis*), for example, or André Frénaud, with *La Sorcière de Rome* (*The Witch of Rome*), which he himself terms an *épopée mythique* ("mythical epic"), although the distinctions remain large—may poeticize biblical scenes ("La Fille de Jephté" ["The Daughter of Jephthah"], *OC*, I, 42–44), *faits divers* ("Les Amants de Montmorency" ["The Lovers of Montmorency"], *OC*, I, 102–105), historical or legendary moments ("Le Trappiste" ["The Trappist"], *OC*, I, 86–93, or "Symétha," *OC*, I, 56–57); or it may choose to "rewrite" poetic texts ("Le Cor" ["The Horn"], *OC*, I, 812–24) or plunge us into vast contemporary social dramas ("La Prison" ["Prison"], *OC*, I, 65–73) or, again, give to personal experience, observation, or thought a huger optic, at once rooted and broadly symbolic ("Le Malheur" ["Misfortune"], *OC*, I, 63–65). Such dramatized poetry can thus take us from Moses ("Moïse," *OC*, I, 7–10) and the Flood ("Le Déluge," *OC*, I, 32–41) to poignant existential miniatures of past and present ("Le Somnambule" ["The Sleepwalker"], *OC*, I, 50–52, and "La Mort du Loup" ["Death of the Wolf"], *OC*, I, 143–45), or, again, to more ample canvasses: of time immemorial, such as "Eloa" (*OC*, I, 10–31), of contemporary Christian colonialism, such as "La Sauvage" ("The Savage," *OC*, I, 133–39), of seething urban modernity, as in "Paris" (*OC*, I, 105–112). "How sweet, how sweet it is to listen to stories told," he will rather pointedly write in the 1820 "La Neige" ("Snow"), from the *Poèmes antiques et modernes* (*OC*, I, 79), emphasizing the fascination with event, the specific, the lived, the incontrovertible, that, indeed, which seems to be caught in that moment of flux between option and destiny, the possible and the fatal.

There is something at once immobile and moving in (hi)story, in time's, presence's slow congealment into "stories of time past" (*OC*, I, 79), a convergence that draws out the narrative and descriptive (Claude Simon will equate the terms) powers of Vigny, yet urges him to push beyond the surface to what he instinctively knows to be an essential depth linked inseparably to it, like meaning to sign, *fond* to *forme*. One could argue, too, that Vigny's conception of the "dramatic" is well attuned to this convergence in that it allows the semi-congealing event to be experienced in all its poignancy, its "movingness"—at that critical instant when the fatal remains unaccomplished, when "destinies" are flowing into their apparently final mold, when history is still life, *récit* still *présence*. The "philosophical" coloring, in a sense, tends to point up the discreet or blatant emotions, or thought, underpinning such ontologically pertinent junctures, showing at once their personal and universal features, their specific exquisiteness and their latent, if irreducible symbolism.

For Vigny's philosophizing, it is important to stress from the outset, refuses systematizing, purely analytical rigor. It is emotional, subjective, and variable, rather than mathematical, logically consistent. It pursues a philosophy in situ, now extrapolating from joy or high aspiration, now from doubt or ignorance, now from anguish or deep anxiety—a practical philosophy, strictly beyond platonic essentiality, though striving to perceive the shifting psychic emblematicalness of given circumstance. In that sense, Vigny's philosophizing—take his views on human evolution and progress in "Paris" (*OC*, I, 105–112), or on woman in "La Colère de Samson" ("Sampson's Wrath," *OC*, I, 139–42), or on God and Evil in "Le Mont des Oliviers" ("The Mount of Olives," *OC*, I, 149–53)—is not amenable to demonstration, to the "reason" of scientific "repetition." It is impulsive, circumstantially pertinent, more Voltairean than Cartesian, though it does have affinities with aspects of existentialist thought, again more Camusian than Sartrean. Of course, though in largely different form—this is Vigny's legitimacy, and claimed originality—Lamartine and Hugo are far from averse to what they themselves call *méditation* or *contemplation*, but Vigny's enterprise is double, even triple, and *fused*. He himself is the first to point out the long distance to be traveled by the poet in moving from prosaic idea, quotidian sentiment, to versified form, and, finally to poetry itself: "thoughts to be put not only into verse, but into poetry," he reminds himself in his drafts for "Eloa" (*OC*, I, 242). It is thus quite insufficient to obtain rich episodic, historical, or documentary material, fascinating "ideas for a poem" ("L'Atelier du poète" ["The Poet's Workshop"], *OC*, I, 322); just as it is quite insufficient to dream up excellent "scenarios" (*OC*, I, 258) or vast notional epic "drafts" (*OC*, I, 285). Poetic fusion is finally needed, and, as we shall see later, this will require a fuller deployment of Vigny's creative and figurative capacities. His poetry may thus lie between experience and archetype, episode and curiously unstable essence, but its ultimate assemblage entails further genius.

Heroism

In the midst of this poetic swirl of thought and drama, woven into the fabric of every text of the *Poèmes antiques et modernes* and *Les Destinées* is a vision of humanity's heroic, and to some extent tragic, nature. Such heroism tends to exemplify itself via the acts and postulations of exceptional individuals, both men and women, but in certain poems, and in an implicit general sense, the entire human project may be so perceived, heroism thus animating the ontology of both the renowned and the anonymous, the poet and the worker, the fiercely resistant and the awesomely crushed. Byron (see "Sur la mort de Byron" ["On the Death of Byron"], from *Fantaisies* [*Fantasies*], *OC*, I, 202–203) may seem to represent for Vigny that melding of dream and social action that also lies at the center of writers like Lamartine, Chateaubriand, and Hugo and that, curiously, is far from foreign to the ideal surrealist *démarche*, the fusion within the "Poète-conquérant" ("Conqueror-poet") of the highest (senti)mental and practical aspiration. But a poem like "La Beauté idéale" ("Ideal Beauty," *OC*, I, 203–205) evokes "la grandeur du coupable et celle de son juge" ("The greatness of the criminal and of his judge"), an heroic, non-Cornelian glory of the collectivity, of the humble, the unfortunate, the "condemned," and not merely the high-placed. The memorable poem "Paris," strategically situated to close the *Poèmes antiques et modernes*, goes even further in positing—though all is tinged with authentic ambivalence in Vigny's poetics—the quasi-absurd, quasi-divine majesty of those blind, swarming, turning movements that, symbolic of all mass proletarian-bourgeois evolution, are inspired by the frenzy and fervor of the postrevolutionary citizens of one of the world's great urban societies. "Tout brûle, craque, fume et coule" ("All is burning, cracking, smoking, flowing forth"), he writes in 1831, in the wake of the July Revolution, and in a tone and expressive mode anticipating certain of Frénaud's equally great poems,

> tout cela
> Se tord, s'unit, se fend, tombe là, sort de là;
> Cela siffle et murmure ou gémit; cela crie,
> Cela chante, cela sonne, se parle et prie;
> Cela reluit, cela flambe et glisse dans l'air,
> Eclate en pluie ardente ou serpente en éclair.
> Oeuvre, ouvriers, tout brûle! au feu tout se féconde! . . .
> Salamandres partout! . . . Enfer! Eden du monde!

> all is
> Twisting, joining, cleaving, all is falling, exiting;
> Things whistle and whisper or groan; things scream,
> Sing out, ring loud, converse and pray;
> Things gleam, flare up and glide upon the air,
> Bursting in ardent rain, snaking in flashes.
> Work, workers, all is burning! in fire all is fecund! . . .
> Salamanders everywhere! . . . Hell! The world's Eden!

> (*OC*, I, 109)

Unquestionably there is irony and anxiety in "Paris," yet he stresses soberly that "ash . . . is never sterile" (*OC* I, 112); that such social and existential turmoil is not scorned as parenthetic or irrelevant by an all-seeing mind, which recognizes the aspiring divinity of such vast unfolding human projects (*OC*, I, 111); that "men of love, doubt and pity," nameless but as real and determining as any celebrated hero/ine, lived, chose, and passed on through, such enigmatic dream-actions as grand as the "rêve symbolique" ("symbolic dream") that Vigny called his own poem (*OC*, I, 1023).

But if certain aspects of the great collective heroic project that Vigny, with Balzac, termed, in "La Maison du berger" ("The Shepherd's House") of *Les Destinées,* "la comédie humaine" (*OC*, I, 127), are well and aptly treated, Vigny's principal elaborative strategy consists in enacting the at once concrete and "philosophic" dramas of self and other, man and woman, freedom and enslavement, choice and fatality, death and suffering, religious intuition and cosmic "silence," doubt and progress, and so on, that "structure" his work, via a marked emphasis upon that exemplary *individual,* engaged in his/her heroic struggle, at the heart of the world's great epic (but philosophically unmeditated, Vigny would maintain) poems or other texts. Thus, the justly famous 1823 "Moïse" will celebrate—the word is not too strong, despite the tragic and even bitter overtones, for Vigny remains, ultimately, as the 1862 "L'Esprit pur" ("Pure Mind," *OC*, I, 166–168) and the 1854 "La Bouteille à la mer" ("Bottle cast adrift") of *Les Destinées show*, a poet, somewhat like Rimbaud, of future option, of as yet unexplored psychic wealth—"Moïse" will celebrate, then, heroic solitude, its anguish and its *gloire* (*OC*, I, 9), the continuous struggle of high wisdom and repressed emotional need, the vast and moving onus of "L'élu du Tout-Puissant" ("The All-Powerful's Chosen One," *OC*, I, 10), a burden both assumed and finally transcended.

The beautiful 1823 "Eloa" (*OC*, I, 10–31), which I shall look at in a little more detail below, will sing the song of, as he puts it at the end of his life, "*une* ange femme et symbole de la pitié" ("an angel woman, symbol of pity," *OC*, I, 949), the song of love's appalling "condemnation" from on high, the absurd fact that heroic and tragic feminine struggle in the face of Satan's seductive charm should be bizarrely necessary in the first place. The elegant and haunting "Le Cor," Vigny's rewriting of the climax of *La Chanson de Roland* (*The Song of Roland*), rather than lamenting the traitorousness of some, praises, between smiling admiration and melancholy, the courage, the instinctive boldness, the simple grandeur of the rare, the extraordinary *preux* that was Charlemagne's Roland. And in "Le Trappiste" Vigny offers discreet but sure commemoration of the inspired and again in a sense tragically absurd heroism of the leader-priest for whom "man has thoughts much greater than the world" (*OC*, I, 87): the sense of honor and principle that can lead to self-sacrifice; or elsewhere, as in "La Flûte" ("The Flute," *OC*, I, 145–49) from *Les Destinées*, that preparedness to struggle on, in blindness and yet noble, "singing desire" (*OC*, I, 148), against all the odds. "Ce Sisyphe éternel," Vigny will declare à la Camus,

> est beau, seul, tout meurtri
> Brûlé, précipité, sans jeter un seul cri,
> Et n'avouant jamais qu'il saigne et qu'il succombe
> À toujours ramasser son rocher qui retombe
>
> This eternal Sisyphus is beautiful, solitary, bruised
> Burned, hurled down, uttering not a single cry,
> Confessing never his bleeding, his collapse
> Ever gathering up his tumbling rock
>
> (*OC*, I, 148).

And let me finally evoke, in this context, two of Vigny's most known and characteristic poems, both from *Les Destinées*, the 1843–1863 "Le Mont des Oliviers" and the 1847–1854 "La Bouteille à la mer." The former pictures Jesus as a high Romantic hero, "triste jusqu'à la mort; l'oeil sombre et ténébreux" ("mortally sad; his eye dark and obscure," *OC*, I, 149)—one thinks of other poems by Hugo and Nerval—sensing all, yet caught in fright and the impotence he feels descending upon his sacrifice, realizing the full significance of that "double accusation/Weighing everywhere upon Creation": evil and doubt (*OC*, I, 151). Here, Vigny manages only faintly to suggest the human need to assume fully the divinity of psychic reality, of our continuing creation of what we are, individually and collectively; rather does the poem privilege the power of that *deus ex machina* that prefers to throw us back upon our own ignorance, the revolt—this is Vigny's heroic choice, expressed in the finally (1863) added stanza "Le Silence," but it is not Christ's— of our own "silence," our obstinate stoicism, but a revolt that inevitably assumes only a limited responsibility for what is, and therefore, it might seem, a limited degree of heroism.

Vigny himself seems to have been fully conscious of this slippage of implication: was Jesus a skeptic and a rebel, not utterly separable from Vigny's (also somewhat heroic) conception of Satan? Was he a man-God or a God-man (*OC*, I, 1103)? To what degree does his submission entail acceptance of being? To what degree do poems like "La Bouteille à la mer" and "L'Esprit pur" transcend such submission and create a positivist revolt, (wo)man assuming the fullest of ontological responsibility? "La Bouteille à la mer," in effect, seems to push Vigny's poetics of heroism one step farther. We are asked to step beyond the somewhat gloomy heroism of "Chatterton, Gilbert et Malfilâtre" (*OC*, I, 153), beyond, too, the traditionally perceived potential of what we might term platitudinously human humanity. If we are asked to assume heroic solitude, like the captain of the sinking ship, and heroic decision-making, it is not merely, like Anouilh's Antigone, to say a desperate "no" to existence's seemingly loaded and fatal absurdity. It is, rather, going beyond sheer stoicism, in a sense beyond doubt and revolt, to assume in purer form the love and hope that, from the outset, have always also animated Vigny's poetics—and thus to take up the possibility of idea, thought, (self-)knowledge in a fuller assumption of the immensity of the psychic project in which we are engaged, individually and collectively, as the poem stresses. To take up, in short, the divinity of the psyche, of mind—"Le vrai Dieu, le Dieu fort est le Dieu des idées" ("The true God, the strong God is the God of ideas"), he affirms in the final stanza (*OC*, I, 159)—and, thus, the divinity and the true, latent "heroism" of the self, of all selves. And yet the final line of the poem lingers on in this newfound mind of ours: God's presence continues, as transcendence? Or does it: is the bottle's/the work's/the idea's buoyancy perhaps, rather, guaranteed by the divinity of Idea, mind, psychic possibility itself? Is, in fact, Vigny not contradicting himself, but affirming the circular logic of his new heroic spirituality?

Woman

Vigny's poetics of the feminine is complex and tensional, much more delicate than a reading of "La Colère de Samson" would induce us to believe, and may even be said to offer an essentially unified emotional texture. Moving symbolically and allegorically between the real and the ideal, the desired and the denied, the claims of purity and those of a sensuality steeped in fault, Vigny's poetics of the feminine determines in large measure the tonality of individual poems and penetrates to the very heart of the ontology his poems construct, being centered upon the "divine light" ("La Maison du berger") that love can cast upon existence both of the self and the collectivity (see the end of "Paris"). Poems such as the early 1819 "La Femme adultère" ("The Adulterous Woman") from the *Poèmes antiques et modernes* (*OC*, I, 45–49) and the 1839 "La Colère de Samson" can paint a disturbing and mixed picture of betrayal, cold calculation, sensual abandonment and ensuing vulnerability; and the celebrated verse, "Et plus au moins la Femme est toujours DALILA" ("And more or less Woman is always DELILAH," *OC*, I, 140), following upon the evocation of man's goodness locked in eternal struggle with woman's impure craftiness, is certainly capable of raising questions of misogyny. The latter poem, of course, may be read in the light of Vigny's relationship with Marie Dorval, but it remains, like many other poems, of blatant biblical inspiration; the former, equally biblical in its origins, offers divine compassion and mystical *voyance* ("seeing") transcending gross, reductive morality:

Vigny

"May any man amongst you . . . cast a stone
If he thinks himself guiltless, may he cast the first,

. . . .

His mysterious hand, above the light sand,
Wrote a language foreign to men"

(*OC*, I, 49).

The obsessions and anxieties persist, of course, troubling for poet and reader alike, but a range of allegorized feminine figures such as Eloa, Eva, Suzanne, along with others, more tragic though admired, such as Jephté or Néra, are proposed by Vigny as symbols at once of radiance, gentleness, protection, and action, and yet of an historic vulnerability and abuse that can haunt and deform, through the acts of men, the intrinsic power and spiritual beauty of women. It is important, perhaps, to give full value to a number of the *Poèmes antiques et modernes* that demonstrate the young Vigny's search to release himself from the "criminality" of the body and the senses, from the multiple religious, social, and moral constraints imposed upon male-female relations, into a mental space wherein the sensual, the sensuous, the rich, voluptuous enigma of femininity might be easily, simply, happily acceded to. The 1815 "La Dryade" ("The Wood Nymph," *OC*, I, 52–56), although redolent of a persistent duality and ambiguity, escapes into an idyllic, male-generated pastoral fantasy somewhat à la Chénier, and ill-appreciated by Vigny's watchful mother; the 1817 "Le Bain d'une dame romaine" ("A Roman Woman Bathing," *OC*, I, 52–58), not unlike certain of Ingres's canvases, and with the sensitivity of a Virgil rather than a Catullus, provides an image of at once transfigured, dreamlike, yet most present sensuality—the 1824 "Chant de Suzanne au bain" ("Song of Suzanne Bathing") from *Fantaisies* (*OC*, I, 199–20) is rather more bold and vigorous, but remains smilingly and appreciatively available for the joys and endless gifts of a woman whose husband will embracingly call her "his sister, his glory, his crown" (*OC*, I, 200); and the mythical, magical, super-feminine Eva of "La Maison du berger," seemingly dedicated to the cherished Tryphina Holmes met in Dieppe in 1827 a few weeks after her marriage, will incarnate, much beyond the specificity of any lived relationship, what François Germain and André Jarry, have called "the luminous double of Delilah": the grace, the bodily presence and yet the purity of a complex, all-redeeming feminine figure, capable of assuming all roles and finely, ideally adapted to Vigny's own complicated, and high, aspiration.

"Eloa," too, via a characteristic intertwinement of symbolic projection linking Eloa to Eva to, even, Stello and other ideal feminine or masculine figures, develops a poetics of the feminine sharing in the essential serenity, purity, here even angelicalness—Eloa does belong to the universe of angels—and lightedness various poems depict, but the poem, as we have already seen above, conveys equally the tensions of spirituality and sensuality, freedom and guilt, and, most pertinently, hints at the intense emotional and moral problematics at the center of that revered yet disquieting "virtue" that Vigny call *pudeur:*

> D'où venez-vous, Pudeur, noble crainte, ô Mystère
> Qu'au temps de son enfance a vu naître la terre,
> Fleur de ses premiers jours qui germez parmi nous,
> Rose du Paradis! Pudeur, d'où venez-vous?
>
> . . . .
>
> Au charme des vertus votre charme est égal,
> Mais vous êtes aussi le premier pas du mal.
>
> Whence are you, Modesty, noble awe, oh Mystery
> That saw in childhood the birth of earth,
> Flower of its first days growing amongst us,
> Rose of Paradise! Modesty, whence are you?
>
> . . . .
>
> To the charm of virtues your charm is equal,
> But you are too the first step to evil.
>
> (*OC*, I, 24)

What is at stake here, in effect, is the very acceptance of the totality of what we are, though Vigny tends to bemoan, via an intricate elaboration of a God/Satan dialectics that poets like Baudelaire, Hugo, and Lautréamont will pursue, the fatality of what we have been given, as if, in a sense, *pudeur*, innocence, "fall from grace," guilt, and so on were not of our human making, our assumable responsibility—although the fact that "Eloa" and other texts pose the problem is a significant step in itself. Finally, too, poems such as

Vigny

"La Fille de Jephté, "Le Somnambule," and even "Symétha" or "Le Bal" ("The Ball," *OC*, I, 84–86), all from the *Poèmes antiques et modernes*, offer, with greatly varying intensity, portraits of woman caught in the ambivalences, the contradictions, the tragic yet humanly—Vigny would say divinely—created absurdities of our long planetary history.

"Le Somnambule," for instance, shows woman swept to death in dream, madness, imagined and also probable infidelity, and yet, astonishingly, her own seemingly undying though lucid love. "Le Bal" conveys tensions of a different order: delight in, and yet irony toward, the swirling, insouciant young dancers of some ball observed in quasi-Laforguean manner, a sense of the "just" deployment of light, fleeting energy as against the very irony employed or, worse, the "moroseness" of frustrated age.

The little-considered poem, "Le Livre" ("The Book," *OC*, I, 213–14) written in 1831–1832, at the height of Vigny's liaison with Marie Dorval but not published until 1925, exposes the full range of emotion transcribed in that "book" which is his "heart" and his "soul," "the love of a woman/alight within a man":

> Désir, délire, transe,
> Ennui, rage, espérance,
> Enfin . . . une démence
> Qui vaut d'être enfermé.
>
> Desire, delirium, trance
> Spleen, rage, hope,
> and then . . . a madness
> Yielding but imprisonment.
> (*OC*, I, 213)

I quote it only to stress two facts: first, that Vigny's poetics of the feminine inevitably devolves from such an impressive sentimental gamut; secondly, that his poetics cannot prevent itself from being fundamentally masculine—I say fundamentally, because Vigny attributed his own finer instincts, such as compassion and poetic impulse, to his "Stello" or "Eva," feminine side of himself. "La Maison du berger" demonstrates Vigny's tendency to wish to feminize the world, for to feminize it was to render it infinitely more livable, more supple, more ideal. From the 1823 "Eloa" on there is unambiguously a horror of life "without love, remorseless in the depths of an icy heart" (*OC*, I, 29), which will, finally, allow Vigny radical differentiation between "satanic" charm and libertinage and angelic bewilderment. The 1831 "Paris" will end by evoking the overriding but half-understood force of "men [and women] filled with love, doubt and pity" (*OC*, I, 112). And the 1843–1844 "La Maison du berger" creates an elaborate dreamscape ready to "cacher l'amour et ta divine faute" ("hide love and your divine fault," *OC*, I, 120) and Vigny's then conception of the feminine is such that only it can provide and initiate ideal existential ambiance, that exculpative, transfigured convergence of soul and body, mind and senses, poetry and nature. Woman, or, better, the primordial love and capacity for love she represents, may, in certain poems, risk diminishment and be linked to misfortune, and Vigny may, too, be tempted by a false and distorting purification of the sensual, anxiety may swamp out confidence; but Vigny's work remains eminently capable of elaborating a worthy and even balanced poetics of the feminine: at once realistic and idealistic, sensitive to historic and contemporary moral limitations weighing upon woman and man alike, and yet aware of the potentiality of the feminine, its power of social and cosmic transmutation. Such a poetics can also at times point to a liberation of humanity via a rethinking and a re-living of the feminine, wherein fatality may be rejected and possibility assumed.

Le Mal

From the earliest moments of Vigny's poetic production (1815–1816, in all likelihood: "La Dryade" and "Symétha"), tensional questions of possession and loss, "idyll" and "elegy," exquisite sensuousness and darker brooding, manifest a latent propensity that will blackly blossom into that obsession with existential problem, unhappiness, and *le mal* which will not only persist throughout his own oeuvre, despite the relative final release afforded by "La Bouteille à la mer" and "L'Esprit pur," but leave its trace upon much of the poetry of the next 130 or more years—from Baudelaire and Hugo to Jouve, Michaux, Frénaud and Char. As, inevitably, with such poets, Vigny's perception of *le mal*—a term I shall largely retain owing to its semantic scope—may be said to center, on the one hand, upon its experiential, practical, social, and therefore epically dramatizable manifestations; on the other hand, upon its philosophical implication, its ontological significance and consequence.

Many poems choose to enact aspects of human experience, direct or indirect, of *le mal:* "Eloa," as we have seen somewhat above, and although it only faintly reflects the myth of Adam and Eve, nevertheless generates the intense drama of fallen angelicism, with the ambivalent logics of both *pudeur* and sensual abandonment, the "satanic"—Satan, too, is depicted as a fallen angel—"sad love of sin! [and] somber desire for evil!" (*OC*, I, 28), the "Nietzschean" and Baudelairean possibility of confusing good and evil without having penetrated the secrets of any newly emergent morality; "Le Déluge," which argues the innate criminality of the human amid paradisiacal purity and fearfully pits already problematized love and innocence against *le mal*, a seemingly impotent hope against the implacable eschatology "destined" to drown the earth; "Le Malheur," an 1820 poem showing a watchful, fear-inducing mentality thinking in presymbolist terms of horror at, and escape from, *présence*, showing, too, the relentless reduction of pleasure to "mourning" in the heart of this "son of pain" who can only cry out in desperate anguish, like so many men and women:

> Malheur! oh! quel jour favorable
> De ta rage sera vainqueur?

> Misfortune! oh! what day of favor
> Will vanquish your rage?
>
> (*OC*, I, 65)

And so the poems unravel themselves: "Le Somnambule" with its bleak, nightmarish madness; "Les Amants de Montmorency" with its all too true story of ecstasy become joint suicide; "La Mort du Loup" with its tale of cruelty and ignominy. The list is indeed long, and for Vigny the implications are largely clear and reflected in both his choice of Shakespeare translations and in his own dramatic creations such as *Chatterton*, though his "terminal" position with respect to existential evil/unhappiness/misfortune seems ultimately to shift in order to echo more amply certain ideas long implicit in his poetry.

Over and above, then, the "philosophic" consequences of inherent human "weakness" and "wretchedness" ("Le Trappiste"), our individual and collective leanings toward ambivalent emotion, to-

ward fear where love might carry the day, toward confidence and
hope where (self-)criticism and (self-)judgment erode our strength,
worse, toward anger, violence, and sadism—over and above such
a "logic" that may be drawn from experience and observation, a
logic in Vigny's case hovering between fatality, intrinsic-ness, "destiny" and "responsibility" (*Les Destinées, OC,* I, 117), assumption of
being and option, the main thrust of his meditation of *le mal* is concerned with questions that "Le Mont des Oliviers" most powerfully
and compactly articulates. "Mal et Doute!" cries out Christ to the
God to whom he will finally submit in anguish,

> Mal et Doute! En un mot je puis les mettre en poudre;
> Vous les aviez prévus, laissez-moi vous absoudre
> De les avoir permis. —C'est l'accusation
> Qui pèse de partout sur la Création!

> Evil and Doubt! In a word I can crush them;
> You had foreseen them, let me absolve you
> From their allowance. —That is the accusation
> Weighing everywhere upon the Creation!

> (*OC,* I, 151)

Vigny boldly confronts divine wisdom and justice, arguing for
the inclusion of (wo)man within the secret knowledge of all cosmic
mystery, for the elimination of uncertainty, for the inauguration of
the divine reign of confidence and finally justifiable hope. The closing stanza of "Le Mont des Oliviers," the 1851 addition entitled "Le
Silence," seems to render the full bitterness that Vigny can feel in
"an, as it were, aborted world." A stoicism, worse "cold silence"
and scorn, constitute the basis of any philosophy he may be said to
elaborate at this time. But this is not a radiant, transcendent stoicism; it is far from any Buddhist inclinations he clearly had in the
mid-1850s; it is, in effect, at a pessimistic, quasi-nihilist extreme of
a highly emotive *weltanschauung* that will tempt many writers and
thinkers of the twentieth century, from Jarry and Dada on.

Le mal seems, then, at this point, ineradicable. The 1849 poem
that opens *Les Destinées* and takes its title (*OC,* I, 115–19) evokes the
options of "responsibility" and "will" that could have been allowed fully to develop in human beings, were divine justice to
have prevailed, and Vigny does succeed in strongly articulating a
desire truly to assume humanity's full cosmic potential. But "mys-

tery" and ignorance offer at best a blinkered, false sense of freedom, the possibility of mere struggle, of mere heroism—of ob-
taining, as Vigny already suggested as early as "Eloa," "in the
common evil . . . / . . . some small delight, and sometimes oblivion" (*OC*, I, 24). In his late poems, especially "La Bouteille à la mer"
and "L'Esprit pur," Vigny appears poised to fully develop a philosophy of spiritual transcendence of *le mal* that, as even "Les
Destinées" and "Le Mont des Oliviers" show, is always maturing
and implicitly available. The "transcendence" affordable through
mind is inevitably largely imminent, but it is also linked to notions
of progress, ideality, purity, and divine spirituality that are not
just, platitudinously, those of the passage of the written from generation to generation. Above all, we might remember that Vigny
understands here to what degree mind, psychic, ontological project can bypass or render inexistent the fear and anguish of *le mal*
by simply recentering attention, by recreating the emotional-psy-
chical focus of our own existence in a manner not entirely Buddhist, but which allows *le mal* to "disappear" in a more luminous
void and silence.

Guilt and Justice

Such a project remains for Vigny, as for all of us, fraught with
difficulty. The conception of evil and misfortune, the common perception of love as "criminal" (as in "La Femme adultère"), as "factitious" and "lying" ("La Colère de Samson"), undoubtedly persist,
with all the concomitant tensions between purity and impurity, se-
duction as delight and as problem, fault and simplicity. They may
be attributed to a certain moralistic resurgence of the *Restauration,*
the puritanical upbringing of Vigny, the relative unhappiness of
his relationship with his at times tyrannical mother, to whom nevertheless he remained deeply attached—and all this despite that
undying aspiration to the joyful, the beautiful, the womanly, which
we have explored in some measure above. But persist they do: "Le
Mont des Oliviers" is a song of accusation and cosmic, divine guilt,
imputing chaos and *hasard* to the creation, and defending the
grandly disdainful, coldly heroic silence of our human response to
the absence of communication and revelation. Even the exquisite
Lettre à Eva (*OC*, I, 119) that is Vigny's equivalent to Baudelaire's
"Invitation au voyage," "La Maison du berger"—even this haunt-

ingly idyllic vision of love cannot avoid mention of threat, taciturnity (*OC*, I, 128, final verse) and the "divine fault" that is at the heart of Eva's barely avowable passion for the dreaming poet. The shepherd's house that will unite them will be a refuge, an escape, a place to "*hide* love and your divine fault," not to sing it to the world (*OC*, I, 120). And, of course, this is to forget the very early, 1816 "Héléna" (*OC*, I, 171–96), finally eliminated from subsequent editions after its appearance in the 1822 *Poèmes:* this poetic text in itself, Vigny's longest moreover, demonstrates the terrible struggle between notions of guilt, crime, shame, expiation that can inhabit the mind of Vigny and challenge his very emotional and moral stability.

Various poems, furthermore, in the face of such guilt, whose origin is at once multiple and intrinsic to being-in-the-world, push to an extreme limit a logic of justice that can appear disturbingly retributive, based upon vengeance or sacrifice leading to a relatively notional equilibrium. "La Fille de Jephté" depicts God in this way, as enforcing some unknowable law carrying off, "in exchange for crime[,] innocence" (*OC*, I, 43). Only an infinitely complex network of karmic relationships would explain such sacrificial equations. "Le Somnambule" projects, as we have seen, a poetics of madness, confusion, and contradiction, in which, as in "Héléna"—and in this Vigny's work is a terrible reflection of male-dominated history— justice is seen not to be done and Vigny's sense of personal and cosmic morality is discreetly outraged. "La Colère de Samson" goes as far as mimetically to invoke that masculine, sovereign judge and deity in order to punish and correct human disorder in the name of some natural, but divine justice. In so doing, Vigny seems to be urging old laws of social and moral balance, problematizing his essential feminine ontology, refusing exploration of the logic of pardon and compassion he will elsewhere espouse.

There are times, however, in Vigny's work, as in "Le Déluge," when he speaks less of the incomprehensibility or the blatant revengefulness associated with divine, fateful justice, than of the latter's capacity for equity and "gathering." Sara and *le pasteur* will thus cry out on Mount Arar: "'Ah! let us praise the Eternal, that punishes yet gathers'/ ... 'Oh Lord, judge us!'" (*OC*, I, 36); and "Le Trappiste," also from the *Poèmes antiques et modernes*, articulates a powerful poetics of self-effacing justice, compassion, and, finally, faith in some transcendent vision capable of righting imbalance upon the purely physical plane. "Dieu seul est juste, enfants," he will exhort via his symbolic/real hero, "sans lui tout est mensonge" ("God alone is just, children, without him all is untruth," *OC*, I, 92).

Elsewhere, Vigny can go much farther in elaborating a vision of justice removed from the hindering logic of guilt, shame, and would-be corrective punishment. And, characteristically, chronology does not seem to be pertinent (as our next section will confirm). Already, in the 1819 "La Femme adultère," Vigny stresses that divine, "mystical" justice predicates itself upon compassion, for the latter demands a self-knowledge leading to forgiveness, nonviolence, love. The "Post-scriptum" to "Les Oracles" from *Les Destinées* (*OC*, 129–33) similarly argues that justice is connected to truth and "self-analysis," a vision and clarity of assessment before the self's conscience that can offer freedom of self and other. "La Flûte," Vigny will argue in *L'Atelier du poète*, is based upon the notion of "l'égalité des âmes" ("the equality of souls") and the Bonnefidian need to eliminate pride, but also shame (*OC*, I, 280), no doubt because both have distinct elements of violence about them, either generating fear or submitting to it. And "La Bouteille à la mer," especially stanza 24, notably suggests that the very discovery, within ourselves, of the instincts of justice, goodness, and beauty is sufficient to allow us to transcend "oubli, morsure, Injustice insensée,/Glaces et tourbillons de notre traversée" ("oblivion, attack, mad Injustice/Ice and whirlwinds in our crossing," *OC*, I, 158–59). For herein lies, with the mysterious ontic, spiritual depths of "(wo)man and nature," "equal in depth" (*OC*, I, 158), that sense, moral but beyond all banal, tit-for-tat equation, of what truly can be our "greatness," our ideal, ideational self-projection and self-destination (*OC*, I, 159).

Tensions and Struggle

In more ways than it can be said of Mallarmé, Rimbaud, or even Laforgue and Lautréamont, Vigny's is "a divided consciousness." He is more Baudelairean, more *fêlé* ("cracked") than at first it may seem, and prefigures many of the taut polarizations and fragile syntheses of twentieth-century literary consciousness. Did not Proust himself admire the extraordinary tension accumulated in the powerful "La Colère de Samson"? I shall not argue that such tension—whether it be between the sensual and the *pudique*, the vision of Delilah and that of Eva, violence and compassion, divine harshness or even sadism and divinely comprehending justice—is a sign either of fundamental emotional or spiritual ambivalence in Vigny or of some intrinsically tragic propensity of his poetics. The carefully meditated and purposive structuring of *Les Destinées* sufficiently belies the latter interpretation, and the former I reject in favor of a poetics, quite achronological and spontaneous, dictated by joy or anxiety, pleasurable anticipation or sudden frustration— a poetics of emotive rhythm, exploratory mythical alternation, typical occidental polarization, as Derrida would have us believe, of ideational category and option. A few samplings are in order.

One of the core tensions of Vigny's poetics is most discreetly visible in that most discreet of poems, "Le Cor" (*OC*, I, 81–90), with its common slippage between smile and melancholy, at times their superimposition one upon the other. "Le Bal" also operates a similar sentimental tautness, at once opposing and melding the light, charming vigors of dance and the sensation of their ephemerality, of the sorrows, moroseness, and sickliness to come. In this he is close again to Baudelaire, less so to Mallarmé or even Verlaine, who tend to separate out their extremes more consistently, but in broad fashion Vigny fronts upon something of the symbolist aesthetic/ethic—"Fatal silence succeeds the dazzling/Orchestra, and disgust the sweet exchanges of dance" (*OC*, I, 85)—with its insistence upon horror, *ennui*. Yet, as with Laforgue, a nostalgia for the gentleness and sweetness of feminine presence remains manifest in the latter's ambiguous "trembling of pleasure" (see *OC*, I, 86, final verse), which Vigny will not hesitate to promote. The "psychology" of Vigny's smile, then, unlike that in Stendhal's *univers imaginaire*, retains a wan, nervous quality, and, although linked to the *recherche du bonheur* underpinning the promise of Stendhalian smile, it focuses more upon loss than future. "Paris" confirms this fragility: "Je souris tristement" ("I smile in sadness"), concludes the narrator/poet, caught between thoughts of revolutionary destruction and dreams of residual possibility (*OC*, I, 111–12).

Many other similar oppositions and paradoxical characterizations structure the poetic texts of Vigny. If Vigny is undoubtedly, like Philippe Jaccottet, a poet of ignorance, blind Dupinian search— "Eternity veils over before our intelligence," we read in "Eloa," but Christ's reported recriminations in "Le Mont des Oliviers" demonstrate that existential origin and purpose are not to be exposed to definite knowledge—we should not overlook the crucial poetics of mind, idea, and spirit that Vigny will simultaneously develop. "To read a book in order to know" does not for Vigny, as it will for André Breton, "denote a certain simplicity." Writing and reading offer the crucial, (wo)man-made, yet mysteriously, divinely permitted, option of exchange, continuity, persistent *présence*. "La Bouteille à la mer" and "L'Esprit pur" make this much clearer. They point to future, to progress available, to potential vision of that "human trinity" he will evoke in his 1838 sonnet, unpublished in his lifetime, "The Human Trinity" of *Fantaisies* (*OC*, I, 219). "Will, Love and Mind," a trinity compared to the holy trinity, but seemingly crushed by narrow-minded contemporary thinking:

> A présent, il ne reste en notre Conscience
> Que deux flambeaux noircis par l'humaine Science:
> —La Volonté méchante el l'Esprit égaré.

> Now, remain in our Consciousness
> But two torches blackened by human Science:
> —Evil Will and the Mind gone astray.

As Vigny writes in "La Maison du berger," "science/Traces about the earth a sad and straightened trail" (*OC*, I, 122). Far from opening and freeing, scientific thought tends to limit because it is systematizing and didactic rather than "fiery" and "enthusiastic" (*OC*, I, 1172). As "La Maison du berger" also clarifies, thought is ideally poetic. "Poésie! ô trésor!" Vigny exclaims, "perle de la pensée" ("Poetry! oh treasure, pearl of thought!" *OC*, I, 123), even though science, in "La Bouteille à la mer" is a "divine elixir," "treasure of thought and experience."

Vigny's conception of thought, in short, is rife with tension and paradox. It can, on the one hand, both be ontologically impotent, intransitive, self-referentially imprisoned like a text for semioticians, *and* generative, revolutionary, transformational, creative; on the other hand, it can be deemed equatable with science seen either as misleading, peripheral, "moralistically" reductive, *or* as a kind of transcendent positivism bizarrely mixed in with mysticism, pure Christian spiritual upsurge, pure poiesis, pure "feu sacré" ("sacred fire," *OC*, I, 1172).

Such tensional imaginative or conceptual "structures" abound throughout *Poèmes antiques et modernes, Fantaisies,* and his entire oeuvre, and they can touch what would seem to be Vigny's firmest notions, feelings, "arguments": stoicism and suffering, the conception of power and authority, questions of nothingness and beauty, the perception of "nature," the dialectics of doubt and compassion. Only the briefest of assessments of one of these preoccupations can be offered here. Vigny's perception of nature, of the natural splendor of the earth, to which Desbordes-Valmore, Lamartine, Hugo, and even Rimbaud will show themselves eminently sensitized, would appear to be determined by his obsessions with human suffering, a certain resultant refusal and (self-)denial that color his "silence" and stoicism. "Le Trappiste" makes it clear that Vigny, like Reverdy, accords priority to the greatness of *antinature,* the superiority of thought over (other forms of) reality; and the oft-cited "La Maison du berger" would make it clear that, if nature offers asylum and a locus of meditation (*OC,* I, 120), it promotes fear, its "theatre" is "impassive," its beauties are vain, futile, cold, shunned in favor of "the majesty of human suffering" (see *OC,* I, 127–8). And yet "Le Cor" will sing with beautifully intense simplicity, "O azure mountains! o adored land"; "La Neige" adopts a tactic of anaphoric crescendo in evoking the wintry world of snow and trees, pallid skies and crows; "Les Amants de Montmorency" spectacularly deploys a landscape of sweet, sunlit air, dreamlike hummings and whisperings, scented foliage, that is in overt communion with the young lovers' brief ecstasy; and, reversing the affective direction of the above-mentioned opposition in "La Maison du berger," where nature can be seen as a "tomb" rather than a "mother" (*OC,* I, 127), even here Vigny can propose a vision of heathland, fragrant flowers, snow-covered slopes, rare moonlit scenes, a vision that only awaits the confirmation of its beauty by the beloved, half-lived, half-phantasmatic Eva to truly assume reality (*OC,* I, 120–21).

Conception, perception, characterization of all kinds remain, in Vigny's poetry, colored by rhythmically alternating or simultaneously experienced tensional and oppositional factors. Vigny is a poet of struggle, of precarious and in a sense purely notional equilibrium, whether he be thinking and feeling from the "positive" to the "negative" pole, or in the reverse direction. For if Vigny's initially (self-)liberating and "happy" sensuality (see "La Dryade" and "Le Bain") is hard-won over repression and taught prudishness, the struggle reverses itself in a dangerous slide toward the ambivalence of *pudeur*, the contradictions of shame and guilt, and the temptation of punishment and exclusively ancient, masculine ethic. Similarly, when love seems nearly achievable for the mind, as in "La Maison du berger," the struggle never lets up. Vigny remains nervous, problem-conscious, unable for long to bathe in the calm of that confidence, certainty, and instinctive hope he feels to have been banished by design from the human psyche.

Struggle is, finally, not merely appalling and emotionally restricting for Vigny, and we should not understate that part of his poetics that would dearly love to eradicate struggle: "Le Mont des Oliviers" is a violent condemnation of the human condition seen as blind, impotent, aimless struggle, but "Le Bain d'une dame romaine" and "La Maison du berger" are the two-pronged extreme *other* demonstration of the intrinsic absurdity of struggle and the desirability of privileged access to bliss. Struggle is also, however improbably, immensely heroic. "Les Destinées" insists upon the Reverdyan dialectics of domination and, while showing the "timidness" and "incompleteness" of humanity, confirms its will to rebellion (*OC*, I, 118) in the face of destiny: "Mais plus forte à présent, dans ce sombre duel,/Notre âme en deuil combat ces Esprits impassibles" ("But stronger now, in this dark duel,/Our mourning soul fights off these impassive Spirits"). If the will for being is not unlike Bonnefoy's, the revolt is, rather, Camusian. The Sisyphian, heroic struggle creates an unstable, rapid slippage between hope and anguish that is very modern in character—one thinks of Dada and the surrealists but also of the existentialists, and, today, of the "struggle" between poetics of meaning and those of absence and autotelism. In an untitled poem, amazingly remaining unpublished until 1975 (*OC*, I, 1159), "Sur la neige des monts ..." ("Upon the mountain snow ..."; *OC*, I, 207–208, from *Fantaisies*), Vigny, not unlike Rimbaud in "Le Bateau ivre," though there is something uncannily Baudelairean in the final stanza—Vigny has the air of a poet sensing both the noble necessity and the quasi-tragic error of struggle, genial though it may be. "Tel," the poem concludes,

> Tel, dans ces régions de gloire et d'harmonie,
> D'un coup venu d'en bas est frappé le génie;
> Tel il cherche à lutter contre la terre; et tel
> Il succombe abattu sous un chagrin mortel.

Thus, in these regions of harmony and glory,
Genius, with a blow from down under, is struck;
Thus does it seek to struggle against the earth; and thus
Does it succumb downcast beneath a mortal grief.

(*OC*, I, 208)

Struggle, if tension and paradox are the modes of one's perception, cannot be thrust aside. The lived symbolic presence of those fatal furies Vigny calls *Les Destinées* ensures resistance and struggle; abandonment and the bliss of some buoyant *dérive* of mind and heart could only come about for Vigny in the fullest of revelations.

God and Destiny

Vigny's conception of God, as many critics have argued, is predicated upon God's sadism or cold indifference, or, again, in the post-Christ perspective, upon God's implacable silence, which draws out Vigny's apparent revolt and bitterly stoical silence, an assumption of a kind of existential anti-responsibility born of frustration and pursuit of self-dignity. The notion of destiny—which Vigny couples both to myth, a seemingly exteriorized reality, and to "philosophy," a personal mode of seeing and thinking accredited somewhat by its immersion in the distant clouds of our supposed collective ponderings—would appear to hinge humanity's ontology to factors of impotence, imprisonment, victimization—predestination, in fact. The plural designation of the concept, moreover, in *Les Destinées*, only adds weight to the feeling of power Vigny attributes to those cold agents of supreme, unknowable divine essence that sow, amongst us, blindness, anguish, and humiliation. And, if Vigny sees the advent of Christ as leading to a sense of human freedom in fraternal/sororal love—and I maintain that a crucial transformation of consciousness does come about in Vigny's mind owing to this critical symbolic signal—he will not hesitate, in "Le Mont des Oliviers" as in "Les Destinées," to thrust upon us what he feels here to be the crushing argument of our "Evil and Doubt!" (*OC*, I, 151), the reclosing of the ontological circle by that fatal (but of course human) reading of the signs of our condition: "C'ÉTAIT ÉCRIT" ("IT WAS WRITTEN," *OC*, I, 119). The *Atelier du poète* points clearly to the fact that Vigny can see doubt as having been irresistibly—affectively and rationally—

made his "destiny," for fate is "immuable et inconnu" ("immovable and unknown," *OC*, I, 250), he argues. In an 1827 poem, from *Fantaisies*, "Le Port" (*OC*, I, 207), he will go so far as to assert the futility of revolt, so great would seem to be his sense of cosmic (pre-) determination and external control, whether chaotic or unknowably ordered:

> Car la force n'est rien, car il n'est point d'asile
> Contre l'onde et contre le sort.
>
> For strength is nothing, for there is no asylum
> Against the wave, against fate.

It is important, however, to recognize two or three pertinent and understated aspects of Vigny's discourse of destiny: first, (Vigny's) ignorance and doubt imply mystery, an ontology of mystery, a living in a force that carries, and carries away—even the dying prisoner of "La Prison," "estranged" as he is from the earth, remains "this son of mystery" (*OC*, I, 73); secondly, destiny, implying some transcendent power, can reasonably—as we shall see, this is crucial—unleash joy *or* fear, confidence *or* distrust: *Les Destinées* essentially opts for the "negative" emotional pole, but this is a *choosing* of a *certain* logic of destiny over others; thirdly, if, as Vigny commonly insists in *L'Atelier du poète*, *Les Destinées* are of largely satirical intent (see *OC*, I, 281, for example), he remains unequivocably sensitized, in "La Maison du berger" and "L'Esprit pur," to a residual and haunting absolute that orients his being, his desire, his poiesis; lastly, *L'Atelier du poète* makes it clear that *Les Destinées* was conceived in the context of a dialectics of "fatality and grace" (*OC*, I, 280–85): grace seems an unquestionably assumable power, transcendent, yet experienceable, internalizable, and those furies of destiny that give their name to the volume and its liminal poem Vigny divides into two kinds, those of "fatality" and those of Christic "grace" (*OC*, I, 285), the latter being linked to the concept of freedom ("The Destinies of Grace . . . alight close to man's heart. —Then the breath of Freedom stirs up their wings," *OC*, I, 285), and, despite their vulnerability, reigning "in God's name," pure "fatality" being now effaced, and *for the good*: "vous détruirez le mal et ferez arriver le bien" ("you will destroy evil and cause good to come," *OC*, I, 286).

L'Atelier du poète also offers some interesting insights as we return now to Vigny's conception of God and divineness. "The inertia of God in human affairs," he will note, "is the idea behind the poem, *The Mount of Olives.* Jesus asks him for certainty, he does not reply" (*OC*, I, 279). Vigny's draft ideas then explain (wo)man's need for self-organization, self-perfection, and stresses what he now feels is the pointlessness of prayer, since doubt is the self's destiny. Later, and most fascinatingly, because it undermines the apparently dominant discourse and links up with aspects of his thought just examined, Vigny will add to these same working notes: "La Fatalité ne voyait pas Dieu.//La Grâce le voit" ("Fate could not see God.//Grace sees him," *OC*, I, 281). Thus might we question assertions, based on certain of Vigny's own statements, of his total lack of "faith." Vigny himself is elsewhere quite unambiguous in his feeling that it is in mysticism that "I have found my best inspiration" (*OC*, I, 915), that he experienced mystical ecstasy in writing "Eloa" (see *OC*, II, 983)—in illness, he notes, as when composing "Une âme devant Dieu" ("A Soul before God," *OC*, I, 205–207, *Fantaisies*). And is it not true that the dialectics of doubt and love/compassion pits against the former an essential ontology of giving, opening, Bonnefidian *confiance,* even faith? In "La Maison du berger," in addition to making woman, here the mythical, composite Eva, a characteristic archetype of divine spontaneous empathy and imprudent encouragement, Vigny will go so far as to highlight the absurd *décalage* between doubt and speech: "He who doubts the soul, believes in his words" (*OC*, I, 124). Sartre will remind us that speech cannot take place without a certain faith in the being that buoys up language.

Going further, one might be tempted to argue the pertinence to Vigny's poetics of godliness of passages such as that in "Le Trappiste," where the hero maintains the truth and justice of God and the need, despite dubiousness, to serve our kings: "servons-les pour Dieu qui nous les a donnés" ("let us serve them for God who has given them to us," *OC*, I, 92). I shall not argue in this way, though there is no doubt in my mind that Vigny's admiration for the Trappist's noble self-immolation, based upon a respect for the divine mystery and implicit though obscure meaning of all ontic configuration, could be given the same attention as that given to the great feminine symbols Eloa, Kitty, and Eva that structure his work like what Char or even Jaccottet might call the "gods" of his imagination, his imagined being. Rather I shall dwell, briefly, upon a number of other characteristic utterances and two little-considered poems that could help us revise our view of Vigny's sense of the divine. "L'Invisible est réel" ("The Invisible is real"), he will trenchantly affirm in his long-meditated (1836?–1844?) "La Maison du berger," in a stanza that powerfully states the all-possessing nature of God, whose logos is also the locus of *our* finest intelligence. The same poem evokes life itself, but with life also love and the simple glory of the sun in the sky, as "d[es] flambeaux divins" ("divine torches," *OC*, I, 123), mysterious forces that may destroy—via death, loss, fire—yet remain unambivalently, despite their "double" potential, essential to our highest being.

The most personal and quite unbiblically inspired "La Flûte" is predicated upon a firm belief in excarnation and in what he terms "la sainte égalité des esprits du Seigneur" ("the holy equality of the Lord's spirits," *OC*, I, 148). Not dissimilarly, and dating from 1853 (revised from 1847), "La Bouteille à la mer" pointedly and twice articulates an appeal to God and the Gods—this, once more, in a highly personal text that contains, with "L'Esprit pur," what is usually held to be a kind of testamentary expression of his poetics. This is striking in that nothing *requires* Vigny, as it does in "La Colère de Samson" or even "Le Trappiste," to allude to a divineness that in "Le Mont des Oliviers" he has seemingly renounced, or ceased to speak of: the "Le Silence" stanza appears to date from 1851. And then let us not forget that moving untitled poem from *Fantaisies*, dated 28 September 1862, but not published until nearly thirty years after Vigny's death:

> Faites, ô Seigneur invisible,
> Que, puisant la lumière en la pure clarté,
> J'agisse dans le calme avec sérénité.

> Let me, oh invisible Lord,
> Drawing light from pure brilliance,
> Act in calmness and with serenity.
>
> (*OC*, I, 226)

In reading such a poem-prayer there is no need to reappraise Vigny's oeuvre in the light of some resurgent Christian principle or instinct, but it is important, as with the texts that follow ("Une âme devant Dieu" and "Prière pour ma mère"), not to neglect in his work an impulse that, as with Jules Michelet or Verlaine or Rimbaud, remains, beyond all skepticism, most essentially mystical. One thinks of Vigny's own creation of Julien L'Apostat, in contact with the essences, or of his evocation, in "La Beauté idéale," of that "Unknown language, like the divine songs of Plato's stars,/Beautiful more than the voices of Homer and Milton" (*OC*, I, 204). "Une âme devant Dieu" opens with this supplication—

> Dis-moi la main qui t'enlève,
> Ô mon âme! et dans un rêve
> Te montre la vérité
>
> Tell me the hand that transports you,
> Oh my soul! and in a dream
> Shows you truth.

—and proceeds to speak of dream's access to other dimensions of the real, other thresholds of consciousness. Vigny notes that he was ill at the time of this dream-poem, feeling himself dead and "going to God." The extraordinary poem, subtitled *élévation* like other texts of the *Poèmes antiques et modernes* and dated 1826, relates "seeing" God, stresses the "rejuvenation" that death occasions, and seeks to conjure up the infinite being spread before him: "I knew it from childhood," he adds, "I spoke it in my nights" (*OC*, I, 206). And he concludes—somewhat along the lines of Christ in "Le Mont des Oliviers" but ecstatically—by articulating his desire to *reveal*, definitively, the seamed, folded continuity of existence in order to dispel sorrow. The 1833 poem "Prière pour ma mère" invites us to meditate upon the mystery of death and the visible coming and going of the soul at the point of its "separation" from the body, "ineffable lueur qui marche, veille et brûle/Comme le feu sacré sur la tête d'Iule" ("ineffable glimmer moving, watching, burning/Like the sacred fire above Iulus' head"). Poems such as these need not be given overinflated significance, but they remain deeply pertinent to that discourse of God, the divine, and the mystical that is at the heart of Vigny's complex poetics. They also show that Vigny belongs firmly to the great tradition of open meditation and contemplation of the 1820–1860 period, and less firmly to that of our modern poetic and literary age, which can often be dismissive of the subjective, the "improbable," the unrepeatable, fearful even of all that is not cautious intellection.

Mind

This said, might it not seem that Vigny's fascination with the powers of the human mind and his structuring of *Les Destinées* to give especial emphasis to "La Bouteille à la mer" and "L'Esprit pur" are in some danger of being understated? Particularly if we consider the implications of the provocative line of the closing stanza of the earlier poem: "The true God, the strong God is the God of ideas!" (*OC*, I, 159). For here Vigny would sing the "greatness" and the nobility of persistent, patient, perhaps implicitly but not necessarily brilliant thought, the moving spectacle of its presentation and propagation via the book, the fact that, though caught up in "fate" and buoyed by divine providence, thought can be chosen, in a sense free. Yes, we can agree to this. Indeed, "L'Esprit pur" elects to make the argument unambiguous. Addressed, like "La Maison du berger," to the mythic and ideal Eva, the poem equates critical being-in-the-world with reflection, *recueillement* (*OC*, I, 167) and writing; "ton règne est arrivé, PUR ESPRIT, Roi du Monde!" ("Your Kingdom is come, PURE MIND, King of the World!"), he will somewhat extravagantly exclaim (*OC*, I, 167), giving mind and spirit not merely apparent privilege, but the privilege of symbolist purity and Mallarméan "azuredness." Curiously, if we look at the epigraph to *Les Destinées*, "C'ÉTAIT ÉCRIT," taken up at the end of the liminal poem (*OC*, I, 113, 119), Vigny would seem also to be implying a trajectory of ontic feasibility, ending up, in "L'Esprit pur," with the insistence upon the contemporary mind's option to write its own history, its own "destiny": "Aujourd'hui, c'est l'ÉCRIT/... Que tu graves au marbre ou traînes sur le sable,/ Colombe au bec d'airain! VISIBLE SAINT-ESPRIT!" ("Today, it is the WRITTEN WORD/ ... That you engrave in marble or pull across the sands,/Bronze-beaked dove! VISIBLE HOLY GHOST!" *OC*, I, 168). Such a writing of the mental is part of Vigny's—any poet's, he will say—"ideal," absolute, for it permits self-knowledge, communication, shared justice, love (*OC*, I, 168).

We should not lose sight, before pursuing Vigny's conception of the mind, of one or two points pertinent to the above. First, there is the interest of this allusion to the holy spirit, which places the poetics of the mental back in the optic of some of the considerations raised in my previous section. Secondly, one month after completing "L'Esprit pur," Vigny, in his *Journal d'un poète* (the night of 13–14 April 1863), will declare how problematic self-knowledge, and hence all thought, is. "Our mirrors are murky," he will conclude (*OC*, II, 1385). Thirdly, the poem not only went through many experimental titles (see *L'Atelier du poète*, *OC*, I, 309) offering quite different stresses, but Vigny also summarized the poem in a manner rarely considered: "Outline of Pure Mind. After-life of a mortal . . . Test of time, Continuity of name through glory" (*OC*, II, 1387). Small factors such as these already destabilize a poetics of mind that we shall now see become even less univocal, though it perhaps would be exaggerated, from Vigny's point of view, to term it, à la Deguy, à la Derrida, *indécidable*.

"La Maison du berger" proposes many clarifications in this regard, all shifting the poetics of mind away from any positivist conception that would dispense with the ethical, the subjectivist, the emotive: 1. the significance of a certain Rousseauistic "peaceful, amorous revery" (*OC*, I, 122), which would clearly link mind's highest functions to meditation and adoration or compassion; 2. mind is not finally equated to science, which traces "about the earth a sad and straightened trail" (*OC*, I, 122); 3. ideal thought is poetic, it is intuition rather than analytical, linear mentation, and centered upon the "divine secrets" of the cosmos (*OC*, I, 123); 4. such poetic thinking is a form of "le pur enthousiasme" available to us, that surging forth of breath, spirit, often feared because of the deep latent meaning of its "graves symboles" (*OC*, I, 123–34); 5. it offers "illumination" of "The slow, tardy steps of human reason," rapid elliptical, multidimensional movement, access to what we have already seen Vigny call "the invisible . . . real."

If Vigny believes, with Hugo and others, in a kind of progressivist, cumulative mode of thought's deployment, he has no sympathy for pure intellectualism—"Experts in long, flowing, inexhaustible speech!/You who teach all, had you learned nothing?" he will say in "Les Oracles." His own didacticism is not deliberately sophistical (*OC*, I, 131) but simply affective, centered both upon felt ethical conscience and aspiring aesthetic ideality (as the "Postscriptum" of "Les Oracles" makes clear; *OC*, I, 133) and always tempered by that personal doubt which he hesitates, interestingly, to deem synonymous with skepticism (see *OC*, II, 1383, for example). The ideal mental project of poiesis Vigny seeks to foster within himself and promote "universally" (*OC*, I, 168) is responsible—as he argues in the 1841 "La Poésie des nombres" ("Poetry of Numbers") from *Fantaisies* (*OC*, I, 221)—for all seeing, all knowing, all symbolizing, and it takes place in freedom and with shrewdness, acting textually as a kind of "talisman," as he calls it in an 1852 sonnet, "A Evariste Boulay-Paty" ("To Evariste Boulay-Paty," *OC*, I, 224–25).

Other texts offer different or otherwise elaborated elements of a poetics of mind shimmering like a cubist prism—or that "diamond" or "crystal" that haunts Vigny's imagination (see *OC*, I, 133, for example): 1. a sense of the continuity of mind exceeding the logic of historical evolution, immersed in the intuition that exchange can take place also via reincarnation/excarnation, an exchange at the soul-level: "Poète-conquérant," he will cry out in "Sur la mort de Byron," "adieu pour cette vie" ("farewell for this life")—an exclamation it is essential to regard as no more rhetorical than any other, apparently less extravagant, declaration in Vigny's poetry or prose, and which thus rejoins his mystical propensities; 2. the poet's insistence upon the convergence, in that "holy trinity" they form, of the poetics and functions of will, love, and mind ("La Trinité humaine"): mind's illumination beyond questions of its contemporary bewilderment and scientific occultation can only be appreciated in the context of these other forces, those of self's desire and effort and those of the (embrace of the) other, as in Bonnefoy's poetics; 3. mental activity seen as "an amicable contemplation . . that sees us in meditation, inclining its head to mine, reading over my shoulder" (*OC*, II, 1366)—the text is remarkable in its seeming division of the mind, à la Valéry, into sub-minds, in its intuition of a presence of some otherness, of the other, that would account perhaps for the very spurting forth of spirit into the physiology of mind, and perhaps what André Frénaud will call "visitation" (we could also go back here to questions of "destiny" and "divine" ontic buoyancy); 4. Vigny's designation of ideal mentation as "pure," his leaning toward essence and factors of high aestheticism and exquisite intelligibility, must be read in conjunction not only with a level of practical emotional problem-solving inherent in his poetic enterprise, but also with a certain sensualization, even eroticization, of thought, idea, myth, ideality: "Where will you lead me, passion for Ideas, where?" he will ask in his *Journal*, "I have possessed some Ideas; with others I have spent nights.//You have given me my imagination as mistress.//The pleasures of the soul are long, moral ecstasy is superior to physical ecstasy" (*OC*, I, 1008). And later, in 1840, he will affirm, "oui, la poésie est une volupté, mais une volupté couvrant la pensée et la rendant lumineuse" ("yes, poetry is a pleasure, but a pleasure covering thought, rendering it luminous," *OC*, II, 1139): if thought can be functional, it is also—perhaps this is even its highest claim to functionality—oriented toward ecstasy, mystical union, a *jouissance* offering, as for Rimbaud and probably Baudelaire, the mutual completion of body and spirit.

From Construction to Dispersal

Vigny's poetical work, both individual poems and particular volumes, may be viewed as demonstrating careful orchestration, painstaking reflection—the publication of the *Poèmes antiques et modernes* covers the period 1822–1841 and the texts of *Les Destinées* span the vast period of 1838–1864. Poems can come and go, being cut out, added, modified in a sharply scrutinized evolution obeying changing plans and conceptions that *L'Atelier du poète* and *Le Journal d'un poète* (*A Poet's Journal*) amply document. The *Poèmes antiques et modernes* are perceived in the triple light of Vigny's conception of epic or drama, philosophy, and poetry itself, and epic is further organized according to its ancient or modern manifestation. *Les Destinées* continues this tactic, but elaborates more finely the philosophical "structures." In broad terms, moreover, more specific organizational features and principles may be readily identified: the recourse to both symbol and allegorical representation whose discretion and arguable objectivity can be made to meld with bold effusion and satire; the widespread use of source materials meditated in the perspective of both obsession and high intent and ideal; a level of presymbolist preoccupation with aesthetics that centers effort upon form, balance, and *beauté idéale* (*OC*, I, 203–205), yet in Vigny's case never sacrificing to some "joli mélimélo" what Denis Roche calls the "combativity" of his literary gesture. If these broad organizational principles can be readily identified, so too can a host of smaller, but crucially structuring phenomena: 1. the use of asterisks or numbers to order the development from section to section or even stanza to stanza; 2. the practice of giving generic (*élévation, mystère,* even *poème*) or explanatory (*conseil à un jeune homme inconnu* ["advice to an unknown young man"]) subtitles to the texts in a further effort of poetic and ideational arrangement; 3. the use of capitalized words or phrases (*LE DIAMANT, L'ÉCRIT UNIVERSEL, L'ESPRIT [THE DIAMOND, UNIVERSAL WRITTEN LOGOS, MIND], OC,* I, 133, 168, 167) to focus attention and give implicit in-depth structure; 4. a similar predilection for abstract terminology to offer explicit culmination to allegory and symbol ("Les Destinées" and "Les Oracles"); 5. a respect for prosodic convention, especially the alexandrine, with heavily purposeful couplets with their *rimes plates,* although Vigny can aspire both to an elegant but limited liberation from such restriction, via *coupes,* enjambments, and to other combinations of meter, rhyme, and stanzaic shapes (the seven-line alexandrine stanza of "La Maison du berger," with its *ababccb* rhyme scheme; the elegant deployment of the *faux quatrains,* with minor but dramatic structural variations, of "La Fille de Jephté" and "Le Cor"; the varyingly composed sonnets of the *Fantaisies,* "Stances" and "À Évariste Boulay-Paty"; the five-syllable line, used as a separate gambit or in combination, as in "Foule immense et vaine" and "Madame de Soubise" [*OC,* I, 215–17, 74–78); 6. the elaborative, "com-pensatory" tactic of metaphor and simile, no doubt underestimated in Vigny, though far less spectacular than with Hugo; "Des fleurs qu'on ne voit pas dans l'été des humains,/Comme une large pluie abondaient sous leurs mains" ("Flowers not seen in the summer of humans,/Like a broad rain abounded before them," *OC,* I, 13, "Eloa") offers, however, a good example of Vigny's capacities for figurative delicacy and nuance and shows how, in his conception of thought, poetic advance and construction can often be infinitely greater if logical, drily objective evocation is bypassed; 7. the application of epigraphs to both volume and individual poem (*Les Destinées,* "Eloa," "Le Déluge"), which allows for a situation, a further networking of idea and event, not dissimilar from metaphoric function and deployment of thought; 8. the use of anaphora, often linked to crescendo effects, as with Lamartine and Hugo, which, in addition to intensifying unfolding meaning, multiplies and diversifies it into a more complex composition (the opening stanza of "La Neige" is a good example, as are the first four *septains* of "La Maison du berger"); 9. the fondness for dialogue or apostrophe (as in "Eloa" or "Le Bal") or, again, the structure of the poem-letter (as in "La Maison du berger"), Vigny having at one point contemplated a whole collection of such epistolary texts; once more, such creative stratagems permit exposition of argument, the flexible coming and going of thought both ordered and less than flatly linear; 10. the profusion, in certain poems, of epithets, in others, of parenthetical clauses, within the strictly observed limits of an elegant syntax, demonstrates equally Vigny's desire to tease out idea, emotion, sensation, all pertinent descriptive, dramatic, or conceptual elements, yet coherently, "developmentally," even if, as his notebooks often remind himself, "poetically"—that is, not merely in versified form. The list could be considerably extended, but will no doubt suffice.

I should like, however, in conclusion of this discussion, to attend to a further series of compositional and stylistic features, some paradoxically taken from the above list, in an effort to show that, if Vigny's tactics of structuration must be respected, so, too, is it proper to remain alert to all that would defy them. Such an assessment will be seen to be readily applicable to many other, if not all, writers, but is particularly pertinent to a poetic *démarche* preoccupied, as is Vigny's, with carefully arranged and surveyed message and form. Let us start with the dates that accompany all the *Poèmes antiques et modernes* in the hope of confirming their generic originality, as he indicates in the 1837 preface (*OC*, I, 5), and the majority of *Les Destinées*. Here—as Vigny's plans, calculations, and notes of the *Journal* show him to be aware—here, we have, imposed, but *en sourdine*, upon the definitively chosen construction of the volumes, a spectral, secondary order, strictly authentic, because embodying the temporal and emotional structure of their creation, yet regarded as a disorder; here we have a dispersal of philosophical artifice, a deconstruction of fictional orchestration, a thoroughly honest reminder of the fragility and arbitrariness, studied as it may be, of what the surrealists themselves called *l'arrangement en poème*, or, here, *en recueil*. Secondly, Vigny's anticipated collection of poems he had tentatively titled *Fantaisies* in 1862—this is the title posthumously retained—offers a conscious logic of fragmentation and *collage* ("des fragments seuls *avec leur date*" ("fragments only, *dated*"), he insists in the "Note sur Héléna," *OC*, I, 1137) in utter conflict with his severe quasi-Parnassian or Mallarméan mode: "un livre tel que je le conçois," he writes in the same note, "doit être composé, sculpté, posé, taillé, fini et limé et poli comme une statue de marbre de Paros" ("a book as I conceive it, must be structured, sculpted, set firm, chiselled, finished, filed and polished like a marble statue from Paros," (*OC*, I, 1136). The capricious, fanciful, whimsical mode loosens and disorders the whole fabric of Vigny's compositional code and permits a rethinking of that poetics of finish and polish he maintains as his major artistic fiction. The very tone of poems like "Rêverie" (*OC*, I, 209), but not unlike "Madame de Soubise" of *Poèmes antiques et modernes* (*OC*, I, 74–78), draws upon this *fantaisiste*, Apollinairean quality—and Mallarmé's many *vers de circonstance* demonstrate an equal *dissémination*, an equally shambling, though stylistically affected, playfulness.

Thirdly, both the *esquisses* ("outlines") and the *esquisses sans lendemain* ("outlines undeveloped"), from *L'Atelier d'un poète*, point in two directions: to the gestures of rounding and structuring seen above, but also to the changeability, the precarious, unstable relative nature of all construction, all artistic congealment of being. Fourthly, symbol, as Michel Deguy has stressed, may be intrinsic to all expression, but it is, as he says, an *être-comme* ("being-as"): throwing two things together (*sum-ballein*), it cannot provide true convergence, true com-position or con-struction, nor can it give us the actuality of being or presence. It is thus doubly immersed in factors of dispersal, even though its project is union and seamless message. Fifthly, metaphor and simile—and, arguably, all elements of poetic figuration—follow this same logic of *l'être-comme de l'être*, as Deguy puts it: engaged in transfer, change, *com-pli-cation*, the folding over of one thing upon the other, albeit in the intention of centering and constructing the elegant edifice of some "philosophy," the metaphor inevitably can be said to destabilize via its very enrichment, deconstruct via its very reordering. And this is not to underline the intensely personal, and therefore decentralizing, nature of all metaphoric discourse.

Some remaining points I shall mention very briefly: 6. Vigny's use of *points de suspension*, his occasional allusion to poems as "fragments" ("Le Bain," "Sur la mort de Byron," "La Beauté idéale," "Prière pour ma mère"), or his creation of rare fragments such as "Faites, ô Seigneur invisible" ("Let, oh invisible Lord," *OC*, I, 226), give to an oeuvre ostensibly predicated upon principles of elaborate artistic closure an aura of openness, incompleteness, and possibility that, far from harming the overall intention, give it aeration and meditative potential; 7. the abundant exclamations to which Vigny resorts throughout his work offer compact, compressed "structuring" of thought and sentiment, but all exclamation entails excess, overflowing, illusory containment, and, as with Desbordes-Valmore or Rimbaud, such a strategy at once succeeds and "fails" in its endeavor to construct an ultimate, but inevitably reductive, expression of essence as experienced; 8. even the very proliferation of speech, the great descriptive or narrative swaths of "Eloa" or "La Mort du Loup," the complex *incidentes*, anaphoric swells or crescendos we have spoken of, the explicative use of the subtitles, or the also examined tendency to multiply clarificatory abstractions—all such proliferation, the very stuff of conceptual and rhetorical order and design, points also ironically, to the impossibility of compacting the changing intricacies of idea and emotion into that perfected compositional emblem that is the verse, the poem, or *le livre*. Grammar and all linguistico-poetical strategy can construct, but they cannot contain except, as Vigny himself put it, in the manner of a "talisman" (*OC*, I, 225), for multiplication, development, parenthesis, explication, all continuation of speech—we might think of Rimbaud's final choice of silence here—is inevitably, at least simultaneously, ontic and "philosophical" openness or osmosis; it is dispersal and deconstruction; it is, to quote Yves Bonnefoy, "la dérive majeure de la nuée" ("The vast drift of cloud").

· FOUR ·

Baudelaire

"Parisian genius," Verlaine wrote of Baudelaire's immense talent, which, he maintained, consisted both in his acutely pertinent representation of "modern man" and his unsurpassed powers of versification. Born in Paris, on 9 April 1821, Baudelaire was to live and die in Paris. His early travel, in 1841, to the Indian Ocean—Mauritius and Reunion—though forced upon him by a stepfather, Aupick, with whom relations were rarely cordial, nevertheless left its mark upon his sensibility and a sensual, fleshy oeuvre both for and against the simple-minded or even transcendent logic of the quest for the exotic. The year 1842 was, further, to launch a lifelong passion for the mulatto actress Jeanne Duval, a passion so complex, and so complicated by financial and family difficulties, as to provoke, in 1845, a suicide attempt. Despite emotional and material disturbance, Baudelaire was already, with the publication of the *Salon de 1845* (*1845 Exhibition*), the foremost aesthetician of his age, and his own slowly maturing poetic genius at once feeds off and reciprocally nourishes his writings on poetry, music, art, and social mores in general. Member of the Société des gens de lettres, as were established figures such as Balzac and Hugo, friend of great artists such as Courbet, Baudelaire oddly never ceases to be a willful marginal, an explorer of the world of drugs, a sufferer, a free yet misunderstood spirit, a *maladapté* knowing the depths of taedium vitae and plunged, finally, into the horrors of aphasia, hemiplegia, dumbness, dying pathetically at the age of forty-six on 31 August 1867, in the arms of a mother sensing only at the last something of her son's painful but exquisite genius.

If Baudelaire's discovery of Delacroix may be said to be determining, so too is his sensitive and elaborate study of Edgar Allan Poe. *Les Fleurs du Mal* (*The Flowers of Evil*), whose first edition, in 1857, was to lead to criminal charges, trial proceedings, fines and suppression of certain poems, is written at the intersection of, on the one hand, romantic and symbolist vision, sweeping ideality and a poetics of centripetal, horror-struck imagination, and, on the other hand, the ironized obligation of compassion, love, hope, and an availability reimmersed in the swirling dilemmas of the quotidian, the dubious, the mortal. Little wonder that Victor Hugo spoke immediately of "un frisson nouveau" or that Rimbaud, in his *Lettre dite du voyant*, refers to Baudelaire as "the foremost seer, king of poets, *a true God.*" Indeed, his reputation has never ceased to grow, not just within France but throughout the Western world. Mallarmé struggles to release himself from Baudelaire's bewitching spell, and great poets of the modern age as different as Reverdy and Deguy, Emmanuel and Frénaud, have found in *Les Fleurs du Mal* or *Le Spleen de Paris* (*The Spleen of Paris*) an energy, a discipline and resilient yet lucid vision of art that, varyingly, has fueled their own individual dynamisms. Lautréamont's designation, "écrivassier funeste," is less derogatory than demonstrative of his own ethical struggle, and Laforgue's almost inevitable reservation is quickly put in perspective: "ni grand coeur, ni grand esprit; mais quels nerfs plaintifs! quelles narines ouvertes à tout! quelle voix magique!" ("not a great heart, nor a great mind; but what plaintive nerves! what nostrils available to everything! what a magical voice!"). Baudelaire would not have complained, one feels. It is perhaps to Yves Bonnefoy, however, that we owe the greatest debt today, despite the great range of subtle critical commentary developed, in our understanding of Baudelaire's precarious and essential balancing of the complementarily valid claims of what he calls *l'image* and *la présence.*

Horror

Towards the end of the posthumously published journal *Mon coeur mis à nu* (*My Heart Laid Bare*, 1897), Baudelaire describes the substantial "tissue of horrors" that every newspaper churns out for our daily consumption: "Wars, crimes, thefts, vulgarities, tortures, princely crimes, national crimes, private crimes, a drunkenness of universal atrocity" (*OC*, 1299). Such an anti-intoxication, wildly, ignobly barbaric, far from the idealizing, potentially transcendent *ivresses(s)* ("intoxications") that Baudelaire will ultimately—though with some irony—recommend to us, accounts for that sentiment of isolation and loss that, as he implies in his other journal, *Fusées* (*Flares*, 1887), marks profoundly his sensibility: "Lost in this wicked world, elbowed by the masses, I am like a weary man whose eye gazes back, in the deep years, upon mere disillusion and bitterness, and, forward, but to a storm containing nothing new" (*OC*, 1264). Baudelaire's vision may be thus regarded as *spleené-tique* ("splenetic"; *OC*, 7, 69–71), constantly beset by the nervous exhaustion caused by what he terms in the first line of the liminal text of *Les Fleurs du Mal*, "Au Lecteur" ("To the Reader," *OC*, 5–6), "la sottise, l'erreur, le péché, la lésine" ("foolishness, error, sin, niggardliness," *OC*, 5); constantly assaulted by that blackness, melancholy, sense of imprisonment and hopelessness, even anguish—"Atrocious despotic Anguish,/Upon my bowed skull plants its black flag," Baudelaire writes in perhaps the fiercest of the four "Spleen" poems of his shattering collection—that seem to swamp enthusiasm and subvert all existential simplicity. Life is not just complicated by *le mal,* as for Vigny; it is in itself, as Baudelaire argues in "Semper eadem" (*OC*, 39), "un mal" ("an evil"); it is "implacably unbearable," as he will suggest in "La Chambre double" ("The Double Room"), from *Le Spleen de Paris* (*OC*, 235), "immorally tedious" (*OC*, 69, "Spleen"), intrinsically and eternally stultifying and "faulted" (*OC*, 93, "Danse macabre"). Existence, in short, is under the sign of Satan, exposing us, seemingly to our own moral, psychological, and philosophical impotence. "C'est le Diable," he affirms from the outset of *Les Fleurs du Mal* in his singularly "modern" quasi-articulation of original sin, "qui tient les fils qui nous remuent" ("It is the Devil who holds the strings moving us," *OC*, 5).

Such a bizarre mixture of criminality and pure *hasard*, as is implied in "Hymne à la Beauté" ("Hymn to Beauty," *OC*, 23–24, especially the first stanza), or of crime and madness, as in "Sonnet d'automne" ("Autumn Sonnet," *OC*, 62), would show Baudelaire hesitating between a poetics of guilt, of moral responsibility, and one of chaos, wild absurdity; other texts would suggest that "indestructible, eternal, universal and ingenious human ferocity" (*OC*, 1287, *Mon coeur mis à nu*) is consciously assumed by humanity, yet can be readily made to dovetail with the logic of time, which, inevitably, would seem to rob us of a significant level of freedom. The latter reduction, with its annihilation and putrefaction, its negative transformation, so powerfully evoked in "Une charogne" ("Carrion," *OC,* 29–31)—"And yet you will resemble this filth,/This horrible infection,/Star of my eyes, sun of my nature,/You, my angel and my passion" (*OC,* 30)—can at times seem to outweigh all specifically human intervention. But Baudelaire's sense of horror at this particular form of *l'irréparable* or *l'irrémédiable* (*OC,* 53, 75) is, finally, easily compensated by that other sensation of all that is consciously abominable, awarely demoniacal in the human. Plunged into existential responsibility or excusable impotence, life remains relentlessly, giddily, horrific, ceaselessly and paradoxically luring the poet, as he says in "La Destruction" ("Destruction," *OC,* 105), "far from God's gaze,/Panting and broken, in the midst/Of the deep, barren plains of *Ennui.*" Even the knowledge gained from inquiry constitutes, Baudelaire argues at his most devastatingly cynical, "une oasis d'horreur dans un désert d'ennui" ("an oasis of horror in a desert of boredom"), the same images of nothingness and *taedium vitae* surging forth unstoppably (see *OC,* 126, "Le Voyage"). And if Baudelaire's poetics will be in part founded upon an aesthetic exploitation of horror— "You walk, Beauty, upon corpses you deride" ("Hymne à la Beauté"), and "of your jewels horror is not the least delightful"— so, also, is it true that, as the exquisite "Les Phares" ("Guiding Lights," *OC,* 12–14) renders unambiguous, art remains for Baudelaire "the burning sob rolling from age to age" in response to the horror of sorrow and suffering; and that *Les Fleurs du Mal,* far from being some gratuitous riot of amorality or spiritual *je-m'enfoutisme,* represents both "l'AGITATION DE L'ESPRIT DANS LE MAL" ("AGITATION OF THE MIND IN EVIL"), as Baudelaire calls it in the *Reliquat et dossier des Fleurs du Mal* (*Residue and Dossier of the Flowers of Evil*), and that "HORREUR DU MAL" ("HORROR OF EVIL") of which he observes such little evidence in the literature of 1857 (*OC,* 181).

Satanism

One could, given the foregoing, be perhaps surprised to find that Baudelaire's work maps out and embraces a poetics of "evil" and *malheur.* For doesn't he declare worrisomely in the paradoxically titled "L'Idéal" ("The Ideal," *OC,* 21), "what this abyss-deep heart needs,/Is you, Lady Macbeth, your crime-powerful soul,/Your

Aeschylus dream blossoming in southerly winds" (*OC*, 21)? And, in "Le Possédé" ("The One Possessed," *OC*, 35–36), also from *Les Fleurs du Mal*, doesn't he cry out, with vigor and seemingly perverse glee, "there is not a fiber of my trembling body/That does not cry: *Oh my dear Beelzebub, I adore you!*" (*OC*, 36)? So that, despite the sense of horrified outrage at life, Baudelaire appears duplicitously to practice what he doesn't preach, to be engaged in an "hermetic" transformation, as he suggests in "Alchimie de la douleur" ("Alchemy of Pain," *OC*, 72–73), not of base metal into exquisitely refined jewelry, but of "gold into iron/And paradise into hell" (*OC*, 73). The following poem in the "Spleen et idéal" ("Spleen and Ideal") section of *Les Fleurs du Mal* pictures "the Hell in which my heart delights" (*OC*, 73, "Horreur sympathique" ["Likable Horror"]) as a locus of apparent pleasure and self-indulgence, but then, even if this is so, we can hardly ignore the fact that the stormy, cloud-torn sky depicted is the emblem of the poet's heart, fascinating though disturbing, sundered though one. Indeed, the poem, despite its would-be bravado, hints at much else that helps us to an initial comprehension of Baudelaire's *satanisme:* the fact, as "L'Irréparable" ("The Irreparable," *OC*, 52–53) makes clear, that, if in the "banal theatre" of Baudelaire's emotions and spiritual impulses, Satan's defeat is actually glimpsed, the poet/narrator "awaits,/Ever, ever, in vain, the gauze-winged Being" responsible for the transmutation of "an infernal sky/[Into] a miraculous dawn" (*OC*, 53); the poet's slippage into "irresistible Night," described in "Le Coucher du soleil romantique" ("Romantic Sunset") from *Les Epaves* (*Jetsam*, 1866), comes about despite a Vigny-like "vain pursuit of God withdrawing" (*OC*, 133); Baudelaire's painful but essential "conscience dans le Mal" ("consciousness in Evil"), a consciousness both moral and spiritual, shows that the various "emblems" of the fall from the divine are by no means offered in gratuitous play (see *OC*, 75–76, "L'Irrémédiable" ["The Inevitable"]); the poet's demoniacal hauntedness, so powerfully evoked in "La Destruction" (*OC*, 105), while leading to desire, also plunges him into confusion, sentiments of guilt, a self-destructiveness "far from God's gaze" (*OC*, 105); the fact, lastly, that Baudelaire realizes to what an appalling extent "satanism" is a generalized phenomenon, the trace of our other "ignoble double," as Jarry will call it, "that mood, hysterical according to doctors, satanic according to those who think a little better than doctors, pushing us irresistibly towards a mass of dangerous and improper actions" ("Le Mauvais Vitrier" ["The Poor Glazier"], *Le Spleen de Paris, OC,* 238–40).

Baudelairean satanism is intimately linked to self-knowledge, as "Allégorie" suggests (*OC,* 109–10), but a self-knowledge steeped in moral, even catholic, conscience with its proddings of guilt, shame, and remorse. The entire city of Paris lying before the narrator of the "Epilogue" of *Le Spleen de Paris* is thus implacably portrayed as being under the sign of Satan, "patron of my distress": "hôpital, lupanars, purgatoire, enfer, bagne,//Où toute énormité fleurit comme une fleur" ("hospitals, brothels, hell, hulks,//Where each enormity flourishes like a flower," *OC,* 310). But Baudelaire, unlike the anonymous woman of "Allégorie," cannot shake off the sense of deep rift thus engendered within his entire being. Certainly, some poems are bolder than others, more defiant, more tinged with high revolt. Thus "Lesbos" (*OC,* 134–36) seems to place guilt and convention in parenthesis in establishing a love, as Nietzsche will say, beyond good and evil, "[a love] mocking Hell and Heaven" (*OC,* 135). Thus, too, though with irony and perhaps even bitterness, can Baudelaire seem to flaunt every bourgeois wish for surface discretion and uncomplicatedness when he writes, in the *Reliquat et dossier des Fleurs du Mal:* "Chaste comme le papier, sobre comme l'eau, porté à la dévotion comme une communiante, inoffensif comme une victime, il ne me déplairait pas de passer pour un débauché, un ivrogne, un impie et un assassin" ("Chaste as paper, sober as water, given to devotion like a communicant, harmless as a victim, I should not be displeased to be taken for a debauchee, a drunkard, a blasphemer and a murderer," *OC,* 188). And we should thus not neglect the fact that "satanism" can also be, for Baudelaire, a mode of existential self-liberation, a provocative instigation of action, struggle and new possibility (see "Assommons les pauvres" ["Let's Knock the Poor"], *Le Spleen de Paris, OC,* 305), a path of "egoism," as his notes on "commerce" in *Mon coeur mis à nu* render explicit (*OC,* 1297), yet an egoism, a self-affirmation, a reaffirmation of a dangerously collapsing self, in the face of the countless social monstrosities that *Les Fleurs du Mal* precisely delineates and that, say, "L'Albatros" ("Albatross," *OC,* 9–10) wastes no time in firmly emblematizing.

A number of factors remain to be teased out. If, for example, "Les Litanies de Satan" ("Satan's Litanies," *OC,* 116–19) can be read as an ironic and antagonistic anti-invocation to an anti-God still inhabited by splendid dream, a darker anguish lingers, beyond defiance, beyond that wild proud, pretentious cursing of the divine Baudelaire himself chastises in "Le Voyage"—an anguish embedded in nostalgia, remorse, and sense of loss. "Oh Satan, pity my long wretchedness" is the persistent refrain of the litany, just as the "Epigraphe pour un livre condamné" ("Epigraph for a Condemned Book," *OC*, 163), finally added to the third edition of *Les Fleurs du Mal*, stresses that, if the book is "Saturnian,/Orgiacal and melancholic" (*OC*, 163), its author precisely needs the understanding, the empathy, the compassion whose lack is at the root of the book's very composition.

Not dissimilarly, the corrosive "L'Examen de minuit" ("Midnight Analysis," *OC*, 168–69), also added to the third edition, while plunging us—the *nous* of the text is no accident—into our contradictions of blasphemy, insult, flattery, stupidity, and materialism, evokes *en filigrane*, spectrally, factors of love, divineness, compassion, intelligence, and spirit. As Baudelaire points out in *Reliquat*, "à un blasphème j'opposerai des élancements vers le Ciel, à une obscénité des fleurs platoniques" ("to blasphemy I shall oppose heavenly upsurgings, to obscenity platonic flowers," *OC*, 181). Indeed, not only is there opposition and *battement*, but an essential equivalence of the two modes, an inseparable discourse, a unified logic and search. "Satanism"—and I place the word in quotation marks to distinguish it from any strictly contemporary appropriation—implies both temptation and horror for Baudelaire, and it is an essential mode of his highest aspiration, his most profound ontological quest. In "Vers pour le portrait de M. Honoré Daumier" ("Lines for a Portrait for Mr. Honoré Daumier") from *Les Epaves* (*OC*, 151), Baudelaire writes:

> C'est un satirique, un moqueur;
> Mais l'énergie avec laquelle
> Il peint le Mal et sa séquelle,
> Prouve la beauté de son coeur.

> He is a satirizer, a derider;
> But the energy with which
> He paints Evil and the like
> Proves the beauty of his heart.
> (*OC*, 151)

There is no doubt that Baudelaire's work is more pained, more distressed, more tragically meditated than Daumier's; but there can equally be no doubt that, for those reasons, his *satanisme* is a sign of the poet's spiritual and emotional "beauty." "Histoire des *Fleurs du Mal*," he notes to himself in *Mon coeur mis à nu*, "humiliation par le malentendu, et mon procès" ("Story of *The Flowers of Evil*, humiliation through misunderstanding, and my trial," *OC*, 1279). Agitation, horror, consciousness/conscience, continuing aspiration—these are the principal elements underpinning Baudelaire's poetics of the "flowers of evil."

One could stress, and with Baudelaire, the specifically aesthetic exploitation of evil and the horrific. Does he not write in his long 1859 essay on Théophile Gautier that "it is one of the prodigious privileges of Art that the horrific, artistically expressed, becomes beauty, and *pain*, rhythmed and cadenced, fills the mind with a calm *joy*" (*OC*, 695)? And is it not blatantly clear that, in *Les Fleurs du Mal*, there is at work a powerful mechanism of distillation, transmutation, and transcendence sufficient to permit the *satanisme* inherent in existence at large to yield to the exquisite antinature of poetry and imaginative form? Beauty, for Baudelaire, is not merely relative (see "Qu'est-ce que le romantisme" ["What is Romanticism?"], *OC*, 879), not merely linked to the genius and originality of the subject ("Salon de 1859," *OC*, 1084), but, for him, "something ardent and sad" (*OC*, 1255), irretrievably sunk in mystery and *malheur* and "satanism," as he argues in *Fusées* (*OC*, 1255).

But as many of these texts suggest or explicitly state, Baudelaire is no cold developer of some exclusively aesthetic consolation. Transcendence there may be, but it occurs within the blatant immanence of all the "satanism" evoked, all the "HORREUR DU MAL" that seeps, thick with painful irony, from every "flower" he has caused to blossom. Satanism and its aesthetic transcendence do not cancel each other out, but they do beg for a world of love and compassion, serenity and joy, to be miraculously fashioned in our hearts. Despite the searing and cautionary onslaught of "Au lecteur," *Les Fleurs du Mal* are framed by their *dédicace* and the *Reliquat*.

Crack, Contradiction, Irony

"My soul is cracked," Baudelaire concludes in "La Cloche fêlée" ("The Cracked Bell") from the "Spleen et idéal" section of *Les Fleurs du Mal* (*OC,* 68) and such crackedness again haunts him as he asks in "L'Héautontimorouménos" (*OC,* 74):

> Ne suis-je pas un faux accord
> Dans la divine symphonie,
> Grâce à la vorace Ironie
> Qui me secoue et qui me mord?

> Am I not off key
> In the divine symphony,
> Thanks to ravenous Irony
> Shaking and biting me?
>
> (*OC,* 74)

Such a cleavage of being, of mind, of heart, manifests itself in various modes: those of simultaneity, multiplicity, alteration, principally, and a kind of resultant betweenness or no-man's-land, which is, precisely, the impossible space of crackedness, of *fêlure.* "You are a lovely autumn sky, clear, rose-hued," he can write in "Causerie" ("Chatting," *OC,* 54), "but sadness wells up in me like the sea" (*OC,* 59). Or, in "Sisina" (*OC,* 58), Sisina herself can be described as "the gentle warrior,/Her soul both loving and murderous" (*OC,* 58), just as the poet-narrator of "L'Héautontimorouménos" will cry out: "Je suis la plaie et le couteau!/Je suis le soufflet et la joue!" ("I am the wound and the knife!/I am the slap and the cheek!" *OC,* 74). This is the self as locus of all pain that is given and received, the site of a riven equilibrium, an ontology *between* blasphemy and divine impulse (see *OC,* 181), lodged in the improbable, inconceivable zone of "buts," "howevers," "ands," where one lives out one's split yet single identity "with delight and terror" (*OC,* 1265, *Fusées*); where, as Baudelaire notes in *Mon coeur mis à nu,* his "feeling of eternally solitary destiny [is,] however, [offset by his] very sharp taste for life and pleasure" (*OC,* 1275); where one can sense the curious sweetness of being "alternatively victim and executioner" (*OC,* 127, *Mon coeur mis à nu*). Such a cracked, multiply divided, yet bizarrely whole condition— "La vérité, pour être multiple, n'est pas double" ("Truth, because multiple, is not dualistic"), he will emphasize in *Salon de 1846*— such a condition Baudelaire understands to be at once singularly his and massively, though perhaps unavowedly, generalized.

Baudelaire

Once more, his journal *Mon coeur mis à nu* is instructive. "As a child," he tells us, "I felt in my heart two contradictory feelings, horror of life and life's ecstasy" (*OC*, 1296); and, a little earlier, we read his famous declaration: "Il y a dans tout homme, à toute heure, deux postulations simultanées, l'une vers Dieu, l'autre vers Satan" ("There are in us all, at any moment, two simultaneous postulations, one towards God, the other towards Satan," *OC*, 1277). This simultaneity-contradictoriness-alternation-betweenness, "what one can call, alas, my wound/And my fatedness" (*OC*, 153, "La Voix" ["Voice"]), and that I have termed Baudelaire's "crackedness," is inevitably linked to various other factors of his consciousness: to what he himself calls, in "Les Dons des fées" ("Fairies' Gifts," *OC*, 256–58), "the logic of the Absurd" (*OC*, 258), to his conception of existential drama, "the natural drama inherent within us all" (*OC*, 1072), to the celebrated opening gambit of *Mon coeur mis à nu:* "De la vaporisation et de la centralisation du Moi. Tout est là" ("The vaporisation and the centralisation of the Self. That's everything," *OC*, 1271).

The whole question of oppositions, contradictions, differences, linked however to its other face—unity, non- or in-difference, Derridian *différance, indécidabilité*—is no doubt central to an appreciation of Baudelaire's profound modernity. One only needs to think of surrealism, cubism, relativity theory, the unconscious, psychoanalysis, reincarnation or simultaneous incarnation theory, multiple personality, to understand the implications of Baudelaire's thought. The poet is fascinated at once by affective and spiritual contradiction and by a need to press, through a persistent exploration of contradiction's various manifestations, to a consciousness both with them and beyond them. With respect to the former exploration, only a few samples need be drawn from Baudelaire's inexhaustible stock: humanity's inexplicable "love of carnage and death," the endless "struggle" in "brotherhood," that "L'Homme et la mer" ("The Man and the Sea") will evoke (*OC*, 18); the choking juxtapositions of the transparently gentle, the exquisitely fructified, and the despairingly rotting and dying, such as "Une charogne" unforgettably portrays; the dizzying coexistence of "mystery" and "absurdity," of meaning and senselessness, that can "wound" the poet-narrator of "Les sept vieillards" ("The Seven Old Men," *OC*, 83–84); the contradictions of either that quasi-madness, evoked in "La Voix," provoking laughter in mourning and sorrow in festivity, or, after delight in natural splendor, those feelings of repulsion or exasperation that well up, as we are told in "Le *Confiteor* de l'artiste" ("The Artist's *Confiteor*," *OC*, 232), unexplainable but real. Contradiction in such lights involves paradox, what Baudelaire calls "réversibilité" (*OC*, 42), difference in confrontations that may even suggest unthinkable equivalence, emotional, moral and spiritual illogicality, madness, and so on.

Yet, for Baudelaire, contradiction is equally a way of access to some totality of consciousness, some spirituality of truth at once permitting relativity to multiply within relativity and yet sensitive to a certain indefinable "eternal" constancy (*OC*, 1154). It is for this reason that the poet, in "Les Foules" ("Crowds," *OC*, 243–44), is seen as generating that capacity to embrace, even become, all alterity, all difference. It is for this reason that Baudelaire admires Hugo, who sees the human, the diabolical, and the divine in all creatures, all phenomena (*OC*, 704). Hugo is thus, though living contradiction, beyond it, "un génie sans frontières" ("a boundless genius," *OC*, 707), a consciousness more cosmic than terrestrial, yet living the infinity of the immanent, the endless contra-dictions of our global, universal discourse. It is for this reason that Baudelaire embraces the horrors and uglinesses around him, just as he will not hesitate, faced with the immense artistic shifts from Daumier to Delacroix to Ingres, to say: "Aimons-nous tous les trois" ("Let All Three of Us Love One Another," *OC*, 818). Such an embrace of what is—despite, even because of, its contradictions—involves an openness identical to the very "crackedness" we began with, but a crack seen less as "wound," less as *plaie*, hurt, pain, horror, than as a great place of availability, healing, love, aesthetico-spiritual transformation.

It is, then, possible to read the countless ironies of *Les Fleurs du Mal* and *Le Spleen de Paris*, as a chosen mode—bitter, grating, and grimacing—allowing the expression of the equally countless contradictions oozing from the "cracked soul" and the divided sensibilities and affinities Baudelaire observes both within himself and without. Irony, in this optic, can include the oft-repeated logic of the dignity of sorrow (see the end of "Les Phares"); the perception of suffering as a "divine remedy to our impurities" (cf. "Bénédiction" ["Blessing"], *OC*, 7–9); the unsatisfied wait for a yet envisage-able reversal of satanism ("L'Irréparable"); the searching empty upward-turned gaze of the blind ("Les Aveugles" ["The Blind"], *OC*, 88); death become consolation, goal and hope ("La Mort des pauvres" ["Death of the Poor"], *OC*, 119–20); even the fleeting yet tense moment when the poet-narrator can write: "I felt my bosom, like an irony,/Torn by the sun" ("À celle qui est trop gaie" ["To Her, Too Merry"], *OC*, 140–41).

Almost every poem carries something of this sharp and bleak ironic flavor. And Baudelaire's stance is fully conscious, stressing "Deux qualités littéraires fondamentales," as he notes in *Fusées*, "surnaturalisme et ironie" ("Two fundamental literary qualities, the supernatural and irony," *OC*, 1256). Elsewhere, in his essay on *Madame Bovary*, he speaks of "the high faculties of *irony* and *lyricism* illuminating to excess *The Temptation of Saint Anthony*" (*OC*, 656). And, furthermore, is it not to Baudelaire that we owe enlight-ened essays on laughter and the comic, Daumier, Vernet, Gavarni, Hogarth, Goya, Brueghel, and other *caricaturistes* (*OC*, 975–93, 994–1013, 1014–24)? Baudelairean irony could be viewed exclu-sively as artistic compensation, a somewhat self-hardening allevi-ation of pain, even an aesthetically transcendent exploitation of the cracks and contradictions of lived being. In this sense, we could regard irony as cynical or coy calculation, a tongue-in-cheek rising above the tiresomeness of existence to a level of play and image that would insulate the poet from the raw bite of *le quoti-dien*. If there is something of this in Baudelaire, however, it is cov-ered by a further layer of irony, as intangible as the first, but knowable and appreciable by virtue of both the sheer intensity of Baudelaire's work and the tone of compassion and saddened love that pervades his vision and dominates his intention.

Irony, in this perspective, tends to render the grating more elegiac, and, rather than settle into some futile trough of either sarcasm or idle playfulness, it moves between the improbable poles of serene smile and tragic gravity. Ultimately, Baudelaire's irony, the twists and turns of poems such as "À une heure du matin" ("One O'Clock in the Morning," *OC*, 240–42) and "Le Gâteau" ("The Cake," *OC*, 249–51) from *Le Spleen de Paris*, center upon an intense desire to em-brace the teeming complications, the crisscrossing folds, creases and crevasses, of that unspeakable force that buoys us up. In this sense, irony is a tactic of ontological fullness, of cosmic truth, of wholeness of vision—a *creative force* in the deepest sense of the term.

Ideal, Beauty, Journey

Baudelaire is no positivist, no social democrat, no political idealist. "Progress" and "perfectibility," as not only the prose poem "Le Joueur généreux" ("The Generous Player," *OC*, 274) but also his essays and journal notes on Hugo would suggest, are not synonymous with Baudelairean notions of ideality, even if Hugo's purer visionary quest and his general cosmic embrace are closer to Baudelaire's personal poetics. The beautiful "Elévation" (*OC*, 10) quickly gives the already bemused reader of *Les Fleurs du Mal* a fuller sense of the *idéal* that, one presumes, lies in majestic opposition to the *spleen* of the first section: the free, ascendant movement of the mind and spirit, their purification and escape, far from "boredoms and vast griefs," into high luminosity and serenity, a movement of self-liberation that yet permits the spirit to "understand effortlessly/The language of flowers and muted things" (*OC*, 10). If Michelangelo may be said to be, as Baudelaire puts it in the *Salon de 1846*, "à un certain point de vue l'inventeur de l'idéal chez les modernes" (*OC*, 915), art in general, the same book argues, is capable of settling both the stomach and the mind back into "l'équilibre naturel de l'idéal" (*OC*, 874)—that state of immanent sanity that is our true condition, ideally. The various poems and texts that, despite spleen and satanism, conjure up those "élancements vers le ciel," the logic of "platonic flowers," that Baudelaire alludes to in the *Reliquat* (*OC*, 181), or the "spiritualité" and "aspiration vers l'infini" of his celebrated definition of romanticism, also in the *Salon de 1846* (*OC*, 879)—such texts would seem to guide us toward a sense of the ideal centered upon high fulfillment, dispassionate *excarnation*, as Bonnefoy says, a flight from the real and the quotidian, the establishment of that same space in which, as Baudelaire says in *Fusées*, "music hollows out the sky" (*OC*, 1251), beyond all anecdote, all evident finitude.

Two factors warn us against opting definitively for this nevertheless pertinent depiction of Baudelairean idealism. The first is Baudelaire's typically ironic, paradoxical, but real *mise en garde* in the poem itself entitled "L'Idéal," where he speaks of "mon rouge idéal" ("my red ideal"), that abysmal, demoniacal aspiration, that seems to flow directly from the poet's impotent gazing after "l'Être aux ailes de gaze" ("gauze-winged Being," *OC*, 53, "L'Irréparable"). Although irony tends to create endless spirals of meaning, it can be reasonably affirmed that Baudelaire's idealism is not simply ethereal angelicism, whether broadly spiritual or tightly aesthetic. The second factor is Baudelaire's insistence, in the *Notes bio-bibliographiques* (*Bio-bibliographical Notes*), upon his "preoccupation with the simultaneous, perpetual relationship of the ideal with life" (*OC*, 1313), that need, expressed so powerfully in "Réversibilité" (*OC*, 42), to place the angelic, the elevating, the potentially transcendent and excarnated, back in the context of anguish, hatred, age, suffering. Those "regions of pure Poetry" evoked in *Fusées* (*OC*, 1261) are not, finally, Baudelaire's, and not only, as he suggests in "Laquelle est la vraie?" ("Which is True?") from *Le Spleen de Paris* (*OC*, 290–91), does he remain "tied, perhaps forever, to the ditch of the ideal" (*OC*, 291), but there is a point of inspection of his entire literary enterprise that would see his idealism, whether angelicizing or diabolic, as even more profoundly caught up in irony, though not as for Mallarmé. When he speaks of Rembrandt as "cette canaille [qui] est un puissant idéaliste qui fait rêver et deviner au delà" ("that riff-raff who is a powerful idealist having us dream and divine beyond," *OC*, 880), we are allowed some finer intuition of that deeper idealism that haunts Baudelaire himself and which is intimately bound up with the logic of crack, contradiction, and irony, with a deep desire for that "universal love" he decrees essential to all pleasure (see "Notes," *OC*, 533–34), with that Hugolian seeing of the sacred and the transcendent within the human and the immanent, with that capacity of Delacroix's to "progress in the way of the good" (*OC*, 815), even though progress is not linear, measurable, material. And, of course, Baudelaire is the last to forget that ideality is concerned less with realization than with movement toward (*OC*, 913), potential, desire, private, intimate spiritual project. "Être un grand homme et un saint *pour soi-même*," he writes in *Mon coeur mis à nu*, "voilà l'unique chose importante" ("Being a great man and a saint for *myself*, that is the only important thing," *OC*, 1289). Baudelaire's idealism is a voyage of the spirit, but it takes place in the *hic et nunc*, dripping with the embraced and assumed tensions of some spiraling self-elevation endlessly traversing and retraversing the "morbid miasmas" of our presence (*OC*, 10, "Elévation").

That beauty—Baudelaire would prefer Beauty—is intimately connected conceptually with the ideal in the poetics of *Les Fleurs du Mal* no one would deny. Beauty—"Je suis l'Ange gardien, la Muse et la Madone" ("I am the guardian Angel, the Muse, the Madonna"), we read in the untitled sonnet "Que diras-tu ce soir . . ." ("What will you say tonight . . ."; *OC*, 41)—is clearly an avenue of poetico-spiritual transcendence, dependent, as the following sonnet, "Le Flambeau vivant" (*OC*, 41), stresses, upon a power of seeing, a "mystical brilliance" that can faultlessly guide, "singing my soul's reawakening" (*OC*, 41–42). The pursuit of beauty, however, Baudelaire is aware, is rigorously exacting. It can enslave, as even "Le Flambeau vivant" avows, and, while perhaps exquisitely purifying, is, as he says in "Causerie" (*OC*, 54), the "dur fléau des âmes" ("the hard scourge of souls"), burning and scouring what residue of wretchedness clings. As with ideality, however, Baudelaire repeatedly affirms his—and, he would argue, our—need to be available, "open to all beauties" (*OC*, 1046, *Salon de 1859*), the divine and the infernal, the joyous and the horrific, as he explains in "Hymne à la Beauté." The wider the sensitivity—"*le beau est toujours bizarre*" ("the beautiful is always bizarre"), he notes in the 1855 "Méthode de critique" ("Critical Method," *OC*, 956)—the greater our capacity for release from that ontic heaviness he evokes at the end of "Hymne à la Beauté." The essential task of the writing of *Les Fleurs du Mal*, he maintains in the *Reliquat*, involved precisely "extracting *beauty* from *Evil*" (*OC*, 185), a task that should not be seen as merely poeticizing, aesthetically framing the uglinesses of poverty, pain, excess, and remorse, but as penetrating with compassion—and of course irony—to the very core of their disturbing realness. This no doubt explains Baudelaire's insistence, in "La Beauté," upon not just the degree of amorality or suspension of our judgment involved in "seeing" the universality of beauty, but also the fact that the apparent "coldness" of beauty is, precisely, a function of this universality, this implacable challenge to our relativity. Like the sickly beggar woman of "À une mendiante rousse" ("To a Red-headed Beggar," *OC*, 79–81)—a poem of blatant celebration of the "minimal," the severely reduced and deprived—beauty needs no artificial beautification. It has its own intense, moving truth in its "maigre nudité" ("skinny nakedness," *OC*, 81), a truth that *is* beauty, a beauty that, as Baudelaire says in "Le Peintre de la vie moderne" ("The Painter of Modern Life," *OC*, 1154), is composed of the relative and the eternal, and wherein the latter renders brilliant and transcendent the former.

Funnily enough, although he often stresses the relativity of beauty—"For me, romanticism is the most recent, the most current expression of the beautiful," he writes in the *Salon de 1846* (*OC*, 879)—Baudelaire only once emphasizes that beauty emanates from our private passions (*OC*, 950, *Salon de 1846*). In this sense, it is self-created, a gift (back) to universality from privacy, a rediscovery of something deeply shared in the at times despairingly relative, a traveling among things with ironic yet open, loving indistinction. "La définition du Beau—de mon Beau," he notes in *Fusées*, "c'est quelque chose d'ardent et de triste, quelque chose d'un peu vague, laissant carrière à la conjecture" ("The definition of the Beautiful—my Beautiful—is something ardent and sad, something rather vague, giving rein to conjecture" (*OC*, 1255).

Baudelaire's conception of the notions of the ideal and beauty implies movement, search, journey, the refusal of a stasis that is, without transmutation, the congealed locus of horror, *ennui, spleen,* and so on. "L'Invitation au voyage" of *Les Fleurs du Mal,* along with its sister prose "version" from *Le Spleen de Paris* (*OC*, 253–55), provides good purchase for an initial assessment of what Baudelairean journey may imply. We can note the following: journey is intimate, it offers sweetness, love, identification, satisfaction and what Baudelaire's refrain calls "order and beauty,/Luxury, calm and voluptuousness" (*OC*, 51). Journey occurs from space here to space there, to a not-here that yet becomes a place of joining of self and other, retaining even, with characteristic irony, the "charming" dubiousness of treachery and sorrow. Journey, here, would seem to offer sensual, aesthetic, and spiritual accomplishment, while remaining tinged with the ambivalences of presently occupied mental and emotional space. A poem such as "Moesta et errabunda," also from the "Spleen et idéal" section of *Les Fleurs du Mal* (*OC*, 60–61), equally demonstrates that journey for Baudelaire is essentially of the mind, the heart, and the soul, and that it permits a distancing from "remorse, crimes, pains" (*OC*, 61), a movement toward some remote "scented paradise" (*OC*, 61), where all is delight, love, joy, "worthiness," purity. As with "L'Invitation au voyage," however, some shadow is cast across this mental path. The last two stanzas, while continuing to build the image of remembered or invented enchantment, question repeatedly its feasibility, its accessibility, edging the reader's consciousness back toward the opening hesitations and the notion, implicit in the title, of intransitive wandering rather than achieved desire. Thus is it that, if journey can offer the possibility of union, healing, "l'infini de la jouissance" ("infinite delight," *OC*, 240, "Le Mauvais Vitrier"), the ecstasy of self-creation, "the pleasure," as Baudelaire writes in "Paysage" ("Landscape," *OC*, 78), "of evoking Spring at will/Drawing a sun from my heart, making/Of my burning thoughts a milk-warm atmosphere" (*OC*, 78), so too can it generate chimera, illusion (see "Chacun sa chimère ["Each his chimera"], *Le Spleen de Paris*, *OC*, 235–36), artificial expansion, the suspect intoxications that, despite Baudelaire's resounding enjoinder—"One should always be drunk. That's everything: it's the only question of significance" (*OC*, 286)—he himself will advise against in his last note of *Fusées* (*OC*, 1270).

Were space permitting, a full analysis could here be undertaken of the extensive writings on opium, wine, hashish and other drugs, "compared as means of multiplying individuality" (*OC*, 323) and seen as an integral part of Baudelaire's poetics of journey. The final poem of the original edition of *Les Fleurs du Mal*, "Le Voyage," serves well, however, as a summary of the complexities of this poetics. The opening section contrasts, with immediate irony, the seeming vastness of existential option and exploration available, with the tight restrictions of remembered experience. Journey is seen as the confrontation of infinite desire and spatio-temporal (but really spiritual) limitation. Moreover, Baudelaire recognizes that if the dream of illumination and unlimitedness can be compellingly real, so too are the endless negative motivations that make journey mere flight, mere refuge, a kind of absent act. The second part, far from building upon the idea of the un-dreamed and unnamable to which journey might offer access, hastens to underscore the spinning, giddying movement journey locks us into, and the pure illusion and madness of all self-displacing purpose, all imaginings that shift the gaze from what Rimbaud will call *la réalité rugueuse* ("rough reality"). Parts 3 and 4 deflate the constructions of the journeying seer, demonstrating the "tautology" of desire, the dissatisfaction, ennui, and nonaccomplishment that await; parts 5 and 6 continue this process of deconstructive anti-revelation, which shows journey to be naive, childish, predicated upon a poetics of frenzied mental images nothing beyond "the tiresome spectacle of immortal sin" (*OC*, 125), anti-visions of human enslavement and foolishness, tyranny and greed, cruelty and sorrow, pretention and arrogance. "A bitter knowledge," the poet-narrator concludes in part 7, "that obtained from journeying" (*OC*, 126), for, although the logic of journey seems founded upon both escape from self (and other) and the dream of an otherness transcending what has been and is, journey, "today,/Yesterday, tomorrow, always, reflects our image:/An oasis of horror in a desert of taedium" (*OC*, 126). If in the final section of "Le Voyage" Baudelaire turns to death and the unknown, potential newness it masks, in an effort to recuperate something from the logic of what underpins all existences to some degree—for journey is desire, hope, quest, effort, work, project, theory—it is a blatantly ironic and tragically colored gesture that places in doubt all human enterprise, even that of art. We should not forget, however, that the whole poem rests upon a visceral and shared desire for some barely conscious transformation; nor should we merely smile with due skepticism at the admittedly ironic verses of the final section:

> Si le ciel et la mer sont noirs comme de l'encre,
> Nos coeurs que tu connais sont remplis de rayons!

> If sky and sea are black as ink,
> our hearts that you know are filled with light!
>   (*OC*, 127)

The poetics of journey is not nihilistic; its very ironies are a resilience and a resistance to that anguish Baudelaire knows to be but one part of his cracked being.

Self and Other

The whole concept of self as opposed to other/ness plunges us into a dialectics that, needless to say, parallels that at the heart of the poetics of journey. To be conscious of the self—the "precocious dandy" Baudelaire considers himself to have been from early youth (see *OC*, 1273, *Mon coeur mis à nu*)—is to take upon oneself the endless questioning of society, of individuality and exchange, of solitariness and sensuality, of love and revulsion, of criticism and charity. A poem such as "La Béatrice" (*OC*, 110–11) on the one hand offers, with such a typical mixture of detachment and intensity, a portrayal of the flooding miseries of self-other relationship; whereas, on the other hand, the lovely "À une passante" ("To a Woman Passing By," *OC*, 88–89) evokes the rich, ever precarious yet ever available potential of all human contacts, however fleeting, however unrealized: "Ne te verrai-je plus que dans l'éternité?/... Ô toi que j'eusse aimée, ô toi qui le savais!" ("Shall I not see you again till eternity?/... Oh you I should have loved, who knew it!" (*OC*, 89).

The modes of movement between self and other are, furthermore, numerous. If Baudelaire, in *Les Fleurs du Mal*, privileges the sensual—"I shall plunge my head, in love with intoxication,/Deep in the black ocean where the other lies closed," he writes in "La Chevelure" ("Flowing Hair," *OC*, 25–26)—other modes may be distinguished: the emotional, the intellectual, the spiritual, the moral, and so on. Ultimately, they merge and blur over—just as the very logic of self's separation can often fuse with factors such as Baudelaire's insistence upon the "self-prostitution" of the self (*OC*, 1247, 1286), the self's bent for adoration and idolatry (*OC*, 57, 1286), even self-oblivion via the other (*OC*, 1294), and a whole discourse, central to *Les Fleurs du Mal*, of complicity ("Hypocrite lecteur," he writes at the end of "Au lecteur" "—mon semblable—mon frère!" ["Hypocritical reader—so like me—my brother!"]) and address, apostrophe: the constantly recurring *tu* of the poems, a turning-away-from-self (*apostrophê*) only to return to what Reverdy deemed the only possible subject of poetry, the self. "Lis-moi, pour apprendre à m'aimer," Baudelaire will cry out in the "Epigraphe pour un livre condamné" (*OC*, 163), "plains-moi! ... Sinon, je te maudis!" ("Read me, to learn to love me/Pity me! ... Else, I curse you!"

In this question of the locked but half-resistant embrace of bodies, consciousnesses, souls, the Baudelairean discourse of self and other-as-woman occupies a somewhat special place. Here, the other assumes its full ambivalence, an ambivalence heightened by Baudelaire's tireless fascination, even obsession, with the feminine. Although it may be dismaying to read, in a poem such as "Tu mettrais l'univers entier ..." ("You would Put the Whole Universe ..." (*OC*, 26–27), of woman's "impurity," of her cruelty and her remorselessness, we should not forget the general harshness Baudelaire metes out to humanity, to all others—mere reflections of the self, moreover, as we have just seen!—throughout his work. "Le Voyage" was explicit:

> La femme, esclave vile, orgueilleuse et stupide,
> Sans rire s'adorant et s'aimant sans dégoût;
> L'homme, tyran goulu, paillard, dur et cupide,
> Esclave de l'esclave et ruisseau dans l'égout.

> Woman, vile, proud and senseless slave,
> Laughless in self-adoration, no disgust in self-love,
> Man, gluttonous, lewd, hard and grasping tyrant,
> The slave's slave and the sewer's gutter.
>
> *(OC, 125)*

Baudelaire's severity and causticness can, indeed, be overpowering and seem intolerably imbalanced and unjust if swallowed without antidote, and at times the misogyny is only comprehensible in the barely comforting framework of a generalized misanthropic satire. However, nor should we overlook almost invariably in the same poem, an evocation, as in "Tu mettrais l'univers entier . . ." of the woman-as-other's "genius" and "sublimeness," or, as in "L'Aube spirituelle" ("Spiritual Dawn," *OC*, 44), of her charm, of her "soulness," of her "lucid and pure" being. And, if the reader is tempted to argue an element of ironic disclaimer attaching to such praise, then surely the same argument is available at the other end of the gamut. Irony floats, rather, rarely blatant, allowing high seriousness and smile, indictment and delight to coalesce, forever uncertain upon their mountings. The other-as-woman is thus the object, simultaneously, of scathing social inquiry and compassion, hatred and love. She is seen in the awful trappings of her historicity and in the light of her eternal soul-beauty: "Hymne" ("Hymn," *OC*, 146), as ever ironic, rises high and unmistakably above the ironic. She is "superb flower" and "volcanic terrain" (*OC*, 288–89, "Le Désir de peindre" ["The Desire to Paint"]. She is, in short, like all other selves, the locus of extreme paradox and tension, "magic and supernatural" despite her artifice and her "abominable nature" (*OC*, 1184, 1272). Baudelaire is far from being Ingres, whom, however, he invites us to love, and in whom he sees the artistic embodiment of "the love of woman" (*OC*, 872). Despite the gravest reservations we may legitimately entertain, I should however argue that Baudelaire's work struggles in the direction of such a love and that the embrace of the other is his highest purpose, and his greatest challenge, for himself, for us.

"Duellum" (*OC*, 34) and "À celle qui est trop gaie" (*OC*, 140–41) render manifest the great spirals of affective ambivalence structuring Baudelaire's conception and experience of love. And "À une madone" ("To a Madonna," *OC*, 55–56) is the poem to end all poems on the dizzyingly enigmatic profundity of love. Such intense self-other relationships, at once sparring and gently idolatrous, are perceived at once as unstable, fragile, completely erodable (see "Confession," *OC*, 43–44), and as offering access to the ecstasy and vastness of those "infinite kisses" of "Le Balcon" ("The Balcony," *OC*, 34–35). Similarly, the "oblivion" occasioned by or sought in love can be either positively or negatively connoted, a vain farewell to the rigors of pure selfness, a desire to "sleep rather than to live" (*OC*, 140, "Le Léthé" ["Lethe"]), or a hope of union, a means of salvation as powerful as art itself (*OC*, 156, "La Rançon ["Ransom"]), a necessary self-transcendence that the rebel-self may refuse the angel-self (*OC*, 156, "Le Rebelle" ["Rebel"], *OC*, 171).

If, then, the self can so often appreciate the intrinsic argument of love—in "Les Petites Vieilles" ("Little Old Women") Baudelaire exclaims: "Monstres brisés, bossus/Ou tordus, aimons-les!" ("Broken, hunchback, twisted/Monsters, let us love them!" *OC*, 85–87)—so, too, can the self—which is both a lived and observed phenomenon, a personal confession and a social critique—regard the movement toward the other as dangerous, criminal (*OC*, 62, 1284), destructive of the self's integrity, an act of "prostitution" as dubious as the "self-prostitution" of art (*OC*, 1247, 1286), as unequal as all "sharing" inevitably is (*OC*, 1249). When Baudelaire notes at the very opening of *Mon coeur mis à nu*, "the vaporisation and the centralisation of the *Self.* That's everything" (*OC*, 1271), it is clear, despite the rich implicitness of the fragment, that his thought is centered upon questions of the coherence of the self, the self's identity, its vulnerability and yet its extensibility, beyond knowable frontiers of being/nonbeing, self/nonself, and so on.

Self-consciousness, the self's consciousness of other(ness) and the other's consciousness of self, clearly binds all concerned into a vast, indefinable network of intense multivalent emotion, where, if the notion of self is valid, so are those that would subsume self within a global structure where, precisely, love and enmity, compassion and dis-passion may be deemed unified states of some larger psychic project beyond the confines of all individuality, yet mediated by the latter. Here, the pain of otherness that pushes the self towards solitary retrenchment (*OC*, 264, "La Solitude") vies with Baudelaire's feeling that the other's sensibility must always be respected, for therein lies his/her "genius" (*OC*, 1258); and it is at this very intersection—of repulsion and movement toward the other—that, as he explains in *Fusées*, Baudelaire feels some deeply paradoxical "victory" may be achieved: "Quand j'aurai inspiré le dégoût et l'horreur universels, j'aurai conquis la solitude" ("When I have inspired universal disgust and horror, I shall have conquered loneliness," *OC*, 1258). Such a victory involves realizing those vast projects of com-passion that are *Les Fleurs du Mal* and *Le Spleen de Paris* in particular and his work in general: a project of painful yet transcendent self-multiplication that he describes in various ways and on numerous occasions: as in, for example, "Les Foules" and "La Corde" ("The Rope") from *Le Spleen de Paris* (*OC*, 243–44, 278–81); as in his essay on Constantin Guys in *Le Peintre de la vie moderne*, where he maintains that the artist, "the lover of universal life," "is a *self* thirsting after the *non-self*" (*OC*, 1161), whose "passion and profession is to *wed the crowd*" (*OC*, 1160).

Baudelaire's complex discourse on self and other can be best read in the light of poems such as "Le Vieux Saltimbanque" ("The Old Tumbler"), "La Fausse Monnaie" ("Counterfeit Coin"), or "Les Bons Chiens" ("Good Dogs"), all from *Le Spleen de Paris* (*OC*, 247–49, 273–74, 306–309). In these poems, the full force of that impulse toward charity can be felt over and above the gusts and squalls of irony. Poets and philosophers, Baudelaire writes in "Les Veuves" ("Widows," *OC*, 244–47), "feel irresistibly drawn to all that is weak, ruined, saddened, orphaned": they are the gift of selfness to otherness. The famous essay on imagination, "La Reine des facultés ("The Queen of Faculties"), from *Salon de 1859*, underlines the profound interconnections of "virtue," "pity," and an imagination that thus is far from exercising some purely gratuitous autonomy or some aesthetic hygiene (*OC*, 1038). And if the danger of ironic excess, or of "buffoonery," is known to Baudelaire—*Mon coeur mis à nu* shows him torn between "the sense of charity . . . the sense of libertinage . . . the literary sense, that of the actor" (*OC*, 1277)—he does not hesitate to affirm, in *Fusées*, "sans la charité, je ne suis qu'une cymbale retentissante" ("without charity, I am merely an echoing cymbal"), asking almost immediately afterward, "ma phase d'égoïsme est-elle finie?" ("is my egoistic phase over?" *OC*, 1268). For a poet who seemed to have staked all upon the high ecstasy of poetic symphony, such notes to the self are powerfully telling. Above all they point to a poetics of com-passionate osmosis rather than aesthetic closure, to that overriding sense that poetry's egoism must, by duty, struggle toward that embrace of the other which Baudelaire, despite all, can quite remarkably convey. "Lord, have pity," he writes at the end of "Mademoiselle Bistouri" (*OC*, 300–3), "pity the mad! Oh Creator! can monsters exist in the eyes of He alone who knows why they exist, how they *have come to be*, and how they could have *not come to be*?" (*OC*, 303).

(Self-)Destruction and Re-Creation

"Un voyage à Cythère" ("Journey to Cythera," *OC*, 111–13) offers the reader of *Les Fleurs du Mal* the most vivid image of the self destroyed, crucified, devoured, and rotting, as a fate overtakes and swamps from the outside, not unlike that to which the poet/great seabird is exposed in "L'Albatros" (*OC*, 9–10). "La Destruction" again pictures devastation as an invasion of the self by forces external to the poet/narrator, forces that are demoniacal, choking, culpabilizing, at once emptying and possessing, annihilating and yet causing intense self-awareness. The poem also evokes that "confusion" which sets up the endlessly swirling dialectics of horror and ideal, "satanism" and love, ennui and purpose, a dialectics at the root of Baudelaire's poetics of journey. Despite the paradox, moreover, a poem such as "Le Goût du néant" ("Taste for Nothingness," *OC*, 72) demonstrates that imposed self-destruction can so readily become destruction chosen. Here, the self ceases all struggle, abandons hope, chooses, as a kind of anti-action, resignation, the opium of *fadeur*, limpness, suicide: "Avalanche, will you carry me off in your fall?" (*OC*, 72). If the desire for destruction—"15th May," Baudelaire writes in *Mon coeur mis à nu*, "Still the taste for destruction. Valid taste if everything natural is valid" (*OC*, 1274)—can lead to a revolt, a refusal, a resistance that connotes residual possibility, the end of "Le Voyage" may be read as suicidal. If it also contains a desperate anti-vision, of *anything, anywhere,* but, after all, of something, somewhere, it is equally true that, as in "Le Goût du néant" sleep can be chosen over life (see *OC*, 139–40, "Le Léthé"), the poet of "Obsession" (*OC*, 71–72) can declare "je cherche le vide, et le noir, et le nu" ("I seek the void, blackness, nakedness," *OC*, 71), in a refusal that, instead of poeticizing life through *ivresse*, seeks the bleak and ultimate poiesis of mindless death, of senseless nothingness. Destruction as (potentially healing) satire, as continuing ontological effort, yields here to a destruction that is always self-destruction, a despairing ontic impotence that he lucidly describes in the *Reliquat:*

> Ne rien savoir, ne rien enseigner, ne rien vouloir,
> ne rien sentir, dormir, et encore dormir, tel
> est aujourd'hui mon unique voeu. Voeu infâme et
> dégoûtant, mais sincère.

> To know nothing, learn nothing, want nothing,
> Feel nothing, sleep and yet sleep, such
> Today is my wish. Foul, disgusting
> Wish, but sincere.

> (*OC*, 189)

That vestigial "charm of a wildly titivated nothingness," an ironic charm of which Baudelaire can still speak in his lacerating "Danse macabre," has seemingly irrevocably crumbled and dissolved. Nothing remains but negation itself, a complete and definitive negation of self's ontic elasticity—the most authentic of pleas for self-destruction.

But desire is not accomplishment, and the writing of surrender and self-annihilation is not self-erasure or even self-abandonment. In reading such texts as "Le Goût du néant" or even the above passage from the *Reliquat*, we are witness to a kind of invisible *battement* of contrary energies that gives us the writing of (self-) destruction *as* resurrection, as continuity, as something, anything. Initially, that is to say in its most minimalist mode, re-creation— which is far from recreation, pure *ludicité*—may be said to be that stepping back from nothingness that allows something to continue, above all an un-ironic "consciousness in Evil" (*OC*, 76), a raw *retournement*—an irony without Baudelairean irony—that tolerates writing *through* the desire for self-destruction. The second "stage" of re-creation is that in which, with full consciousness and with his full range of irony, from the most bitter *bouffonnerie* through the characteristic tautness of fiercely personal satire to the somewhat rare smile of wry compassion, Baudelaire can mount aesthetic transformations, shifting horror into its "floral" mode, crude being into the endless analogies and *correspondances* of what Deguy calls *l'être-comme* ("being-as"), going from existential stasis or quasi-nothingness to alchemical "discovery" and "construction" (*OC*, 72-73, "Alchimie de la douleur"), "kneading mud and making gold from it," as Baudelaire says in the *Reliquat* (*OC*, 177), repeatedly, eternally transforming the world just like the sun, "quand, ainsi qu'un poète, il descend dans les villes,/[Et] ennoblit le sort des choses les plus viles" ("when, like a poet, it descends upon cities,/Ennobling the fate of the vilest things," *OC*, 79, "Le Soleil" ["The Sun"].

What Baudelaire calls his "wound/And [his] fatality" (*OC*, 153) can, in such an *assumed*, chosen optic of (self-)creation, be transcended. Death, (self-)destruction can be in turn obliterated by the power of art. "Fancioulle proved to me," Baudelaire writes in "Une mort héroïque" ("An Heroic Death," *OC*, 269–73), "in peremptory, irrefutable fashion that Art's intoxication is more apt than any other to veil the terrors of the abyss; that genius can act itself out at the tomb's brink with a joy preventing it from seeing the tomb, lost as genius is in a paradise excluding all notion of tomb and destruction" (*OC*, 271). What counts above all in the logic of (self-)re-creation is will (*OC*, 98, "Rêve parisien" ["Parisian Dream"]), projection of the mind's light (*OC*, 1044, *Salon de 1859*), the manipulation and orchestration of what is, rather than its passive endurance (*OC*, 1044). And it is at this "point" that we can see Baudelaire comprehend, not just the aesthetic function of mind and imagination, but their deeper ontic function. For the imagination is suddenly seen to be the agent of all creation, of The Creation—"one can reasonably say that, I think," Baudelaire notes, "even in a religious sense" (*OC*, 1038)—and the specifically continuous nature of the creative process, of (self-)re-creation, is perceived as the "model" for aesthetic creativity (*OC*, 1043). The same essay, *Salon de 1859*, can refer to the *fiction* of being (*OC*, 1045) and argue the entire relativity of beauty (*OC*, 1076), but, far from endeavoring to deflate the significance of the self's intervention, Baudelaire again seeks to heighten awareness of the exquisite opportunity, the deep personal involvement, even commitment, such an intervention implies. The 1855 "L'Héautontimorouménos" and the 1857 "Paysage" show Baudelaire already fully sensitive to the deeper meaning of these questions of self-creation, of self-assumption, of self-willing and self-responsible being. His famous cry

> Je suis la plaie et le couteau!
> Je suis le soufflet et la joue!
> Je suis les membres et la roue!
> Et la victime et le bourreau!
>
> I am the wound and the knife!
> I am the slap and the cheek!
> I am the limbs and the wheel!
> The victim and the executioner!

is not just a clever irony; rather is it the negative expression of that law of self-assumption and self-creation which his essays on the imagination in the *Salon de 1859* will broadly develop into a poetics of endlessly possible ontic self-structuring. And is not the very late "Mademoiselle Bistouri," refused for publication a second time in the last year of Baudelaire's life, a clear trace of this poetics of ontic self-choice: "Ô Createur! peut-il exister des monstres aux yeux de Celui-là seul qui sait pourquoi ils existent, comment ils *se sont faits* et comment ils auraient pu *ne pas se faire?*" ("O Creator! can monsters exist in the eyes of He alone who knows why they exist, how they *have come about* and how they might *not have come about?*") (*OC*, 303).

Being, for Baudelaire, is not congealed, horribly definitive, impossibly incontrovertible. Being is, rather, his, as it is mine, ours. It is mental, psychic, while "settling" itself into matter. Baudelaire's entire life-long discourse on and through creation is a discourse less of idle hope than of hopeful striving and actual (self-)re-creation. "L'homme finit par ressembler à ce qui'il voudrait être" ("Man ends up resembling what he would like to be"), he writes in *Le Peintre de la vie moderne* (*OC*, 1153); in this desire alone he, like all humans, can sense the truth of our self-malleability. "Choisissons" ("Let us choose") is an implicitly common watchword of *Fusées* (*OC*, 1266). And when he notes to himself—"Prayer, Myself, the Century" (*OC*, 1309)—it is not to offer some smiling self-aggrandizement à la Woody Allen, but to show himself that the relationships of all equations are movable, rethinkable, remakable.

Fencing, Passion and Pertinence: Poetry

"Le Soleil," from the "Tableaux parisiens" ("Parisian Paintings") of *Les Fleurs du Mal*, speaks of the poetic act as "ma fantasque escrime" ("my whimsical swordsmanship," *OC*, 79), a gesture of whimsy, unpredictable, eccentric, fencing with the barely existent, that "abyss," that emptiness that, Baudelaire argues in "Le Gouffre" ("The Abyss," *OC*, 172), invades all, "action, desire, dream,/ Speech!" (*OC*, 72). The same "Le Soleil," as if to emphasize the point, evokes the "hazards of rhyme" and the lexical stumblings to which the poet is prey despite his will to shape and control (*OC*, 79). If such a text can give to poetry an air of unreality and spectral presence, Baudelaire is eager at times to confirm the degree to which "the phantoms of [poetical] imagination . . . are . . . beings and memories" (*OC*, 598), substantial psychic presences that inhabit one's very being. It is for this reason that he writes, in his essay on Pierre Dupont, that true poetry always involves "incarnation" (*OC*, 606) and, elsewhere, that "tout bon poète fut toujours *réaliste*" ("any good poet was always a *realist*," *OC*, 636, "Puisque réalisme il y a" ["Since Realism There Is"]). Poetry, for Baudelaire, is steeped in an essentially Bonnefidian logic of *présence*, despite the paradoxical idealization of the *imaginaire*; it "describes" being, material, moral, and psychic states in flux (see *OC*, 620, "Les Drames et les romans honnêtes" ["Honest Dramas and Novels"]), even though its "description" is rather a "narration of the possible," a plunging into the poet's "collective soul that questions, weeps, hopes, and sometimes divines" (*OC*, 711, "Victor Hugo"), a description of all that is most urgently felt, sensed, intuited, but a living creation nevertheless, and, in consequence, only verifiable in turn through feeling and empathy. "It is through feeling alone that you should understand art," Baudelaire declares in the *Salon de 1846* (*OC*, 875). Thus is it that the real and the unreal, *présence* and some element of psychic, spiritual (self-)transcendence, reach that precarious but sure poetic equilibrium Baudelaire evokes in "Puisque réalisme il y a": "La Poésie est ce qu'il y a de plus réel, c'est ce qui n'est complètement vrai que dans *un autre monde*" ("Poetry is the most real thing, it is what is only completely true in *another world*" (*OC*, 637).

Toward the end of *Mon coeur mis à nu*, we come upon that celebrated injunction-cum-affirmation: "Glorify the cult of images (my great, my unique, my primitive passion)" (*OC*, 1295). Such a journal entry would seem to give to poetry and its constructs, its *worlds*, as Bonnefoy would call those autonomous fictions in which being risks losing itself, a degree of antinatural separation, of at once formal and mental esotericism and pure, excarnate symbolism. And when, in the *Reliquat*, Baudelaire states that *Les Fleurs du Mal*, "an essentially useless and absolutely innocent book, was not written with any aim other than to divert myself and exercise my passionate taste for difficulty" (*OC*, 185), we again risk being confirmed in this sense of poetry as exercise, as autotelic game, as irrelevancy. However, we should not be led astray by such ironic disclaimers, despite an essential truth attaching to them in the light of our earlier discussion. Art *is* useful, it *has* purpose and pertinence (*OC*, 620), but it is self-justifying, anti-didactic, open and dependent upon the reader's critical intervention (*OC*, 653, "Madame Bovary"). Its "aim" is, rather, "de mystique nature" ("of mystical nature") (see "La Mort des artistes" ["Artists' Death"], *OC*, 120), filtering into all domains, all feelings, all modes of being (*OC*, 186), a "prostitution" of the self that is synonymous, however, with "charity," with love (*OC*, 1247, 244), no doubt to the extent it can project upon the gashes and gaping wounds of the real "its dim opalescent brilliance," as Baudelaire puts it in his essay on Flaubert (*OC*, 655). Immanence does not, then, disappear into the fanciful reconditeness of the imaginary; rather does the latter, art, "correct, embellish and rethink" (*OC*, 254, "L'Invitation au voyage," *Le Spleen de Paris*) nature in the mysterious and mystical light of some absolute compassion. Poetry, with its "cult of images" (*OC*, 1295), can thus be guided safely by that "queen of faculties," imagination (*OC*, 1036), precisely because, although it proceeds by metaphor, symbol, and analogy, it does not withdraw from the real into the echo-chamber of its areferential and nonmeaningful *signifiance*. Rather is the imagination, for Baudelaire, linked to "moral sense," to the infinite, to the exploration of the spiritual (*OC*, 1037, 1038, 1044, *Salon de 1859*); its realism is "passionately visionary," as was Balzac's (*OC*, 692). Art is not for art's sake; the "immoderate" pursuit of form is self-defeating (*OC*, 627, "L'Ecole païenne" ["Pagan

School"]); the poetics of "prosody" that truly touches Baudelaire is one of the soul rather than of pure "classical theory" (*OC*, 186, *Reliquat*). If he can say, in his essay on Gautier, that "there is in the word, in the *logos*, something *sacred* that forbids making it a game of chance" (*OC*, 690), this does not mean that Parnassian orchestration and mental "sculpting" à la Gautier reassume paramount importance, but rather that poetry is *conscience* in every sense of the term, a deep psychic self-other project whose origins Baudelaire regards as sacred, mystical.

Forms of Modernity: The Poem

With the publication, in 1857, of *Les Fleurs du Mal* and, in 1869, of *Le Spleen de Paris*—or *Petits poèmes en prose* (*Short Prose Poems*) as they are often termed, after Baudelaire's other potential title—something shifts unmistakably in the evolution of French poetry. Gone, in broad measure, are the pastoral and mythologically tinted odes, epistles, and elegies of great poets like Chénier. Gone is the pure lyricism of Desbordes-Valmore or Hugo. Gone, too, are the "new" epics of Vigny or Hugo, or the vast texts of Lamartine. Gone the geographically or culturally exotic, the blatantly biblical or historical inspirations, even, largely, the smaller circumstantial work that few poets of Baudelaire's century will seek to eradicate. And, in the place of this vast poetic program, two compact collections with, as Hugo puts it in an 1859 letter to Baudelaire, "un frisson nouveau" ("a new sensation," (*OC*, 1666). Before turning to a necessarily telescoped assessment of the rather more formal aspects of this modernity—and Baudelaire has just warned us of the perils of such an attachment—let us look at some of its more general features: 1. the broad, symbolic influence of Hugo: if Baudelaire's notebooks betray an irritation with the concept of poet as priest and prophet, his long essay on Hugo (*OC*, 701–713) shows that Hugo is nevertheless *génial*, exemplary, and emblematic—more so than Gautier, despite the dedication of *Les Fleurs du Mal*—of the *vast potential and the cosmic mystery of the poetic*, even in Baudelaire's framework of highly compacted vision and form; 2. the allegorical, symbolic mode of Baudelaire's poems: distinctly beyond Vigny's fusion of myth and philosophy, and intimately tied up with his conception of the (poem as) *image*, a fetishistic talisman yet possessing great power within the context of daily existence, of *présence*; 3. the rich, syrupy, yet lucid sensuality of Baudelaire's language, quite unknown in French poetry; 4. the related criterion of *correspondances*, or what, in his essay on Hugo, Baudelaire calls *"universal analogy"* (*OC*, 705), a criterion that has its effect and pertinence at once on the stylistic level in the plethora of exquisite metaphoric fusions and on the psychic or spiritual level, where synesthesia emblematizes that "expansion of infinite things," that "dark and profound unity," of his most famous programmatic poem, "Correspondances" (*OC*, 11); 5. Baudelaire's discourse on love, on self-other relations in general: although one could place this in a vast poetic tradition extending from Villon, through Du Bellay, Scève, Louise Labé, to Racine, Saint-Amant, Chénier, and Baudelaire's contemporaries, the poems of *Les Epaves* are sufficient to demonstrate the subtlety, the complexity, the fierce acerbity of a consciously new sense of *galanterie*; 6. the fact that poetry, with Baudelaire, is prepared to push itself to the limits of the grotesque, of *bouffonnerie*, while retaining its urgent claim to high seriousness, high pertinence; 7. the relentless depiction of modern life, of its inner realms, its searing contradictions, its banalities, its horrors, its residual wonder and mystery; 8. Baudelaire's hyper-modern marriage of irony, skepticism, disgust, *satanisme*, on the one hand, and, on the other, deep sincerity, enthusiasm, the instinct of *élévation*, or even what he can wryly call mere "work" (*OC*, 1265, *Fusées*), an unflagging sense of spiritual mission; 9. an interesting collection of ideas on questions of artistic finish or completeness: the need to perceive the work in its entirety (*OC*, 481), the difference between the "finished" and the "made," openness and closure in art, reading and authorial voice (*OC*, 850), creation as continuing or closable process (*OC*, 1043); 10. Baudelaire's consciousness of the tensions between poetic creations and readings based on the *justesse* of structural, quantifiable relationships and those based on intuition, feeling, which he preferred (*OC*, 614, 627); 11. that emphasis upon the degree of *"indispensable obscurity"* (*OC*, 704, "Victor Hugo") essential to (nevertheless uncontrived) poetic expression, an emphasis that will lead to the divergent hermeticisms of Mallarmé and the surrealists, or to that practiced by his many admirers and co-theoreticians, from Reverdy to Char; 12. that modernism which will push Baudelaire beyond verse straight into the poetry of prose—in the wake, as he admits of Aloysius Bertrand (*OC*, 229), but in the vanguard not only of experimentation of poets from Mallarmé to

Claudel, Perse, and all our contemporaries, but of that transgeneric explosion—visible today in the writings of Cixous, Hyvrard, Giraudon, Gleize, Atlan, even Duras—which Baudelaire seems to have been vigorously plotting to explore (see *OC*, 513–23, "Liste de titres et canevas de romans et nouvelles" ["List of Titles and Sketches for novels and short stories"]).

In turning to a very brief analysis of certain formal features of Baudelaire's two major poetic works, it would not be unhelpful to read his verse at least in the light of earlier commentaries directed toward Lamartine and Vigny, especially. Many categories of evaluation remain constant, for the formal constraints and options have not essentially modified. We can grasp here Baudelaire's own reticence with regard to "le goût immodéré de la forme [qui] pousse à des désordres monstrueux et inconnus" ("the immoderate taste for form leading to monstrous and unheard-of disorders," *OC*, 627) for artist and reader.

First, regarding *Les Fleurs du Mal*, let me stress Baudelaire's system of numbering the component texts of what he clearly regarded as a collection of at once autonomous and unified poems, some titled, others not. Such an ordering, as with Vigny, reveals an overall intention, a will to be read in some accordance with Baudelaire's sensibility and *weltanschauung*. The section titles, in particular, give shape to the latter and compensate for that arguably paradoxical disruptive gesture which led to disordering and reordering the original edition to include not only the *pièces condamnées* but others, too. The notion of an absolute form and structure is thus shaken by such ultimate remodelings and even major reorchestrations and repositionings. The intention to direct remains, however, and, if relativity creeps into the sacrosanct, the meaning of *Les Fleurs du Mal* continues to lie in part in their disposition and evolution within the volume. Secondly, *Les Fleurs du Mal* is a formally, sculpturally sensitive volume with regard to its attention to meter, stanzaic form, rhyme, length of poem, and so on. Essentially, all the texts are fixed-form texts, although fluidity and suppleness do not disappear. Baudelaire generally prefers compact metric and stanzaic structures, though never anything that could be deemed fragmentary, aesthetically uncaressed, unmolded. The sonnet dominates—with fifty-nine in the first edition of *Les Fleurs du Mal*, upon which my analysis is based—and even beyond this preference, the quatrain, or *faux quatrain*, is Baudelaire's principal formal vehicle. Apart from the sonnets, which are almost all built on the 2-quatrains/2-tercets model, the number of poems organized exclusively in quatrains is as follows: 5 poems of 4 quatrains, 3 of 5, 6 of 6, 6 of 7, 3 of 8, 1 of 9, 5 of 10, 1 each of 11 and 12, 3 of 13, 1 of 14, 4 of 15, 1 each of 19, 21, and 36. In addition, both the quatrain and the sonnet can appear within longer structures: 6+4, 8+8+4, 4+24+8+2, 2+9+13+4, 4+14+12, 14+12, and so forth. Other stanzaic configurations pale into statistical insignificance set against such an artillery, but they inevitably remain aesthetically crucial, giving aeration and variation to stanzaic and textual structures that could otherwise have been somewhat stifling. One may note in particular the lilting 5-line stanzas in poems of varying length: 1 poem each of 4, 5, 7 and 10 stanzas, 2 of 6. Further "disarticulation"—though highly engineered—comes from various tactics of stanzaic and textual orchestration. A few examples will suffice, and will overlook the more conventional dispositions: "Le Masque" ("The Mask," *OC*, 22–23) with its 7-9-3=9-3-5 arrangement; "Tu mettrais l'univers entier . . .": 8+9+1; "Franciscae meae laudes" (*OC*, 59–60): 11 3-line stanzas; "Les Litanies de Satan" (*OC*, 116–8): 15 structures composed of a couplet plus one-line refrain. To this rigorously controlled and at once conservative and flexible exploitation of essentially traditional forms, Baudelaire brings an additional double effort of discreet aesthetic modeling, in metric deployment and in the realm of rhyme.

Here, the alexandrine prevails majestically, as with Marceline Desbordes-Valmore, Lamartine, Vigny and Hugo, but it can also be used in conjunction with other meters: 12+8, as in "Une Charogne"; 12+7, as in "Le Poison; 12+5, as in "La Musique" (*OC*, 65). The traditional 10-syllable and 8-syllable lines can also appear, especially the latter, but, once more, a certain loosening can occur, above all with an 8-syllable line, as in the 8+5 combination of "Le Serpent qui danse" ("The Dancing Snake," *OC*, 28–29). The 7-syllable *impair* meter can be favored, too, as in "Chanson d'après-midi" ("Afternoon Song," *OC*, 57–58) and may combine with the 4-syllable line, as in "À une mendiante rousse," or with the 5-syllable *impair*, as in "L'Invitation au voyage." These variously destabilizing metric effects remain cautious and judicious, and give rhythmic suppleness around the anchoring alexandrine: 10, 11

(7+4), 13 (8+5), 14 (7+7). Baudelaire's rhyme schemes, too, show discreet ingenuity, while rendering homage to the ancient conventions of *rimes plates, rimes croisées,* and *rimes embrassées.* The quatrains freely exploit all three modes. The sonnet tercets display great variety—*eff/egg, eef/ggf, eef/gfg, efe/fgg, eef/fgg, efe/ffe*—though, again, the results are subtle, at times barely discernible in the midst of other sound effects such as alliteration and other interior harmonics. The 5-line stanzas opt either for *ababa* or *abbab,* but, once more, various additional effects are crucial, and Baudelaire is fond of the full line echo, quite apart from his use of the refrain. Many other features of rhythm could be similarly assessed, particularly the *coupes* and enjambments.

A third global factor of interest in this discussion of form is the syntax of Baudelaire's poems and the linguistic strategies preferred. Here, were space permitting, one could examine the relationship of sentence to stanza; the deliberate highlighting of each component member of the sentence via a masterly command of punctuation and a syntagmatic buildup that is quite extraordinary in its slow, rhythmic insistence; the proliferation of adjectival phrases; the deft use of parentheses, appositions, anaphoras plus development; the use of subordinate clauses; the play of pronouns, especially *je/tu;* the combination of exclamation, imperative, question, and firm description/narration; the uses of present and future tenses; and so on. Fourthly, no appreciation of Baudelaire's "form" could be complete without an examination of the lexicon of *Les Fleurs du Mal,* including metaphor and simile. Here, if it cannot be said, as he himself said of Hugo, that Baudelaire has swallowed the dictionary of the French language, it does not escape us that adjectives are thickly pertinent, whether sensual or remote; verbs are chosen either for their evocative, concrete power, or for their startling intensity and simple directness; nouns can be humanized, no matter how abstract, and never fail to portray with dense and unflinchingly contemporary vividness the multiple colorations of Baudelaire's scenes and dramas.

As for the metaphors and similes of *Les Fleurs du Mal,* they are determining in the constitution of the volume's special atmosphere: "un soulier pomponné, joli comme une fleur" ("a titivated shoe, pretty as a flower"), "la ruche qui se joue au bord des clavicules,/Comme un ruisseau lascif qui se frotte au rocher" ("the ruche playing around the collarbones,/Like a lascivious stream rubbing up against a rock"), "quelque vieux désir./. . . Te pousse-t-il, crédule, au sabbat du Plaisir?" ("does some old desire/. . . urge you, credulous, upon a sabbath of pure Pleasure?"), "le gouffre de tes yeux . . ./Exhale le vertige" ("your eyes' abyss . . ./Breathes out vertigo"). Such images, taken from "Danse macabre," give some idea of the swirling unpredictability, the fierce irony, the terrible relevance and the sheer visionary quality of Baudelaire's teeming metaphors. But, if we seem rather far from the base logic of Baudelaire's "Correspondances," behind such an apparent circus of figurative interchange is a real discourse on equivalence, unity, symbolic com-passion, which renders the Baudelairean image utterly undecorative and gives it its true spiritual depth.

In conclusion, a few words on the form of *Le Spleen de Paris:* 1. as prose poems, they are not an absolute innovation, but a profound shift in available expressive option, due mainly to their tone, their density, their intense but distanced deployment of a most particular sensibility; 2. these are compact texts, averaging one-and-a-half pages each, requiring rapid centering, continuous exploitation of every resource, from adjective to capital letter to semicolon: in this, they differ little from *Les Fleurs du Mal;* 3. the poems carefully balance the different stylistico-formal claims made upon them: *récit,* narration, or anecdote (yet as Reverdy will say, they are *antinatures* not related in any evidently novelistic manner à la Balzac, Stendhal, or Hugo), description of a very particular order, and reflection that avoids didacticism and blatancy; 4. dialogue and "quotation" can play important roles, and tend to decenter the discourse, render it rather more enigmatic, even though "real," apparently situated; 5. these poems tend to avoid contextualization, surging forth from that precious "margin of silence," as Max Jacob puts it, yet, at the same time, they seek what Reverdy terms the essential *justesse,* or poetic appreciability, of the "world" they invent; 6. it is possible to study the process of moving from poem to prose to poem, by examining, say, "L'Invitation au voyage" in its two "versions," that of *Les Fleurs du Mal* and that of *Le Spleen de Paris;* 7. similar useful analyses can be conducted for both volumes with respect to all those features, and more, I alluded to above: sentence structure, parentheses, subordinate clauses—this in an effort to determine the specificity of the prose poem; 8. the same could be done for metaphor and vocabulary; 9. the role of the verse epilogue remains to be characterized in the context of form.

Mystery and Mysticalness

No reading of Baudelaire can be rounded off with impunity. He is a poet all too alert to that "mystère divin que l'homme n'entend pas" ("divine mystery ununderstood by man," *OC*, 194, "Incompatibilité"), all too conscious that the world is composed of endless human types, among which "les amoureux de la solitude et du mystère" (*Le Spleen de Paris*, *OC*, 264). Looking back over the preceding pages, one might be tempted already to see "mystery" in Baudelaire's conception of the real, its troubling oppositions and yet its *correspondances*; in the fact and nature of desire, sensual and mental, moral and emotional; in his related poetics of journey; in the power of the imagination and Baudelaire's discourse on (self-) re-creation. Speaking of Hugo, he suggests how exceptionally gifted the author of *La Lëgende des siècles* is to express "le *mystère de la vie*" (*OC*, 704)—life's depth, variegation, harmony, obscurity: "He sees mystery everywhere. And, in effect, where is it not?" (*OC*, 706). For, to press forward into things with the mind, the senses, the emotions, and the soul—Baudelaire never hesitates to use the word—is to discover abyss upon abyss (*OC*, 706), to understand that *all* that is seen, discovered, remains of the order of mystery.

The Beautiful that so orients Baudelaire's attention, includes the ugly, the weak, the reduced, the wretched. This "multicolored and multiform beautifulness," as he puts it in *Exposition universelle de 1855* (*1855 Universal Exhibition*), "moves within the infinite spirallings of life" (*OC*, 955). All of presence, our experience of presence, is caught up in infiniteness, in a conception of being decidedly beyond flat materialism, systematization, rationalism. It is for this reason that Baudelaire is concerned by the threat of technology to "the spiritual part" of life (*Fusées*, *OC*, 1263); that he plans, in *Mon coeur mis à nu*, "a large chapter on the art of divination, through water, cards, examination of the hand, etc." (*OC*, 1288); that he criticizes Voltaire for his off-handed dismissal of the mystery of birth and the "immortal soul" (*OC*, 1282, *Mon coeur mis à nu*); that he argues, in the same journal, the need to go beyond life's "silly curiosities" and ask ourselves the essential questions:

"Où sont nos amis morts?//Pourquoi sommes-nous ici?// Venons-nous de quelque part?" ("Where are our dead friends?//Why are we here?//Do we come from somewhere?" *OC*, 1275–76); that he can say, in *Fusées*, that "there is in prayer a magical operation. Prayer is one of the great forces of intellectual dynamics" (*OC*, 1257).

Given the foregoing and given, too, Baudelaire's evident desire, both in *Les Fleurs du Mal* and *Le Spleen de Paris*, to at once polarize and unify those twin "postulations" toward God and toward Satan (*OC*, 1277), it should come as no surprise to find Baudelaire noting, and purely for himself: "Dès mon enfance, tendance à la mysticité. Mes conversations avec Dieu" ("From my childhood on, tendency to mysticalness. My conversations with God," *OC*, 1299, *Mon coeur mis à nu*). If Baudelaire's thought can at times appear unaligned with this important propensity—"Dieu est un scandale," he writes in *Fusées*, "—un scandale qui rapporte" ("God is a scandal, a scandal that rakes it in," *OC*, 1258)—it is because, on the one hand, he distinguishes drastically between clericalism or organized religion and intimate spiritual thought, and, on the other, he gives himself, at once experimentally and authentically, to that plunge into "satanism," into the contradictions of self, which he regards as crucial to lucid self-knowledge. Religion, seen as a reflection of true and pure individual aspiration, may be nevertheless deemed the "highest fiction of the human mind" (*OC*, 1045), and he can go as far as to declare, in *Mon coeur mis à nu*, "religions are the only interesting thing upon earth" (*OC*, 1290).

For a man whose spiritual point of departure is a sentiment of relative horror before daily existence, this should, nevertheless, occasion little surprise. *Fusées* and *Mon coeur mis à nu* remain riddled with notations of intended or actual spiritual self-improvement: "Do one's duty every day and trust to God, for the morrow" (*OC*, 1267), "every morning make my prayer to God, *reservoir of all justice, to my father, to Mariette and to Poe*, as intercessors" (*OC*, 1269–70), "*calcul en faveur de Dieu.*//Rien n'existe sans but//. . . Il faut . . . prier ce quelqu'un [plus savant que moi] de m'éclairer" ("*calculation in favor of God.*//Nothing exists without purpose//. . . I must . . . ask this someone [more knowing than I] to enlighten me," *OC*, 1273), and so on. And, if Baudelaire can say, at the beginning of *Fusées*, that "God is the only being who, in order to reign, does not even need to exist" (*OC*, 1247), we may prefer to read this "absence" as, rather, a transfer of divineness, responsibility, freedom, (self-)creativity to the individual. To some extent, Baudelaire hints at this at the close of *Fusées*, when he notes: "Que de pressentiments et de signes envoyés déjà par Dieu, qu'il est *grandement temps* d'agir, de considérer la minute présente comme la plus importante des minutes . . ." ("How many intuitions and signs sent already by God, that it is *high time* to act, to consider the present moment as the most important . . ."; *OC*, 1265).

Whichever way we look at it—and we, as readers, are faced with the same "dilemma" Baudelaire faces—he does not hesitate to conjure up a mystical depth, at once within us and without, that requires a rethinking of the platitudes, the troughs and the miseries of being, in the light of a logic of profound ontic option whose origins remain unknown. It is not surprising, then, that Baudelaire interests himself in the various forms of mysticism and that "superstition," for him, is linked to truth (*OC*, 1273). The greatness of Hugo is tied up with his perception of an ubiquitous cosmic mystery. And Heine, "that delightful mind," would be, Baudelaire maintains, a genius, "if he turned more often to the divine" (*OC*, 985). That Baudelaire himself, in turning toward *le Mal* and "satanism," is taking the rough and rocky "low road" toward an exploration of the self's—every self's—difficult and often obscure divineness, I would see as centrally pertinent to his entire opus. "There is a universal religion," he writes in *Mon coeur mis à nu*, "made for the Alchemists of Thought, a religion given off by man thus deemed to be a divine memento" (*OC*, 1290). Here, we reach back to that notion of the self as divine agenda, mystical project, self-transforming program. If, in one of Baudelaire's last entries in *Mon coeur mis à nu*, a rather tenser note is struck, the profound simplicity of both mystical aspiration and human frustration cannot escape us:

> Dieu et sa profondeur.
> On peut ne pas manquer d'esprit et chercher dans Dieu le complice et l'ami qui manquent toujours. Dieu est l'éternel confident dans cette tragédie dont chacun est le héros.

> God and his depth.
> One can not be without wit and seek in God the
> absent accomplice and friend. God is the eternal
> confidant in the tragedy of which we are all heroes.
>
> (*OC*, 1298)

The "divineness" of each of us, however, as the subsequent entry reveals, resides in the "immortality" of our every trace, the authentic, unrepeatable pure psychic struggle and release of our every thought and (self-)re-creation (*OC*, 1298).

· FIVE ·

Hugo

"The Master," as Verlaine was to call Victor Hugo in his later writings on contemporary poets, was born in Besançon on 28 February 1802. After years of traipsing with his brothers and unsettled parents from one military garrison to another, he was to found, in Paris, a fervent and intensely active *Conservateur littéraire* (*Literary Conservative*) around which his immense and already precocious creative and socially conscious genius was to develop—if not explode. *Bug-Jargal*, not published until 1826, was written at the age of seventeen and already demonstrates a singular and exotically visionary brilliance. At this time he met, too, Adèle Foucher, with whom he became secretly engaged, marrying in 1822. His literary production flowers from this point on, in endless forms, registers and genres, in the most prolific of ways: *Odes* (1822), *Han d'Islande* (*Han of Iceland,* 1823), the *Tablettes* (1823), the founding of *La Muse française* (*The French Muse*), *Ballades* (1825), *Odes et ballades* (1826–1828), *Cromwell* (1826) and on and on into substantially transformed visions and modes such as those deployed in the forbidden *Marion de Lorme* (1829), the scandalous *Hernani* (1830), the stupendous *Notre-Dame de Paris* (1831) written under the most trying of emotional circumstances, *Les Feuilles d'automne* (*Autumn Leaves,* 1831), *Les Chants du crépuscule* (*Songs of Dusk,* 1835), *Les Voix intérieures* (*Inner Voices,* 1837)—the creative verve is seemingly inexhaustible and the bibliography unrivaled.

Literature, for Hugo, rapidly becomes the place of all experience, all desire, all possibility: aesthetic, certainly, but social, moral, spiritual, political, individual and collective, historical, legendary and future, microcosmic and universal. Powerfully productive years; years of exhilaration; years of disillusion, tragedy, and yet recuperation, resilience, reenergizing. Hugo knows already marital bliss and dissolution, the death of his children, the madness of his brother, and, soon, the long exile of 1851–1870. Since 1833 Hugo has also known the strange turbulence of his lifelong liaison with the actress Juliette Drouet. The 1840s see him become member of L'Académie française; a peer, in 1845; exposed to public cries of adultery, the same year, due to his blatant relations with Mme Biard; plunging into his *Choses vues*, the preparation of *Les Misérables*, parliamentary endeavor, and spiritual self-interrogation. The coup d'état of 1848, its repression and reactionariness, lead him to overt and clandestine political resistance whose failure forces him into flight for Brussels, then Jersey and Guernesey.

Exile ushers in a vast period of creative production: *Les Châtiments* (*Chastisements*, 1853), *La Fin de Satan* (*Satan's End*) and *Dieu* (*God*)—superb, unfinished visionary explorations—*L'Ane* and abundant material of *La Légende des siècles* (*Legend of the Centuries*), the panoramic, quasi-encyclopedic yet deeply personal *Les Contemplations* (*The Contemplations*, 1856), *William Shakespeare* (1864), *Les Chansons des rues et des bois* (*Songs of Streets and Woods*, 1865), *Les Travailleurs de la mer* (*Workers of the Sea*, 1866), *L'Homme qui rit* (*Laughing Man*, 1869).

Back in Paris upon the proclamation of the Republic during the 1870 Prussian siege, he is elected to an Assembly he quickly judges inadequate to the country's sociopolitical needs. *L'Année terrible* (*The Terrible Year*, 1872) bears witness at once to these frustrations and to more personal anguish. Retiring briefly to Guernesey, Hugo writes his magnificent *Quatrevingt-Treize* (*Ninety-three*). His 1876 election to the Senate confirms him in his struggle to create a politics of compassion, love, and bloodless (r)evolution, and his writings of this fertile period all speak of such convictions: *L'Art d'être grand-père* (*The Art of Being a Grandfather*, 1877), for example, and *L'Histoire d'un crime* (*History of a Crime*, 1877). After the stroke of 1878, all writing became excessively difficult, though from that time on until his death on 15 May 1885—and even up to and beyond the centenary of his birth!—earlier written but unpublished work continued to appear in rather astonishing and genial quantity: *La Pitié suprême* (*Supreme Pity*, 1879), *Religions et religion* (1880), *Les Quatre Vents de l'esprit* (*Four Winds of the Mind*, 1881), *Torquemada* (1882), *Toute la lyre* (*Full Lyre*, 1888–1893), *Dernière gerbe* (*Last Sheaf*, 1902). The Massin edition of Hugo's work (1967–1969) also reveals the writer as one of the century's greatest painters.

Even the stinting praise of Jules Laforgue yields before the power of Victor Hugo: "The most extraordinary poet ever to appear." Admired openly by Lamartine, somewhat grudgingly by Vigny, Hugo was best characterized by an awed, if elsewhere finicky Baudelaire: "the most gifted man, the most visibly chosen to express through poetry what I shall call the *mystery of life.*" Rimbaud sees him as headstrong, *cabochard*, but a poet of real and rare visionary power in his "later work." Lautréamont, despite predictable reservations, appreciates his sheer poetic force, and especially his poems about children; Péguy, his great "pagan" spirituality; Aragon, in *Hugo, poète réaliste*, his undying commitment to the cause of the people; Ionesco, ironically, in his *Hugoliade*, the paradox of "great genius" and life's more banal substrata. And René Char sees, among his "Grands astreignants," a Hugo who, despite what he characteristically regards as certain dispensable and "impossible" sides, retains an "ineffable touch" and an ability to leap with admirable wildness and yet the highest of metrical sensitiveness. To Reverdy is left the privilege of perceiving Hugo's vast, "oceanic" poeticity, but beyond even that a generous human and ethical commitment barely recognized, he felt, even in 1946—and, might one say, still today?

Totality, Progress, Oceanity

In "A mes odes" ("To My Odes"), from the 1822–1823 section of *Odes et ballades*, Hugo writes in an apostrophe to his own poetic "songs":

> Vous disiez, dans votre délire,
> Tout ce que peut changer la lyre
> Tout ce que l'âme peut rêver.
>
> You said, in your delirium,
> All that the lyre may change
> All that the soul may dream.
>
> (*OB*, 98)

A poetics of totality is thus consciously elaborated from the beginning of Hugo's vast creative production; his voice becomes multiple, infinitely focused and refocused both in space and time. "Muse," he affirms in "Histoire" from the same collection, "there is no time your gazings do not embrace" (*OB*, 100). Indeed, such totality of fascination and embrace is sensed to be part of some divine adoration rendered singularly possible, and spiritually—rather than merely aesthetically—pertinent, via the placing of "my thousand-voiced soul . . . / . . . at the center of everything like a sonorous echo" ("Ce siècle avait deux ans . . ." ["The Century was Two Years Old . . ."], *FA*, 193). Nothing is too microscopic, too banal, too fleeting, in this replenishing and revalidating optic. "All is great," as he says in *Les Contemplations* ("A M. Froment-Meurice" ["To Mr. Froment-Meurice"], *C*, 60), which he accordingly describes in his 1856 preface, written in Guernesey, as "all impressions, all memories, all realities, all vague ghosts a consciousness may contain, laughing or funeral, come back, recalled, flash by flash, sigh by sigh, mingled in the same dark cloud" (*C*, 11). Such totality thus implies no absolute clarity, no final grandiose structure or ultimate vision, but rather, as Hugo suggests in the 1831 *Feuilles d'automne*, an intoxication with the teeming abundance of things. "Enivrez-vous de tout, enivrez-vous, poètes" ("Drink in everything, intoxicate yourselves, poets"), Hugo declares in his exquisite "Pan" (*FA*, 325–28), well in advance of Baudelaire, but in contradistinction to the latter's poetics of compensatory *ivresse* and rather in a gesture of deep, global penetration of the otherness of being, *partout* ("everywhere"; *FA*, 326), an ubiquitous, somewhat Apollinaire-like penetration that allows for a "merging [of] all your soul with the creation" (*FA*, 327). Hugo's poetics of totality thus eschews the platitudes of egoism and pride in its desire to be, to experience, all (see "Ire, non ambire," *LS2*, 342); endeavors to avoid the pitfalls of "moroseness" and "silliness" while "tasting everything" in a spirit of simple self-dedication to the gifts of what is ("Post-scriptum des rêves" ["Post-scriptum to dreams"], *CR*, 80); prefers, willfully, as in "Jour de fête aux environs de Paris" ("A Holiday Near Paris"), from the 1865 *Les Chansons des rues et des bois* (*CR*, 66–67), the plunging of the self into the endlessly spawned vicissitudes of coexistent states, emotions, all thought, felt, experienced in their intrinsic innocence, their spurting difference-together, their deep imbrication. For totality implies both multiplicity and connectedness, a separation and a continuity of which "Le Lapidé" ("Stoned to Death"), from *La Légende des siècles*, speaks with characteristically moving eloquence:

> Et moi qui sais que tout a pour racine tout,
> Que, si l'un est couché, c'est que l'autre est debout,
> Que l'être naît de l'être, et sans fin se transforme,
> Et que l'éternité tourne en ce cercle énorme
>
> And I who know that all has all at its root,
> That, if one is down, the other is thus up,
> That being arises from being, in endless transformation,
> That eternity turns in this vast circle
>
> (*LS2*, 153)

Such factors of continuous (self-)transformation, unified being, and mingling of the eternal and the mortal, the seemingly exclusively specific, inevitably hold implications for that cornerstone of Hugolian ethics and ontology: progress. Progress implies many things throughout Hugo's poetry, though, largely through his poetics of totality and oceanic movement, it retains a complex coherence beyond its apparent Vigny-haunted elementariness. Certainly, progress is that movement Hugo calls, in *Les Chansons des rues et des bois*, "L'Ascension humaine" ("Human Ascent," *CR*, 169); certainly it implies therefore the need to "unlearn [our] backward steps," as he writes in *La Légende des siècles* (*LS2*, 279, "Paroles dans l'épreuve" ["Words in the Trial]"), to seek betterment and center upon ideal here below in a kind of Charian "sufficiency of going." And certainly Hugo's poetics of progress is founded upon the viscerally inalienable feeling that "winter leads to spring and hatred to love," as he puts it in *L'Année terrible*—a feeling already not so readily available, moreover, progress involving a faith in some natural cosmic flow both external and internal to us, a flow which not only means that progress at least always "hobbles" along ("Patrie" ["Homeland"], *AGP*, 683), but that it is predicated upon a persistent sense of the originality-now, the possibility-now, of all events, all time. "Est-ce un écroulement?" he asks in *L'Année terrible*, only to answer instinctively, "non. C'est une genèse" ("Is this a crumbling? No, it is genesis," *AT*, 463). No wonder, then, that Hugo's logic of progress can leap beyond the limits of some purely sociohistorical dialectics, for even though *Les Châtiments* (*Chastisements*), for example, connotes faith in (r)evolution (*LCH*, 270), progress via overthrow, transfiguration comes about—and is assured as a "bearing up of the flag, [a] bearing up of the ark" ("La Caravane," *LCH*, 295)—by virtue of mind(s) being in constant movement, in constant going-forth or ontic genesis. "The great mysterious thread of the human labyrinth, Progress," as Hugo calls it in the 1857 preface to the first series of poems for *La Légende des siècles* (*LS1*, 60), may thus be seen as a linear process, evocative of the logic of difference in the context of totality; but it also may imply that Hugolian sense of simultaneity and synonymy which allows for his sense of the "sisterhood" of brutishness and gentleness ("Le Crapaud" ["The Toad"], *LS2*, 314) or of the equivalence of "abyss" and "source," void and being ("Les Mages" ["Magi"], *C*, 450). Progress can thus be deemed, as in *Dieu*, that "luminous disaster" (*D*, 330) fusing existential problem and illumination, resultant anxiety and surging vision (*D*, 322), a sense of chaos and a sense of divinity, infinity, recuperation ("Le Noir" ["Blackness"], *LS2*, 16).

There is, then, a crucial Hugolian perspective in which progress, although we may fight for it, is natural, to be taken for granted, in need merely of something like consent and (transformation of) being. The 1819 ode, "Premier soupir" ("First Sigh," *OB*, 223–24), invites one to "be happy, o my sweet friend /. . . Let the waters follow their course." The natural movements—of seasons, days, elements, but feelings, too, and thoughts: "Oui, c'est la vie. Après le jour, la nuit livide" ("Yes, it's life. After day, livid night)," we read in *Les Orientales* (*Orientals, LO*, 148)—allow our being to fully manifest its natural becoming and flowingness, the latter entailing, unquestionably for Hugo, fulfillment, completion, some ultimate and resplendent harmony. The apparent "oceanic" chaos of humankind thus contains a "grandeur" that is not purely rhetorical (*C*, 149); "nothing is terrible, frantic, free; /Convulsive, aghast, mad, but for balance," he insists in *L'Année terrible* (*AT*, 390), where the logic of the flowingness of being merges with that of some vast oceanic totality wherein balance of difference and global purpose work themselves out. The poetics of oceanity suggests that being is, as it were, already complete; filled with contradiction, paradox, imbalance, and, perhaps above all, our belief therein, yet complete. "Ces oiseaux sont dans leur fonction," he insightfully writes in *Les Contemplations*, "laisse-les" ("The birds are in their function, let them be," *C*, 62, "Les Oiseaux" ["Birds"]): their continuity and complementarity of purpose is certain; it is sufficient that they be (left to be). And even in more struggling, outraged moments, the latter are seen to be part of a vaster enterprise of peace and love: "To chastise/Is to love," Hugo clarifies in "La Paternité" ("Fatherhood") from *La Légende des siècles*, "the haughty Ocean remains whole,/ Whatever hurricane abysses cast upon it" (*LS1*, 496).

The great posthumous poems of *Océan, Dernière gerbe*, and *Toute la lyre*, deploy in exemplary simplicity this vast "entireness" of being and vision, the seething yet gentle unity of infinite parts, moments, differences washing one over the other in endless interchange, in streaming com-position of some immense symbolic whole. Progress floods and ebbs, but its movements are as certain as life itself, inescapably caught up in something beyond mere temporality, linear sociology, and psychology. "Nothing is outside of being," Hugo writes in *Dieu* (*D*, 342) and the principle of contained, yet infinite oceanic flowingness permits an inevitable sense of the interlocking, simultaneous, equivalent nature of all manifestations of being, feeling, consciousness. "No! All beings are, and were, and will be," he affirms in the same—no doubt intentionally unfinished, and thus infinite—volume (*D*, 337). Aspect may change and fluctuate, yet a profound unity remains, Hugo argues in *Les Contemplations* (see "Les Mages"). Such unity, at once riverlike and tidal, oceanic, is clearly, for Hugo, most manifest at the soul level of existence ("Ecrit en 1846" ["Written in 1846"], *C*, 300) and ultimately rests upon the deep nondifference of self and other. Does not Hugo cry out, in the very preface of *Les Contemplations*, "Ah! insensé, qui crois que je ne suis pas toi!" ("Ah! madman, believing I am not you!" *C*, 12)? And does he not declare, in the beautiful "Oui, je suis le rêveur; je suis le camarade . . ." ("Yes, I am the Dreamer; I am the Friend . . .") of the same collection, his "conversing/With all the voices of metempsychosis" (*C*, 78)?

To understand Hugo is not to brush aside such statements, but to meditate their fullness of meaning, for him, for ourselves, for all being(s). The discourse of totality, of progress, of oceanity, is perhaps ultimately one of com-prehension: the seizing of the multiplicity of aspect in the optic of union, with-ness, love. "To understand is to love," Hugo tells us in "Je lisais. Que lisais-je? . ." ("I was Reading. What Was I Reading?" *C*, 162–63), insisting, "the lily understood within you blooms": the reading, of the infinite contra-dictions of the universe, or of Hugo, as a com-prehension, a seizing and flooding love of (our) oceanic totality.

Earth

The reading and com-prehension of Hugo's immense poetic oeuvre plunges us quickly and inescapably into an experience of "blades of grass [and] sleeping lizards," caught in Durassian "summer rain" (*OB*, 267, "Pluie d'été" ["Summer Rain"]), of spiders and nettles manifestly in need, as Hugo emphasizes, of our com-passion, our com-prehension, our love taking them up together, resplendently equal in the vastness of being (*C*, 204, "J'aime l'araignée . . ." ["I Love the Spider . . ."])—an experience, in short, of the ugly with the beauteous, the tiny with the immense, within that realm we term earth. Such a range of telluric focus as is Hugo's is by no means limited to insects, plants and small animals: the poetics of earth engenders a discourse of multiple, infinite, timeless telluric fascination. The 1823 "A un passant," from the *Odes et ballades*, clearly predating Baudelaire's celebrated sonnet, sings the mystery of earth's ephemeralness and ineffable anonymity (*OB*, 301–302); others commemorate "seen things," lived events, *faits divers* gleaned from papers, documents, letters—I think of "À un martyr," from *Les Châtiments*, recording the murder of a missionary in China (*LCH*, 54–58), "A quatre prisonniers" ("To Four Prisoners") from the same volume singing passing event both in and beyond its sociopolitical context, or, again, "Chose vue un jour de printemps" ("Something Seen One Spring Day"), from *Les Contemplations*, recounting the pathos of orphanage, à la Rimbaud, yet showing the links between lack and hunger, and prostitution, theft, violence, illness. Yet other poems center upon personal event, poems such as "À Villequier" ("At Villequier") caressingly dated 4 September 1847, four years to the day after the traumatizing drowning of Hugo's beloved daughter, Léopoldine, during her honeymoon with Charles Vacquerie, for whom several moving poems were also written in the following years. The trying ways of the earth and the earth's still exquisite presence merge their discourses in the poet's fusion of immanence and implicit though difficult transcendence: "Now softened by these divine visions," he writes, "plains, forests, rocks, vales, silvered water,/Seeing my smallness and seeing your miracles,/I take up once more my reason before the vastness" (*C*, 270).

The complexity of the Hugolian poetics of earth can no doubt already be glimpsed, as it skips from lizard to nettle, from a fleeting face at night to his at once absent and present daughter, from the specific naming of "Pauline Roland," with its commemoration of revolutionary hero(in)ism (*LCH*, 203–207), or of "Eblouissements" ("Dazzlements") with its condemnation of corrupt "judges" (*LCH*, 230–36), to the evocation of the near-ineffable experience of what, in the 1840 "Le Firmament est plein . . ." ("The Firmament is Full . . ."), from *Les Contemplations*, Hugo calls "the hosanna of forests, rivers and meadows"—the earth as song of ecstasy, worship, "prayer" (*C*, 23–24).

The range of telluric discourse is thus typically vast, at once reminiscent of Marceline Desbordes-Valmore and Lamartine, yet in anticipation of writers as diverse as Michelet and Flaubert, Rimbaud and Zola. It is in the contemplation of what we think of as nature, that Hugo's most immediate expression of the earth's intrinsic sublimeness of logic occurs—though this neither excludes occasionally darker brooding nor the inclusion of the "human" within this intrinsicalness. The "divineness" of what is (*C*, 114, "Je sais bien qu'il est d'usage . . ." ["I know that it is customary . . ."]), of the earth's simplest evidence, gives to Hugo's telluric poetics both a resiliency and a power of unruffled trust unparalleled in this century. Thus is the "language of birds" indistinguishable from the "language of the angels" in his experience of nature's innocent *présence* (*C*, 100, "En écoutant les oiseaux" ["Listening to the Birds"]); thus are nature's constructions at once stupendously negligible yet implicitly more magnificent than the greatest of cathedrals—one thinks of Francis Ponge's "Notes pour un coquillage" ("Notes for a Seashell"; (see *C*, 134, "La Nichée sous le portail" ["The Nestful under the Portal"]); thus would the world, without roses, be quickly reduced to "very little" (*C*, 115, "Je sais bien qu'il est d'usage . . ."). For, in the final analysis, this poetics of what might appear to be simple externality or passing materiality, rides upon a logic of universal consciousness, universal and divine—both privately and collectively lived—"spirituality" and meaning. "Ce que dit la bouche d'ombre" ("What the Shadow's Mouth Says," *C*, 462–87)—the earth's dark maw—tells us, at the close, almost, of *Les Contemplations*:

Hugo

Arbres, roseaux, rochers, tout vit!
                    Tout est plein d'âmes.
Trees, reeds, rocks, all is alive!
                    All is soul-filled.

The earth may be otherness, perhaps black and fathomless, but Hugo's comprehension of it is animated by a logic of shared vibrancy, shared awareness à la Nerval ("Vers dorés" ["Gilded Lines"]), or à la Baudelaire ("Correspondances"), or even à la Gautier ("Affinités secrètes" ["Secret Affinities"]). And this logic of reciprocated consciousness—"La tremblante forêt songe, écoute et regarde" ("The trembling forest dreams, listens and looks"), Hugo writes in "Le Groupe des idylles" ("The Idylls") from *La Légende des siècles* (*LS2*, 122)—slips easily into his poetics of the non-difference, the merging of self and other, the earth and the "I." In this optic, nothing "mechanistic" attaches to Hugo's poetics of earth (*D*, 370). All is inherent purpose, meaningful function, from cell to sun. Breaking down and restructuring are one, "through the magnificent rending of veils,/Nature confirms and proves unity" (*LS2*, 123, "Bion"). Burial and creation form a single telluric discourse, as Hugo tells us in the great "Abîme," from *La Légende des siècles* (*LS2*, 411–16): earth is abyss and generative spring, its poetics recuperates the chemical within the psychical, chaos within infinity. The most banal—"the creaking of a trestle bed"—is paradisiacal, he argues in "Paupertas," from the *Les Chansons des rues et des bois* (*CR*, 30–33), for "earth, swollen by sap,/Is a holy, mysterious and/Sublime place" (*CR*, 31), beyond all futility, all intrinsic platitude, every instant, as he notes like an Yves Bonnefoy in "L'Ascension humaine," being traversed by eternity (*CR*, 174).

None of this means that Hugo's particular *poétique de la terre* avoids or seeks to avoid what I will term horror, politics, struggle. Hugo's entire oeuvre, poetic, dramatic, novelistic, and even, artistic, painterly, seeks rather to incorporate perceived social problem and nagging metaphysical questioning into the framework of a telluric discourse thus simultaneously lucid, informed, frank, and visionary, recuperative, ideal. Certainly, the temptations of *angélisme*, aestheticism, or some ardent, pure spirituality are known to Hugo; but, as the 1823 "Paysage," from *Odes et ballades*, makes plain, the youthful impulse to "flee of a narrow world the impure turbulence;/[For] there crawl the heartless, there reign the wicked" (*OB*, 241) may be real, but it yields to the urge to love. Earth's discourse can fragment into the contra-dictions of what, in *Les Châtiments*, he terms "supplices, couperets, billots, gibets, tortures" ("torments, cleavers, blocks, gallows, tortures," *LCH*, 35, "Nox") or, in *Les Contemplations*, earth's filth, imprisonment, grief, strict materiality (*C*, 168–69, "Explication" ["Explanation"]). Yet, as in these two poems, the principle of oceanity prevails and the poetics of earth finds restored to itself some notion of radiant, smiling concord (*LCH*, 35), the splendor of reawakening, of spirit within our being-here (*C*, 168–69).

Other poems might appear cut off from recuperation, their poetics anchored in the eclipse of loving presence ("What matter green woods, harvest, hill . . .," we read in the Rousseauist or Lamartinian *complainte* of *Odes et ballades*, "Le Voyage"), in the apparent refusal to "attach one's heart to passing things" ("Les Tronçons du serpent" ["The Snake's Stumps"], *LO*, 123–25), or in the obsession with that Babel-like "lugubrious Tower of Things" (evoked in the liminal "La Vision d'où est sorti ce livre" ["The Vision From Which This Book Came"], from *La Légende des siècles*). But, even here, it is important to note Hugo's manifest desire to insert, into the ideality—the lived and felt ideality, for we are far from Mallarmé or even Baudelaire—of the poetics of earth, its pain, its social and spiritual difficulty, and not in an embrace that truly refuses, but in one that struggles to reconcile, even transfigure. "Les Tronçons du serpent," from *Les Orientales*, is finally a poem that speaks the passing, even while pondering the wisdom of such speaking. Hugo's poetics of earth never really wavers; a poetics of stark and exquisite mortality, its consciousness of the vulnerable inevitably includes, is indeed synonymous with, a consciousness of the sacred, the meaningful.

Hugo's logic of earth(liness) thus meshes with his abiding sense of what he terms, in *Odes et ballades*, "universal Being" (*OB*, 173, "Le Poète"). Just as time is shot through with eternity (*CR*, 174), so is earthliness traversed by universality, by nonfiniteness. Hugo's beloved granddaughter, Jeanne, is thus "surnaturelle": not metaphorically, but really, her *présence* being, to speak like a Lyall Watson, naturally supernatural, simple but infinitely stunning (*AGP*, 681). Thus does, for Hugo, our mortal, human song-of-earth mingle with the "eternal hymn" of being (*OB*, 222, "Jéhovah"). Thus does the beautiful "La Terre," from *La Légende des siècles*, sing the inexhaustible energies fueling the fusion of birth and apotheosis, collapse and continuity, affirmation and negation, physical multiplication and intuited sacred purpose. The poetics of earth can be plunged into "monstrosity," as "Le Satyre" ("The Satyr") writes (*LS2*, 13), for all, at times, may be felt to be swirling, swarming visceral mystery. Yet, as the same poem insists, such mystery is, as for a Char, the primary source of our sense of telluric sacredness and meaningfulness: "Oh gods!" he exclaims, "The tree is sacred, the animal is sacred,/Man is sacred; respect to the earth profound!" (*LS2*, 17). Despite—indeed, incredibly, *with*—"all that is bad in the earth and humankind," our earthliness remains still sublime and beautiful (*FA*, 294, "Bièvre"). No doubt in its very vulnerability, its precariousness, in the sense we can have, with Hugo, of its ever-surging absoluteness, its ever-original inimitableness— experienced in its very passingness. "Qu'importe!" he writes, dismissing in his very embrace of them the trials and assaults of the earth,

> J'ai pour joie et pour merveille
> De voir, dans ton pré d'Honfleur,
> Trembler au poids d'une abeille
> Un brin de lavande en fleur"

> My joy and my wonder is
> To see in your Honfleur meadow,
> Quivering beneath the weight of bee,
> A sprig of lavender in bloom.
> (*CR*, 188, "A un ami")

Horror, Sociology, Struggle

"L'Enfant," from *Les Orientales*, bears the epigraph from *Macbeth*, "O horror! horror! horror!" (*LO*, 101) and evokes, emblematically, a vast fascination and ethico-spiritual response deeply pertinent to Hugo's global poetics. It is a question not solely of the awesome mystery of the earth, "the inexpressible horror of prodigious places" (*LS1*, 129), nor of, say, for some, death's reductive, leveling logic of despair and nothingness ("L'Epopée du ver" ["Epic of the Worm"], *LS1*, 279–93); at stake, also—and equivalently, perhaps, awe joining fear and outrage—is a persistent sentiment of horror before the actions and choices of some that transform our "sociology" into a logos of terror and abomination, exploitation and suffering. The premature deaths of Hugo's own children, the madness of Adèle, his own long exile, and the trials and tribulations of strictly private emotion—it is not of such experience, profound and moving as it is, that I speak. Horror, for Hugo, implies more essentially a poetics of public ethics, and to some almost inevitable degree of public metaphysics, for all is vision, mind, spirit(uality) for this most dogged and inspired of strugglers.

Les Châtiments, of course, details much that is crucial here, but it is important to realize: 1. the extent to which the texts overflow—especially for us today—their specificity and join with the numerous other poems, as well as plays and novels, that document the world's monstrous absurdities and atrocities, of Hugo's century but of all time; and 2. the perspective of hope and faith in which they are relentlessly written. *La Légende des siècles* is exemplary in this respect, as is *La Fin de Satan* (*Satan's End*). The feeling of "horror for this earth," that even *L'Art d'être grand-père* can articulate (*AGP*, 584, "Parfois, je me sens pris . . ." ["Sometimes I feel caught . . ."]), finds, then, in *Les Châtiments*, a full and ample, urgent and visceral voice. "Nox" (*LCH*, 21–35) decries unambiguously the indiscriminate and cowardly massacre of men, women, and children by those who reign by terror, backed by the church; "Souvenir de la Nuit du 4" ("Memory of the Night of the 4th," *LCH*, 81–83) recounts with intense yet sober realism the mindless political murder of a politically innocent child of seven; "A l'obéissance passive" (*LCH*, 90–102) deplores the slippage from basic soldierly honor and dignity to that mercenary servility generated by a Louis-Napoléon whom Hugo contemptuously calls "that omnipotent dwarf,/Presiding over triumphant filth and orgy,/Fermenting massacre and exhaling/The awful gasp of blood!" (*LCH*, 100); "Eblouissements" (*LCH*, 230–36) culminates in an indictment of the abominations of heartless deportation around the then colonies, leaving children and adults to "die in agony, burned up with fever and vermin." The litany of chastisements is long sung, and appropriately so in such an encyclopedic opus such as Hugo's. The logos of social and political reality—its ideals, its laws—is so pathetically undercut by easy corruptibility, so that a logos of protection and nourishment slumps to one of exploitation, domination, suppression, as the 1853 preface suggests (*LCH*, 13). It may be "the last hour of Kings, [the] first hour of men [and women]" (*LCH*, 348, "La Fin" ["The End"]), but privileged, closetted, and cossetted "people of war and people of church," as Hugo calls them in the powerfully eloquent "Les quatre jours d'Elciis" ("The Four Days of Elciis"), from *La Légende des siècles* (*LS1*, 445–70), continue to profit from violence and fear:

> They blanket with their good honor, law, republic,
> The charter of the people and the gospel's work,
> Progress, firm hope of the desolate;
> They are odious
>
> (*LCH*, 158)

The last poem of *L'Année terrible*, "Le Vieux Monde" ("The Old World," *AT*, 471–72), evokes both the clinging anachronisms of a sociology arguably surpassed in the minds and hearts of ordinary people and yet not yet swept irrevocably away: wretchedness, ignorance, sense of despair, of nothingness, male dominance, high privilege, superstition, fatality. If, then, the horror of wide-scale planetary slaughter described so compellingly in "L'Egout de Rome" ("The Sewers of Rome," *LCH*, 284–87) ever lingers in Hugo's mind, he is, too, sensitive, beyond the problem of what is materially, to what we think and feel. "Question sociale" ("Social Matters"), for example, from *La Légende des siècles* (*LS1*, 374–75) speaks of "hunger, thirst, horror, shadow, and immense *ennui*," and it is this last detail that allows us to sense the degree to which Hugo's poetics of horror and sociological problematics folds back upon purely mental and affective factors that may in fact block (self-)assumption and (self-)transformation.

Horror may provoke shrinking, withdrawal, the impotence of an ennui that this century's literature knows so well; but it is simultaneously occasion for change, action, rebirth, according to Hugolian dialectics. "The world springs green in mourning and horror," Hugo affirms in "Loi de formation du progrès" ("Law of Progress' Development"), from *L'Année terrible* (*AT*, 362–70), "each flower is first dung, and nature/Starts by eating its own rottenness." Thus is it that the poetics of social horror can be stood on its head. That "instinct [that ever] brings me/To know the depths of human suffering[,]/The abyss of pains" (*C*, 350, "Les Malheureux" ["The Wretched"]) is not predicated upon prurience or even mere compassion, but upon a vision of contrast between "fate and soul," a vision in which "the ugliness of trial becomes beauty" (*C*, 355, "Les

Malheureux"), a vision of (r)evolution that is "only the formula/Of horror accumulated in twenty reigns" (*C*, 296, "Ecrit en 1846"). Thus can a "pale dawn" burst through the cracks of the tomb of Hugo's deceased son, Charles (*AT*, 459–61, "O Charles, je te sens . . ." ["Oh Charles, I Feel You . . ."]); thus, in the very fine "Magnitudo parvi" (*C*, 210–37), can Hugo deem "one soul [to be] greater than a world"; thus, in "Le Poème du Jardin des Plantes" (*AGP*, 598–616), is the horror of "beastliness," even the "Satanic," balanced by splendor, by the divine—and indeed with the balance tipped in the latter's favor. The "zodiac of tyrants" still burning in humanity's "gloomy sky," as Hugo writes in "Horror" from *Les Contemplations*, is not a fixed astrological construct: our human destiny, our socio- and eco-logy is assumable, in Hugolian poetics, and thus always a psychological construct, which we are free to create.

Hence the logic, ever visible from the earliest odes to the last "heap of stones," of struggle, of protest, of outcry, of naming, of exposure. And, as the 1831 preface to *Les Feuilles d'automne* (*FA*, 183–90) clarifies, if struggle involves questioning, rethinking, (self-)upheaval, these in turn demand that exemplary (poetic) action at the intersection of detachment and concern, independence and commitment, measure and unambiguousness. Struggle, for Hugo, is nonviolent, loving combat and, if necessary, chastisement; its action is poetic, spiritual, creative. And it demands that perseverance and fidelity, that improbable admixture of indignation and serenity, of which "Ultima verba," from *Les Châtiments*, simply and eloquently speaks (*LCH*, 333–35). As the title of the third book of *Les Contemplations* reminds us—and as with the logic of horror—struggle and dream go hand in hand. To struggle is to have purpose, meaning, to know them blindly, impulsively, but illuminatingly, without knowing the specifics of end, of achievement, caught even in an endless dream, an endless progression, an endless transformation of being. The poetics of struggle certainly implies a deployment of energy *against* "social" doubt, (r)evolutionary doubt, "metaphysical" doubt, and the pride of generalized skepticism (*D*, 336). But it implies more importantly an orientation *toward, for*. Chastisement may be a "terrible gaze," as "Ce que dit la bouche d'ombre" tells us (*C*, 475), but it is buoyant, confident, curiously consenting because predicated on love. Cutting through discouragement, the poetics of struggle affirms, rejects negation, looks to future and truth. "Ne croyez pas," Hugo writes in "Les quatre jours d'Elciis,"

> que je me décourage.
> Je ne fais pas ici le bruit d'un vent d'orage
> Pour n'aboutir qu'au doute et qu'à l'accablement.
>
> . . . .
>
> Tout luira . . .
> . . . Tous les peuples sont vrais, même les plus niés
>
> Do not believe that I am discouraged.
> My storm and wind here are not made
> To end up in doubt and dejection.
>
> . . . .
>
> All will gleam forth . . .
> All peoples are true, even the most denied
>
> (*LS1*, 469).

Struggle emphasizes equality, not just of peoples but of human, sun and fly ("Jeunesse" ["Youth"], *CR*, 92); it inserts itself in a vast, patient, and confident continuity going from Plato and beyond to Luther to Pascal to Rousseau (*AGP*, 685, "Persévérance"); it occurs in solitariness and "fraternity"/sorority (*AGP*, 687); its socio-logy is both ethical and "naturally" spiritual. And, most crucially, as Hugo argues in "Le Groupe des idylles," when thinking of Beaumarchais, there is nothing finally tragic in all of this (*LS1*, 134). Struggle can be an acquiescence to the vicissitudes of love, a trust in—and not just an engagement in—the natural impulsive movement of mind and spirit ("Tout le passé et tout l'avenir," *LS2*, 210).

Freedom, Innocence, Child and Peace

Everything rides upon freedom, mine, yours, that of each of us (see *FA*, 201, "Rêverie d'un passant à propos d'un roi" ["Revery of a Passer-by about a King"]): freedom "bears up" our possibilities. It is therefore Hugo's most flown flag, as he suggests in "Ultima verba" a flag for political, collective life and a flag for art, a flag of "light" and "purity," made for storms and glory alike, as the 1823

"La Liberté" from *Odes et ballades* renders clear (*OB*, 113). Freedom is not an object of Hugolian struggle, however, in order that anarchy may reign, nor, evidently, to permit the abusive power of the masses to replace that of absolute tyranny. Freedom is conceived as accompanying "order" (*OB*, 40, the 1829 preface) and as involving measure and collaboration, cooperation (*FA*, 189, preface). While stemming from a visceral hatred of oppression, the poetic song of freedom, like that of struggle, envisions realization and assumes itself as a "duty" to the defenseless and the anonymous ("Amis, un dernier mot . . ." ["Friends, One Last Word . . ."], *FA*, 331–33). The poetics of art's, or poetry's, liberating gesture, depends a priori upon a freedom and independence of voice that gives the poet or artist a special role to play in social and ethico-spiritual matters. Thus poetic freedom may be lightly evoked— "nuage errant" ("errant cloud"), he writes in *Les Feuilles d'automne,* "Ma haute poésie/Vole capricieuse et sans route choisie" ("my high poetry/Flies fanciful and without chosen path," *FA*, 213)— but such fancy and whim are by no means simply aesthetic. The freedom that, in *Les Contemplations,* leads to revolution in rhyme and lexicon, is the same freedom that allows for all (self-)transformation, (self-)discovery or recovery (see *C*, 32, "Réponse à un acte d'accusation" ["Response to an Accusation"]). Freedom, aesthetic, social, spiritual, arises always from "your song free and saying all" (*CR*, 23)—from a freedom of speech permitting the saying of what one likes, how one likes.

This poetics, however, while predicated upon "boldness" and "endeavor," as Hugo stresses in "Plein ciel" ("Full Sky"), is equally rooted in what the same poem terms "holy rage" (*LS2*, 385). Again, freedom combats anarchy and chaos (*AT*, 400, "Paris incendié" ["Paris on Fire"]); it may root itself in irony and, as we shall see, laughter—"Rupture avec ce qui amoindrit" ("Breaking with Diminishment") sings the praises of "ces divins passants" such as Diogenes, Swift, Rabelais, Diderot, Voltaire (*LS2*, 357); but freedom is, for Hugo, clearly never gratuitous, never contrary to love and compassion, never outside a sense of the general good. It thus possesses a power of nonabusiveness and, as for Bernard Noël today, is always to be assumed essentially as an action for and upon the self. Certainly, "no one has the right to take/My freedom, my goods, my blue sky, my love," as Hugo affirms in *Les Châtiments* (*LCH*, 110–11,

"Ainsi les plus abjects . . ." ["Thus the Most Abject . . ."]), even though collective freedom demands in his eyes order, justice, equity. To die for one's freedom and that of others oppressed remains undoubtedly, in Hugo's mind, a noble—because, precisely, free and chosen—act: "Pauline Roland" is amply eloquent in this regard (*LCH*, 203–207). And the ghosts of the crushed are, for Hugo, "freedom [itself] hovering above" (*LS2*, 78, "Le Régiment du baron Madruce" ["Baron Madruce's Regiment"]). But the poetics of freedom is not of death, but of life, of historical and spiritual redemption, a poetics worthy indeed of the aspirations of "l'ange Liberté" ("The angel of Freedom") of *La Fin de Satan* (*FS*, 278).

The Hugolian poetics of freedom may be said to be intimately linked to three other questions or phenomena that obsessively draw Hugo's attention: innocence, childliness, and peace. Enacted, realized freedom of self and other, beyond abuse and imposition, involves already a sense of the innocence—the harmlessness, the ontic simplicity, the intrinsically pure sacredness—of all. "Rien ne touche un esprit que Dieu même a saisi" ("Nothing touches a mind that God himself has grasped"), Hugo writes in *Les Feuilles d'automne*. Innocence is residual despite perversion, reduction, degradation (*FA*, 233); belief in inherent purity, grace, and sublimity is essentially unshakable (see "Ô mes lettres d'amour . . ." ["Oh My Love Letters . . ."], *FA*, 239); it harkens to an original, maternal simplicity of heart, beyond bitterness, to that sense of love and plain greatness Hugo feels within and without in "Aux arbres" ("To Trees"), from *Les Contemplations* (*C*, 199–200). The means of attaining to innocence now are endless, but I might particularly stress Hugo's insistence upon laughter and joyfulness. This, for example, is the essence of his "advice" "À André Chénier" ("To André Chénier," *C*, 25), and indeed *Les Contemplations* as a whole shows that innocence in struggle comes not from self-righteousness but from love, joy, serenity; from an understanding of nature's innocent and loving mingling of all with all (see "Après l'hiver" ["After Winter"], *C*, 124–26); from a sense of the urgency of our assumption of "gaiety, joy, laughter, marriage" ("Le Groupe des idylles": "Beaumarchais," *LS2*, 134). And from our will to forgive, to let go, to focus upon the present: "Moi qui pourrais mordre," he writes in *Les Chansons des rues et des bois*, "je ris" ("I who could bite, am laughing," *CR*, 34, "Hilaritas").

Severity, as the very next poem of the same 1865 collection argues, runs contrary to our sacred innocence, which is borne up rather by "joy and forgiveness" (*CR*, 35, "Meudon"). Innocence—mine, your, ours, all things'—demands effort, struggle, an acquired consciousness of the depth of the principle of freedom. *L'Année terrible* emphasizes this effort—"Je tâche de comprendre afin de pardonner" ("I try to understand so as to forgive"), we read in "Expulsé de Belgique" ("Expelled from Belgium," *AT*, 411), where com-passion, con-structiveness, and creativeness are privileged—and shows that if innocence is a "right," it may be "abdicated," and its reign must be paradoxically self-empowering yet powerless (see "Pas de représailles" ["No Reprisals"], *AT*, 385). Only the intrinsic spiritual power of innocence and forgiveness matter: they imply no control, yet embrace all. "Forgiveness is greater than Cain, and overlays him," Hugo notes in *Dieu* (*D*, 327). Innocence is the powerless, all-empowering simplicity of one's vulnerability; it leads to the joy recounted in "La Cicatrice" ("The Scar") of *L'Art d'être grandpère*, written for Jeanne—and himself (*AGP*, 620). The logic of innocence means that even Satan's cry for recuperation and redemption is unerringly heard (see *FS*, 275, 288 and passim).

"Lorsque l'enfant paraît..." ("When the Child Appears . . ."), from *Les Feuilles d'automne* (*FA*, 252–54), reveals the deep discourse of smile, simplicity, joy, and innocence immediately available within us all via the at once real and emblematic presence of the child; just as the exquisite "Claire," from *Les Contemplations*, points to the child—albeit just deceased—as a locus and a sign of lightness, ephemeralness, origin, of "la sereine clarté des paradis profonds" ("the serene brilliance of deep paradises," *C*, 401). The child, for Hugo, is the enigma of pure assurance and contentedness (*AGP*, 611, "C'est une émotion étrange . . ." ["It is a Strange Feeling . . ."]), the enigma of some deep truth beyond our material platitudes. "Kings," he writes in "Le Comte Félibien" ("Count Félibien") from *La Légende des siècles*, "truth is a child; you are chimeras" (*LS1*, 193). More significantly even, the child is the enigma of pure ontic emergence, of our ceaseless coming-into-being-from-nothingness—or what we may be tempted to think of as nothingness (*C*, 453, "Les Mages"). The child is thus an implicit sign of meaning, purpose, pro-gress, (r)evolution, new origin now.

In "L'Idylle du vieillard" ("Old Man's Idyll"), from *La Légende des siècles*, the very voice of the infant is "innocence in our midst, bountifulness"; it represents wisdom and faith and love as a language ever to be spoken (*LS2*, 137). Even the pure babblings of children, beyond decipherable message, are "ce dessus divin de la vaste harmonie" ("The divine overlay of the massive harmony," *AGP*, 583, "Georges et Jeanne"). The "Fonction de l'enfant" ("Child's Function"), as Hugo titles one of his texts of *La Légende des siècles* (*LS2*, 372–73), is thus clear: it gives flesh and energy to the pure theory of godliness, it helps us sense our individual and collective divine createdness, a love and reason, a truth and clarity traversing our being and upon which we can draw if we wish.

The celebrated but utterly unpretentious "Sur une barricade . . ." ("On a Barricade . . ."), from *L'Année terrible*, thus leaps beyond the fatuity and contradiction of adult ideology to the visceral honesty and innocent noncomplexity of the child (*AT*, 424–25). As Hugo declares without hesitation in the same pain-racked volume, and in a poem, "À petite Jeanne" ("To Little Jeanne"), far removed from any sense of aesthetic self-importance,

> the most famous authors have written nothing better
> Than the thought half-blossomed in your eyes,
> Than your strange, scattered, obscure revery,
> Gazing upon man with the ignorance of the angel
> (*AT*, 305).

The child, indeed, is a locus and a symbol of what, for Hugo, it is worth believing in. "I believe in children as people believed in the apostles," he declares in the 1877 *L'Art d'être grand-père* (*AGP*, 597). Such a belief, distinct from dogma, form, and the power of structure, joins that of his earlier, equally delightfully confessed credo articulated in *Les Chansons des rues et des bois*:

> Maintenant, je te l'avoue,
> Je ne crois qu'au droit divin
> Du coeur, de l'enfant qui joue,
> Du franc rire et du bon vin.
>
> Now, I confess to you,
> I believe but in divine right
> Of the heart, of the child at play,
> Of open laughter and good wine.
> (*CR*, 129)

The child is a symbol not just of nonviolence, of nonpower, of nonabuse, but of all that is blatantly positive and affirmative and that rests upon a principle of peace and harmony. Peace is perhaps the ultimate "justice" we can give to the world and to each other; it is clearly beyond revenge and reprisal, as the splendid poem "Le Parti du crime" ("Crime's Side," *LCH*, 247–52) confirms. Peace, freedom, ideal, and what Hugo often alludes to as "marriage," *hymen, hyménée*, go hand in hand ("La Caravane," *LCH*, 296). The enactment of peace demands generosity, forgiveness, Hugo's refusal of capital punishment and returned violence in general. That dreamed "concord between citizens," that still eludes us, nationally and internationally, involves the blossoming, "in the depths of our hatreds," as Hugo writes in "Aux rois," of a "hymn of peace issued from a divine mouth" (*LS2*, 98–100). "Men of peace," as Hugo calls them, cannot be simultaneously "men of war" (*LS2*, 295–97, "Les Hommes de paix aux hommes de guerre"), even though poets "struggle" and Hugo once wrote that he would have perhaps been a soldier, if he had not become a poet (*OB*, 236, "Mon enfance" ["My Childhood"]).

The poetics of peace ushers in a time when "war, shadow, envy" simply "die," irrelevant before the poet's—the creator's—"gentle chasing of men towards life" (*LS2*, 216, "Changement d'horizon" ["Change of Perspective"]). When Hugo urges us to "employ in the service of peace/The warrior, truth" (*CF*, 205), he wittingly highlights the joinedness and yet the difference of truth centering upon problem, and truth centering upon solution. To assume fully the poetics of peace, and innocence, childliness and freedom, is not to dwell upon fear, mourning, imprisonment, degradation. Rather does it involve the tautological living—the thinking and feeling—of peace. Peace is peace and the synonyms of peace, love, harmony, and that joyous recognition of consciousness everywhere which a poem such as "Mugitusque boum" from *Les Contemplations* so simply and splendidly evokes (*C*, 333–34).

Satan, God, Transfiguration

In turning our attention to Hugo's obsession with the satanic, there is no need to elaborate the full detail of this crucial consciousness, which roots itself firmly in that of all other major poets of the

century, now more historically, culturally focused, now more spiritually, metaphysically, or simply psychologically attuned. "Evil
appeared before me, potent, joyous, sturdy,/Triumphant...,"
Hugo writes in "Ecrit en 1846," from *Les Contemplations* (*C,* 296),
thus emphasizing the vigor of the monstrous, the demonic, its resiliency, its hallucinatory power and tempting ecstasy. The satanic
can seem to be fundamental to existence, innate, one of those "two
beings ... within us," of which *La Légende des siècles* speaks, "one at
ease, the other foul" (*LS2,* 209). Satan is thus pride, egoism, cruelty, hideousness, the teeming knot of vipers that Baudelaire and
Mallarmé, Jarry and Lautréamont, Freud and latter-day atheistic
Darwinists lay bare before us—as us. Sociologically speaking, evil
may be traced by Hugo to poverty, hunger, inequality. Beyond sociology, but in parallel fashion, "Satan is the night of God," as we
read in a fragment from the never finished *Dieu* (*D,* 429). Satanism
is the dark time of our utopia, the as yet unlit face of our feasible
"divinity." And as Hugo also insists in *Dieu,* "Good and evil [are]
mysterious mirrors," caught up in some interpertinence, some reciprocity, some logic of unity (*D,* 365).

   Baudelaire, Mallarmé, Lautréamont, the surrealists, Freud, Jarry,
Reverdy, Ponge, Michaux, Jouve—all have their modes of res-
ponding to the varyingly focused consciousness of the "satanical":
angélisme ("angelicism"), hermeticism, *l'imaginaire,* the surreal, suppression, *objoie,* and so on. Hugo's own response is multiple though
coherent, and inevitably rooted in factors to which we shall turn
later in this same section. *Les Contemplations* can stress human
responsibility—and therefore option—in *our* creation of the real
(*C,* 464, "Ce que dit la bouche d'ombre"); and can therefore suggest
that thought—mind, spirit—is not inherently problematical, but
can be inappropriately materialized and concentrated (*C,* 465). In
this sense, Hugo can recognize that "evil"—*le mal* covers all "sins,"
from massacre and pillage to simple feelings of depressiveness, or
the death of an aged parent, or a minor misunderstanding—is subsumed in creation (*C,* 466), a kind of "strange enigma,/Misspelling
of God," as he puts it in *Les Chansons des rues et des bois* (*CR,* 157,
"Les Enfants lisent ..." ["Children Read ..."]). And, yet, as the
same volume suggests, what is occurring upon the physical plane is
equivalent to what is being accomplished off it, in the aerial wings
of its theater (*CR,* 177, "L'Ascension humaine"). It is no doubt for
this reason that evil demands our pity in Hugo's eyes, for unhappi-

ness belongs most to the evildoer, he argues (*C,* 204, 358), and aggressive condemnation comes close to entrapping oneself in that which one condemns.

On top of this, Hugo's entire poetics of the satanic is predicated upon its progressive disappearance. The logic of revolution is not sound because the means justifies the end, but because it is contained within an unstoppable logic of transcendence of evil (*C,* 296, "Ecrit en 1846"). *La Légende des siècles,* as Hugo explains in its 1857 preface, is thus structurally, conceptually related to *La Fin de Satan* and *Dieu* (*LS*1, 62). Not only does Hugo's oeuvre reveal a constant "adjourning of Medusa and Satan" (*CR,* 26, "Paulo minora canamus")—to show the divine, now, here, in all that might seem insignificant to a casual or cynical eye—but it reveals, too, globally, the extent to which we are urged, motivated, "pushed towards the ideal by our evils, by our vows" (*LS*2, 280, "Paroles dans l'épreuve"). Construction thus lies deep within seeming destruction (*CR,* 179, "L'Ascension humaine"), birth gushes from evil's "Sepulcher" (*AT,* 368, "Loi de formation du progrès"). The whole logic of *La Fin de Satan* is movement, becoming, reintegration—better, the self-rediscovery of the satanic as the divine.

Polarities cease, division crumbles, the "ebb and flow" between good and evil ends—is thought, "seen," and felt as ending (*FS,* 266). In a sense, the very nonexistence of the satanic is demonstrated, as some have suggested, by "Satan dans la nuit" ("Satan in the Night," *FS,* 269–78), where love dominates, is confessed: "Je l'aime. C'est fini" ("I love him. It is over," *FS,* 269). This deeply felt core of love at the heart of satanism allows Hugo—who certainly traversed trials, observed tribulations, and never idly dismissed the slightest adversity—to recenter his whole poetics of the satanic, refounding it upon the basis of intrinsic universal goodness and (self-)fulfillment. "De tout ceci . . ." ("Of All This . . ."), from *L'Année terrible,* is unambivalent: "All is Well," he affirms, adding in a later section of the same poem, "complaint is a futile cry, evil a hollow word" (*AT,* 465, 469). *L'Art d'être grand-père* confirms this realization always within him, *le mal* being a face of *le bien,* just as beauty commonly reveals itself—as with Baudelaire, though less ironically, less anguishedly—as "ugliness" (*AGP,* 578, "L'Exilé satisfait" ["Content in Exile"]). And, of course, the writing of *Dieu* follows upon that of *La Fin de Satan.*

Philosophy, Hugo writes in his 1824 preface to *Les Nouvelles Odes* (*New Odes*), might have been radically rethought by genius in the light of the divine (*OB*, 31). A strict rationalism, a distrust of experience, a lack of simplicity and openness (*OB*, 299, "Les deux archers" ["The Two Bowmen"]), a refusal to stand, without hasty judgment and at ease, with Hugo, "upright, but leaning towards mystery," as he writes in "Veni, vidi, vici," from *Les Contemplations* (*C*, 267)—these are just some of the pitfalls blocking access to what Hugo calls God, an ubiquitous divineness, and a kind of "religion naturelle," as he puts it in *Les Chansons des rues et des bois* (*CR*, 189, "Clôture" ["Closure"]. This is a religion, no doubt inspired by the great principles of Christianity, faith, hope, charity, yet far from human reduction of the divine to idol (*FA*, 267), to political weapon and material justification. "The true God, distinct from the jealous God," he writes in *L'Art d'être grand-père*, beyond punishment, retribution, spiritual hierarchy (*AGP*, 627); a divineness beyond the deadly effect of unnatural, nonpersonal, ideologized religion (*FS*, 269).

Hugo, as almost any two or three poems will show, is essentially pantheist; though his sense of the divine, again, refuses system, pomp, power, theoretical glibness. Divineness, quite simply, resides in all—this is indeed the very logic of the antisatanic. "L'Extase," from *Les Orientales* (*LO*, 168), unwaveringly articulates this thesis, which provides "altars for every god" in every phenomenon (*OB*, 24, "À mes amis"), sees divineness in foliage, in the sun, flowers, caves, scents, brambles (*CR*, 13, "Orphée, au bois du Caystre . . ." ["Orpheus, in the Kaustros woods . . ."], *LCH*, 84, "Oh sun, oh divine visage . . ."). Divineness is life itself, and livingness is in all things, in the glory of a blade of grass (*FA*, 203, "Que t'importe, mon coeur . . ." ["What matter, my heart . . ."]), in and beneath stones, as for a Nerval (*C*, 437, "Les Mages"), in "a little bird beneath the leaves,/[That,] singing, sufficiently proves God" (*CR*, 99, "Ecrit en 1827" ["Written in 1827"])—a line explaining fully Hugo's feeling of affinity to Marceline Desbordes-Valmore. And as with the recuperative discourse of satanism, (wo)man "is nothing else/Than the synonym of God" (*CR*, 175, "L'Ascension humaine"). All phenomena are as metaphors of the divine, realized transfers of the divine, a process in which the latter is at once exterior and interior, transcendent and immanent, here and beyond our ordinary vision of being-here.

Hugo

"Tous les êtres sont Dieu" ("All beings are God"), then (*D*, 338): what is, is in all that is, spirit or soul breathed into the tiniest cell, the vastest cosmic conglomeration. To contemplate the divine is thus always, in part, a self-contemplation, a sense and remembrance of our soul-ness, the divineness of our every gesture or emotion (*FA*, 261). To contemplate being is to realize the extent to which all is *religio,* mystery, sacredness, deep authenticity. "Tout est religion et rien n'est imposture" ["All is religion and nothing is imposture"), he writes at the close of *Les Contemplations* (*C*, 498, "À celle qui est restée en France" ["To the Woman Remaining in France"]. The divine is intimate, private and immanent, and of necessity, upon a plane of existence that concerns us now, pragmatically, and via, always, *my, your, her* specific experience; and for Hugo, our most pressing collective, but always individual need involves, as he says in "Je lisais. Que lisais-je? . . .", "taking account of God. To understand is to love" (*C*, 163); it involves claiming the divine everywhere, in oneself, "conquering one's own mystery" (*C*, 366, "Ibo"); realizing one's every word is a divine logos, regardless of certain appearances (*C*, 39, "Suite" ["Continuation"]); realizing that, while "God will want" (*LS2*, 211, "Tout le passé et tout l'avenir")—while the divine implies an always-wanting, an implacable impulse of (self-)fulfillment—such wanting (of ecstasy, peace, love) remains to be assumed more consciously. Divinity may buoy up being, may *be* being, as "L'Elégie des fléaux" ("Elegy of the Scourges," *LS2*, 291) suggests, but its "support [of] all that bends" demands, still, our vision, our consent, for its greatest "progress."

"The eternal principle, simple, vast,/That thinks, being, that of all is the place./And that, for lack of a greater name, I call God": thus writes Hugo in the midst of all that weighs upon him and many others in *L'Année terrible* (*AT*, 323, "À l'évêque qui m'appelle athée" ["To the Bishop Who Calls Me Atheist"]). God—divineness—is thus a transcendent principle, yet one intuitively lived via Hugo's psychological and sensory immanence. It is not known, felt, thought, elsewhere than here, and if its pertinence is infinite, because, like God, "conjecture" (*D*, fragment, 404), it is manifestly existential, sociologically, ecologically urgent and immediate. No line of Hugo is written for an out-of-this-world. The experience of the divine is the experience, now, of "light" and love (*D*, 348), the placing in parentheses of fear—in a sense a giving of oneself to the pure divineness of just being, in confidence. "Are you afraid then to see the world go along by itself?" he asks in "Les Voix du seuil" ("Voices of the Threshold," *D*, 371): the ineffable "runs" itself, we need merely to trust to being, difficult as the first step may seem. Our theorizing upon the divine constructs, he argues, no more than "smoke" (*D*, 360) that tends to screen the manifest, shroud the blatancy of spontaneous recognition. "No one has the alpha, no one the omega," he proclaims; the name of "God" is unnamable, "vast, unheard of, refractory" (*D*, 364). "God," like *Dieu*, like all being, is (in) constant creation, becoming, expansion: it, they, remain unfinished, beyond "conclusion," specific end, being already, for Hugo, pure moving purpose, meaning, direction, indecipherable yet revealed *sens*. The ninth, unwritten part of "Solitudines coeli," from *Dieu*, bears merely a parenthetical, provisional title: "[Ce qui n'a pas encore de nom. Deus]" ("[That Which has yet no name. Deus]," *D*, 348). The divine is an ever-unfinished, ever-(self-) fulfilling creation for this most pragmatically, terrestrially focused of visionaries, Hugo.

Writing, poetic creation, may be, for Hugo, consolation of the other (*OB*, 46, "Le Poète dans les révolutions" ["Poet Amidst Revolutions"]), a sacred mission pursued because sacredness has been understood and assumed (*OB*, 136, "À M. Alphonse de L." ["To Mr. Alphonse de L."]), a "magic reflection," in the mind and heart, of all that is, and thus is divine (*LO*, 166–67, "Rêverie"), a speaking whose effect is not unlike that of "prayer," both finite and infinite (*FA*, 312, "La Prière pour tous" ["Prayer for All"]). Perhaps above all, however, Hugo's writing centers itself upon a consciousness of, and a will to, (self-)transformation, the possibility of (self-) transfiguration, now, here, in privacy, for a privacy, but aware of its effect upon the collectivity. Thus is his seeing of "constellations" in a beggar's sackcloth an at once resolute and intuitive leap beyond the socioeconomics of being (*C*, 317, "Le Mendiant" ["The Beggar"]); thus, when speaking of a young girl washing "des torchons radieux" in the Marne, does Hugo pierce through materiality to the exquisite heart of *présence* (*CR*, 73, "Choses écrites à Créteil" ["Things Written at Créteil"]); thus can he tell of "the pure kiss of the Ideal," falling from some deathly Baudelairean *inconnu* (*C*, 417, "À celle qui est voilée" ["To the Woman Veiled"]); thus can he eerily sense "that in all places, life/Dissolves evil, mourning, winter, night, envy" (*C*, 408, "Eclaircie" ["Clearing"]). Where disintegration and ruin seem to risk prevailing, apotheosis and deeply symbolic reaffirmation emerge, the satanic is reintegrated, the paradox of exchange, transfiguration, and strange unity is enacted. The "great blessing" upon everything, which "Les Mages" evokes, improbably imposes its never-lost discourse, occasioning a (psychological, affective) mutation and illumination of our "most desperate uglinesses" (*C*, 486, "Ce que dit la bouche d'ombre").

The poetics of transfiguration is thus founded upon the tripartite logic of ever-available possibility, of implacable progress, of will. "This vision," Hugo writes in "La Vision d'où est sorti ce livre," the liminal text of *La Légende des siécles*, "begun in night, ended in glowing light" (*LS1*, 68). Transfiguration is essentially synonymous with being—"le grand souffle vivant, ce transfigura-teur" ("the great living breath, the transformer"), he declares in "Le Satyre" (*LS2*, 19)—but, as elsewhere too, it thrives and accelerates on our assumption of its (nonabusive) power. Hence Hugo's encouragement to self-transfiguration—a process that demonstrates the utter privacy and immanent immediacy of its simple, unpretentious practice. "Come!", he urges, "you were good one day, be forever happy./Enter, transfigured" (*LS1*, 369, "Sultan Mourad"); and later in *La Légende des siècles* we are delightfully pressed to take upon ourselves our soul-ness, our improbability, our buoyancy, our intrinsic lovingness. "Transfigure yourself! go on! be more and more your soul!" he smilingly challenges (*LS2*, 21, "Le Satyre"). One moment of love transforms all, unblocks all, as "Sultan Mourad" suggests (*LS1*, 369); "all is saved!"(*LS2*, 394, "Plein ciel") may be a statement about eternal being in Hugo, but it is also temporally relevant to the extent that action is always crucial, in an existentialist manner.

The poetics of transfiguration, moreover, while stressing our soul-ness, thus remains anchored in corporality, yet a corporality sensing its available sublimation. The contradiction of oppositions and polarities, which Hugo can vaguely lament, as in "Fiat voluntas" from *Les Rayons et les ombres* (*Rays and Shadows*)—for he knows well the difficulty of transfiguration—is ultimately absorbed by the discourse of apotheosis and transfiguration, a discourse affirming unity, availability, paradox, the mystery of an "ascension" that may even at times feel like a "fall" (*AT*, 374, "Le Deuil"). "Vivify and transform," as we are told in *Dieu* (*D*, 375), is an imperative for all seasons, all dimensions of being; and it is an imperative lying deep within us, for transfiguration and vital breath are synonymous.

Shadow and Light

"Et toute l'ombre avec tout le rayonnement" ("And all the shadow with all the radiance"), Hugo writes in "Le Firmament est plein . . ." ("The Firmament is Full") from *Les Contemplations* (*C*, 24): perception of a world of antitheses, physical, symbolical, yet wherein the notion persists of a coexistence (*avec* ["with"]), a juxtaposition, and an interpenetration, a logic of synthesis. The separation of the world, indeed the universe, into shadow and light, leads to a search for the divided but inevitably joined meaning of such binary opposites. "I sought to know, trembling, pale, bedazzled," he records in another poem from *Les Contemplations*, "whether No says the shadow to the star that says Yes" (*C*, 296, "Ecrit en 1846"). To some degree Hugo may be said to inherit the symbolic emotional weight of categories in his initial projection of such division: designation is already meaning, answer to his search—though perhaps not a final answer, as we shall see.

Initially, then, light and shadow exist because polarities, categories, seem natural, given, ineluctable: yes and no, up and down, fullness and emptiness. "Antithesis everywhere! one just has to accept it," he notes in *L'Art d'être grand-père* (*AGP*, 605, "Encore Dieu, mais avec des restrictions" ["Again God, but with Restrictions"]). Shadow becomes negation, or diminishment, imperfection, obstacle, nonideality: the "night of fate," the "shadow of duty" (*C*, 285, "À Aug. V." ["To Aug. V."]), "Satan [as] the night of God" (*D*, fragment, 429), "everything [that] is not smile and light" (*CC*, 352). "Human is shadow," he will go so far as to say in *La Légende des siècles* (*LS2*, 161, "Il faut boire et frapper la terre . . ." ["One Should Drink and Strike the Earth . . ."]); shadow is ours, it is natural and it is linked to doubt, he confirms in *Les Voix intérieures* (*Inner Voices*, *VI*, 406). Conversely, in this initial adherence to the seemingly given—but embraced, assumed, continuingly projected—symbolic of category and opposition, light is godly, truthful, God is radiation and illumination (*RO*, 424); poetry's movement is "towards light faithful to all,/Towards innocence, and the azure!" (*VI*, 374). The imagination, followed closely by the emotions, leaps to the dichotomies of "sky" and "mud" (*RO*, 432), existential shadowiness and luminous after-death experience (*RO*, 450), and imposes everywhere their apparently absolute reign.

This said, however, it is essential to observe the degree to which Hugo's poetics undercuts and deconstructs its own factors of categorical antithesis. Various tactics and perceptions are involved, and culminate in a much transformed conception of shadow and light—and, in consequence, of being itself. On the one hand, as in "Aimons toujours! aimons encore! ("Let Us Love Always! Let Us Love Once More!") from *Les Contemplations*, shadow, however human, is understood in its full preciousness, its irreplaceableness: the shadow of the one loved, "cast upon my book/When you lean across me" (*C*, 122, "Aimons toujours . . ."). Shadow, with its "sacred *pudeur*," may suddenly become a place of refuge for the dreamer (*AT*, 412); it may offer peace, as light offers joy, among the things of the countryside (*AT*, 433, "À Vianden" ["At Vianden"]). On the other hand, in accordance with Hugo's discourse of progress and oceanity, shadow gives way, can yield up its seeming fixity, become relative, superseded by greater, vaster discourses. "Shadow passes, love remains," he notes in *La Légende des siècles* (*LS2*, 181, "L'Océan"); it is from "frightful shadow" that "glory" emerges (*LS2*, 38, "Les Chutes"); the "fatal black work will whiten by degree," he affirms in *L'Année terrible* (*AT*, 448, "Flux et reflux" ["Ebb and Flow"]); shadow again assumes a holiness and deep paradoxical potential for its otherness in that, as in the beautiful "Mariée et mere" ("Married and Mother"), "il est dans l'ombre sainte un ciel vierge où se lève/Pour on ne sait quels yeux on ne sait quel soleil" ("there is in holy shadow a virgin sky where rises/For what eyes I know not, I know not what sun," *AGP*, 673).

To some extent, such perceptions are marked by a movement from dark and shadow to light that implies reintegration, a recovery of origin, of source—of that very force which casts shadows by virtue of its primordial luminous intensity. "And this dreadful place is shadow-filled," Hugo thus observes in *Les Contemplations*, "because of God's greatness" (*C*, 397). Shadow, like Satan, is locked into an original transcendent discourse of divine light: reunification, re-fusion, is thus always implicit. What Hugo, in his bracketed subtitle to Part 2 of *Solitudines coeli*, from *Dieu*, calls "*le manichéisme. Duplex*" ("*Manichaeism. Duplex*") thus reveals itself capable of imaginative synthesis, either progressive or, as it were, instantaneous—the kind of realization that occurs in *La Légende des siècles*, where "Shadow is [known to be] a Soul," integral, innocent, a perceptual-affective form as living, as divine, as experiential, as that of "light" itself (*LS2*, 272, "Les Enterrements civils" ["Civil Burials"]). In this optic, not only may shadow move to light in a logic of continuous dawning and luminous transformation or reintegration ("N'insultez jamais une femme qui tombe" ["Never Insult a Woman Fallen"], *CC*, 343, or "À propos de la loi dite . . ."; ["About the Law of . . ."], *AGP*, 669), but shadow is known to be light in a somehow distorted, even misperceived form.

Thus can Hugo declare, in "Je lisais. Que lisais-je? . . ." from *Les Contemplations*, that "all is full of daylight, even night" (*C*, 162). "Ténèbres et rayons/Affirment à la fois" ("Gloom and lightrays/Both give affirmation," *C*, 430, "Voyage de nuit"). Gloom and shadow are, ultimately, not nonbeing, diminished, demoniac; they, too, are caught in the global ontic affirmation that is, or can be, ours. The "divine enigma" of which Hugo speaks is simultaneously lighted and shaded, *nuit* and *clarté* (*LS2*, 193, "Le Temple"), but this seeming polarization does not need to carry with it symbolic exclusion, affective paralysis, and many of Hugo's poems thus reverse the poles or operate a paradoxical fusion of some kind. Léopoldine's death can thus transcendently "fill . . . /My entire destiny with the light/Of [her] coffin" (*C*, 459, "En frappant à une porte" ["Knocking at a Door"]). God may become a "black cloud," one of the infinite "Voices of the threshold" (*D*, 372); "the world," we are told in *Les Chants du crépuscule*, "is half-covered in a shadow wherein all is light" (*CC*, 322, "Prélude"); shadow does not necessarily retreat into itself but can be filled with the "flaring of the wise," as Hugo writes in "Persévérance" from *L'Art d'être grand-père* (*AGP*, 685). Such a discourse of meeting, of merging, of nonpolarized ontology is, ultimately, at the heart of all Hugolian antitheses, founding a poetics of recuperation in oneness, of combination, collectivity, collaboration in difference. "Day plunges to the darkest of the abyss, seeking/Shadow," the beautiful "Eclaircie" asserts, "and kisses its brow beneath the somber, haggard water./All is gentle, calm, happy, soothed; God gazes on" (*C*, 408–409). The logic of shadow and light is—can be if we will it, perceive it willfully—a logic of love, a logic of fine distinction caught within a transcendence of thought and emotion.

Contemplation, Legend, Vision

The 1831 preface to *Les Feuilles d'automne* speaks of the collection as the textual concretization of "a melancholy and resigned gaze, cast here and there upon what is, above all upon what has been" (*FA*, 188). Poetry is a verbalized gaze cast upon being, but a gaze manifestly and consciously steeped in emotion, in experiential tone. If, here, Hugo's gaze seems dulled and languishing, it does not affect its essential purpose and action: it is not just that emotions may change and "contemplation fills my heart with love," as he writes in "Aux arbres" (*C*, 199), for ultimately all emotion is attention, projection, an embrace of trees that thrill or a joining of other phenomena at other moments that sadden. *Les Contemplations* themselves might have been titled, Hugo tells us in the 1856 preface, "les Mémoires d'une âme" (*C*, 11), the poetically chronicled memoirs of the shifting emotions, thoughts and beliefs of a soul. These memoirs are "serene," no doubt because poeticized, written up at an aesthetic distance—the poet, Hugo often notes, "contemplates, serene, the ideal and the beautiful," even in a poem entitled "Melancholia" (*C*, 144)—and yet they are curiously enthused, ecstatic, intoxicated. "Ma contemplation," he writes in a very Baudelairean line in *L'Art d'être grand-père*, "mon parfum, mon ivresse" ("My contemplation, my perfume, my intoxication," *AGP*, 622, "Ma Jeanne, dont je suis . . ."). Poetic contemplation thus maintains, in the midst even of dire adversity, a reflective and aesthetic tranquillity—"the contemplator, sad and bruised, but serene" (*C*, 498)—and a zest and ardor of the spirit.

Contemplation can be so buoying and reinvigorating because, as Hugo suggests in the superb "Magnitudo parvi," its splendor derives from a fusion of dream and reality, a fusion whose logic applies equally to matter and word. Contemplation produces both "dreamed world! [and] real ideality!" he exclaims (*C*, 213, "Magnitudo parvi"). "Soleils couchants" ("Sunsets"), from *Les Feuilles d'automne* (*FA*, 298–304), is overtly predicated upon this poetics, but we realize, further, that contemplation is not just the gazing upon and recording of the multitudinous phenomena of being, here clouds passing in their endlessly changing form; nor is it just ensuing mental and emotional transmutation matching the metamorphoses of externality; nor just poetic, textual metaphorization modeled upon, or even projecting, metamorphoses of mind or matter. Contemplation, for Hugo, goes further; it dips into its deep etymology: it is con-templ-ation, action-with mind, words, and matter in the temple, the templum, the sacred place of all that is, of all possibility, of all creation. Contemplation not so much exceeds plain physical seeing, or imagination, "vision" or poiesis, poetic creation matching, perhaps simultaneous and synonymous with, createdness; rather does it incorporate them all into an action and a (place of) consciousness cherishing the strange mystery of all modes and perceptions of being. "The contemplation that is his life," as Hugo writes in *Les Rayons et les ombres* (*RO*, 418), is a gazing-glimpsing-seeing-feeling-thinking-meditating-intuiting-envisioning action, coextensive with life itself, personal yet not narcissistic, a kind of *magnificat* à la Guillevic, sung by the senses and the mind, the spirit and the writing hand—a song of adoration of the divineness of being's forms and channels, as "Tristesse d'Olympio" ("Sadness of Olympio") hints (*RO*, 451).

The logics of contemplation, legend, and vision are thus intertwined. The prefatory poem of *La Légende des siècles*, "La Vision d'où est sorti ce livre," sketches out a linked poetics of observation, imagination, and socio-ethical and spiritual visionariness. The vast legend of human evolution recounted is thus predicated upon the "contemplation" of "chains, voluptuousnesses, evils,/Death, avatars, metempsychoses/And ... /Satan, the poacher of God's forest" (*LS1*, 67). The poetics of legend is thus anchored in the physical and the corporeal, circumstances and event; legend chronicles and records, it is narration and bio-graphy. It tells the story of war cries, pirates' adventures, battles, "the nun's legend" (*OB*, 317–27), just as it captures the movement of clouds, the shape of hills, the stirrings of insects, the sounds of unnameable birds. But legend goes further than mere documentation, just as Balzac or Flaubert cannot rely upon a poetics of strict mimesis and reproduction; their worlds, like Hugo's, turn to invention, imagination. For legend joins contemplation, and history is always beyond history in Hugo's work, no matter how remarkably evocative the stunning descriptive-narrative specificity of his lexicon may be. But then the intuited truths of myth, romance, fable, gest—whether in *Les Orientales* or *Les Châtiments*, *La Légende des siècles* or *Dieu*—are absolutely as valid as those of what we term history, and no less "conjectural," as he affirms in the 1857 preface to the first series of poems for *La Légende des siècles* (*LS1*, 60). The logic of Hugolian legend is the logic of the contemplation of being's forms, movements, "progress." This contemplation, even if "fictional" in its written mode, involves no "fabrication" (*LS1*, 61), but invents, poetically sees and sings, the authenticity of existential unfolding that is everywhere—and nowhere if not within each living consciousness, now. *Les Rayons et les ombres* offers, as Hugo himself stresses, a vast oceanic production of some of the infinite forms of legendary, poetic creativity; it is a collection that is a part of "the great mysterious epic a song of which lies within each of us" (*RO*, 419, Preface). Any real poet, he feels, "should contain the sum of ideas of his time": ideas, not facts, for history is legend, a structuring, and here an all the more creative structuring, an assemblage of the notions, emotions, perceptions, and beliefs of our reading (*legenda, legere*) of the world, of our being.

Such an immense narrative enterprise implies, then, not merely a retelling of the documentable, but an exceeding of the sensory, the strictly rational, the banally scientific—a plunging into the unlimited from which the finite emerges, an adventure that is psychic and psychological more than it is systematically, constrainedly intellectual. Like Rimbaud's—Rimbaud was to feel not enough, though he is much closer to Hugo than to Baudelaire—Hugo's work operates a simultaneously "conscious" and "unconscious" penetration of being, *voyance* or poetic seeing occurring for both poets at that Reverdyan intersection of dream and reality—or of "adventure and order," as Apollinaire terms it. Universal being, Hugo maintains as early as "Le Poète," from *Odes et ballades,* is attained to by virtue of the poet's "awesome vigil, within his holy visions" (*OB*, 173). Contemplation and poetic, "legendary" truth demands "eyes [that] plung[e] further than the real world," as he writes in "Mazeppa" from *Les Orientales* (*LO,* 160). But their seeing is an act fusing the gains of inner and outer sight, "vision" and "vigil," giving to the real a depth and perspective, essentially psychological and spiritual, that platitudinous visual recording cannot provide. Hugo's injunction in "Pan" to "everywhere . . . /everywhere . . . /go, see, sing" (*FA*, 326) encourages the respect and honoring of our deep poetic impulse; to see is to be a seer and a creator, if we so will it. It means *believing* (*FA*, 207, "Ce qu'on entend sur la montagne" ["What is Heard upon the Mountain"]), as did Rimbaud in "Le Bateau ivre," in what is seen, its reality and its sublimity, its immediacy and its "future"—perhaps, as so often in *Les Châtiments,* the shabbiness of the observed and the felt certainty of the visionary. The poet, like Phtos gazing into the abyss, "voit les vérités qui sont les visions" ("sees the truths that are visions," *LS1*, 129, "Le Titan"), giving back to banality or torment its ontic splendor, its meaning, restoring to consciousness its multidimensional quality, its vast, perhaps infinite, capacity for communication, dialogue, interconnection (*C*, 462, "Ce que dit la bouche d'ombre").

Hugolian vision, then, is not just a question of peering, in unilinear fashion, into a future, a "Vingtième siècle" ("Twentieth Century," *LS2*, 377–95), a finally devolved "progress"; its journeys may begin with history and physical phenomena, but they quickly become affective, psychic, journeys of the soul. "L'âme, invincible voyante" ("The Soul, invincible seer"), Hugo writes in "Shakespeare" (*LS2*, 129), yet understanding that all consciousness is truth and all truth consciousness, or soul-ness. For truth itself, he stressses in "La Vérité" ("Truth"), is at once "la regardée et la voyante énorme" ("that looked upon and the vast seer," *LS2*, 247). In this way, seeing or vision(ariness) and what is seen are interlocked—one soul consciousness gazing into another. Hugolian vision is above all a realization of that infinite network of being, meaning, and consciousness of which his own seeing soul is but a fragment—a fragment, nonetheless, of profound and curiously infinite proportions. When Hugo writes in "L'Âme à la poursuite du vrai" ("The Soul in Pursuit of the True"), from *L'Art d'être grand-père*, "I shall go off in the dark chariots/Of dream and vision" (*AGP*, 691), we can thus readily conjure up the great visionary works of *La Fin de Satan* and *Dieu*. But we should not forget the *equally* visionary status of his humble, quotidian, seemingly insignificant, idling gaze cast upon a leaf, an insect, a faint sound, a trembling color. Here, too, vision dwells, great vision, if multidimensional consciousness inhabits the gazing eye, become soul. Vision implies an assumption of a divineness within the gazer; such a gazer, like God, "looks, and that is all. Seeing is enough for the sublime" (*D*, 344).

Conceptions and Means

Faced with a poetic oeuvre as vast as Hugo's, I have opted for a number of itemized observations pinpointing important, broad features of his overall poetics, his conception of the poetic act and its feasibility, followed by a necessarily telescoped series of remarks more strictly pertinent to formal means.

The poetics of Hugo is multiple in its conceptual play, and 1. despite his insistence at times upon the aesthetic dimension of writing, tends— a crucial "initial" position, as his 1822 preface to the *Odes et ballades* shows—to privilege less 'the form of ideas [than] the ideas themselves, poetry [being] everything that is intimate in everything" (*OB*, 20): ideas, thoughts, shifting, personal yet symbolizing themselves in things/words, are intrinsically poetic; form follows thought, but it is the poetry of the creation of ideational symbols that fascinates Hugo from the outset, not the niceties of technique, poetic exteriority, the rhetoric of formal means. Hugo's poetics is 2. focused upon a double, but linked sense of divineness: on the one hand, poetic speech is deemed intrinsically "divine," multidimensional (*OB*, 32, 1824 Preface) both because, as Hugo says in *Les Contemplations*, "Dieu dictait, j'écrivais" ("God dictated, I wrote," *C*, 488, "À celle qui est restée en France") and because all that exists, with which poetry is intimately bound up, is equally divine in its essence and "encodement" (*RO*, 418, 1840 Preface). On the other hand, poetry itself redivinizes flagging human consciousness, reintroduces the metaphysical into a physicality that appears and threatens to prevail. Hugo's is thus a poetics of the restoration of the divine soulness in all, despite all (appearance) (*RO*, 418, 1840 Preface).

As so many of Hugo's prefaces and poems insist, his poetics is 3. one of broad and ubiquitous liberation: the principle is related to the process of redivinization just mentioned (a freeing of our thought and spirit from strict physical encasement), but in fact extends to all matters. Classification of poems generically is thus of little importance, he will affirm in his preface of 1826 to the *Odes et ballades.* Transcendent values such as truth and beauty render such distinctions interesting but rather humdrum, and the "dramatic" and the "lyrical" know no formal, stylistic bounds (*OB*, 33). Besides, if order exists, it flows from a logic, a poetics, of freedom and choice (*OB*, 35), all great art remaining beyond system, fixing, reduction (see February 1829 Preface to *Les Orientales, LO*, 26). The "independence" that Hugo claims for literature, while not excluding that critical passion Baudelaire recommended—writing and art are based upon affinity, attraction—nevertheless imposes upon the writer a detachment—"nul engagement, nulle chaîne" ("no commitment, no chain"), he declares in *Les Rayons et les ombres* (*RO*, 418)—which places his action at that same intersection Michel Deguy speaks of: "attaché/arraché." This constitutes an intersection where purpose and liberty meet, where a distance may be taken even from one's own emotions in this juggling of transcendent, com-passion-ate, and personal, local urgencies. This, in turn, may be seen in the light of 4. a poetics of infinite poetic pertinence and concern: "All is subject-matter," he notes in the January 1829 preface to *Les Orientales*, "All is within art's demesne; all is free to dwell in poetry" (*LO*, 19). Poetry embraces, but in its preparedness to embrace all, it sets up a poetics of intrinsic innocence and equivalence guaranteed by detachment. Poetry thus tends, in multiplying indefinitely its subject-matter, to argue all cases. Oceanity is the poetics, the deep meaning of all—despite all reservations; it recuperates, as will Baudelaire and Rimbaud, Apollinaire and Perse in their own ways. The logic of ubiquitousness and simultaneity is a logic giving back to the banal, the insignificant, the ugly, the terrible, their inherent poeticalness, the caress of a divineness we might have thought had vacated them. *La Fin de Satan* is generated by such a poetics; *Les Châtiments* moves toward its implementation; mere domestic flies bask in its glory (*RO*, 459, "Ecrit sur le tombeau . . ." ["Written Upon the Tomb . . ."]).

Growing out of this is what I shall term 5. a poetics of nonfixity of designation, and therefore of inner meaning. Thus can the Middle Ages be deemed "modern," our notion of "antiquity" be transferred easily to the Orient (*LO*, 24). Such a poetics is one of living, ever-rethought, ever-contemporary pertinence (*VI*, 368). This sensitivity to the freedom of our conceptualization of existence and reality places us at the heart of a paradox. Hugo's 6. poetics of essential nondidacticism is simultaneously one of civilizing poetic function. To enlighten those that doubt, as he writes in *Les Contemplations* (*C*, 80, "Il faut que le poète . . ."), is never to inculcate, to indoctrinate. Illumination remains open, inspirational, mystical or predicated upon high, uncentered truth, rather than dogma, ideology, unsupple morality. To record and "teach," as *Les Voix intérieures* has it (*VI*, 368, 1837 Preface), is not, again, to imprison. The dreamed art of that volume, "which delights, . . . which civilizes" (*VI*, 407), merely fosters meditation in the other, divine inspiration—a remembrance of the divine which is infinite, both shadow and light. Certainly, 7. a poetics of affront, challenge, confrontation and revolt may be espoused, as in *Les Châtiments*, but it is doubled from the outset by a logic of sharing, of representation, of emblematic resistance à la Char, as "Au moment de rentrer en France" ("At the Time of Returning to France") makes clear (*LCH*, 16). Such a poetics only seems to hinge upon flat revenge; its ambition transcends egoism and all individuality—or rather sees in the injustice meted out to many, though one would do, sufficient cause for response. This, then, is a poetics of the improbable but very real power of poetry itself, of all voice raised in purity and sincerity. For, as "Caeruleum mare," from *Les Rayons et les ombres*, points out, any poetics of "problem"—whether political, socioeconomic, or ethical, spiritual—is simultaneously a poetics of eternity, of the transcendence of problem, if we can rise to this perception within ourselves (and symbolizable without) (*RO*, 459). All confrontation demands benevolence, gentleness, and compassion in Hugo's poetic discourse—no matter what the odds (*RO*, 466, "Sagesse").

Two or three clusters of significant elements remain to be specified. The first of these groups together 8. Hugo's omnipresent poetics of truth, of nonexaggeration—"That is what he has done," we read in "Le Parti du crime" from *Les Châtiments*, "I exaggerate nothing" (*LCH*, 248), a poetics of noninflation, scrupulous reason and balance, yet in accord both with the logic of invention, fiction, vision, and that of passion and intervention; 9. Hugo's finely held equilibrium—equivalence even—of "dream" and "study," imagination and observation, subjectivity and objectivity. "There is moreover," he writes in *Les Rayons et les ombres*, "no incompatibility between the exact and the poetic" (*RO*, 420); and 10. that telling poetics of laughter, noninflating, not so much deflating as capable of maintaining emotional balance and spiritual buoyancy. Hugo's poem, "À André Chénier" (*C*, 25), elaborates this crucial logic of ease, familiarity, unprecious gusto that allows poetry to laugh as easily as it may cry. Laughter is as true, as precise, as proper, as poetic as all else; to accept it is to remain in the way of insight, to refuse it is to block the blossoming fullness of our inner being.

The second cluster of factors would have us 11. see the poetic act as that kind of *phalène* of which Deguy speaks: a going-forth-into-the-world based upon fascination with and adoration of our boundless external symbols—trees, petals, bees, dust, warm evening haze—and yet a world, *une terre* as Bonnefoy would say, of rich interiority to which, too, our listening must go (*C*, 21, "Le poète s'en va . . ." ["The Poet Goes Off . . ."]). Such a poetics of going forth without and within, of "search" at once physical, sensual, and psychic, psychological (*CC*, 348), depends upon Bonnefidian will or Reverdyan, Frénaldian "effort" (*VI*, 369), but it fuses rapidly with 12. a poetics of passage, of becoming—poetry, as Hugo's epigraph to *Dieu* indicates, that offers a moving forth through mind and matter, but a "return to God," a shifting, flickering illumination of what we can achieve in sight and vision, and that is all. A divine and simple *summum*, reabsorbed by the greater realities in which we participate. Furthermore, this poetics of change slips into 13. a not dissimilar logic of broad poetic exchange. The poetics of search and *phalène* implies ceaseless modification of discovery and revelation, and its textual translation, its publication, its becoming-public, equally opens up poetry, exposes it to further inner and outer journeying, further, near-infinite ex-change, taking and giving out again, incessant, living *devenir*. When Hugo urges: "take this book and make of it a divine psalm" (*C*, 497, "À celle qui est restée en France"), he fosters a deep consciousness of textual liberation via the plurivalence, the infinity of readings constantly repossibilizing the poem, yielding up its divine creative exchange. Moreover, such an insistence always pushes the Hugolian conception of poetry to 14. a position beyond aesthetic dalliance. The "horse" of poetry, in "Au Cheval," need feel no compulsion to "linger with beauty" per se (*CR*, 203). Poetry is the intrinsic creative energy in all reality, its *poiein*, and thus leaps conventional niceties, even strict verbality. "Oh fields, what a verse is the periwinkle!/What a stanza is the eagle, oh skies," Hugo writes in "Sagesse." Poetry transcends language, opts for any symbolism that speaks to the heart and the soul of the boundless poeticity of all of (our) being.

Finally, the third cluster may be said to generate a poetics of general purpose, perceptible in everything, in all antithesis, all contradiction, all pain, all apparent gratuitousness. The brief "À L." ("To L.") from *Les Rayons et les ombres* (*RO*, 459) eloquently voices such a position, just as "Fonction du poète" ("Function of the Poet") from the same volume (*RO*, 421–24) imposes royally an umbrella logic of love, of com-prehension, of the infinite directionality of the soul, of the utopian power of thought, of the inalienable meaning of poetic listening and speaking.

Hugo

It would be possible to write very many pages on the formal means espoused in Hugo's immense and shifting oeuvre. If a few compact observations will have to suffice, it can be appreciated at least, from the above, that Hugo himself, despite occasional insistence, rides freely and easily upon a technical and stylistic genius second to none, preferring questions of high vision and purpose to matters of form and textual detail. This said, let me race through the bare bones of certain points whose examination, in the light of my more extensive analyses devoted to Lamartine, Vigny, Baudelaire, and others, would yield a good deal of fruit: 1. modal or generic questions can interest Hugo, who is eminently conscious of their subtleties. The ode may thus be "any purely religious inspiration, any purely antique study, any translation of a contemporary event or of a personal impression" (*OB*, 32, 1826 Preface), whereas the ballade may range from "tableaus, dreams, scenes, accounts [to] superstitions, legends, popular traditions" (*OB*, 32). Almost infinite modal patterns are practiced: melodies, *musiques*, dialogues, micro-theater, grouped "idylls," vast visionary texts with all manner of components and surprising, improbable juxtapositions, even a prose-poem; 2. globally, transgeneric, transmodal factors may be said to transcend any effort of banal limitation. Hugo's modal unity stems from its persistent diversity, from a generic, formal and "atmospheric" mobility that becomes even more vertiginous if one takes account of those often vast subtexts swarming with deletions, additions, endless textual possibilities, the variants and fragments that the still ongoing editing of Hugo's work staggeringly reveals; 3. stanzaic and overall poem structure may demonstrate great variations, while retaining a broad constancy characteristic of the verse poetry of the entire century. Thus *Odes et ballades* often centers upon 4-line, 6-line, 8-line, and 10-line stanzas, with 6 and 10 dominating and rare 12-line and 20-line structures, even rare sonnets. And yet 5-line and 7-line stanzas are common, the former very prevalent, with specific forms focused upon exclusively or imbricated with complementary structures. Length of poem, too, is quite variable, though rarely less than 30 lines and rarely in excess of 160. A collection such as *L'Art d'être grand-père*, however, opts for largely different formulas: many poems of medium length (60 lines) or more, with varying stanzaic structures such as continuous blocks of free, intuitive, personally disciplined organization such as 17+9+6+16 ("L'Exilé satisfait,"

AGP, 578–79) or 28+7+1+40 ("Georges et Jeanne," *AGP*, 581–83); quatrains forming texts of medium length or quatrains in combination: (4+2)×9 ("Choses du soir" ["Evening Things"], *AGP*, 594–95), 1+(4×7) 1 ("Ora, ama," *AGP*, 643–44); traditional 10-line stanzas (×4 up to ×30), 6-line stanzas (×5, ×9, ×10); a plain 8-line poem, a dramatized, delicately articulated 8-line text complete with "stage" directions ("Ce que dit le public" ["What the Public Says"], *AGP*, 601–602); a single-structure sonnet; 5-line stanzas (×7), 9-line stanzas (×2, ×9); and so on; 4. Hugolian meter, like stanzaic structure, is in a sense remarkably supple, spontaneously generated, but always in traditional molds to the extent that all disciplined, systematized rhythmic structure depends upon a principle of repetition, beat, established and manifest number: the ever-present alexandrine, the commonly used 6- and 8-syllable structures, the infrequent 10-syllable line; and the quite widespread, pre-Verlainean *impairs*, especially the 7-syllable line, but also the 3-, 5-, and 9-syllable rhythms, usually applied consistently, but at times in combinations (7+4, for example).

Added to these strategies and liberating them, opening them up to their innermost rhythmic elasticity, without ever destroying syntactical stability, are Hugo's wonderful uses of enjambments, of *coupes*, of crisp punctuation, of tripartite alexandrine meter, of anaphora, accumulation, crescendo and descrescendo, sudden release or stoppage, internal and end-rhyme and so on; 5. rhyme in Hugo's poetry as a whole again displays immense variety and yet disciplined constancy. All imaginable mathematical interlacings may be applied in a given volume, though the great, swelling swaths of alexandrine verse that can be found throughout his oeuvre, from *La Légende des siècles* to *Dieu*, almost irresistibly opt for the *rimes plates* of Lamartine's *Jocelyn* or Rimbaud's "Les Poètes de sept ans." Of course, Hugo's rhymes can be as surprising as Laforgue's, as charming or as aggressive as Baudelaire's; they can be "rich" or barely "sufficient," boldly repetitive or homonymic, studied or off-handed, frequently lexically astonishing. His claim to have "taken and demolished the Bastille of rhymes" (*C*, 33) is thus legitimate in the sense of a great liberation of and plunging into the many resources of rhyming strategy; but it implies no demolition giving way to the free verse of the minor *symbolistes*, or the ampler *verset* of Claudel and Perse, or, again, prose *consciously* assumed as poetry.) I stress the need for that deliberate redefinition of poetic means and mode, for it would not be unreasonable to deem much of Hugo's novelistic work as generically transgressive—as with, say, a Hélène Cixous, a Chantal Chawaf, or even a Marguerite Duras of our time; 6. Hugo speaks, also in *Les Contemplations*, of placing a "red cap upon the old dictionary" whose words he has thrust into "equality" and "freedom" as they suddenly are forced to reach their "majority," their intrinsic maturity (*C*, 31, "Réponse à un acte d'accusation"). Such a liberation demands a truly unsurpassed lexical mastery, a "swallowing" of the dictionary as Baudelaire writes, but a digestion, too, a com-prehension, a penetration of both the semantic specifics of language and its deep, swirling symbolic logic. Hugolian lexicon does not depend upon Laforguean neologism ("a sad resource for impotence," *OB*, 36); it offers precision of observation and evocation as well as quick, though never phantasmagorical, surrealist metaphorical pertinence, and thus brushes aside the "spirals" of periphrasis à la Chénier, or of the early Lamartine and Vigny; it adores the clash and juxtaposition of seeming opposites, though such very linkings often question difference and imply greater transcendent categories; its quality may verge on the simple, the transparent, only to veer toward thundering power, great range, or technicality, but it is never really arcane or esoteric, and in this one can see affinities with Balzac, Flaubert, and Zola: context and application remain clear, just as Hugo prefers "fresh" metaphors à la Petrarch (*CC*, 361) to convoluted semantic interiority. Even the great "visionary" texts manifest this lexical centering, this option for stable, coherent reference, allusion, and symbol—an option that denies neither subtlety nor depth of "seeing," moreover.

Much more could be said. It would be possible to focus, for example, upon 7. tone and register, again immensely variable in Hugo, though without either the extreme self-derision found in Frénaud or the impersonal cubist manners of Reverdy. Irony is rare, though the intensity of frontal satirical attack is common, and, always, even at the lightest, the most easeful of moments, deep seriousness is manifest, a sense of that ubiquitous poetic purpose I have spoken of. Too, 8. the structuring of individual volumes and, indeed, the entire poetic oeuvre, would yield significant insight into Hugolian scriptural tactics. The compositional logic of *Les Châtiments* is far from that of *Les Contemplations*; a volume such as *Les Voix intérieures*, whose chronology is very compact and little tampered with, is radically distinct in structural logic both from *La Lé-gende des siècles*, written over fifty years, its component texts jostled and juggled, the final collection deemed to be a "whole" rather than a series of fragments, yet held to be merely a "beginning" (*LS1*, 59), and from *Dieu*, whose "ordering" and even "intention," according to Jean Gaudon, remain fundamentally impossible to determine given its incompleteness, its massive array of accompanying fragments. Such analysis, in turn, could lead to 9. a penetration of the teeming relationships between Hugolian form and structure, and what may be termed content, the status and "reliability" of Hugolian discourse, or one might be led to focus upon the related tensions between "traditional" and "organic" form. And so on: great fields remain open to cultivation.

Thought and Love

"Ma Pensée est un monde errant dans l'infini" ("My Thought is a world wandering in the infinite"), Hugo declares in "L'Âme," and it is appropriate to circle back from matters of form to a final consideration of the role and nature of thought, and the latter's relation to love, in the poetics of "this pensive, mysterious and gentle man" as he terms himself in *Les Rayons et les ombres* (*RO*, 450). Mind, thought—consciousness, the "unconscious," spirit, soul-ness—is always at stake, always "stirring in life," as Hugo puts it in "L'Âme." Our thinking-dreaming of the real, of being, is everywhere, day and night ("Rêves"), and the link between consciousness and matter, interiority and exteriority, is intimate ("Fantômes" ["Ghosts"], *LO*, 150). Thought, as he suggests in "Mazeppo," constantly "traverses all fields of the possible," within and "without the real world," but such traversal is never inauthentic, never fatuously or idly unreal, even when pure imagination seems to be involved.

To dream, to think, is, as Hugo demonstrates in more concrete terms in "Oui, je suis le rêveur..." ("Yes, I am the Dreamer...") from *Les Contemplations*, to accompany, to be (with) the things of one's consciousness. The deep complexity of being *is* that of the infinite wanderings of thought (in its many supple forms). "Monde rêvé! idéal réel!" ("Dreamed world, real ideal!), he can exclaim (*C*, 213), *realizing* the full creative power of the mind's, the soul's, swarming production. "King," Le Cid cries out in "Le Roi défiant" ("The Wary King") from *La Légende des siècles*, "I am my cage/And I am my key" (*LS1*, 165). Thought is liberation from reality, because it can be consciousness of our continuous generation of reality. Thus may the "inner eye," as Hugo calls it in "Shakespeare" (*LS2*, 129), project the self's "trajectory" of being that is at once "ideal and real" ("Là-haut" ["Up Above"], *LS2*, 114), mental or psychic and yet also vibrantly, even materially possibilized. Is not *Les Chansons des rues et des bois* a perfect example of the logic of Hugo's *turning* of the mind to beauty, of the (senti)mental (ideal: *idéal, idéel*) *construction* of simple, innocent splendor when other, more oppressive reals could have been brought into focus only too readily?

Thought, then, as Hugo makes clear in "Dicté en présence du glacier du Rhône" ("Dictated by the Rhône Glacier," *FA*, 213–15), is free, impulsive, poetic, metamorphic. Its "dictation" is not a tyranny, but rather a teeming creative impulse or instinct within us, a free yet divine arising of ontic option within: "Au gré du divin souffle ainsi vont mes pensées" ("At the pleasure of divine breath, so go my thoughts," *FA*, 215). Thought may be gentle or "rugged" (*LCH*, 31, "Nox"), assume the force of "prayer" (*FA*, 307–324, "La Prière pour tous"); it may seek to "complete knowing by intuition" (*LS2*, 219, "La Comète" ["Comet"]), realizing the power of rationalization and egotistical focus yet sensing the beauty of its capacity to "burst into flames" (*CR*, 15, "Le Poète bat aux champs" ["The Poet Takes to the Fields"]). Linked to Hugo's conception of progress (*AGP*, 686, "Progrès"), thought embodies intrinsic individual and collective purpose (*C*, 298, "Ecrit en 1846"); thought "illuminates and shines forth" (*LCH*, 239, "Luna"); it is inner sight, psychic quest, a continuous, "bridging" expansion (*LS2*, 182, "L'Océan") of mind, heart, and soul (*LS2*, 349, "Par-dessus le marché . . ." ["Into the Bargain . . ."]). Passing through language's physical symbols (*C*, 37, "Suite"), thought clearly is not limited by the latter and always, to quote Yves Bonnefoy out of context, "exceeds the sign." The rolling stanzas centered upon the explicative logic of Hugo's *puisque*, for example, both sketch out trajectories of real, rooted consciousness, yet never contain the fullness of his, or anyone's thought, for, as Hugo reaffirms in the 1853 preface to *Les Châtiments* (*LCH*, 14), the latter is not confinable, is ever-resistantly free (in a way exceeding even the logic of *Les Châtiments*); it "signals" and then returns to its freedom, its becoming, its expansion, its inherent "pensiveness" (*LCH*, 149, "Ce que le poète disait en

1848" ["What the Poet Said in 1848"]). Thought may, then, ensnare itself, may seek specific articulation, but, to maintain its "ideality," it avoids all closed systems, breaking out from its own "cages" into the impulsiveness of a greater, perhaps infinite openness. "Méditer, c'est le grand devoir mystérieux" ("Meditation is the great mysterious duty"), Hugo writes in "À L'homme" ("To Man"), from *La Légende des siècles* (*LS2*, 187); but meditation is manifestly ongoing, consciously unfixed, though inevitably caught in a web of intimacy with its swarming objects and phenomena.

It is in the latter context that I have chosen to close my reading of Hugo by showing the degree to which thought and love embed themselves one into the other. Thought as being (with) its objects/subjects, constitutes an act of com-prehension of others, of the other, a drawing-inward and a going-toward that, Hugo recognizes, follows the logic of love. Love, he suggests in "Ama, crede" from *Les Chansons des rues et des bois*, is the first, essential step in thought's comprehension, in the experience of the other via consciousness (*CR*, 143); and in *Les Contemplations* he forthrightly maintains, "to understand is to love" (*C*, 163, "Je lisais. Que lisais-je . . . ?"). Ideal, maximally supple and infinitely open, becoming thought is synonymous with love, for Hugo, and although it involves knowing, access, it moves above and beyond the restrictive criteria and categories of judgment. Such love-thought is, indeed, a "divine sun" (*OB*, 233, "Le Nuage" ["The Cloud"]) and "the greatest of happinesses" (*OB*, 213, "À toi" ["To You"]). Such love-thought may maintain a consciousness of difference, of separate identity, while offering a sense of convergence or unity or equivalence. It is the only true need of the divine (*FA*, 320, "La Prière"), an ideal, but realizable movement from soul to soul (*LCH*, 166, "Ceux qui vivent . . ." ["Those Who Live . . ."]), utopian, Christic (*LCH*, 55, "À un martyr") yet socially practical, implementable (*LCH*, 34, "Nox"). "Ne rien haïr, mon enfant," Hugo writes in "À ma fille" ("To My Daughter"), "tout aimer,/Ou tout plaindre" ("Hate nothing, my child, love all,/or pity all," *C*, 20): com-prehension, compassion, love-thought as multitudinous (senti)mental embrace.

Curiously, too, our individual and collective "progress" via love's consciousness seems, for Hugo, to be inherent to being itself. "To live is to love," he argues in *Les Chansons des rues et des bois* (*CR*, 28, "En sortant du collège" ["Leaving College"]) and, in *Les Contemplations*, "everything," he maintains, "conjugates the verb to love" (*C*, 87, "Premier mai" ["May First"]). Effort and will may thus be deemed important, but thought and being carry within such intrinsic buoyancy. All things cry out for love—for the caressing thought of the other—(*C*, 205, "J'aime l'araignée . . ."), yet love, as consciousness, as being itself, constantly and equally flows out from and to, all that is (*C*, 298–99, "Ecrit en 1846"). Hugo thus feels, in his own contemplation of nature, "the kiss of unlimited being" (*C*, 334, "Mugitusque boum"), the infinite poetry of consciousness with its "stanzas of love" manifested as light, birds, flowers, but through the mind of the self, too (*C*, 23, "Le Firmament est plein . . ."). "Aimer. Aimer suffit" ("To Love. To love is enough"), Hugo can, not surprisingly, declare, "pas d'autre stratagème/Pour être égal aux dieux que ce mot charmant: j'aime" ("no other strategem/for equalling the gods than these delightful words: I love," *LS2*, 128, "Pétrarque"). His ultimate, indeed sole, function, as man, as poet, thus reverts constantly to love (*AGP*, 587, "Je prendrai par la main . . ."). Love generates consciousness, deepens being, gives meaning to belief (*C*, 121, "Aimons toujours . . ."). It offers "com-prehension of the universe to the soul," as he puts it in "Je respire où tu palpites" ("I Breathe Within Your Quivering"), from *Les Contemplations* (*C*, 129).

If love and consciousness are intrinsic properties of being, however, Hugo understands well the blockages that can dam up, in a given life, the channels of our ontic liberty. Thus is it that his entire poetic oeuvre articulates a long summoning to love and thought; thus is it that he urges upon us an awareness of the need to "let oneself love" (*CC*, 349, "Hier, la nuit d'été . . ." ["Yesterday, Summer's Night . . ."]), for love-thought is first and foremost freedom, a remembrance of our possibility, our option. Thus is it, too, that our assumption of (our) love—our lovableness, our lovingness—is an assumption, and an inner proof, of (our) godliness (*RO*, 447, "Mille chemins, un seul but" ["A Thousand Paths, A Single Goal"]).

· SIX ·

Mallarmé

Born in Paris on 18 March 1842, Stéphane Mallarmé was catapulted, upon the premature death of his mother and the relative indifference of his father, into a quasi-institutional childhood in Sens.
A brilliant student, though nervously failing his first attempt at the
baccalauréat in 1860, he was soon to find headier compensations in
the work of Baudelaire and Gautier, his own budding poetic genius, and the translation of Edgar Allan Poe. Escaping to England
with his wife-to-be, Maria Gerhard—they were married in 1863—
his expertise in English was at once to assure his livelihood—teaching in Tournon, Avignon, Besançon, and Paris—and frustrate his
higher ambitions. Early friendships with Des Essarts, Banville, and
the Provençal poet Mistral were to expand upon his coming in 1871
to Paris, to the Lycée Fontanes (Condorcet). Initial encounters with
Manet, Zola, Verlaine, and others were—in 1890, in part due to
Verlaine's praise of Mallarmé in his *Poètes maudits* (*Accursed Poets*)—to blossom into those remarkable *Mardis* during which the
little-published and self-doubting Mallarmé bewitched writers
such as Laforgue, Gide, Kahn, Huysmans, and Claudel. "Nobody,"
said the latter, "has spoken like Mallarmé." The year 1879, however, with the death of Mallarmé's eight-year-old son, Anatole, left
its indelible mark upon the consciousness of the poet and his conception of poetry's powers of transcendence. Earlier and subsequent stays in the countryside, at Valvins, where Mallarmé was to
die on 9 September 1898, provided solace and serenity, a kind of
refuge that his oft-anticipated early retirement for reasons of ill-
health was to provide in 1894. His later years would see him attend
or even preside over poetic banquets such as that organized to celebrate the 1892 publication of Hugo's *Toute la lyre*; interest himself
as ever in theater, ballet, and music; give densely convoluted lectures on poetry in Oxford and Cambridge; attend the première of
Jarry's *Ubu Roi* (*King Ubu*); and find himself promoted upon the

death of Verlaine, in 1896, to the esteemed rank of "Prince of Poets."

Despite the relative sparseness of Mallarmé's published oeuvre—from the early texts accepted in 1866 by the *Parnasse contemporain* (*Contemporary Parnassus*), through the incomplete *Hérodiade,* the slowly gathering *vers de circonstance*, the little cluster of prose poems and "last sonnets," to the slim but quintessential *Un coup de dés* (*A Throw of the Dice*) and the posthumous and improbably condensed *Igitur*—Mallarmé's impact upon both his contemporaries young and old, and poets as different as André Breton, Valéry, Reverdy, Claudel, Ponge, not to mention France's new novelists and whole areas of poetics, literary theory, and linguistics, has been, directly or indirectly, very considerable. Broadly, Mallarmé's poetic practice can be deemed to represent, as in *Un coup de dés*, the exploration of the extreme limits of art's capacity for autotelic, nonreferential, pure symphonicalness. It is for this reason that Yves Bonnefoy can call it the epitome of "l'ancien movement d'espoir de la poésie" ("poetry's former movement of hope")—a pinnacle of dreamed transcendence, but an impasse, and, as Mallarmé himself knew, a kind of ultimate "failure."

Azure and Impotence

It was in 1859, at the age of sixteen, that Mallarmé wrote "Cantate pour la première communion" ("Cantata for First Communion," *OC*, 3–4), whose opening stanza begins: "Anges à la robe d'azur" ("Angels azure-robed,"*OC*, 3). This very early poem, which Mallarmé made a point of preserving and even briefly annotating, shows an imagination already fired, albeit seemingly serenely, by a notion, a symbol, which, while shifting in its emotional content, will not cease to haunt and obsess: *l'azur* ("azure"). Emblem of purity, high spirituality, improbably accessible "angelicism," the azure quickly becomes associated with poetic dream and endeavor. The 1862 "Contre un poète parisien" ("Against A Parisian Poet," *OC*, 20–21) already offers us, "pailletés d'astres, fous d'azur, les grands bohèmes" ("star-spangled, azure-crazed, the great bohemians," *OC*, 21). Such a wildly glorious desire, however, is soon vitiated by accentuated feelings of difficulty of attainment, frustration, and so on. Desire is transformed into "begging" from the outset of "Le Guignon" ("Ill-luck," *OC*, 28–30); the azure mocks and "laughs" in "Renouveau" ("Renewal," *OC*, 34); all "childish" delight in what Mallarmé calls, in "Las de l'amer repos..." ("Weary From Bitter Repose...," *OC*, 35–36), "l'azur naturel" ("natural azure")—the true sky in its dazzling presence—fades into insignificance before the tantalizations of the "soul's sighing" and aspiration toward a pure poetic heaven ("Soupir" ["Sigh"], *OC*, 39). The 1864 "L'Azur" (*OC*, 37–38) provides both an intense expression of Mallarmé's continuing poetic ambition and obsession, and an indication of the extreme creative embarrassment he is experiencing. Little wonder that the dramatic poem, "Hérodiade," which Mallarmé was working on at the same time, can have its heroine declare her hatred of "the beautiful azure" (*OC*, 48) and plot a self-inhumation that, in a certain illuminated and transfigured way, will become the hallmark of Mallarmé's later poetics.

The earlier written poems of the *Poésies* (*Poems*), essentially from the *Parnasse contemporain* period, while symbolically setting forth a program of poetic accomplishment, simultaneously lament the sense of sterility Mallarmé feels, the bitterness that inhabits him, the ironic hiatus between hope and felt barrenness. *Felt* barrenness, because, if Mallarmé writes and publishes, the thematics of these poems is one of nonachievement and, to a certain degree, Mallarmé deems them to be performed *failures*. "Renouveau" (*OC*, 34) thus sings "impotence stretching in a long yawn" (*OC*, 34), a lack of poetic self-renewal only accentuated by the tiresomely reliable productivity of nature in springtime. "Las de l'amer repos..." (*OC*, 35–36) evokes "le terrain avare et froid de ma cervelle,/Fossoyeur sans pitié pour la stérilité" ("the cold, greedy terrain of my brain,/Pitiless gravedigger of sterileness," *OC*, 35); "L'Azur" (*OC*, 37–38) conjures up a piteous image of the "soul's emptiness," of an "impotent poet cursing his genius/Across a sterile desert of Pains" (*OC*, 37)—an image of self-contradiction and potential self-destruction. Mallarmé's short tripartite essay on Gautier, Baudelaire, and Banville, "Symphonie littéraire" ("Literary Symphony"), also written in 1864, speaks blatantly of the "modern Muse of impotence that has so long forbidden me the familiar treasure of Rhythms" (*OC*, 261). It seems to imply the possibility of inspired creativity under the sign of recognized poetic genius, but the essay, in addition to this acknowledgement and a certain taking-heart at perceiving such variously possible poetic brilliance, implicitly articulates that feeling of blockage that recurs whenever Mallarmé seeks to write in an exclusively personal, original mode. Recognition of existing genius and true creation are radically separate gestures in Mallarmé's mind, even though he realizes, as in his 1862 review of Emmanuel des Essarts' *Les Poésies parisiennes,* that "great minds have begun via pastiche" (*OC*, 251). Bitterness can be seemingly acute, as in "Les Fenêtres" ("Windows," *OC*, 32–33)—"ô, Moi, qui connais l'amertume" ("Oh, I who know bitterness," *OC*, 33)—and leads to sentiments of extreme deprivation, even exile. The "repose" described in "Las de l'amer repos . . ." is far from that aspired to in the achieved haven of an absolute "tombal" poeticity. "Le Guignon" (*OC*, 28–30) and "Le Sonneur" ("The Bell-ringer," *OC*, 36) even speak of that desperate resort of Nerval—as, indeed, of other seekers of the absolute, such as Jacques Vaché: suicide.

The azure, then, is a symbol of all that, poetically, aesthetically, and therefore ontologically, is at once of the utmost desirability and the utmost impossibility. It is a supreme and "serene irony," as Mallarmé writes in "L'Azur," catching the poet between an illusion and a disillusionment, both of his own making—a self-created nightmare and dream fused inextricably, unlockable only via a similar trick of the mind, a truly new "play" of thought and language that Mallarmé will be able to deem transcendent. Other ironies may emerge, just as others had been, prior to that represented in poems like "Les Fenêtres" or "L'Azur." I am thinking here of the youthful sense of the ironic (death's intrusions into childlike grace, the persistence of suffering and poverty in the world, and so on), a sense counterbalanced, however, by Mallarmé's earlier spirituality or by sheer compassion ("Sa Fosse est creusée! . . ." ["Her Grave is Dug . . ."], "Sa Fosse est fermée" ["Her Grave is Shut"], "Galanterie macabre" ["Macabre Attentiveness"], *OC*, 4–6, 7–10, 15–16). The ironies of the *Parnasse contemporain* poems, and certain others, are, however, more radically insistent. It will take all of Mallarmé's life to exorcise and transcend them, and others will sprout up in their place, not unlike those "cursed fragments of an absurd sentence" implacably popping up in the mind of the narrator of "Le Démon de l'analogie" ("The Demon of Analogy," *OC*, 272–73).

Flight, Rebirth and Tomb

Flight, escape, is a dynamic force in the elaboration of Mallarmé's early poetics and remains an essential element of his entire poetic enterprise. "Je fuis et je m'accroche à toutes les croisées/D'où l'on tourne l'épaule à la vie" ("I flee and cling to every window/At which one turns one's back on life"), he writes in "Les Fenêtres," where evasion implies, beyond its negative connotations, the desire to accept risk in the attainment of some high visionary ideal. Flight can be presented also as a desperate movement away from the piercing irony of *l'azur* itself, so that it can appear as a self-contradictory gesture; but to the extent that the azure remains a symbol of poetic dream-space and glimpsed artistic originality beyond both preexisting world *and* word, it remains, too, that remote zone of accomplishment toward which flight occurs. Of the *Parnasse contemporain* poems, "Brise marine" ("Sea Breeze," *OC*, 38) offers the most complete and insistent articulation of Mallarmé's poetics of flight, and it can profitably be thought of alongside similarly, though far from identically, inspired poems of Baudelaire ("Invitation au voyage") and Rimbaud ("Le Bateau ivre").

Mallarmé's poem, however, is far less centered upon the specifics of ultimate poetic (and ontological) accomplishment, and is thus far from any capacity to report upon the characteristics and direct feelings emanating from the experience of such dreamed possibility, while, at the same time organizing such desire around the various negations that escape entails: the negation of the familiar, the old, the conventional, the lived and felt; the negation of impotence, sterility, blockage of the self's as yet merely dreamed originality; the "negation" of the givens of human attachment and love. "Brise marine" is, however, a characteristic poem of conceived failure, of the possible nonaccomplishment of the poetic task, of its dangers as well as its exotic allurements, of its perhaps intrinsic irony. Flight, escape, is for Mallarmé an act of multiple exclusion and farewell: exclusion of "the real because vile," as he puts it in "Toute l'âme résumée . . . ("The Entire Soul Summed up . . ."; *OC*, 73), an exclusion based upon "Baudelairean" horror—"the horror of ground where plumage is caught," we read in "Le Vierge, le vivace et le bel aujourd'hui . . ." ("The Virgin, the Hardy, the Lovely Today . . ."; *OC*, 67–68)—but seeking to transcend it in more exclusively aesthetic terms: the "exclusions" of "hieroglyphics" (*OC*, 257, "Hérésies artistiques" ["Artistic Heresies"]), poetic closure, hermeticism, and, inevitably, the consequent exclusions of an art of "disdainful" rarity and "aristocracy" (*OC*, 259–60, "Hérésies artistiques"). Flight is an act of at least strong initial, if

not continuing, negation, "in oblivion of existing at a time surviv-
ing beauty," as he says at the end of his prose poem "Le
Phénomène futur" ("Future Phenomenon," *OC*, 270). Ideally, it
leads to an accomplishment, as he writes in his by now "escaped,"
retreated mode, in "Bucolique" ("Bucolic," *OC*, 401–405), "hors la
vue et dans un congé de tous" ("outside sight and in a leave taken
of all," *OC*, 403).

The logic of Mallarméan flight is the dark side of that light-filled,
"vague and beautiful" aspiration which is that of the mind's
dream-movement toward *l'azur* (*OC*, 34, "Renouveau"). Flight-as-
dream can be "martyrdom" (*OC*, 30), or, as Mallarmé expresses it
in "Quand l'ombre menaça . . ." ("When Shadow Threatened . . ."),
"tel vieux Rêve, désir *et mal* de mes vertèbres" ("a certain old
Dream, desire *and malady* of my entire body," *OC*, 67, my italics).
But, despite these difficulties of realization, despite the bareness,
the fragility, the quasi-inexistence of the poet's "scattered dream"
(*OC*, 45, "Hérodiade"), despite, too, in the midst of that accomplishment performed by "L'Après-midi d'un faune" ("Afternoon
of a Faun," *OC*, 50–53), the sudden hesitation that can surge forth—
"Did I love a dream?" asks the faun, elaborating its exquisite patterns of altered vision (*OC*, 50)—despite, then, such self-created
obstacles placed in the way of flight-as-dream, the latter continues
to seduce and allure to a degree well confirmed by a number of the
delightful *poèmes en prose* Mallarmé composed from as early as
1864 and as late as 1887. One thinks, less of "Plainte d'automne"
("Autumn Complaint," *OC*, 270–71), where the positivity of dream
is offset by sadness and even "despair," than of the ebullient "Un
spectacle interrompu" ("Interrupted Spectacle," *OC*, 276–78), with
its surrealist notion of "a newspaper observing events in a dream
optic" (*OC*, 276); or the exquisite "Le Nénuphar blanc" ("White
Water-lily," *OC*, 283–86), with its Rousseauesque mental drift, "the
mental somnolence in which my lucidness veils over," and the
"imaginary trophy" it produces: the poem itself (*OC*, 285–86).

Mallarméan flight, then, moves beyond negation and exclusion
to the inner niceties of its intricate accomplishments. It aims at
infinity rather than contenting itself with finite constraints (*OC*, 14,
33): a kind of oddly simple vision that yet remains unlimited and
renders being itself boundlessly elastic. "To perceive oneself, simple, infinitely upon the earth," Mallarmé writes at the conclusion of
"Bucolique." Such flight is predicated upon a desire for, at once,

Baudelairean *ivresse* and Rimbaldian *voyance.* "Avide d'ivresse" ("Avid for drunkenness"), as Mallarmé writes in "L'Après-midi d'un faune," the poet seeks fulfilment in the intoxication of poetry (*OC,* 264), of art (*OC,* 307)—in short, of that otherness, that otherworldliness, that transformation of the self, which, already, poems such as "Le Pitre châtié" ("Chastised Clown," *OC,* 31) and "Les Fenêtres" powerfully evoke. Mallarméan escape is a self-evasion, a kind of ascetic self-intoxication that permits access to "the unknown foam and the skies" (*OC,* 38, "Brise marine") or what, in "Eventail" ("Fan," *OC,* 58–59), he happily calls—reversing the bitterness of the azure's earlier mockery—"the laughter of flowering intoxicated" (*OC,* 59): the joy, albeit still vaguely Baudelairean in its expression of traversing *le mal* of desire (*OC,* 67, "Quand l'ombre menaça...") and emerging as flower, as transformed, poetic ecstasy. Flight can leap high and long beyond negation, for its aim is ultimately that half-bowed (self-)"salvation" evoked at the end of (the unfinished) "Hérodiade" (*OC,* 49, "Cantique de Saint-Jean" ["Canticle of Saint John"])—a "salvation" similarly offered at the threshold of the final, posthumous 1899 edition of *Les Poésies:* "Salut," a greeting that, by 1893, could be vaguely deemed also an accomplished salvation, a flight having transmuted negation into some spiritual access.

That flight occurs *from* circumstances held to be dismaying or anguishing, needs hardly to be stressed. I shall merely affirm intensely elaborated thematics of distress and *ennui* in, especially, the poems of the *Parnasse contemporain* period and, to a lesser extent, those of his youth. If time can be seemingly transcended at an emotional level in some of Mallarmé's *dons de fruits glacés* ("Gifts of Glazed Fruit") and *autres dons de nouvel an* ("Other New Year's Gifts")—so that time can seem a "lie" (*OC,* 120, "Ces vers qui se ressembleront..." ["These verses that will look alike..."]) and friendship's presence, "smile, grace, other genius" (*OC,* 128, 137) can switch ephemeralness into some vague eternity—and if the same effect is beautifully produced in the unusually personal sonnet, "Ô si chère de loin et proche et blanche..." ("Oh so dear from afar and near and white..."; *OC,* 61), where, once again, the female smile (this time addressed to Méry Laurent, rather than Madam Whistler) is the center of a timelessness evocative of Gautier's "Affinités secrètes"—if, then, such transcendence is possible, even, seemingly, outside poetry, time is more often deemed a constant "adieu funèbre" ("a funereal farewell"), as he puts it in one of his earliest texts, "Sa Fosse est creusée! . . ." (*OC*, 4–6), "yesterday! . . . that was my life [. . .] a mere word!" (*OC*, 6).

Suffering and death, similarly, are often powerful agents of evasion, haunting and prodding consciousness from the earliest moments of poetic production. If some tentative possibility of their traversal remains initially available—"Who knows? an angel may lose its way amongst us," Mallarmé can write in the 1859 "Sa Fosse est creusée! . . ." (*OC*, 5)—already joy adjacent to pain and sorrow seems a barely tolerable juxtaposition (*OC*, 9); and, by 1861, the powerful "Galanterie macabre" reveals the fullest irony of a wretched, unwept death, in some nameless hovel, of a poor young woman—"without sacraments and like a dog,—said her neighbor" (*OC*, 15). By the time of "Angoisse" ("Anguish"), "Las de l'amer repos . . ." and "Hérodiade," death has become such an integral part of the Mallarméan *univers imaginaire* that it is both abhorred and, symbolically, embraced as an escape from all that, in daily existence, it represents.

The flight from the very "lassitude" (*OC*, 34, 35) and "incurable *taedium vitae*" (*OC*, 35) that block or stymie poetic self-purification and ideality appears, even as early as the *Parnasse contemporain* poems, to meet with some brief success. Does not "Les Fenêtres" speak already of actual rebirth, of self-angelicizing, of a dying to the world-as-it-is?—even if the achieved élan is short-lived, "Herebelow [being] master: its obsession/Com[ing] to sicken me at times even in this safe refuge" (*OC*, 35). And "Le Pitre châtié" (*OC*, 31), written a year later, in 1864, seems equally ready to document a "seeing" steeped in the "simple intoxication of rebirth"—a rebirth of the self as other, in otherness, in the deathly innovations of disappearance and virgin reappearance. What "Le Pitre châtié" makes clear, however—and "Hérodiade," begun in the same year and worked upon as late as May 1897, perhaps even up to Mallarmé's death in September 1898, pushes this logic to an extreme though enigmatic point—is the completely interlocked nature of Mallarmé's poetics of rebirth and that of the tomb. For it is in the cold, remote separateness of "a thousand sepulchers" that "virginity," new origin—and originality—only can be found (*OC*, 31). Creation, which is at once poetic creation and self-re-creation, the founding of a new ontology, requires what Mallarmé, in "Prose pour des Esseintes" ("Prose for Des Esseintes," *OC*, 55–57), terms

"Anastase!"—*anastasis*, resurrection. The poems Mallarmé offers Poe, Baudelaire, and Verlaine at the time of their deaths, are not just *hommages* and commemorations; they are, as he says, and in the fullest Mallarméan sense of the word, *tombeaux*. Tombs: places of repose from the tumult of time, imperfection, grief; poetic, aesthetic retreats from self, nature, being-as-nothingness, to (the self's) otherness, antinature—a kind of *nature morte*—nothingness-as-being: tiny zones of essential death and rebirth, "spiritual instrument[s]," like the Book, "offrant le minuscule tombeau, certes, de l'âme" ("offering the minute tomb, certainly, of the soul," *OC*, 379, "Le Livre, instrument spirituel" ["The Book, Spiritual Instrument"]). In an 1891 interview for *L'Echo de Paris*, Mallarmé is utterly explicit: "For me, the case of a poet, in this society which does not allow him to live, is the case of a man who isolates himself so as to sculpt his own tomb" (*OC*, 869). That such a tombal flight and resurrection is vibrant and offers a true, transfigured homeland to Mallarmé, can be amply understood via a reading of the section of his "Symphonie littéraire" devoted to Baudelaire's *Les Fleurs du Mal*: "I have closed the book and my eyes," he writes, "and I seek the homeland. Before me arises the ghost of the learned poet who shows it to me in a hymn shot forth mystically like a lily" (*OC*, 264).

Non-Purpose and Purpose

Without plunging into a full appraisal of the poetic ambition of Mallarmé, I should like to touch upon a number of factors that have not yet emerged or that may require some clarification. First, Mallarmé's artistic purpose may, not unreasonably, be stated in negative terms. He is decidedly not a romantic lyricist; not a poet of epic, nor even of brief anecdotality. The nearest his poetic purpose comes to some mode of *récit* is in the emblems of poems such as "Les Fenêtres" or "Brise marine," or in the framed pseudo-discourses of the *Poèmes en prose* (*Prose Poems*); not a satirist, nor a *moraliste*, nor a polemicist, nor a philosopher; not an impassive descriptivist, even though an admirer of Leconte de Lisle. Such negation, however, is far from dismissive. Not only can he remain sensitive, as will Rimbaud and Verlaine, and later the surrealists, to the exquisite purpose of high emotion in Desbordes-Valmore or Lamartine, but his unspoken debt to Vigny remains manifest, his admiration for Verlaine unwavering, despite his shift from the relatively impersonal and esoteric to punchy invective, his praise for Zola essential and cordial. Mallarmé's deep inner purpose lies elsewhere. Not for him, either, the art of quick pleasure or wide appeal. Exclusion is, once more, his nonpurpose, a contentment with "the suffrage of the sanhedrin of art" (*OC*, 259) is enough; difficulty, intricacy, an opaque yet new-glistening redeployment of "the words of the tribe" seal his elitist and "proud" tactic (*OC*, 54, 260), his anti-purpose. Exclusion, negation, and "suicidal" farewell characterize, too, as we have seen, Mallarmé's attitude to life, to nature, and to self. The intrinsic *hasard* of the latter is thus willfully denied, parenthesized, finessed. And the self, dying, too, slipping into the 'tombs" of its spectral creations, shuts out the light of the quotidian, the ephemeral in a seemingly anti-existential gesture as futile as the futility it would renounce.

Of course, all non-purpose, unless utterly nihilistic—but even the demolitions of Dada were inspired, Tzara tells us, by "une volonté d'atteindre à un absolu moral"—is merely apparent, and merges, seamlessly, with an implicit higher intention, or, in the case of Mallarmé, with a certain specific elaboration thereof. I shall content myself with noting the following: 1. much of Mallarmé's anti-purpose is a negative expression of pure aesthetic ambition, of that high artistic purism animating the Parnassian and the symbolist dreams: in Mallarmé's case it tends to hermeticism and a kind of exquisite formalism in which "symphonic" music can ultimately prevail; 2. it is clear that, at least in crude terms, Mallarmé's purpose is associated with that of a number of his contemporaries: Poe, Gautier, Baudelaire, Banville, especially, but also writers as apart in their purpose as Flaubert, Verlaine, the Goncourts, not to dwell upon the parallel motives of, say, Wagner, Whistler, Manet, Berthe Morisot, and so on; 3. not unlike Francis Ponge in some respect, Mallarmé dreams of that "new duty" of things, to which things will be called in poetry (*OC*, 56, "Prose pour des Esseintes"), a duty that, as he will explain in "Crise de vers" ("Poetic Crisis," *OC*, 360–68), involves "transpos[ing] a fact of nature in its vibratory quasi-disappearance according to the play of speech . . . so that its pure notion may emanate therefrom" (*OC*, 368)—a transposition of the "simple," the ephemeral for the purpose of some remote, original "initiation" (*OC*, 524, "Deuil" ["Mourning"]); 4. Mallarmé's desire is oriented toward what he calls in his 1873 "Toast funèbre" ("Funereal Toast") to Gautier "une agitation solennelle par l'air/De paroles" ("a solemn agitation through the air/Of words," *OC*, 55): Mallarméan play is solemn, serious, profoundly ontologically pertinent to the extent that it "installs, via science [the science of poetry],/The hymn of spiritual hearts" (*OC*, 56, "Prose pour des Esseintes")—the hymn, as we have seen, of the "resurrected" being of the self and all things; 5. Mallarmé's poetic purpose is not, therefore, gratuitous, fancifully "playful," for it entails, as he noted in his commentary on Emmanuel des Essarts' *Les Poésies parisiennes*, being "lived," experienced, beyond any "love of the beautiful verse, the worst of things" (*OC*, 251)—a distinction of crucial significance, to which we shall return in a discussion of Mallarméan *présence*; 6. as "Crise de vers" also makes plain, Mallarmé's poetic practice is predicated upon a distinction as to the "state" of language, "brut ou immédiat ici, là essentiel" ("raw or immediate here, there essential," *OC*, 368), a distinction that tends to draw a sharp line between the referentiality of words and their purely "fictional" character, their potentiality or pure "virtuality"—their poetic option of polysemic, unspecific relation of facts that turn out not to be facts; 7. if it is true that Mallarmé insists upon the ethical, philosophical, and metaphysical nonpurpose of the poetic, his note to Charles Morice about Poe clarifies what, in effect, always remains evident in Mallarmé's work: "I add," he says of such a "philosophical" or similar purpose, "that it is required, included and latent" (*OC*, 872, "Sur Poe" ["On Poe"]): a "philosophy" of poetic idealness and absolutism will underpin the text, at once manifest and yet beyond all dogmatism: Poe may be for Mallarmé "the absolute literary case" (*OC*, 531), but his poetry is beyond all blatant thesis, infinitely irreducible; 8. the question of the relationship of emotion to poetic function and purpose is more complex than any simplified Parnassian or symbolist project might lead us to believe: Mallarmé's work may push toward the "death" of the self, its otherness, its pure textualization, that serene transfiguration of which his essay on Gautier speaks ("Symphonie littéraire," *OC*, 262), yet it is clear that for Mallarmé nonaesthetic emotion, that emotion other than what Reverdy will call *cette émotion appelée poésie*, remains pertinent: a) in Mallarmé's reaction to reading Baudelaire (*OC*, 263); b) in his desire to love the world upon reading Banville (*OC*, 264); c) in the sheer "thematics" of much early work, from the compassion of "Galanterie macabre" or "Pauvre enfant pâle" ("Poor Pale Child," *OC*, 274–75) or, again, the bitterness and desire of, say, "Les Fenêtres" to the deeply purpo-sive affection that drives, finally, much of Mallarmé's work. One thinks of the sonnet "Dame/sans trop d'ardeur . . ." ("Why,/With-out Excess of Passion . . ."; *OC*, 60), the endless *vers de circonstance*, the *tombeaux, hommages, toasts* and *dons*—sober texts, yes, though tender, already moved, and *texts for the other*, not just for the transfiguration of the self. "Toute émotion," he writes in *Crayonné au théâtre* (*Pencilled at the Theater*), "sort de vous, élargit un milieu; ou sur vous fond et l'incorpore" ("All emotion leaves you, broad-ens out an environment; or upon you sweeps, incorporating it," *OC*, 309), thus stressing the unity of all emotion, natural and anti-natural, "raw" and "essential" or aesthetic, the seamless slippage from state to state, from life to art and back again; 9. the very earli-est scriptural purpose of Mallarmé's poetry—that of the *poèmes d'enfance et de jeunesse* (*Poems of Childhood and Youth*)—can be linked to his more refined and mature poetics, but it has a dynamic char-acter all its own which cannot be separated from what follows with impunity and honesty.

Spirituality and Ideality

The language and metaphors of Mallarmé's poetry are profoundly imbued with spiritual and even religious overtones, initially no doubt out of some essentially catholic conviction, later by transfer. Art becomes the locus of high worship, spiritual fervor, a mode of penetration into the mystery of the soul, a certain sacredness of be-ing. A glance at the compositions of great artists like Mozart, Beethoven, or Wagner reveals the "severe, chaste and unknown" *signs* of such ritual penetration (*OC*, 257, "Hérésies artistiques"), the "hieratic formulas" permitting aesthetico-spiritual access to regions of being otherwise perhaps unattainable. I say perhaps only so as not to overlook all that is spiritual but unwritten for Mallarmé, but which his writing can at times evoke: friendship, love, idle summer drifting at Valvins in his *yole*, and so on—all that, as "Brise marine" indicates, will not prevent a higher pur-pose. As he points out in "De même" ("Likewise," *OC*, 395–97), "nothing . . . will reveal itself exclusively lay, because the word pre-cisely elects no meaning" (*OC*, 397). If, then, spirituality clings to everything, art remains the privileged and rare way of attaining to its most intense and ecstatic experience. Mallarmé's lovely "Ballets" (*OC*, 303–307) thus offers us dance as the "mysterious sacred interpretation" of a climactic but fleeting embrace (*OC*, 305). Creation for him, in theater, in all of art, involves "fashioning divinity" (*OC*, 314), as he puts it in another text from *Crayonné au théâtre;* and the stage is that "majestic opening upon the mystery of things, whose greatness we are in the world to contemplate" (*OC*, 314). The poet or writer may in this way come to regard his or her work as a "système agencé comme spirituel zodiaque" ("system ordered as a spiritual zodiac"), as he says in an 1893 fragment (*OC*, 850), and he himself/she herself becomes "the spiritual histrion" of his/her own raw existential events (*OC*, 370, "Quant au livre").

For spirituality, while conceptually linked to what he calls in "Symphonie littéraire," "the eternal repertoire of the Ideal of all time" (*OC*, 262), remains for Mallarmé a deeply private, though shared, phenomenon—a mental assuming of the "divinity" already fashioned or about to be fashioned. It remains an "ascension into the spiritual skies" that preexist in Banville's book (*OC*, 264), yet require the reader's taking up within the self of his or her (cor)responding "spiritual being." "Perhaps all that was divine and extraterrestrial in me," he writes in the same piece, this time in reference to Gautier, "was summoned up like a fragrance via this unimaginably sublime reading" (*OC*, 262). An experience such as this, whether it be theatrical, textual, or musical, entails, therefore, a participation in—and a memory of—what, always, remains available within us, if we care to bear it up, assume its pure mental, spiritual reality, its capacities of self-renewal, its power of refounding our origin now. "Ce spirituellement et magnifiquement illuminé fond d'extase, c'est bien le pur de nous-mêmes par nous porté" ("This spiritually and magnificently illuminated ecstatic basis is the purity of ourselves borne up by ourselves"), Mallarmé writes in "Solennité" ("Solemnity"), from *Crayonné au théâtre* (*OC*, 334). Spiritual ecstasy is not somewhere else; its otherness is already ours, within us; it is our essential mode of being, plunged so often into oblivion or incoherence.

The "superstition of a Literature," of which Mallarmé speaks to his March 1894 Oxford and Cambridge audiences (*OC*, 643), may well hint at the "fictional" and purely mental character he associates with "music and letters," but it should not be thought that such fictionality diminishes in any way the intensity of the spiritual experience involved. The "mental situation" or "mental pursuit" of any artistic gesture (*OC*, 294, 648) is not fictional in the sense that it is nonexistent or unreal; but it is at once *idéal* and *idéel*. It is steeped in the pure aspirations of our idealness, our thought—and felt—spiritual, mental absoluteness, and notional, virtual, precisely because belonging to mind, to the endless shifts and impulses of idea, to the mobile, nonmaterial dimension of being. Here, in this *mentale poursuite* ("mental pursuit," *OC*, 648), self may indulge in a self-reflection significantly richer than that available in daily discourse. Art is the soul music of the self, the mental symphony within us. "Every soul is a melody," Mallarmé will go so far as to affirm, beyond any trace of elitism, "we are here to take up; and for that, are the flute and viola of each one" (*OC*, 363, "Crise de vers"). This pursuit of the pure ideality, the highest mentality or spirituality of the self, plunges poetic language, or theatrical gesture, or operatic music, into its essentiality, its nonrepresentationality, away from that *"fausse apparence de présent"* (*"false appearance of presentness"*) that, equally, we might seek or see in it (*OC*, 310, "Mimique" ["Sign Language"]).

Thus, ballet, rather than anchoring Mallarmé in muscles and anecdote, "simule une impatience de plumes vers l'idée" ("simulates an impatience of feathers towards idea," *OC*, 306, "Ballets"). Thus, Shakespeare, rather than wallowing in history and specific relation, is "fashioned according to the theater of the mind alone" (*OC*, 300, "Hamlet"). Thus, Mallarmé is irresistibly drawn to the ideal flower, "l'absente de tous bouquets" ("the absent of all bouquets"), the pure possibility of flower-ness, rather than to an overt celebration of, say, some hawthorn blossom immersed in temporal and spatial circumstance. "Not the wood intrinsic and dense of trees," he writes in "Crise de vers," but some filtered suggestiveness, some mere allusive trace, some subtle offering to the mind, to the spirit—"that has no other function beyond the musicalness of everything" (*OC*, 365–66).

Ideality takes place in a "mental cloister" (*OC*, 406, "Solitude") wherein words glitter with "une réciprocité de feux" ("A reciprocity of fires," *OC*, 386) not found in pure unilinear, firmly transitive discourse. Poetic or artistic discourse, for Mallarmé, consists in favoring and celebrating the "marriages of mind" (*OC*, 406), "the nuptial proofs of Idea" (*OC*, 387), which can occur precisely via mental multiplication, "suspension" and "vibration" (*OC*, 386, "Le

Mystère dans les lettres" ["Mystery in Writing"]), rather than by limitation, narrowing, focus. Ideality seeks the object in its transcended, rather than its manifest rootedness. "The moment of an object's Notion," Mallarmé explains in his 1869 "Notes," "is thus the moment of the reflection of its pure presentness within itself or its present purity" (*OC*, 853). If "fictionality" seems, then, to be "le procédé même de l'esprit humain" ("the very process of the human mind," *OC*, 851, "Notes"), its essential mode of self-affirmation, it is no less true that it is concerned with a level of ontic presence of things to the mind, the soul, the heart. Ideality appears to be tightly "cloistered," but it opens the self to its depths and its mysteries within the limits of the mind's cast light.

Play, Interiority, Self-Reflexiveness

Halfway through "La Musique et les lettres" ("Music and Letters," *OC*, 642–57), the text of his Oxford and Cambridge talk, Mallarmé asks, "À quoi sert tout cela?" ("What's the use of all that?")—referring to the high niceties of the literary enterprise he has just evoked. His answer is succinct: "À un jeu" ("It is a game," *OC*, 647); poetry is a "game," the play and interplay of fiction and reality, the pleasure of their interface, the "trick" of projecting into ideality "the conscious lack in us of what up above bursts forth" (*OC*, 647). In this act of playing, and in this object of mental interplay that is the poem, can burst forth that fiery interchange, those "nuptials of mind and spirit" (*OC*, 396–97, 406) of which we have just spoken. For Mallarmé, all art indulges in such play, and therefore even his earliest "Cantate pour la première communion" (*OC*, 3–4) may be said to practice it. "Le Château de l'Espérance" ("The Castle of Hope," *OC*, 23), written in 1863 and the last of the so-called *poèmes d'enfance et de jeunesse*, shows how far Mallarmé has already moved along that implacable line of his poetics of ever increasing self-contained (inter)play. By the time the later sonnets and *Un coup de dés* come along the movement is complete: the text's ludic interiority is firmly established as the ground of all poetic event, semantically swirling, unstable and provocatively open upon its inner spirals, yet manifestly closed to its remaining referential potential. Play can take various forms, and, before turning to its extreme mode, it is useful to give some attention to those poems where the mode is at once blatant and yet relaxed, where the logic of play is both committed and delicate, light, almost Verlainean at times, and less definitively tombal, less rigorously interior in its gaze and purpose: the *Loisirs de la poste* (*Leisures of the Post, OC,* 81–106), the *éventails* (*Fans, OC,* 107–110), the *offrandes* (*Offerings, OC,* 111–14), *dons* (*OC,* 117–30), *photographies* (*Photographs, OC,* 115–17), *autres dons* (*OC,* 130–139), *oeufs de Pâques* (*Easter Eggs, OC,* 139–41), *fêtes et anniversaires* (*OC,* 141–46), *albums* (*OC,* 147–50), *envois* (*OC,* 150–81) and other *vers de circonstance* that constitute half of what may be considered as the strictly poetic output of Mallarmé. Here, the logic of play is centered upon leisure, diversion, a poeticization of the circumstantial—such as gift, celebration, exchange, and so on—whose veiling of ennui is not just less anguished, but commonly spirited, jovial, predicated upon the simple delight of a poetic communication steeped in presence and movement toward the other. A balance is thus reached *between* the claims of strict poetic interiority and those of the text's osmotic impulse. The latter focuses upon that other level of play which is less the "ideal flight" of textual, mental interiority "shaking itself" within the book *whether it is ever read or not* (*OC,* 418, "Sauvegarde" ["Safeguard"]) than the anticipated (inter)play of reader and text, the commun(icat)ion, purposefully warm and loving, of different mentalities within that nonspace and nonobject that is the "mentality," the interiority, the self-reflexiveness of that box of mirrors: the poem.

The poem, then, as *loisir, don, envoi,* offers itself as the performance of its semiosis, its semioticity, as a production of "boxed" and "presented" mildly spinning sense, but, beyond this enactment of itself, it seeks to play *with* the other, to go out of itself toward that "circumstance" in which the other is involved—offering its own otherness, its intrinsic poeticity, to the other. The signature of the poem may be the same as that of "Une dentelle s'abolit..." (*OC,* 74) or *Un coup de dés,* but its signs point more overtly both within and without. Yet, each *don* or *envoi* is "le très pur résultat" ("the very pure result," *OC,* 309, *Crayonné au théâtre*) of a play of written but essentially mental forms, symbols; further, each is predicated upon an inner play, moving toward its outside, without which it would not exist nor be complete. In Bonnefoy's terms, textual *excarnation* demands, in this particular logic of play especially, an incarnation or reincarnation Mallarmé anticipates quite beyond the "ideal flight" of signs.

"Hérodiade" is a poem whose discourse, willfully elliptic, obscure, and convoluted, seems nevertheless centered upon notions—Mallarmé speaks of "impressions très fugitives" in an 1865 letter to his friend Cazalis (*OC*, 1441)—of refusal, withdrawal, death, coldness, virginalness. Mallarmé perceived it from the outset as a starkly tragic poem, opposed in its wintriness to the summery enthusiasm and headiness of "L'Après-midi d'un faune." Moreover, the poem's mission is clearly seen as attaining to that language of quasi-immateriality, of essentiality, depicting, as he writes already in 1864, "not the thing, but the effect it produces" (*OC*, 1440)—a depiction going well beyond Verlainean nuance, just as his desire to have "Hérodiade" become a veritable "symphony" (*OC*, 1441) transcends Verlaine's poetics of music in a way we shall seek to define. I speak of "Hérodiade" here in order to draw attention to its thematics of interiority and self-reflexivity, and to show that Mallarmé himself is fully aware of the "contradictions," dilemmas, and practical difficulties such an elected poetics implies. This is not to reduce the poem in any way, its "subject" having been fairly often alluded to, but never specified, in correspondence or elsewhere. We do know that it causes suffering and even despair for various reasons, its subject being "frightening" (*OC*, 1440); that the poem is abandoned, yet never ceases to fascinate; and that its tragic strangeness is judged finally more suited to poetic reading than the originally planned dramatic performance. What remains central in "Hérodiade" and obsesses Mallarmé to the end of his life, is that interlocked feeling of the *potential* of (poetic) purity and the *terror* of near-disincarnation, entombed virginity, high mystical yet self-denying obsession. "J'aime l'horreur d'être vierge . . ." ("I love the horror of my virginalness"), proclaims Hérodiade before her *nourrice* (*OC*, 47), who has already described her charge as that

> Triste fleur qui croît seule et n'a pas d'autre émoi
> Que son ombre dans l'eau vue avec atonie.
>
> Sad flower growing alone, without emotion other
> Than its shadow seen atonic within the water.
> (*OC*, 46)

Mallarmé seems to be articulating, throughout "Hérodiade," the extreme tensions of a poetics that has not yet found its full equilibrium, its adequate modus vivendi, and lies taut and tormented, between, on the one hand, the logic of some unthinkably ultimate Parnassian abolition of the self and the consequent attainment to "the unknown splendor/And the vain mystery of [one's] being" (*OC*, 46) and, on the other, the highly perilous adventure that this inevitably implies, its highly esoteric nature. Poems such as "L'Azur," "Brise marine," and "Les Fenêtres," all written around the same time as "Hérodiade," can be easily "read into" the 1864 poem seen in this light. "Hérodiade" is in many ways an emblem of all that haunts Mallarmé at this period, but above all it pierces deep into the young poet's nervous, frustrated, and experimental poetics of ideality and tombal rebirth. Tinged, almost even soured, by impotence and ennui, such a poetics of self-destruction becomes double-edged, leading to true poetic rebirth, self-discovery in pristine transcendence, or to sheer nihilism or, better, to a kind of self-attention as sterile as the sterility of impotence, a narcissism that can entrap the self as surely as death. When Hérodiade affirms, "Oui, c'est pour moi, pour moi, que je fleuris, déserte!" "Yes, for myself, myself, do I flourish, deserted!" *OC*, 47), all equations are conjured forth and, no doubt, all *simultaneously and fused*. For the glacial, unlit solitude to which Hérodiade aspires and the self-mirroring effects of her icy quasi-tomb are clearly, within the poem as a whole, the object of concern, even traumatizing obsession, even if the "Cantique de Saint-Jean," which forms the third part of "Hérodiade," succeeds in evoking, through decapitation, the notions of an "eternity," a baptismal "illumination," a "salvation" immensely pertinent to the whole Mallarméan discourse of death and rebirth.

Interiority and self-reflexiveness, then, are clearly central symbolic structures within this great unfinished poem, though the nature of "farewell" and death remains utterly ambiguous. This is in accordance with Mallarmé's very poetics of textual interiority, which demands essential closure, the kind of indefinite prismatic verbal/mental play that one can imagine—and only the imagination can show us its reality—in a closed box, or tomb. Such endlessly deferred interior signification—is it an accident or a trick of fate that deprives us of all allusion to the specificity of the poem's "subject-matter"?—could risk resulting in the creation of what in

"Ses purs ongles . . ." ("Its Pure Nails," *OC*, 68–69) Mallarmé calls an "aboli bibelot d'inanité sonore" ("abolished trinket of sonorous inanity," *OC*, 68), a movement (I am using the phrase as a metaphor) of sound and form beyond all retrievable sense with which to play.

Although Mallarmé shows little concern for manifest intelligibility, the intelligible in its most arcane, mentally challenging, and spiritually exalting mode is precisely what he remains fascinated by. The intelligible become unintelligible is not part of his poetics. Interiority and textual self-reflexiveness involve "giving a purer sense to the words of the tribe," as he puts it in "Le Tombeau d'Edgar Poe" ("Tomb for Edgar Poe," *OC*, 70), offering language and thought a hermetic context within which their self-exaltation can follow upon their derealization, their debanalization. Here, in this specifically nonspecific, poetic context, meaning is generated by language's/thought's endless self-mirroring productivity. If the self exists in this nonspace—as Francis Ponge or Bernard Noël might say today—this zone of pure idea and ideal, then it would be like the light caught, but endlessly shifting, in a play of mirrors, like the being of "Madame . . . , l'inconnue à saluer" ("a Lady . . . , unknown, to be greeted") whom Mallarmé evokes in "Le Nénuphar blanc" ("The White Waterlily") (*OC*, 283–86): ". . . elle avait fait de ce cristal son miroir intérieur à l'abri de l'indiscrétion éclatante des après-midi . . ." (". . . she had made this crystal her inner mirror, sheltered from the brilliant indiscretion of afternoons . . .; *OC*, 284). Here, in this self-reflexiveness of language, thought—and light, illumination—the self finds its undreamt otherness, unnamed though worded, for still essential, "virtual," though articulated, symbolized. A multiplication of the self exploding its habitual constraints, attaining, via what Mallarmé calls in the "Cantique de Saint-Jean," "son pur regard" (*OC*, 49), to something of its still indefinable otherness. As he says of Gautier's poetic manner, "de ses jeux combinés résulte la seule lucidité" ("from its combinatory interplay comes its sole lucidness," *OC*, 262).

Perception comes from the interiority of language's/thought's pure self-enactment—not from theory, explanation, strictly channeled meaning, but, as Mallarmé writes in *Crayonné au théâtre*, from that art, "l'unique ou pur qu'énoncer signifie produire: il hurle ses démonstrations par la pratique" ("the unique or pure where to enunciate is to produce: it screams its demonstrations through practice," *OC*, 295). Interiority is the dance of dance (*OC*, 304), the play of art—poetry, music, theater, ballet—itself. "Nothing is taking place," Mallarmé argues in the same writings (*OC*, 305), other than the perfection of art itself, "beyond all possible life" (*OC*, 307). Interiority is that pure artistic expression which—"fontaine intarissable d'elle-même" ("endless fountain of itself"), as Mallarmé says of Loïe Fuller's dancing (*OC*, 311)—points continuously to itself, its self-reflecting productivity in which self and its infinite otherness combine in ideality. It provides an exquisite, jewel-like compacting and "simplification" of being, as this celebrated passage from "La Musique et les lettres" well shows:

La Nature a lieu, on n'y ajoutera pas; que des cités, les voies ferrées et plusieurs inventions formant notre matériel.

Tout l'acte disponible, à jamais et seulement, reste de saisir les rapports, entre temps, rares ou multipliés; d'après quelque état intérieur et que l'on veuille à son gré étendre, simplifier le monde.

Nature takes place, it will not be added to; but for cities, railways and several inventions forming our materialness.

Entire available action, forever and only, remains seizing relationships, between times, rare or multiplied; according to some inner state and that one wishes, to one's taste, extend or simplify the world.

(*OC*, 647)

Sign, Verse, and Book

Certain arts such as historical drama, though all arts may move in this direction, highlight temporality, temporal meaning, finite message. Ballet, for Mallarmé, on the other hand, is "emblematic" (*OC*, 306, "Ballets"); like the poetry he dreams of and ultimately creates, it tends toward the delivery of sense not as explainable specificity but as pure signification at once beyond reduction and infinitely visionary. The ballerina, he writes, also in that collection of essays gathered under the delightful title of its liminary text, *Crayonné au théâtre*, "delivers to you via the last veil that always remains, the nudity of your concepts and silently will write your vision in the manner of a Sign, which she is" (*OC*, 317, "Le Genre ou des modernes" ["Genre or Modernity"]). Art, as conceived, willed, and projected by Mallarmé, pushes the sign to the point of its least transitive function, to the expression of what he calls in the same essay its "signifiances idéales" ("ideal signifyings," *OC*, 314–15), a play or performance of its forms, inevitably entailing an articulation of *signifiés* or signifieds, but as oblique, as remotely allusive as possible, just as its referents, incapable of totally shedding their "gazes d'origine" ("original gauzes"), will nevertheless fade to near-vaporousness in that "envol tacite d'abstraction" ("tacit flight of abstraction") that writing accomplishes (*OC*, 385, "Le Mystère dans les lettres"). Mallarméan art—ballet, poetry, music—seeks consequently to create what he describes, in "Autre étude de danse" ("Further Dance Study," *OC*, 307–309), as "a virginalness of place not dreamed, that the figure isolates, building and decorating" (*OC*, 308), a place of signification wherein context, time, space are evacuated and a pure, aesthetic flowering of unrestricted sense, of signification rendered infinite, of sign become a dance of pure semiosis, may come about. Ballet, theater, poetry may become "hieroglyphs" (*OC*, 312, "Le seul, il le fallait fluide..." ["The Only One, Needed Supple..."]), but they are not hieroglyphs that aspire to some linear decipherment; rather do they invite us to plunge into their hieratic encodements as zones of infinite (un)decipherability.

Even in the theater this is conceivable for Mallarmé, hence his initial enthusiasm for "Hérodiade." Maeterlinck can convey "the essential" (*OC*, 330); Henri Becque, perhaps surprisingly, can attain to "bourgeois allegory"—rather than tautological representation of being (*OC*, 316); and Jarry's *Ubu roi*, at whose opening performance Mallarmé was present, with Yeats, seems partly to conform to the poet's vision of a theater "vierge de tout, lieu, temps et personne sus" ("virgin of all, place, time and person known," *OC*, 544, "Richard Wagner"). Mallarmé's abandonment of the theatrical mode for "Hérodiade," on the other hand, may well stem from a feeling that theater required too much referential rooting and semantic delimitation of the sign—his friend Banville urges him toward "dramatic interest" and a practical "actability" (*OC*, 1441)—whereas the poetic mode retains utter freedom, offering a pure figuration of and to the mind. Certainly, the need to make the sign blatantly, crudely accountable, is an idea not made to please Mallarmé. Such a level of signification he is quick to advise against at the beginning of "Le Mystère dans les lettres," where he promotes rather the generation of "un sens même indifférent" ("an even indifferent meaning," *OC*, 382). Accountability is thus viewed in the purest terms possible: "merely an exact account of being's pure rhythmic motifs, which are its recognizable signs," he writes at the close of "Notes sur le théâtre" ("Notes on Theater," *OC*, 336–45). "It is my pleasure everywhere to decipher them" (*OC*, 345), he says of the signs of being, of *présence*, of our ephemeralness, which are yet perceived in their highest spiritual form, as pure but recognizable, ontic abstractions, as nonfigurative configurations of our essence. It is in this perspective that we can understand Mallarmé's regular insistence upon authorial absence. As he says of Whistler's work, such a manifestation of signification attains to the eternal, "plays at miracles and denies the signatory" (*OC*, 531, "Whistler"). The notion of "mystery" in "letters" is thus a notion that points "beyond verbal value as much as that purely hieroglyphic, of speech or of book of spells" (*OC*, 855, "Notes"), to a level of symbolic function of language, which, as Mallarmé hints in the same 1895 essay, is strangely evoked in that "secret direction confusedly indicated by spelling which moves mysteriously towards the general pure sign that must mark verse" (*OC*, 855). Poetry and art accede, ideally, to a non-naming of things (*OC*, 869: "*Nommer* un objet...le symbole" ["*To name* an object...symbol"]), wherein language's signs represent the pure symbolic nature of themselves and the envelopment of all being within this mysterious and pure symbolicalness. Such transformation of the practice of the sign is largely realized in the later sonnets of the mid-1880s such as "Une dentelle s'abolit..."; more efficaciously still in the 1895 "À la nue accablante tu..." ("To the Cloud Overwhelming...."; *OC*, 76); and immaculately in the 1897 *Un coup de dés.*

The sign as Mallarmé sees it is intimately connected with a perception of totality, of harmony of separate constituent signifying elements, which, in their endless mental interlacements, elaborate a symbolic space-time one could, equally well, call a sign, a rhythmic, "versified" unit of infinite or semi-infinite sense. "Ainsi lancé de soi," he writes in "Solennité," "le principe qui n'est—que le Vers! attire non moins que dégage pour son "épanouissement (l'instant qu'ils y brillent et meurent dans une fleur rapide, sur quelque transparence comme d'éther) les mille éléments de beauté pressés d'accourir et de s'ordonner dans leur valeur essentielle. Signe!" ("Thus self-launched the principle that is—but Verse! attracts no less than releases for its blossoming [the moment they glitter and die therein in a rapid flower, upon some transparency as of air] the thousand elements of beauty hastening along to an orchestration in their essential value. Sign!" *OC*, 333). Such a global sign—which could be a poem, a book, or naturally a movement in a ballet—permits an orchestration of what might at times seem fragmentary, disparate, elliptical, and yet, simultaneously, a highlighting of the mysterious "individuality" (*OC*, 328) of the global sign's sub-signs. "À la nue accablante tu . . ." thus "signifies" both via the mystery of its flickering compactions, truncations, and consequently illuminated decontextualized syntagms, and via the latter's coming together in the evident wholeness of the sonnet, in some strange poetic synthesis or *sym-bole*—"not without similarity," as Mallarmé argues in "Crise de vers," "to the abounding cries of an orchestration that remains verbal" (*OC*, 361).

What Mallarmé senses in language is its intrinsic capacity for some sort of orchestral signing of the essence of being—a signing that is at once a self-signing, for the poem/book will contain the most precious elements of the self, and a signing-off of the self, because "the minute tomb of the soul" and because an act of existence moving toward essence. "The musicality of everything" (*OC*, 366), as Mallarmé writes in the same essay, implies, poetically, the genius of symbolic orchestration. "L'acte poétique consiste à voir, soudain qu'une idée se fractionne en un nombre de motifs égaux" ("The poetic act entails seeing, suddenly, that an idea fractures into a number of equal motifs"), he argues, thinking principally of the power of rhyme (*OC*, 365), yet evoking a more global poetic strategy which constantly deals with the syndesis and disjunction of form, sound, meaning, and so on. Such an orchestral "respiration," as Jacques Dupin might say, of the poem's components, entails for Mallarmé the strictest organizational vigilance. Orchestration, or what I have called simply verse, occurs in order to symphonize signs or sub-signs into global Sign, in order to render the poetic space watertight: "a prescription of the book of verse dawns innate," Mallarmé writes, though the logic equally applies to the individual poem, "or everywhere, eliminates chance" (*OC*, 366). Such a "prescription" engenders a kind of poetic necessity that—"imply[ing] the elocutory disappearance of the poet [and] yield [ing] the initiative to words, mobilised via the crash of their inequality" (*OC*, 366)—does not, nevertheless, founder upon chaos.

The "reciprocal glitterings" (*OC*, 366), set up by poetic choice, free language, open it to its infiniteness, but within the finely sculpted destiny of the poetic "tomb." What Mallarmé creates, casting aside the finite lyricism of the self, is the endlessly teeming lyricism of language, of thought, of pure being, within the closure of some chosen, few, but richly emblematic symbols.

These symbols—of a given poem such as "Le Vierge, le vivace et le bel aujourd'hui . . ." or of a book, even the Book—seek a perfection that is synonymous with ideal orchestration, a perfection—"le paraphe amplifié du génie, anonyme et parfait comme une existence d'art" ("the amplified flourish of genius, anonymous and perfect as an artistic existence," *OC*, 367)—that attains to an internal harmony, rhythmic self-containedness, and symbolic self-logic which is a synechdochic image of "l'ensemble des rapports existant dans tout, la Musique" ("the totality of relationships existing in everything, Music," *OC*, 368). What Mallarmé thinks of, then, as verse, poiesis, orchestration, involves a symbolic vers-ification—a working of those "turns," "stirrings," furrows, and lines—"of the relationships between everything" (*OC*, 378), but as "hymn, harmony and joy, as pure grouped ensemble in some fulgurant circumstance" (*OC*, 378, "Le Livre, instrument spirituel").

It is difficult not to think a little of Lamartine, when reading such lines, and yet only to the extent that Lamartine's hymn may be said to address itself to its own intrinsicalness, and not just the harmonies of being itself. That the artist, for Mallarmé, is the "servant, a priori, of rhythms" (*OC*, 401) is certain; Lamartine's poetics cannot be stated in those terms. That "Poetry, near idea, is Music, par excellence" (*OC*, 381) is indubitable but for the allusion to the musicality of idea, for Lamartine's poetics, as we have seen, is far less serene in its contemplation of thought's ideality or essentiality. Various passages in "Crise de vers" and "Le Livre, instrument spirituel" indicate fairly plainly that *Un coup de dés* is "modeled" on Mallarmé's slowly elaborated poetics of symbolic symphonization or musicalization, a poetics centered upon language's capacity to figure, nonrepresentationally, nonimitatively, but by the sheer majesty of its infinitely shimmering interior play, the ideality of all consciousness. "Tout devient suspens" ("All becomes suspension"), we read in the former of the two essays, "disposition fragmentaire avec alternance et vis-à-vis, concourant au rhythme total" ("a fragmentary ordering with alternation and opposition, working towards total rhythm," *OC,* 367); and, in the second essay: "Pourquoi—un jet de grandeur, de pensée ou d'émoi, considérable, phrase poursuivie, en gros caractère, une ligne par page à emplacement gradué, ne maintiendrait-il le lecteur en haleine, la durée du livre, avec appel à sa puissance d'enthousiasme: autour, menus, des groupes, secondairement d'après leur importance, explicatifs ou dérives—un semis de fioritures" ("Why—a spurt of greatness, thought, emotion, considerable, continued sentence, in large character, a line per page with graduated location, would this not keep the reader breathless, throughout the book, with appeal to one's power of enthusiasm: around, small, groups, secondarily according to their importance, explanatory or driftings—a sowing of fiorituras," *OC,* 381). *Un coup de dés,* read in this light, is the orchestral performance of some major idea, emotion, *état d'âme,* shattered, but symphonically, into its endless yet imbricated sub-ideas, -emotions, *-états d'âme,* a pure symbolic figuration of the complexity and infinite relationalness of being.

For the book—*Un coup de dés,* for example, for Mallarmé never completed, it seems, the Book as he dreamed and knew it within him (*OC,* 663)—must possess that subtlety and all-embracing pertinence of "life" itself (*OC,* 318). The book/Book represents, for him, an act and place of our ultimate human capacity to contain the world, symbolically, to have and be all that is, mentally, spiritually, via language—and despite the radical divorce between word and world. "Everything, in the world, exists to end up in a book," he writes with seeming presumption in "Le Livre, instrument spirituel"; but this necessity exists—and the parameters of the "necessity" differ among artists—only in proportion to one's desire to know and embrace the world. "Quelle représentation!" ("What a performance!") Mallarmé writes in "Solennité," "le monde y tient; un livre, dans notre main, s'il énonce quelque idée auguste, supplée à tous les théâtres, non par l'oubli qu'il en cause mais les rappelant impérieusement, au contraire" ("the world is there; a book, in our hands, if enunciating some august idea, stands in for all theaters, not by the oblivion of them it causes but imperiously recalling them, on the contrary," *OC,* 334). One can well understand why he speaks of "the necessary talisman of the Book" (*OC,* 343), for it is evident that the book/*Livre* does not operate its magic in a vacuum, but in the world, because of the world, *ultimately,* in spite of all we have seen, *moving back toward the world.* I shall return shortly to this matter, but wish, here, to stress equally that, for this "return" to be faintly feasible, artistic or poetic endeavor must, paradoxically, be exclusively concentrated upon artifice, play, fiction, a narcissistic, self-reflexive exploitation that would, initially, seem to confirm nothing but itself. "The book," Mallarmé defines in "Le Livre, instrument spirituel," "total expansion of the letter, should from itself draw, directly, a mobileness and, spacious, via correspondences, institute a play, or the like, confirming fiction" (*OC*, 380). The book, writing itself, establishing a fictionality continually and increasingly drawn from its own shifting, crisscrossing patterns of symbolic form, "boot-straps" itself into a spectral or ideal mental existence henceforth generally available. "Pas de devoir" ("No duty"), Mallarmé charmingly puts it in "Solitude," stressing this purely notional, virtual, idea-l character, "que produire un livre favorable à ces noces d'esprit, ou camarade acquiescement de poignées de main pensantes" ("other than to produce a book favorable to these mental weddings, or comradely acquiescence of thinking handshakes," *OC*, 406).

The Mallarméan Book then, as tomb, yes; but also as pure celebration of mind, à la Ponge. Indeed, Mallarmé's aspiration was great, exceptional. His autobiographical letter, addressed to Verlaine in 1885, goes further than any other text in expressing the serene fervor and the immense ambition that the notion of the book/Book—" [le] Grand Oeuvre" ("[the] Great Work," *OC*, 662)—could conjure up in Mallarmé's genial mind:

un livre, tout bonnement, en maints tomes, un livre qui soit un livre, architectural et prémédité, et non un recueil des inspirations de hasard fussent-elles merveilleuses. . . . J'irai plus loin, je dirai: le Livre, persuadé au fond qu'il n'y en a qu'un, tenté à son insu par quiconque a écrit, même les Génies. L'explication orphique de la Terre, qui est le seul devoir du poëte et le jeu littéraire par excellence: car le rythme même du livre, alors impersonnel et vivant, jusque dans sa pagination, se juxtapose aux équations de ce rêve, ou Ode.

a book, quite simply, in many tomes, a book that is a book, architectural and premeditated, and not a collection of chance inspirations, though marvellous. . . . I shall go further and say: the Book, convinced basically that there is only one, attempted unwittingly by whomsoever has written, even Geniuses. The orphic explanation of the Earth, which is the only duty of the poet and the literary game par excellence: for the very rhythm of the book, thus impersonal and alive, even to its pagination, is juxtaposed with the equations of this dream, or Ode.

(*OC,* 662–63)

"Autobiographie" (*OC,* 661–65) renders once and for all explicit that literary play and the meaning of being are inextricably linked in Mallarmé's poetics, which only demands the strictest meditation and orchestration in the hope of drowning out *le hasard* via the exquisite intricacies of some ultimate *intelligible.* Such a book eluded Mallarmé, as it has eluded all those (few) writers who conceived it to be even thinkable. Mallarmé's express wish, addressed to Verlaine: "to prove by the portions done that this book exists, and that I have known what I shall have been unable to accomplish" (*OC,* 663).

Presence, Nothingness, Homology

It might seem strange to speak of *présence* in the context of a poet whose work often seems devoted to its suppression. A number of important elements of Mallarmé's poetics, commonly neglected or underestimated, remain, however, to be teased out. Not the least of these would involve stressing the impossibility of any project of exclusion of presence in presence, of being in being, as well as the related evacuation from one category of thought (art as nonpresence, fiction, nothingness) of other categories upon which the former conceptually depends. On top of this, for I shall come full circle ultimately, Mallarmé's poetry and writings on art and poetry reveal many facets that might lead us to question any idea of outright rejection of *présence* in the poetic equation. Here are a few random samples: 1. the insistence of "Le Sonneur" upon passage, time, the instant of "an angelus amidst lavender and thyme" (*OC,* 36); 2. the many early poems thick with a Baudelairean and even Verlainean sensuality, that, while working itself out, operates a still powerfully anchoring, temporal, and nonessentialized effect: "L'Enfant prodigue" ("The Prodigal Child," *OC,* 14–15), "À une petite laveuse blonde" ("To a Fair Young Washerwoman," *OC,* 16–18), "Le Château de l'Espérance," "Angoisse," even to some extent "L'Après-midi d'un faune"; 3. Mallarmé's entire early discourse, especially but not exclusively in the *Parnasse contemporain* poems, is the discourse of presence: suffering, time, irony, and so on; 4. Mallarmé's stressing, in his 1862 essay on Emmanuel des Essarts, of the trap of the aesthetic without "livedness" (*OC*, 251); 5. art's, the Book's need to possess the depths and subtleties of life itself (*OC*, 318, "Le Genre ou des modernes"); 6. Mallarmé's reaction to the reading of Banville, as he expresses it in "Symphonie littéraire" (*OC*, 261–65), a reaction leading to an experience of "la terre heureuse" and a veritable adoration of being's munificence spurring on his own poetic desire ("J'aime les roses..."; *OC*, 264–65): poetry and presence in rhythmic counterplay, endlessly fostering each other; 7. even Mallarmé's sailing days, fondly recalled in the "Autobiographie" for Verlaine (*OC*, 664–65), but, as we know, intimately incorporated—transfigured but present in their high otherness—into poems such as "Le Nénuphar blanc." The samples could proceed indefinitely, accompanied, naturally, by counterarguments, and I shall return to one or two shortly. However, abundant, too, are those powerful texts that would seek to strike through such feasibility—with the "reservations" I note, however: 1. "Mimique" (*OC*, 310), with its privileging of idea over presence, its insistence upon *fausse présence* ("false presence"), the installation of "un milieu, pur, de fiction" ("an environment, pure, of fiction"), nonmimetic, self-miming or miming some intrinsicalness of being—but of being; 2. Mallarmé's characteristic claim, in "Solennité," that the poem "replaces everything only because of the lack of everything" (*OC*, 335), a claim, like Reverdy's and Char's, that, while centered upon art-ificial substitution and the nonpresence of presence, stresses equally the desire for "everything," the desire to have and be what, seemingly, one has and is not; 3. the notion that language and things are joined on only a "commercial" base, as Mallarmé says in "Crise de vers," and that, in literature, pure "allusion" and ideal abstraction are the order of the day—even though art is concerned with "incorporating" the "quality" of presence into idea (*OC*, 366); 4. the closing paragraph of "Crise de vers," which evokes the power of original, "incantatory" verse to "complete the isolation of speech: denying, in a sovereign sweep, chance clinging to terms despite the artifice of their alternate tempering in meaning and sound" (*OC*, 368): a denial of *présence*, yes, but one that language itself resists; 5. Mallarmé's famous expression, in the same essay, of language's magical summoning forth of pure spectral, ideal anti-presence, or antinature as Reverdy will say ("I say: a flower! and, out of the oblivion to which

my voice relegates any contour, as something other than known ca-
lyxes, musically rises forth, suave and very idea, the absent of all
bouquets," *OC,* 368): yet an antinature quite unthinkable without
presence and thus finely dependent upon it; 6. the beautiful passage in "Magie" of similar intent ("Evoquer, dans une ombre ex-
près . . ." ["To evoke, in a shadow purposely . . ."]; *OC,* 400), where
Mallarmé exposes with wonderful concision and delicacy his poetics of magical illusoriness, yet, as ever, with reference to the sup-
pressed phenomenality that yet underpins his poetic otherness,
silence, and essence. Here, too, the list could be extended relentlessly.

Many of Mallarmé's poems emphasize, self-reflexively, the movement toward "nothingness" that he sees them, ideally, accomplish-
ing. The liminal text of the *Poésies,* "Salut" (*OC,* 27), wastes no time
in underscoring this essential(izing) transition—"Rien, cette écume,
vierge vers" ("Nothing, this foam, virgin verse")—where poetry's
pristine purity and frothy antinature or absence of all that does not
belong to ideality, is immediately stressed. "Prose pour des Esseintes" is predicated upon the puffy nonexistence of matter
dreamed yet "resurrected." "Eventail de Madame Mallarmé"
("Madame Mallarmé's Fan," *OC,* 57–58) plunges the reader into textuality as pure symbolicalness: "Avec comme pour langage/Rien
qu'un battement aux cieux" ("With as for language/Nothing but a
flapping in the skies," *OC,* 57): a symbolicalness that is the rhythm of
some spiritual nothingness. "Surgi de la croupe et du bond . . ."
("Arisen from the Rump and Leaping . . ."; *OC,* 74) similarly deploys
images depicting the abolition of an object never evoked, just as
"Une dentelle s'abolit" affirms from the outset the pure disappearance, "dans le doute du Jeu suprême" ("in doubt of the supreme
Game," *OC,* 74), to which all materiality is subjected in the implacably orchestrated sprawl of the imagination's liberated ideality. What
is occurring is, as Mallarmé writes of the ballets he observes, nothing: "rien n'a lieu" ("nothing takes place" (*OC,* 305), "l'atmosphère
ou rien" ("atmosphere or nothing," *OC,* 309). "Crayonné au théâtre"
gives a fairly explicit expression of this central factor of his poetics:

Le sot bavarde sans rien dire, et errer de même à l'exclusion d'un goût no-
toire pour la prolixité et précisément afin de ne pas exprimer quelque
chose, représente un cas spécial, qui aura été le mien: je m'exhibe en l'exception de ce ridicule.

Mallarmé

The fool chatters saying nothing, and to wander likewise excluding a noto-
rious taste for verbosity and precisely so as not to express something, represents a special case, which will have been mine; I display myself as the
exception to this ridiculousness.

(OC, 298)

What is "absurd" about Mallarmé's scriptural gesture, he thus
maintains—yet what is exceptional in it, too—is its desire for
"nothingness," its refusal to say anything, any thing, its disappearance into pure fictionality ("La Fiction ou Poésie" ["Fiction or Poetry"], *OC*, 335, "Solennité"), the kind of orchestral miming of the
infinity of silence that Mallarmé evokes in "Mimique" (*OC*, 310)
and that is the realm of pure mentality or notionality. "L'abîme
d'art" ("The abyss of art"), he already writes in "Ballets" (*OC*, 303),
yet such nothingness is not that of idleness, banality, or sheer
sterility; it is a "nothingness" aspired to, a "nothingness" capable,
like the Book, of containing the world, of being all, everything, of
satisfying spiritually that "hunger which feasts upon no fruits
here," as he puts it in the 1887 sonnet, "Mes bouquins refermés..."
("My Books closed up...; *OC*, 76). The poem or work of art is, in
short, the achieved "imaginary trophy" inflated with its only exquisite "vacancy" (*OC*, 286, "Le Nénuphar blanc"): the accomplishment of some pure spiritual and evacuated place of being-as-non-
specificity.

Poetic "nothingness" may be said to be that one non-place and
non-time where *présence* is transmuted into what is, for Mallarmé,
the true place of being. It is, in a sense, Mallarméan presence. It is,
moreover, not just a question of language's "dragging along" of its
gazes d'origine, the veils of its rootedness; Mallarméan presence is
the "present pureness" of things (*OC*, 853, "Notes"), a taut equation,
even equivalence, of time and intemporality, transcendence and
persistent *hasard*. How could "the orphic explanation of the Earth"
(*OC*, 663) not include the world, its dyingness, its ephemerality, within its project of transcendent symbolization? "All is
smoke,/Spanish tobacco and French verse," we read, on the one
hand, in the very early "À un poète immoral" ("To An Immoral
Poet," *OC*, 19–20); on the other, in the 1895 "Bucolique," some
thirty-four years later, Mallarmé speaks of that great dream, forever haunting him, of "perceiving oneself, simple, infinitely upon
the earth" (*OC*, 405): a poetics caught between, in a fusion of, the

wispy fleetingness of existence and the latter's magical, "imaginary" or spiritual infinitization, the symbolic "simplification" or essentialization of telluric presence.

To opt for the symbolic is to opt for the homological functioning of text—but via the mind's immersion therein—and earth, word and world. What is *Un coup de dés* if not a symbolic, textual universe at once apart and embracing presence via its otherness, its spiritualization, equivalent in functional complexity to the world itself? "The Book . . . is sufficient with many most new processes," Mallarmé writes in "Le Genre ou des modernes" (*OC*, 312–21), "analogous in rarefaction to life's subtleties" (*OC*, 318): the homology, the analogousness—the difference and sameness—of the mystery, enigma, subtlety of Book and Earth. "Avec *comme* pour langage" ("With *as* for language") begins the "Eventail de Madame Mallarmé" (my italics). This homological symbolization offers what Mallarmé calls, in "Richard Wagner" (*OC*, 541–46), "une réciprocité de preuves" ("a reciprocity of proofs"), yet a reciprocal proof—the poem or Book "proving" primariness, which "proves itself" in the shimmering (non-)reflections of the symbol—plainly of the mind, the soul, and hence a being plunged back into its equation with "nothingness," "fiction," absence. "Some illusion equal to the gaze," Mallarmé writes in "Magie." He may well insist upon poetry purging from itself the "vain . . . residue" of "objects" ("La Musique et les lettres," *OC*, 655, variant), but his principal ambition remains a poetic—textual-mental—"illumination" of the world's "fundamental rhythm," a homologue of being raised to its highest form of symbolic figuration, parallel to, embracing, even containing, presence, yet different from it, "sa pureté présente" ("its present purity," *OC*, 853)—as Deguy would say, *l'être-comme* ("the being-as") of what is. "Avec comme pour langage" (*OC*, 57).

Poem, Prose and Music: Forms

Mallarmé's *poèmes d'enfance et de jeunesse* gives us a pertinent foretaste of what the next forty years hold in store, formally, stylistically. The 1858 "Cantate pour la première communion" (*OC*, 3–4) may not be metrically innovative (8+8+12+8+6+6 for the refrain, octosyllabic structure for the other stanzas), but nor is it stylistically sluggish, with its choral concept and not unambitious shaping. Poems such as "Sa Fosse est creusée! . . ." (*OC*, 4–6) and "La

Prière d'une mère" ("A Mother's Prayer," *OC*, 10–14) similarly rise above their stable, but still shifting metric and stanzaic patterns to offer tripartite organization, and a concordant cosmic conception thereof in the latter poem. The seven-syllable *impair* sometimes later chosen may not be found here, but the alexandrine and the eight-syllable line dominate, as in many of the sonnets and other poems of the mid-1880s and the final years. The sonnet form, as in "Contre un poëte parisien" (*OC*, 20–21), already claims Mallarmé's attention—his "worship . . . for the antique verse" (*OC*, 456) does not waver—as does the 16-line poem ("Le Château de l'Espérance" and "Soleil d'hiver"). In addition, other foreshadowings may be seen in "À un poëte immoral," with its forceful enjambments and *rejets;* in "Mysticis umbraculis" (*OC*, 22), with its Magritte-like sub-title ("Prose des fous" ["Madmen's Prose"]) and its bold, yet hu-morous use of the tercet in a quasi-fragmentary, or simply compacted, form; in "Le Château de l'Espérance," with its Baude-lairean quality, yet also its propensity for ellipticalness, forced allu-siveness rather than plain evocation.

The *Parnasse contemporain* and *Parnasse satyrique* poems are de-lightfully preceded in the final edition of *Poésies* by "Salut" (*OC*, 27), which dates them, no doubt both wittingly and ironically. Seven sonnets may be counted among these poems of Mallarmé's early maturity, plus one or two near-sonnets such as "Apparition" (*OC*, 30) and "Brise marine" with their sixteen-line structures. The poems of this period are, rather surprisingly, written exclusively in alexandrine meter; quatrains and tercets or terza rima dominate, with rare exceptions such as "Las de l'amer repos . . ." with its ten-line and eighteen-line stanzas, and the ten-line "Soupir" (*OC*, 39). Most of the poems retain a sufficiently discursive strain to be read-ily distinguished from both the formally similar poems of the 1880s and the blatantly rethought mode of the later sonnets.

The unfinished dramatic poem "Hérodiode" is structurally tri-partite, though metrically stable, if finally varied: alexandrine, ex-cept for the "Cantique de Saint Jean," where the stability of its 6+6+6+4 meter and its *rimes plates* is belied by that total lack of punctuation (save the final period) which characterizes the very late production, sonnets, and *Un coup de dés.* "Hérodiade" is stylis-tically, modally, uncompromising. Dense, often ambiguous due to the relatively uncontextualized discourse, the abstract language, and the arcane usage, this enigmatic and hermetic poem is only exceeded in its willed esotericism by the varying modes Mallarmé gives to *Igitur* and *Un coup de dés*. "L'Après-midi d'un faune," from the same period as "Hérodiade," may possess its own strongly elliptical and idealizing features, but it remains a manifestly lyrical *églogue*, a true song of life, light, and desire, with blatant continuity and focus. Its alexandrine form, complete with *rimes plates*, almost mocks, however, the vigor of its symbolist modernity—which, in turn, winks in complicity.

The later sonnets divide themselves into two groups, largely mirrored by chronology: those of the mid-1880s, such as "La Chevelure" ("Hair," *OC*, 53); "Dame/sans trop d'ardeur ...."; "Quand l'ombre menaça..."; "Le Vierge, le vivace..."; "Victorieusement fui..." ("Victoriously Fled," *OC*, 68); "Ses purs ongles..." (*OC*, 68–69); and those of the mid-1890s, such as "Hommage" (*OC*, 72); "Toute l'âme..."; "À la nue..."; and "Salut." "Une dentelle s'abolit..." belongs in mode to this latter group but was written in 1887. The earlier 1880s sonnets show some hesitation between earlier forms, punctuated and metrically conventional despite their firm retreat into pure allusiveness and notionality supported by telescoped syntax, and, on the other hand, that complete liberation from punctuation, contextualization, linear discourse, anecdotality, traditional prosody which "À la nue..." enacts to perfection, offering the reader a mini-version of the symphonic swirl to come in *Un coup de dés*.

Other forms and modes appear in the *Poésies*: the *petits airs* ("Little Airs," *OC*, 65–67), with their late sonnet style and mildly modified structuring (4+4+4+2); the "Chansons bas" ("Songs Low," *OC*, 62–64), often single quatrains equipped with titles, but also, like the "Billet à Whistler" ("Note to Whistler," *OC*, 65), sonnets in the 4+4+4+2 mode ("Le Savetier" ["Cobbler"] and "La Marchande d'herbes aromatiques" ["Woman Selling Herbs"], *OC*, 62–63); and the two fixed-form rondels, scrupulously respected as part of that rich panoply of "antique verse" Mallarmé worships, yet to which he brings that curious mixture of quirky preciousness and often astonishingly convoluted, self-reflexive modernity.

The *vers de circonstance*, written continuously from 1881 on to Mallarmé's death, number close to six hundred. Approximately five hundred of the poems are single quatrains, almost always rhymed *abab* and never in *rimes plates*, most often electing the 8-syllable line, at times the 7-syllable *impair* (as for an occasional late sonnet), rarely some other meter. The couplet is also used somewhat, especially for the *envois,* with close to seventy poems in this manner. And there are very occasional longer circumstantial texts, as well as an odd rondel and sonnet, and five fixed-form triolets read upon performance nights at the Valvins Theater—which Mallarmé also inaugurated with a sonnet. The tone of most of these poems remains jovial, often witty or charming, at times even cockily Verlainean. Never *zutiste,* however. Rhymes and rhythms, especially in the *Loisirs de la poste,* can at times be manhandled, at once with humorous improbability and grace, and disarticulations that push poetry to a more modern musicality are far from uncommon.

Before dealing with Mallarmé's *Poèmes en prose,* his *Igitur,* and the crowning *Un coup de dés,* let me note a few matters as yet unattended to: 1. Mallarmé's poetry tends, consciously and simultaneously, to simplification and complexification (*OC,* 327); 2. his form and style appeal to a "mind open to multiple comprehension" (*OC,* 283); 3. a poem, even a book, is always seen as a unified totality of elements that is appreciable; 4. those "délicieux à-peu-près" ("delightful approximates") he speaks of in "Crise de vers" are at once the spiraling nuances of meaning or thought, and the forms of poetry liberating itself from still-venerated traditions; 5. Mallarmé's aestheticism, even preciousness, does not prevent him from vaunting that "high liberty acquired, the newest" (*OC,* 363) available to every individual ("toute âme est un noeud rythmique" ["every soul is a rhythmic knot"], *OC,* 644), nor from founding, with *Un coup de dés,* a new era of poetic form, an era still very much ours one hundred years later; 6. Mallarmé's post-Baudelairean, quasi-Verlainean, but also presurrealist and ultramodern sense of the deep metaphoricity of all of language's relations, and his desire to make poetic expression the constant place of exploration of the "between-ness" of symbol, the "tiers aspect fusible et clair présenté à la divination" ("third aspect, fusible and bright, presented to divination") in the conjunction, sym-bolization, of separate "realities" (*OC,* 365); 7. the insistence, in the midst of polysemic signification, upon the "guarantee" of syntax (*OC,* 385)—which may be traditional or visually rhythmic, as in *Un coup de dés,*—and the hyperconscious orchestration of poetic effect or "surprise" (*OC,* 384), even though, for Mallarmé, poetic form tends toward the simultaneous—because complexly rational—presentation of the poem's myriad elements (*OC,* 654).

Igitur was begun relatively early, around 1869, and was never chosen for publication by Mallarmé. Its themes or obsessions are at once obvious and yet immensely complex, perhaps unfathomable in the sense of their logical irreducibility, despite the poem's title. *Igitur* is deeply engaged in that "orphic explanation of the Earth" (*OC*, 663); it is a prose poem of the most intricate expository complexity. The thematics is familiar and tends to organize itself according to oppositional tensions: time and timelessness, possibility and impotence, chance and divine creative power ("Elbehnon"), presence and absoluteness, nothingness and infinity, emotion (misfortune, anguish, neurosis, ennui) and heroic pure ontic interiority, and so forth. The poem or "tale"— nothing could be less anecdotal than *Igitur*, though this *is* the story of the essential logic of an exceptional, dreamed (but profoundly "lived") existence—moves repeatedly through such "themes," both in the five parts, their "Introduction" and their "Argument," and in what have come to be known as the *Scolies* (*Scholia*). Moreover, if the poem is the poem of ultimate "thusness" (*igitur*), it is also the poem of "madness" (*la folie d'Elbehnon* ["Elbehnon's Madness"]): a poem of the conscious, the will, but also of the unconscious, what constantly leaks out from known intention, known mental and other parameters. As such, *Igitur* is also a poem of immaculate effort, beset and undercut—but also buoyed up, even created—by irony, parenthesis, doubt, "repetition," incompleteness. Its astonishing density, abstractness, and involution—at the semantic but also the phonological level—make it a poem of pure intellectuality struggling with the entire range of both existential and purely notional phenomena. Its meaning is in many ways purely emblematic, a pure, yet performed symbolics of the human capacity to proceed symbolically; fragments may leap out at us with clarity and focus, but return to the seething swirl of self-reflexive reflection, wherein so many terms—"absolute," "infinite," and so on—elude plain definition, just as the "thusness," the logical linearity, of the poem is constantly reabsorbed into that kind of vast mental "constellation" which, by different formal means, *Un coup de dés* creates and endlessly enacts. *Igitur* is a remarkable, unprecedented dramatic prose poem, but its very privileging of pure mentality over aesthetic consideration may well account for Mallarmé's decision not to publish it as part of his achieved poetic oeuvre.

Mallarmé

Four of the *Poèmes en prose* appeared in the 1887 edition of Mallarmé's *Album de vers et de prose*, all twelve finally appearing, with other prose texts, and none as strict *inédits*, in the 1891 *Pages*. Let me rapidly note the following features: 1. the writing of the poems covers close to twenty-five years, and this slowly caressed meticulousness is most evident in their textuality, each poem "a work of mystery closed like perfection" (*OC*, 532), as he says of Whistler; 2. Mallarmé's prose poems are preceded by Baudelaire's *Le Spleen de Paris* (1869); Rimbaud's *Une saison en enfer* (1873), which was never actually distributed; Lautréamont's *Les Chants de Maldoror* (1874; first integral edition), which Mallarmé, like most readers, of the period, does not seem to have discovered; and, in 1886, Verlaine's *Les Mémoires d'un veuf* and Rimbaud's *Les Illuminations:* the essential influence here is Baudelaire, Mallarmé's production remaining largely of his time; 3. the poems can contain dialogue, may incorporate his own verse poetry ("La Chevelure . . ."; *OC*, 53), and may vary both in length and structure: single paragraph, two or several paragraphs, paragraphs of greatly contrasting length or paragraphs become quasi-stanzas ("Pauvre enfant pâle," *OC*, 274–75), rhythmically intercalated parenthesis ("Frisson d'hiver" ["Winter Shudder"], *OC*, 271–72); 4. the texts betray varying degrees of hermeticism, by and large pushing further Baudelaire's practice, yet quite distinct from Rimbaud's in their often longish and complex sentences, their subtle appositions, inversions and, other syntactical eccentricities; 5. there is a measure of linguistico-aesthetic play, fronting occasionally upon the consciously humorous, always the charming, which, while utterly remote from the prose of *Igitur*, ties in with the stylistic modes of much of Mallarmé's other prose writings and the *vers de circonstance*, not to mention his correspondence; 6. a careful scrutiny of the rhetoric of Mallarmé's prose would be most interesting, especially if laid over, palimpsestlike, the structures inhabiting the verse poetry; 7. Mallarmé holds "versification," rhythmic play, to be everywhere present in language (*OC*, 867), prose being merely a particular state of verse (*OC*, 644), given the presence of that essential factor: "effort au style" ("stylistic effort," *OC*, 667); 8. perhaps in consequence, Mallarmé sees prose as far from a purely linear practice: it can "play . . . according to a thousand turns" (*OC*, 654)—*Igitur* reveals this perhaps better than any of the *Poèmes en prose*; 9. "Prose pour des Esseintes" can be read as a play on much of this thinking, a winking anti-*poème en prose.*

Un coup de dés is the crowning achievement of Mallarmé's poetic oeuvre. It perhaps is the *Grand Oeuvre* of which he dreamed, though Mallarmé's ideal Book could clearly contain many books. What is most remarkable about *Un coup de dés* is the extent to which it leaps over all existing poetic enterprise to found a space of new, high, demanding though feasible poetico-spiritual communion, yet one which does not seek, anarchically, iconoclastically, to break with the other modes Mallarmé has explored and pushed to exemplary limits. The poem is inevitably read in the double light of Mallarmé's preface to it and his reasonably extensive writings on poetry and art in general; and yet it rises serenely above such limitations especially as to its ceaselessly swirling and circulating "symphonic" meaning. The white space, everywhere present, is a space of immense mental potential known to all poets since Mallarmé—one thinks of Reverdy, Guillevic, Noël, Du Bouchet, but all modern and contemporary poets bear the mark of "whiteness," aeration, "constellation." Reading is caught in a process of textual respiration at once similar to that of traditional prosodies (including that of Mallarmé's own unpunctuated last sonnets) and yet transcending them all. Meaning is both simplified—to the extent attention can legitimately be focused upon fragments, "images of themselves" (*OC*, 455)—and infinitely complicated, to the extent that "multiple comprehension" (*OC*, 283) is required: simultaneous perception, relational sensitivity, a reading of some unspecifiable, endlessly elusive totality curiously "there" in the text.

As Mallarmé suggests, the poem's meaning or Idea is "prismatically" (un)focused (*OC*, 455); it projects itself as intimation and by diverse visual and not merely discursive means, via a typographical, even painterly syntax at once coherent and discontinuous. Thought is thus more "hypothetical" or, as Mallarmé says at times, "virtual" (*OC*, 455): its trace or design is musical, a "partition" of suspended yet essentially available symbolics, a "symphony" Mallarmé describes as being "le cas de traiter . . . tels sujets d'imagination pure et complexe ou intellect" ("the case of treating . . . certain subjects of pure and complex imagination, or intellect" (*OC*, 455–56). All of Mallarmé's poetic oeuvre may be an exploration of the possibility of transcending *le hasard* and acceding to some (non) time-space of ideal and ideational purity, and *Un coup de dés* may be deemed to be the place of recognition of the failure of this project. "Toute Pensée émet un Coup de Dés ("All Thought Emits a Throw of the Dice," *OC*, 477); and yet, as we read at the linear point of conclusion of *Un coup de dés*, "watchful/doubting/rolling along/shimmering and meditative," thought's (poetic) movement may reach a moment of constellar congealment deemed "sacred," which we call the text or poem. But the latter, while caught in its closure and per-fectedness, may equally be said to reach a pure liberation of mind as it releases us into a world of meaning infinitely in flux, ever original, curiously intensely present as it rolls through our minds, yet ever-virtual in its endlessly performable play.

· SEVEN ·

Verlaine

On 30 March 1844, in Metz, there came into the world that person whom Oscar Wilde, in *De Profundis*, was to consider, at once improbably and perceptively, the "greatest Christian poet" France had ever known: Paul Verlaine. Verlaine's indifferent studies did not prevent him from sending his early adolescent poems to Hugo, nor did his unenthused dabblings with law school, his youthful drinking bouts, the influence of poets such as Banville, Villiers de l'Isle-Adam, Baudelaire, and Hugo, prevent him from publishing, in 1866, his groping but still newly toned *Poèmes saturniens* (*Saturnian Poems*), which he offers also, and emblematically, to the slightly senior Stéphane Mallarmé. The year 1870 finds him working at the Hôtel de Ville in Paris, with the 1869 *Fêtes galantes* (*Feasts of Love*) under his belt, and marrying his adulated but underestimated recent seventeen-year-old fiancée, Mathilde Mauté, to whom he offers the brief freshness of *La Bonne Chanson* (*Good Song*). The following year sees Rimbaud come to Paris at Verlaine's invitation, and the marriage rapidly deteriorates in a manner mirroring the poet's equally continuing inability to resolve other than via temperamental abusiveness his relations with his mother. Verlaine's exalted and wild adventures with Rimbaud, in England, Paris, and Belgium, culminate in the Brussels gunshots that lead him to the self-analysis and willed self-transformations amply documented in the later *Mes Prisons* (*My Prisons*). The years following his liberation give rise to the publication of *Romances sans paroles* (*Wordless Romances*, 1874) and the now maligned, but lauded *Sagesse* (*Wisdom*, 1881). There is an attempted but failed reconciliation with Rimbaud in Stuttgart; years of teaching in London, Lincolnshire, Bournemouth; a bold adventure with one of his Rethel students, Lucien Létinois, whith whom he idyllically sets up farming in Juniville, only to return to Paris two years later and resume his literary life—and, with it, the carousing, unpredictability, slumps to regretted violence, of more youthful days. Further imprisonment, rising poverty and squalor and illness, broken by occasional splurges from new successes, but bolstered by the undaunted kindness of friends and the love and compassion of women whose affections he reciprocated in his inimitably bitter-sweet, at once clumsy and exquisite fashion—such was the pattern of Verlaine's quickly dissolving last years.

These experiences, far from diminishing his poetic production, goaded it to mixed heights, both new and repetitive forms, both deep and slender fascinations. The last ten years or so of his life see the appearance of *Jadis et Naguère* (*Yesteryear and Latterday*, 1884), *Amour* (*Love*, 1888), *Parallèlement* (*In Parallel*, 1889), *Bonheur* (*Happiness*, 1891), *Chansons pour elle* (*Songs for Her*, 1891), *Liturgies intimes* (*Intimate Liturgies*, 1892), *Odes en son honneur* (*Odes in Her Honor*, 1893), and other more polemical or autobiographical books. His death, on 8 January 1896, had been preceded by lecture trips to Belgium and England, and colored by a deep, psychologically complex friendship with the painter Cazals. In 1894, upon the death of its holder, Leconte de Lisle, Verlaine had been elected "Prince des Poètes." Such praise from his contemporaries, far from ideal, did not succeed in attaching him to anything describable as a "school" or would-be avant-gardist creative mode. Rimbaud appreciated him as an individual, "a true poet," as did Mallarmé. Valéry regarded him as "un primitif organisé" ("an organized primitive"), naive but "skilled [and] conscious," yet neglected his sheer affective and spiritual complexity. Today, poets such as Deguy and Bonnefoy are still powerfully drawn to his work for both its technical subtlety and its psychical emblematicalness.

Saturn and the Devil

If we set aside a handful of poems and fragments—of which "La Mort" ("Death") is the most memorable, Verlaine having sent it to Hugo in 1858 at the age of fourteen—1866 marks Verlaine's definitive entry into a poetic arena whose already changing spectacles he will modify at once modestly and inimitably. The *Poèmes saturniens* are provided with a compact verse preface by their twenty-two-year-old author in which he argues "the logic of a malignant Influence" (*OPC*, 57) dictating the bilious anxieties, the boiling visceralness, the seething unhappiness underpinning his artistic imagination. A reading of the collection largely confirms this apparently fatalistic, but dramatically lucid, self-analysis. The *Poèmes saturniens* evoke dismaying scenes of urban misery and hostility, of cunning, cruelty, and deceit, of rottingness and death, of danger and coldness, of dream plunged back into grievous reality. Visions of high intent are swamped out by feelings of lassitude and exile. Later collections may vary in tone, but this initial diagnosis lingers cloyingly, in part assumed, as in "Un projet de mon âge mûr" ("A Plan for My Maturity"), from the 1891 *Bonheur*, where moral laziness, anger, pride, carnality, and a host of other "sins" are liberally confessed (*OPC*, 673–75); in part attributed to his intrinsic astrological determination—"I have ruined my life, and I know," he will write in the 1889 *Parallèlement*, "That all blame will rain down upon me:/To that I can but reply/That I really was born Saturnianly" (*OPC*, 498)—or what he calls, "less baudelairely," in his 1893 half-page "Autobiographie" (*PR*, 424), "le train-train de l'existence"/ "the humdrum of existence." Over all of Verlaine's work—and despite his humor, his aspirations, his poetic resistance—there hangs a pall of what he himself can often term ennui and moroseness ("L'Ennui de vivre..." ["Life's Boredom..."], *Bonheur*, *OPC*, 691–93), *spleen* (*OPC*, 205), and "autumnal" consciousness. One of his earliest poems, "Un soir d'octobre" ("October Evening") written in 1862 when he was eighteen, spells out powerfully this seasonal affinity:

> Oh! c'est bien là ton heure et ta saison, poète
> Au coeur vide d'illusions,
> Et que rongent les dents de rats des passions,
> Quel bon miroir, et quelle fête!

> Oh, that's your hour and season, poet
> Whose heart has no illusions,
> Eaten away by the rat-teeth of passion,
> Lovely mirror, and what fun!
>
> (*OPC*, 20)

And if this poem speaks of a certain happiness, it is also feverish, improbable, associated with that stagnation, harshness, and death so often to arouse an almost chronic melancholia in Verlaine. The saturnian bent gives rise, already in his first collection, to endless "sad landscapes" (*OPC*, 69–74) where the "Autumnal Song" may be exquisitely formed but remains pained, "suffocating" (*OPC*,

72–73, "Chanson d'automne" ["Autumn Song"]), where the banalities of the real become the "shifting ghosts . . . [of] the drunken poet's/Thought, or his regret, or his remorse" (*OPC*, 71–72, "Nuit du Walpurgis classique" ["Classical Walpurgis Night"]). Gentle or depressive sadness is, then, an ongoing sign of the Verlainean sensibility. It can pertain to external events, as in "Il pleure dans mon coeur" (*OPC*, 192) or "Ô triste, triste était mon âme . . ." ("Sad, oh Sad, was my Soul," *OPC*, 195), both from the 1873 *Romances sans paroles*, but, as the beautiful "Je ne sais pourquoi . . ." ("I know not why . . .") from *Sagesse* suggests, it remains unfathomable, instinctual:

> Je ne sais pourquoi
> Mon esprit amer
> D'une aile inquiète et folle vole sur la mer.
> Tout ce qui m'est cher,
> D'une aile d'effroi
> Mon amour le couve au ras des flots. Pourquoi, pourquoi?

> I know not why
> My bitter spirit
> Dips disquiet and wild over the sea,
> All that to me is dear
> My fright-winged love
> Broods to the waters tight. Why, oh why?

> (*OPC*, 280–81)

That Verlaine struggled, throughout his life, against a deleterious saturnianism is manifest. His many texts written from hospitals and prisons, resiliently cheerful and self-uplifting, show him intent on following the conclusion of that versified comedy "Les Uns et les autres" ("These and Those") from the 1884 collection *Jadis et naguère* (*Yesteryear and Latterday*): "What matters is not to be/Morose and melancholy./Is life a thing/So grave and real?" (*OPC*, 355). He understands well that the end results of his worst proclivities—(self-)doubt, cynicism, scorn (*OPC*, 246, 424)—are self-waste and self-annihilation (*OPC*, 245–46, "Malheureux! Tous les dons . . ." ["Wretched! All Gifts . . ."]), a moral and emotional suicide that his entire oeuvre symbolically and really prevents. For Verlaine's writings not only trace out, with honesty and persistence, the turbulent shifts "from gloomy chasm to flaming skies,/

From skies flaming with every joy/To chasm shadow-filled and evil," as he puts it in the 1894 *Dans les limbes* (*OPC*, 843, "Un fiacre, demain..." ["A cab, tomorrow..."]); they also demonstrate in their spiritual tension the vast effort of self-transformation to which "this poor old chap named hell-hole" (*OPC*, 843) never ceased to give himself.

Saturnianism does not lead to surrender any more than it does to sadism or to "satanism" ("Ma Candidature" ["My Candidacy"], *PR*, 426). This is, moreover, his view of Baudelaire, as expounded in his 1865 essay (*PR*, 604). Artistic "pretense" or "caprice" are responsible for any such erroneous impressions we may have (*PR*, 352, 604). The short 1891 text "Le Diable" ("The Devil") lays bare, with humor and modesty, the massive contradiction that lies at the heart of his *satanisme*, when what deeply drives him, and his admired Baudelaire, is the high design of art, "cet ange par-dessus les Archanges, la nommée Littérature" ("this angel above Archangels, aforesaid Literature"), with its "light" and "life" (*PR*, 305–307). Saturnianism, melancholia, and depression could have led to nihilism and self-destruction. That they did not is a credit to the poetic stubbornness of Verlaine, to the fact that, as he said of Baudelaire's *Fleurs du Mal*, "these strange verses" are written by a poet who knows "the language of angels" (*OPC*, 876)—by one of those rare "holy poets/Their hair wreathed in madness and verbena," as he prophetically wrote at the age of sixteen (*OPC*, 20, "À Don Quichotte" ["To Don Quixote"]).

Parnassianism, Impressionism, Naturalism, Symbolism: Poetry's Modes

"À Don Quichotte," dated March 1861, offers the earliest ars poetica of a poet who, while not theoretically inclined nor keen to "belong," remains sensitive to the logic of his own demarche. The "saintliness," curiously allied to the "madness," of the artistic creation, based in turn upon intuition rather than "inept reason" (*OPC*, 20)—all these factors seem to be removed from the "poetics in two words" that his 1866 "Vers dorés" ("Gilded Verse," *OPC*, 22) elaborates. Here, Verlaine's early Parnassianism is articulated programmatically: poetry is to be beyond (the) sentiment (of romanticism) and reflects a haughty indifference to the tiresomeness of raw emotion, which risks dominating the creative spirit. "Un égoïsme de marbre" ("A marble-like egoism") is preconised (*OPC*, 22). The 1861 "Aspiration" (*OPC*, 14–15) is a wonderful song of presymbolist enthusiasm, and yet, while seeking transcendence and decrying immanence, it is not predicated upon poker-faced self-control. Because such self-control remains implicit, though, "Aspiration" marks itself off from the poetics of wilder dreaming that underpins "À Don Quichotte."

As Verlaine writes in "Souvenirs sur Leconte de Lisle" ("Memories of Leconte de Lisle," *PR*, 434–37), there is in the marmoreal coolness of the Parnassian mode "something really somewhat odd in a century full of nerves and emotions" (*PR*, 436). At the end of his life, in 1895, he will even write a witty, tongue-in-cheek series of "Trois épilogues en manière d'adieux à la littérature personnelle" ("Three epilogues by way of Farewell to Personal Literature"), the first of which begins:

> Ainsi donc, adieu, cher moi-même
> Que d'honnêtes gens m'ont blâmé,
> Les pauvres! d'avoir trop aimé,
> Trop flatté (dame, quand on aime!)
>
> Farewell, then, farewell, dear me
> How good folk have blamed me,
> Poor dears, for loving so,
> Flattering so (lord, when one loves so!)
> (*PR*, 577)

Initially, however, Verlaine's poetry associates itself with the rather loose principles of those poets publishing in *Le Parnasse contemporain* (*Contemporary Parnassus*), founded in March 1866, and to which Verlaine himself offered seven poems in April of the same year. Verlaine never submits to any outside orchestration of his own poetic discipline. Vaguely Parnassian influences upon his youth and early manhood came from the work of Vigny, Baudelaire, Hugo, Mallarmé, and, to a lesser extent, Gautier and Leconte de Lisle. The *Poèmes saturniens,* teasing out some of the concepts of the earliest writings, center upon poetry as an overridingly aesthetic act. The "Prologue" (*OPC*, 58–60) speaks of "exiling the world" in order to pursue the high "ideal" of "the love of the Beautiful." Such a pursuit entails extreme attention to form and style, "chiseling and cutting," as Gautier puts it, to poetry as production and not some means of pure affective *défoulement*. It is no surprise that the "Epilogue" to the same collection (*OPC*, 93–96) insists upon the roles of prosody, rhyme, image, "obstination," and "will" in the "sculpting of the virgin block of the Beautiful/With the chisel of Thought" (*OPC*, 96).

If art, as Verlaine argues in his essay "Charles Baudelaire" (*PR*, 599–612), remains amoral, apolitical, and aphilosophical, it is hardly mindless. The great virtue of the Parnassian consciousness lies in its focusing of attention upon the immense labor, self-discipline, and technical mastery underpinning the expression of any description, feeling, intuition, or vision. The notion of sheer impassiveness is, rather than a reality, a Parnassian reminder of this "invisible" mental infrastructure. *Poèmes saturniens* abounds with thought and sentiment, and Verlaine knows that, belonging to those poets who "[font] des vers émus très froidement" ("[make] emotional verse most coldly") (*OPC*, 95). "Romantic emotion" does not disappear, but it does dissociate itself from "undisciplined" gushing and assume an ironic, self-analytical, or tightly allegorical mode within a poetics of strict aesthetic consciousness.

Above all, Verlaine adores that poetic freedom which Hugo demanded in *Les Orientales* and which Verlaine himself evokes in his Baudelaire essay (*PR*, 604). Already in *Poèmes saturniens* various other poetic modes such as the impressionist and symbolist fuse with the would-be Parnassian ideals. Nothing, however, remains clear-cut, finely theorized in Verlaine's supple aesthetics, where we find the same kind of modal blendings and nuances that he recommends in "Art poétique" ("Poetic Art," *OPC*, 326). A glance at this later text, written in 1882, from the 1885 *Jadis et naguère* will prove helpful, its criteria being: 1. the essential musicality or prosodic integrity of the poem, over and above the thoughts and sentiments conveyed; 2. the lilting, disarticulating quality available via the *impair*; 3. the necessity of ambiguity, of the marriage of the specific and the indeterminate; 4. the preference for nuance and graduation, allowing discourse to dream itself; 5. the need to avoid the polemical, sharply satirical, or didactic; 6. the abhorrence of "eloquence"—of pure rhetoric unallied to substance, emotion, and meaning; 7. the pitfalls of rhyme and assonance—that halfway house to vers libre; 8. the desired rhythmic lightness of poetic expression, its adventurous "anti-literary" aspiration.

While we can see the pertinence of certain of these criteria to Verlaine's earliest affinities, it is easy to observe, too, the slippage into preoccupations that allow us to read his work as symbolist or even impressionist. Criteria 1, 4, 5, 6, and 8 may be viewed in this double light; and a number of the *Poèmes saturniens* are indicative of impressionism: "Effet de nuit" ("Night Effect," *OPC*, 67–68), where parataxic descriptive splashes combine to produce an "impression," half-emotional, half-visual, wherein the anecdotal merges with something beyond telling to produce a poiesis only half *pictura;* the various "paysages tristes" ("sad landscapes," *OPC*, 69–74) where impressionism melds with expressionism, edging toward symbolist allegory while preserving that desire to seize an ephemeral reality. Thus we have "the Dusk/[That] reddens and quivers at the ardent horizon" (*OPC*, 70, "Crépuscule du soir mystique" ["Mystical Evening Dusk"]); "the vague mist conjuring up a great/Milky ghost, desperate and/Weeping with voice of teals" (*OPC*, 70–71, "Promenade sentimentale" ["Sentimental Walk"]); "Here, dwarf roses sharpened by learned taste;/Further, yews cut into triangles. A summer/Evening moon over it all" (*OPC*, 71–72, "Nuit du Walpurgis classique").

Romances sans paroles can give "landscapes," "simple frescoes," "watercolors," in which the visual dominates, quickly etched in its broad, fugitive lines. Poems such as "Walcourt" (*OPC*, 197), "Bruxelles" (*fresque* I) (*OPC*, 198–99), and "Malines" (*OPC*, 201) can be read in this perspective. That this "impressionist" mode of Verlaine's can fade into a purer symbolism, and that it is always tinged with an expressionism à la Van Gogh, is undeniable. And that it flows into a purer fascination with the real should not really surprise us. Again, the global lesson of Verlaine is that poetry's modes are multiple, more interlocking than is generally admitted, and tend to cock a snoot at pure theory.

"Le Soldat laboureur" ("The Soldier Ploughman," *OPC*, 356–59) is included in *Jadis et naguère*, in the *vers jeunes* (*young verse*) section. It is a narrative and descriptive poem of some sobriety, reminiscent of and perhaps influenced by Vigny and Hugo, even Lamartine; it dates back to 1863, when Verlaine was nineteen. In a sense, it is not particularly removed from the Parnassian ideals of self-erasure and cool evocativeness. But this Parnassianism may be seen as a poetic reflection of the novelistic aesthetics of Flaubert and Balzac, and later Zola and the Goncourts. Verlaine admired the former two "masters" (*PR*, 947, 1028) but had mixed feelings for the latter two. Zola, despite "very great beauties," is psychologically insensitive and too given to the enactment of his "systems" (*PR*, 1036–1044), a "splendid dullard" (*PR*, 778). The Goncourts can be "exquisite" yet "cruel" in their overly clinical and finicky "description" (*PR*, 1037). "Le Soldat laboureur" avoids sentimentalism and excessive dissection, psychological reduction and systematization; yet that fundamental realism, so prized by Baudelaire and the young Rimbaud, betrays its deep affinity with the aspirations of the century's great novelists. "L'Angélus du matin" ("The Morning Angelus," *OPC*, 363–64), from the same section of *Jadis et naguère*, emphasizes this youthful and insistent gaze upon the world, as does the 1871 "La Soupe du jour" ("Soup of the Day"), originally published in *Le Parnasse contemporain* and dedicated to Huysmans (*OPC*, 365–66). Here Verlaine's gaze, while evading all idealism, zeros in on the essential factors of *présence:* the "one bed, a ramshackle chest, four chairs,/White curtains covered with the droppings of bugs," "an old rusty gun hanging from a nail," "a few dust-laden tomes . . . / Piled at the back of a rickety chest of drawers," signs of privation and reduction pushing the couple nearer to sheer animality, "the children, their fists in their closed eyes,/Snoring over their plates in the likeness of great sobs." Discretion, intensity, and compassion are the signs of Verlaine's quasi-naturalist poetic mode—a mode that will come and go throughout his oeuvre, and that tells us to what degree his poetry remains focused, despite pain and dismay, on the teeming specificities of life.

The shifts from Parnassianism to the various symbolist modes proliferating in France from, say, 1865 to 1895 are subtle, differently perceived by the poets themselves. The great poets of this "symbolist" period—Verlaine, Mallarmé, Rimbaud, Laforgue—tend to move their poetics from self-erasure to unfolding forms of allegorized subjectivity—open and vigorous in Verlaine and Rimbaud, persistently ironic in Laforgue, esoteric in Mallarmé. In Verlaine's case, as his "Art poétique" has shown, the symbolist mode profits from the insistence not only upon "nuance" and ambiguity but also upon the "musicality" of the text, its nonutilitarian delight in its rhythmic logic. Thus Verlaine, in "À Albert Mérat" ("To Albert Mérat," *OPC*, 326), the poem preceding "Art poétique," can exclaim: "Let's live in a dandyism in love with Rhyme alone"; thus will he insist upon the dominance of Desbordes-

Valmore's prosodic genius over her affective merits (*OPC*, 642); thus does he privilege the notion of the "magical," strictly poetic— Valéry would say "charming," bewitching—transformation of the given in "Images d'un sou" dedicated to Dierx (*OPC*, 331–33); thus, at the outset of *Les Poètes maudits*, does he seek to stress the "accursedness" afflicting the work of Corbière, Rimbaud, Mallarmé, Desbordes-Valmore, Villiers, and himself, but equally the "absoluteness" that haunts their endeavor: "Absolute through imagination, absolute in expression, absolute like the *Reys netos* of the best centuries" (*PR*, 637). Absoluteness is the desire to reign artistically over nature, the feeling that the analogies, emblems, and metaphors of poetry can truly permit metaphysical illumination. Such supreme ambitions clearly underpin the work of Rimbaud and Mallarmé. In Verlaine they persist, more humble, demystified, or smilingly ironised, yet forever haunting in poems even from his first collection, *Poèmes saturniens*.

"Chanson d'automne" is an exquisite example of Verlaine's purest symbolist mode, offering us sensitive analogical slippages that paint inner and outer states in a lilting arythmia so delicately controlled, and supported by onomatopoeia, alliteration, inner rhymes and assonances that almost allow music its complete ascendancy over all else. "Le Rossignol" ("The Nightingale"), from the same first collection (*OPC*, 73–74), deploys somewhat different prosodic means. The ten-syllable line is allied to the *rime plate*, yet its twenty lines create, via the finest control of enjambment, *coupe*, parenthesis, present participle, subordinate clause, the most lovely emblem, a symbolist *blason* that yet remains so unpretentious. Other, later poems could be looked at in this way: "Clair de lune" ("Moonlight"), from *Fêtes galantes* (*OPC*, 107); "Intérieur" ("Interior") or "Allégorie" from *Jadis et naguère* (*OPC*, 322, 328), and so on. The purest texts in this mode belong to the earlier years, though what "Vendanges" ("Wine Harvesting") calls that "discreet and distant music" (*OPC*, 331) never ceases to haunt the work of "[ce] symboliste inexpecté" ("that unexpected symbolist"), as he called himself in "Le Diable" (*PR*, 307).

Let me conclude by underlining a number of additional factors: 1. an analysis of Verlaine's opus reveals that poetry can turn itself to many subjects and overflow the limiting modal chambers we have just discussed. For example, a contrasting of *La Bonne Chanson, Sagesse, Parallèlement, Odes en son honneur,* and *Invectives* produces a firm appreciation of the extent to which Verlaine's poetics is *une poétique éclatée*, never hesitant to *be* "la bonne aventure/ Eparse au vent crispé du matin" ("a simple adventure/scattered upon the morning's puckering wind," *OPC*, 326, "Art poétique"); 2. art may be deemed a "nothingness," but it remains Verlaine's *gift* ("Un scrupule qui m'a l'air sot . . ." ["A Scruple Seeming Daft to Me . . ."], *Bonheur*, *OPC*, 689–90). As such, it is "for the benefit . . . of Life" ("J'ai dit à l'esprit vain . . ." ["I Have Said to the Futile Mind . . ."])—an act of fundamental existential import, self-liberating but no longer self-exiling (see "Ô toi triomphante . . ." ["Oh Triumphant You . . ."], *Odes en son honneur*, *OPC*, 780–81, final stanza); 3. art involves assuming one's totality and complexity: "l'art, mes enfants, c'est d'être absolument soi-même" ("art, my children, is being absolutely oneself" ("J'ai dit à l'esprit vain . . ."). Art is a kind of "walking straight ahead/—Without hiding, dawdling, being distracted" (*OPC*, 900, "L'art poétique ad hoc" ["Ad Hoc Poetic Art"]), yet it also involves a consciousness of art's ubiquitousness, a need for "everything to be something" (*OPC*, 850); 4. if Verlaine would lead us to believe that poetry is mere play (*OPC*, 843, 849), it is important to remember all that, for him, is visceral and urgent in the poetic act; 5. Verlaine may have opposed the proliferation of assonance and blank verse (*OPC*, 854–55, "J'admire l'ambition . . ." ["I Admire Ambition . . ."]; and *PR*, 696–701, "Un mot sur la rime" ["A Word About Rhyme"]), for he was not prepared, at the end of his life, to "think of supreme dives" (*OPC*, 855); yet he adored aesthetic liberty, lived and wrote with debonair impulsiveness, despite the "work" involved, and has given us singularly powerful prose poems.

Body

Verlaine's 1865 essay praises Baudelaire for his bold and original depiction of "modern physical man, such as the refinements of excessive civilization have made him, modern man, with his sharpened, vibrant senses, his painfully subtle mind, his tobacco-saturated brain, his blood burned by alcohol, in a word, the *bilio-nervous type* to a tee, as H. Taine would say" (*PR*, 600). Verlaine's own exploration of human physicality is no less intense and is his most particularizing way of penetrating the full essence and meaning of *présence*, ephemerality, possibility.

"Dahlia" (*OPC*, 81), from the 1866 *Poèmes saturniens*, shows Verlaine "writing" the body—the female body almost invariably, though we should not understate the corporeal sensitiveness of "Le Soldat laboureur" and "La Soupe du soir" (*OPC*, 365–66). Verlaine does so à la Vigny, coolly evocative and emblematic in manner:

> Fleur grasse et riche, autour de toi ne flotte aucun
> Arome, et la beauté sereine de ton corps
> Déroule, mate, ses impeccables accords.
>
> Full, rich flower, about you floats no
> Fragrance, and the serene beauty of your body
> Unfolds, matte, its perfect harmonies.
>
> (*OPC*, 81)

Such an early posture before the body of the other (not until his "hospital writings" will Verlaine turn his sharp eye upon his own physicality) betrays that sense of distance, mystery, and awesome discovery that Vigny knew. The 1869 *Fêtes galantes* continues to show discretion before the body, which is, however, now caught up in pastoral enchantment, theatrical, balletic movement. "Pantomime," "Les Ingénus" ("The Naive"), and "Colombine" ("Columbine, *OPC*, 107, 110, 118–19) reflect this sensual alertness and expectancy in, for instance, the fluttering hands, hearts, and mouths in the dance of the "masques et bergamasques" ("masks and bergamasks," *OPC*, 107; see also "À la promenade" ["Out Walking"], *OPC*, 109). The body, here, is steeped in dream, youthful desire and fascination, a quick but gentle Watteau-like "vertigo" (*OPC*, 113) of laughter and tears. If "En sourdine" ("Muted," *OPC*, 120) conveys the ideality of such a soft and innocent physical idyll—"Let us merge our souls, our hearts/And our senses in bliss,/Among the vague languors/Of pines and cane-apples" (*OPC*, 120)—so can Verlaine burst this magical bubble of the mind. His closing poem, "Colloque sentimental" ("Sentimental Colloquy," *OPC*, 121), following "En sourdine," picks up on the latter's final note of anguished passion and plunges into the "dead," "soft," collapsed physicality of an ironic future, where all is disillusion, negation, harsh correction of youthful dream and hope.

The 1880 *Sagesse* reflects Verlaine's long meditation on the joys and storms of the body: the dissolution of his marriage to Mathilde

Mauté, after the sensual-spiritual promise of *La Bonne Chanson;* the excesses of Paris, London, and Brussels; the confinements of prison; the separations forced and self-imposed. *Sagesse* looks back upon "our days of carnal spirit and sad flesh" (*OPC*, 249) and perceives the body, with compassion and dismay, as a site of almost independent life. "La tristesse," he declares,

> La tristesse, la langueur du corps humain
> M'attendrissent, me fléchissent, m'apitoient.
> Ah! surtout quand des sommeils noirs le foudroient,
> Quand les draps zèbrent la peau, foulent la main!
> . . .
> Triste corps! Combien faible et combien puni!
>
> The sadness, the languor of the human body
> Stir a tenderness, a pity within.
> Ah! more so when black sleeps strike with lightning,
> When sheets crease the skin and twist the hand!
> . . .
> Sad body! How weak and how punished!
>
> (*OPC*, 282).

No independence is involved: the whole logic of *Sagesse* is predicated upon awareness of the self's full, integrated potential. Yet simultaneously, Verlaine acknowledges the self as a locus of schism and contradiction, Baudelairean "crackedness" and difficult equilibrium, as *Jadis et naguère, Amour,* and especially *Parallèlement* remind us. The body's omnipresence, its pressing drives and raison d'être, are constantly known to us, as "our blood . . . sings [in the head],/When memory is absent" (*OPC*, 331, "Vendanges"). "Un conte" ("A Tale"), from *Amour* (*OPC*, 410–12), relates the fall and rise of "a lover in the full sense of the term:/Having known all flesh, foul or virgin,/And the monstrous depth of epiderm"—a lover who remained, "despite all vice, all his crime and all else,/A most simple man decorated at least by his candor" (*OPC*, 411).

Parallèlement shows Verlaine once more in his full force as *the* poet of the body, and, as he says in "À la princesse Roukhine" ("To Princess Roukin"), as its priest, slave, and master (*OPC*, 490). "Auburn" (*OPC*, 493–94) sings the body's parts like a Renaissance *blason*, in adoration. But other texts focus upon the stark realities of abortions (*OPC*, 505); the "hunting and preying," objectifying obsession of the physical—"toute fleur, tout fruit, toute viande" ("every flower, every fruit, every meat," "L'Impénitent" ["Impenitent"], *OPC*, 510–12); the "unscrupulous" and "orgiac" plunge into the corporeal ("Laeti et errabundi," *OPC*, 522–25). And then the pendulum will swing: *Bonheur* will—"après la chose faite" ("after the thing done," (*OPC*, 659)—endeavor to impose the "parallel" optic of spiritual remembrance, aspiration, self-purging, release. "L'Homme pauvre d'esprit . . ." ("The Poor in Spirit . . ."; *OPC*, 663–65) records the history of the body as a place of struggle and self-regeneration. The passage beginning "Ton corps est un lutteur, fais-le vivre en lutteur" ("Your body struggles, have it live in struggle," *OPC*, 664) recognizes the need for a certain self-"hygiene," and the need to assume, in faith, "this lightened, free, near-glorious body," the latter's possible grace, virtue, lovableness/lovingness. Such a gesture represents the understanding of the error of guilt and (self-)condemnation and the embrace of the beauty of forgiveness.

Woman

Women were centrally significant in Verlaine's truncated personal life, and they are ever-present in his work. Not a single collection omits to speak of them; many are entirely devoted to that "muse mine . . ., woman mine [who] unbinds/Both my tongue and my soul" (*OPC*, 838). In the early "Voeu" ("Wish," *OPC*, 62–63), woman—who tends to become a vast feminine force, at once reduced and amplified in her presence—is pictured as the very antidote to solitariness, as lover, beloved, sister, and mother, giver of warmth, gentleness, thought. The beautiful sonnet "Mon rêve familier" ("My Familiar Dream," *OPC*, 63–64), opens as follows:

> Je fais souvent ce rêve étrange et pénétrant
> D'une femme inconnue, et que j'aime, et qui m'aime
> Et qui n'est, chaque fois, ni tout à fait la même
> Ni tout à fait une autre, et m'aime et me comprend.

> I have often this strange and penetrating dream
> Of an unknown woman, that I love, loving me
> And who is, each time, neither quite the same
> Nor quite another, understanding, loving me.

Woman, here, is dreamed, ideal, un-present, and yet real within the mind and heart. She lies somewhere between Baudelaire's *passante* and the surrealists' dream-woman to whom one's *disponibilité* can give reality. As in "Voeu," woman remains a locus of potentiality, aspiration, and need.

Other early poems, such as "Marco" (*OPC*, 86–87), show Verlaine's perception of woman to be fixated initially upon her remoteness, power, mystery, otherness. Even "Sérénade" (*OPC*, 80–81), in which Verlaine addresses himself to a "mistress," bases itself upon a hesitation between woman as an object of veneration and superior power ("Mon Ange!" ["My Angel!"] and woman as possession, as object of self's domination ("Ma Gouge!" ["My Gouge!"]).

La Bonne Chanson (1870) contains twenty-one poems offered to "my beloved Mathilde Mauté de Fleurville," whom Verlaine married in August of the same year. In this young woman, his *"Child Wife"* (*OPC*, 207), Verlaine sees and hopes for many things. She is/can be companion, soul-mate, "Being of light," the definitive Other—a paradisiacal presence. Beyond irony, steeped in nature at large, capable of arousing tenderness, spirituality, and not merely sensual response, this woman is thought to allow him to rediscover both self and world. She is a *charm*, a magical catalyst, but still a largely dreamed being, unable to play the role Verlaine himself cannot play, for himself. Although Verlaine's poetry can be accused of egoism, it might be more generous to deem it self-blindingly desiring. He views their love as simply unmatured, as a profound opportunity wasted. If *"Child Wife"* is uncharitable, he can readily understand elsewhere his own responsibilities, and the poem remains a testimony of unquestionable love. His pure desire, when tested in personal intimacy, does not always have the fortitude of his less than pure desire. In *Parallèlement* Verlaine speaks of the "Neuf environ! Sans m'occuper du casuel,/Des amours de raccroc, des baisers de rencontre,/Neuf que j'aimais et qui m'aimaient" ("Nine about! Without mentioning the casual,/Fluke loves, fleeting kisses,/Nine I loved, who loved me," *OPC*, 513, "Prologue supprimé à un livre d'Invectives"): woman has decidedly become women, but although invoked as a plurality, she is almost always celebrated, or occasionally criticized, as an individual.

Perhaps the most touching and mature portrayals of women may be found in Verlaine's late collections, *Chansons pour elle, Odes en son honneur, Elégies, Dans les limbes,* and the posthumous and more eclectic *Chair* (*Flesh*, 1896). Here he sings the praises of Philomèle Boudin, whom he was close to marrying, and of Eugénie Krantz, whose love, kindnesses and buoying company he never forgets, despite the disputes and infidelities. Woman, for Verlaine, emerges in all her nobleness, strength, and dynamism. Any foibles he sees as mirroring largely his own. In these two women he finds, in the last years of his life, much of that equilibrium and maturation he had long sought in himself. These late poems retain a power and grace all their own; they are often witty, moving, frank, and reflective. They deserve the attention of the heart and the soul, and not just the dry gaze of the aesthete. By way of example, let me mention "Quand tu me racontes..." ("When You Tell Me...;" *OPC*, 778), "Compagne savoureuse ..." ("Savory Companion," *OPC*, 710–11), "À mon âge, je sais ..." ("At My Age, I Know ..."; *OPC*, 787–89), "Oui, tu m'inspires ..." ("Yes, You Inspire Me...; *OPC*, 837–38), "À ma femme" ("To My Wife"), and "À Eugénie" ("To Eugénie," *OPC*, 992–93, 1026–27). If such poems cannot correspond to the high dream of *Bonheur*'s "J'ai dit à l'esprit vain..."—"A worthy man, lover and brother of the Woman/Raising her children for here below and for/Their lot duly earned in the higher Abode" (*OPC*, 684–85)—nor do they sink to the projected horror of "La Soupe du soir," a poem in which Verlaine yet articulates the implicit beauties of female-male companionship.

In these late poems, woman is lauded, both with honesty and gentle lucidness, and with love and compassion. Man's shortcomings are far from overlooked, but the vast potential of union with woman is constantly laid before us. Poems such as "Ballade en l'honneur de Louise Michel" ("Ballad in Honor of Louise Michel," *OPC*, 425–26) and "Marceline Desbordes-Valmore" should be remembered, too, in this context, as should many passages from his autobiographical prose. A paragraph from *Onze jours en Belgique* (*Eleven Days In Belgium*) springs to mind, where Verlaine writes of the *béguines* or nuns of Gand: "I much admired these dear and discreet persons and I envy their happiness with all my heart" (*PR*, 419). They demonstrate well that, if Verlaine could be an excessive man, his sensitivity to purity of soul, gentleness, compassion, nobility of spirit—qualities he almost invariably finds in women—never diminishes. Woman remains for him a symbol of high aspiration; and, despite all, no other male poet of the century has written so extensively, so frankly, and with such compassionate realism of woman.

Aspiration, Hope, Self-Renewal

One of Verlaine's earliest poems is "Aspiration." In many ways a beautiful expression of pure utopian dream, it remains also a poem of Baudelairean refusal, of escape from matter, *présence*, "far from all that lives" (*OPC*, 15). The aspiration is problematized by its spirit of negation, even though it is centered upon the edenic and eternal. No wonder that Verlaine's "moroseness" and "biliousness" have drowned out that "sad Ideal collapsing" (*OPC*, 57), that his dream is "half-rotten" (*OPC*, 75), and that, even in "Çavitri" (*OPC*, 78), where he reminds himself of the need to retain "in the soul . . . a high design," the dream has slipped, resulting in the superiority of "impassiveness"—of art, artificiality, mask, play, ironic *dandysme*—over the "movingness," the terrible hurly-burly of existence.

Curiously, even the high aspirations of *La Bonne Chanson*, though far more anchored in reality, seem complicated and threatened by virtue of a certain idealization of the real:

> Mais plutôt je ne veux vous voir,
> L'avenir dût-il m'être sombre
> Et fécond en peines sans nombre,
> Qu'à travers un immense espoir.

> But rather do I wish to see you
> Were future fated dark
> And fecund with countless pains,
> But through a hope immense.
>
> (*OPC*, 151)

To some extent, aspiration and hope cannot fail to blinker the expression of their desire, and must entail refusal and partiality.

The poems of *Sagesse*, following upon the "dark future" that "J'ai presque peur . . ." ("I am Almost Afraid . . .") from *La Bonne Chanson* has just evoked, are crammed with Verlaine's reformed hopes and ambitions: hope for "the promised forgiveness and peace" (*OPC*, 245), the aspiration to that love which can restore him to life (*OPC*, 247), the hope contained in prayer (*OPC*, 248), the aspiration to the self's "simplicity" (*OPC*, 256, 280) and the "wisdom" of loving serenity (*OPC*, 273). Although such elevated desires center upon the salvation of "my eternal and divine being" (*OPC*, 502), the acts that lead to the poems of *Sagesse* should be seen as uncluttered with thoughts of hope and aspiration. The impulse that thrusts Verlaine to the floor of his cell, sobbing, unclad, incredulous (*PR*, 349, *Mes Prisons*), is visceral yet transcendent; it is, in itself, pure instinctual aspiration. The book is an after-hope or after-aspiration, "wept over, suffered through" (*PR*, 428, "Ma Candidature"). These Christian poems, however, return again, like "Aspiration," to the "vileness" of life (*OPC*, 264), the desire "not to know anything more of this world/Than the obscure adoration of mystical wisdom" (*OPC*, 412, "Un conte"), the sense that "[l'âme] est *en peine* et *de passage*" ("[the soul] is in purgatory and passing through," *OPC*, 256). The last text of *Jadis et naguère*, "Amoureuse du Diable" ("In Love with the Devil"), dedicated to Mallarmé (*OPC*, 393–97), speaks of intoxication in not dissimilar terms. If knowledge, mystical seeing, or "otherness" is achievable, Verlaine's hope and aspiration are equally predicated, as with Baudelaire and Mallarmé, upon oblivion, victory *over* life, transcendence.

Such desire is stymied, transformed into, merely, "our immense effort from amid this mire" (*OPC*, 431, "Délicatesse" ["Delicacy"], *Amour*). But Verlaine knows that, within himself, he does have the resources to allow the self's ideal logic of communion and high accomplishment to prevail ("Adieu," *OPC*, 424–25, *Amour*). If hope and aspiration are plunged back into that struggle between Verlaine's good and "bad angels," the latter insidiously "rayant le pur, le radieux/Paysage de vols étranges" ("striping the pure and radiant/Landscape with strange flights," *OPC*, 673), at least he can look to Desbordes-Valmore's example and know that hope and aspiration are transitive, transformational powers (*OPC*, 640–42), and that his own sense of hope in "mon immense douleur" ("my immense pain") is equally real (*OPC*, 428, "Saint Graal" ["Holy Grail"]). Many subsequent works will testify to this sense, but especially the 1892 *Liturgies intimes* (*Intimate Liturgies*), which contain allusions to Baudelaire's crises and aspirations.

In conclusion, *Liturgies intimes* shows Verlaine's tendency to write by means of imperatives, self-exhortation. Already *Sagesse* had opted at times for this mode: "Ah! rather forget/Your own madness!" ("Du fond du grabat . . ." ["From My Poorman's Bed . . ."]);

OPC, 274–78); or, in "La Bise se rue . . ." ("The North Wind Rushes In . . ."; *OPC*, 283), "up, my soul, quickly, let's get along/ . . . Go, my soul, to vast hope!" Verlaine inaugurates here a process of self-encouragement and self-renewal. He knows that only the self can define self: "notre coeur sait/Seul ce que nous sommes" ("only our heart knows what we are," "Conseil falot" ["Droll Advice"], *OPC*, 372–74). It is not just that "l'enfer, c'est les autres" ("Hell is other people"), as Sartre puts it; what matters is the future truth of the self, to which the self can really aspire through thinking the self anew. "Prière du matin" ("Morning Prayer"), the opening poem of *Amour* (*OPC*, 405–407), goes far in this process, opting for self-destruction leading to self-renovation. "Ah! kill my mind," we read, "and my heart and my senses!/Make way for the soul believing, feeling and seeing" (*OPC*, 406). If Verlaine's *point d'ancrage* is a Christian God, his fundamental mysticism allows him to sense that divineness must be assumed, because it must be in (his) life, which he must "risk" (*OPC*, 689, "Un scrupule qui m'a l'air sot . . ."). The self's aspiration "beyond" the self is an act of self-centering and self-assumption. "Âme vers Dieu, pensez à moi" ("Soul toward God, think of me"), he cries out in "L'Affreux Ivry . . ." ("Frightful Ivry . . ."; *OPC*, 460). "Commence par prier pour toi" ("Begin by praying for yourself") is the response he gives himself. The beginning is here and now, and inevitably with the self—an act in which the self transforms its selfness, understanding its potential correspondence to hope, aspiration, self-definition. As we shall now see, Verlaine can push this logic to a refreshingly extreme limit.

Gods

"Les Dieux" ("The Gods") is one of Verlaine's very early poems (*OPC*, 17), and it stresses, beyond all doctrinal attachment, the continuing presence of the divine among us, a divine at once multiple and in need of our vigilance and adoption. Such gods "have not abdicated, tightening their nervous grip/On stubs of scepters, and prowling in the winds" (*OPC*, 17); but divineness is in the air we breathe, ubiquitous. In "Enfance chrétienne" ("Christian Childhood"), a much later (1889?) but undated autobiographical fragment speaks of the poet's childhood in Arras and of "the poor chapel of Sainte-Agnès" where took root within him what he calls "ma conception mystique ("my mystical conception of things," *PR*,

587–89). This youthful sense of the divinity of being is brought into question as early as 1866, with the publication of *Poèmes saturniens*, partly by its thematic absence and partly due to Verlaine's "Epilogue," where he aligns himself with those "Supreme Poets/Who venerate the Gods and do not believe in them" (*OPC*, 95). Such fencing continues throughout *Fêtes galantes*, and even in *La Bonne Chanson* Verlaine's poetics is so fixed upon the passage of that "Being of light," Mathilde Mauté, that all transcendence is plunged back into immediacy: "Et vraiment je ne veux pas d'autre Paradis" ("And truly I want no other Paradise" ("Puisque l'aube grandit . . ." ["Since Dawn Grows Large . . ."], *OPC*, 144).

Verlaine's sense of the divine is critically modified from the moment of his 1874 revelation and conversion in his Mons prison cell—"je croyais, je voyais, il me semblait que je savais, j'étais illuminé" ("I believed, I could see, I seemed to know, I was filled with illumination," *Mes Prisons, PR*, 348). That this experience affects his art is manifest in *Sagesse* and other collections: Catholicism, dogma, liturgy, feelings of guilt and shame, the need for forgiveness, the aspiration to purity. The divine now becomes in part concentrated in the God of Christianity, Mary, and Jesus. The telling experience is not just mystical, but a specific visitation, "la foudre de Dieu" ("a thunderbolt from God" (*OPC*, 433). Prayer and intercession are focused on Catholic emblems (*OPC*, 456). The "impenetrable designs" may be adored, but they belong again to an identifiable, external Christian God (*OPC*, 451). On the other hand, Verlaine's general sense of the "mystery" of being is increased, even though linked to notions of acceptance and "resignation" (*OPC*, 267, "Vous êtes calme . . . ["You are calm . . ."]), and everywhere present in *Sagesse* is an understanding of the centrality of love—of God, self, other—and its power of creation.

As Verlaine says in 1889, some fifteen years after this inner transformation, "I could at least reflect and grasp/ . . . The reasons for my eternal and divine being" (*OPC*, 502). Imprisonment in Belgium led, over and above what was *given*, to a self-giving whose profundity and meaning never leave him. Certainly, Verlaine will—as in "J'étais naguère . . ."—slip into "melancholy doubt" (*OPC*, 852) and evoke his tiresome fickleness, "sans cible humaine ou but divin" ("without human aim or divine goal," *OPC*, 853). And, certainly, he is fully aware that his hesitations and ennui can lead to that moroseness and irony ready to further undermine his higher ambition and his mystical sense of the ordinary. Yet, equally characteristic is that will to self-consciousness that can lead to self-(re)determination, self-elevation. With such consciousness, as he says in "L'Ennui de vivre . . .", "then my speech sings and my eyes smile/Where divine certainty has cast its glow" (*OPC*, 691). If, then, in the strict Catholic sense, and in comparison with the heady days of Mons, Verlaine can say, in the 1891 *Chansons pour elle*, that "je fus mystique et je ne le suis plus" ("I was a mystic and I am so no more," *OPC*, 727), he remains that poet "haunted by a mystical wish" (*OPC*, 668).

I am not thinking here of those 1893 texts published after his death, "Visites" ("Visits") and "Oxford" (*OPC*, 1000–1001, 1007), where he speaks of the miracle of grace and the resurgent desire to "become once more the thing/Pleasant to the Lord . . ." (*OPC*, 1007). Much more fascinating are those numerous and touching late poems in which the notion of divineness is fully taken upon the self, who, in turn, scatters it like a blessing upon the two women he cherishes and who return his love during the difficult final years of his life. *Le Livre posthume* (*The Posthumous Book*) thus evokes that "divine fate" which is none other than that "tender and touchy past" (*OPC*, 817) of their joint lives—all the pain, deprivation, argument, as well as the joy understood to be true divineness by a "poet and man [who] have placed their faith [in woman]" (*OPC*, 817).

The reader may be tempted to view such texts as hyperbolic. Verlaine appreciates that, yet warns against it in "J'ai magnifié . . ." ("I have magnified . . ."; *OPC*, 818); when he speaks of "your divine kindness" (*OPC*, 819), this is a solemn and significant statement, for Verlaine has never toyed with such language. The divineness he attributes betokens a final deep understanding of what divineness truly can be: an assumable, perceptible, givable, and receivable grace. If the reader remains skeptical, given Verlaine's elderly slippages between Philomène Boudin and Eugénie Krantz, let him or her remember the difficulties of intense human relationships, and read "Vers en assonances," which appeared in *La Plume* (*The Quill*) in the February following Verlaine's death:

> Que vient faire l'hypocrisie
> Avec tout son dépit amer
> Pour nuire au coeur vraiment choisi,
> À l'âme exquisement sincère.

Qui se donne et puis se reprend
En toute bonne foi divine.

What is hypocrisy doing
With all its bitter spite
Hurting the truly chosen heart,
The exquisitely sincere soul.

That gives and then takes back itself
In all divine good faith.

(*OPC*, 891)

Divineness, like life itself, is an ebb and flow of being, of struggle, choice, love. It is not surprising that Verlaine, in "À ma femme," can speak so simply of (probably) Philomène in the following terms:

. . . te voici car Dieu nous veut voir, car il aime
À nous voir toujours, avec ou sans emblème,
Unis, ce qui nous fait des anges à ses yeux.

. . . there you are for God would see us, loving
To see us ever, with or without a ring,
United, making us angels in his eyes.

(*OPC*, 992)

For Verlaine's "mystical conception" (*PR*, 587) and his sense of divine mystery attain not merely to incarnation, exceeding symbol and concept; they are embraced as thoughts that he can give (back?) to the world in love, sincerity, and hope. Just as self-definition is possible, so is definition.

Loves

Verlaine's first three collections, *Poèmes saturniens*, *Fêtes galantes*, and *La Bonne Chanson*, show various facets of his conception and experience of love. All, however authentic, remain tinged with aestheticism, fancy, idealism—the colors of disguise and dream. Not until *Romances sans paroles* do we receive, in "*Child Wife*," an acknowledged sense of the rigors of love, "a brave and strong love,/Joyous in misfortune, grave in happiness,/Young till death" (*OPC*, 207). This is a love not known, except notionally, due to fear on the part of Mathilde and high thoughtlessness on the part of Verlaine. "I have a passion for love," he writes in *Amour,* "my weak heart is wild// . . . I have a passion for love. So, what then? Ah, let it be then" (*OPC,* 445–46).

Initially, however, Verlaine will not let things be, for he is over-taken by events. In prison, following the desperate 1873 scenes of Brussels, not to mention those of 1871 in Paris, the "voices" of pride, hatred, and flesh fade before God's "terrible voice of Love" (*OPC,* 259). This voice that "wounds with love" (*OPC,* 264), demands the death and rebirth of self via a renewed comprehension of the "universal" logic of divine love (*OPC,* 269). All earthly loves Verlaine now perceives and redefines as "deleterious": "toutes ont la guêpe et le ver"/"all have the wasp and the worm," he declares in the 1880 *Sagesse.* Such a statement of futility and implicit horror is ironically not far from his earlier Parnassian anti-love, which he will re-express in the 1884 sonnet "À Albert Mérat": "Vivons dans un dandysme épris des seules Rimes" ("Let's live in a dandyism in love with Rhyme alone," *OPC,* 326). With greater stability, Verlaine's 1888 *Amour* returns us to "ce mystère d'amour" ("this mystery of love"), not that of *Sagesse*'s Christian mysticism (*OPC,* 271) but rather the loves and friendships of the past twenty years. Mathilde, Rimbaud, Georges, his son, Elisa, his cousin, Valade, De-lahaye, Morice, Hugo, Lucien Létinois: the list is very long. Here, in *Amour,* Verlaine is deluged by that "torrent of love from the God of love and gentleness" (*OPC,* 428), and he begins to understand the "innocence" of love and pain ("Ballade en rêve" ["Dream Ballad"], 423–24), the need for simplicity and broadness of view in friendship (*OPC,* 430), the fact that the entire logic of existence is centered on such matters: "l'égoïsme hideux/Que nargue ce prochain même qu'il faut qu'on aime/ Comme soi-même: tels les termes du prob-lème" ("Hideous egoism/Flouted by the very one one must love/As oneself: such the terms of the problem," he writes in "À Ernest Delahaye" ("To Ernest Delahaye," *OPC,* 433–34).

Parallèlement, published a year later, in 1889, not surprisingly pushes further Verlaine's mellowing and compassionate discourse on what he elsewhere calls "L'amour multiforme et large" ("Broad, Multiform Love," *OPC,* 543, "En 17 . . ."). Love is "the Alpha and . . . the Omega" of being (*OPC,* 684); it manifests itself freely and yet mystically, regardless of reigning taboos, as "*Per amica silentia,*" from the section *Les Amies* (*Women Friends*) suggests: "Love, love, oh dear Solitaires,/Since in these unhappy days you still/Are crowned with glorious Stigma" (*OPC*, 487). The language is strong, self-confident, compassionate. Verlaine is moving toward that conception of love and friendship which will allow him to pierce through surface detail to see the joined "splendors of their souls" ("Mon ami, ma plus belle amitié..." ["My Friend, My Loveliest Friendship ..."], *OPC*, 676–79). Love, beyond all wretchedness and peril, is always a fortune, an honor, a type of grace ("*Money!*" *OPC*, 888–89). Love may be experienced, as in Mons, in apparently pure spiritual terms, but even then the mystical traverses the body, makes it shake and sob. "Sois de bronze..." ("Be of Bronze..."), from *Bonheur*, brings home the exact and mysterious equivalence of "Creator" and "creature," the need to assume our "fleshiness": "sois de chair et même aime cette chair..." ("be of flesh and even love this flesh..."; *OPC*, 675).

The glorification of that somewhat wrinkled but noble love in such late volumes as *Chansons pour elle* and *Odes en son honneur* can be thus seen as the high achievement of Verlaine's long-evolving poetics of love. "Vive l'amour et vivent nous" ("Long live love and long live us"), he writes in "Tu n'es pas du tout..." ("You are not at all ..."; *OPC*, 709). What matters is love itself, and "our" free movement via it, in tender companionship. Love gives access to the heart's divineness (*OPC*, 710, "Compagne savoureuse"); it is natural and innocent, "like running water, like a bird singing" (*OPC*, 715, "Que ton âme soit..." ["May Your Soul Be..."]); it thrives on brightness and honesty (*OPC*, 722, "Je ne suis plus..." ["I Am No Longer..."]); it understands its sublimeness even in distress and injury (*OPC*, 766, "La Sainte, ta patronne..." ["The Saint, Your Patron..."]); it may prefer reciprocity, but it bathes in its own simple, passing presence (*OPC*, 779, 782). As Verlaine suggests in one of the posthumous poems entitled "Pour E..." ("For E...") ("J'aime ton sourire" ["I love your smile"]), love can transcend difference and unevenness, if it broadens into a love of life itself:

> And I love your soul
> That loves not me
> To death.
>
> . . . .
>
> For I love your life,
> And mine, too
> (*OPC*, 1025)

Love may vary in its focus, intensity, and mode, and Verlaine's poetry leads us through its many enchantments and disenchantments. But it does not vary inherently, he comes to understand; its modes are the "differences of the same," as Michel Deguy would put it. The Creator's love can be lived via the "creature," who "creates the Creator" (*OPC*, 681) in an endless origination, the logic of love being tied to the logic of self-determination and self-renewal. In terms of daily experience, love is absolute despite the "relativity" it embraces; it renders the world innocent, begins it over, constantly: "You must put up with me thusly, love me thusly/Rather, for I need you to love me" (*OPC*, 963–64, "Mon Apologie" ["Self-Apology"]).

Parallels, Unity, Innocence

In his "Avertissement" for the 1894 edition of *Parallèlement*, Verlaine writes that the collection is "en quelque sorte *l'enfer* de son Oeuvre chrétien" ("in some way the *hell* of his Christian Work," *OPC*, 483), and indeed for many years he had perceived his poetics as one of alternation, simultaneity, equivalence in difference. His mortality, as he says of Rimbaud, is that of "ange ET démon" ("angel AND demon," *OPC*, 601, "À Arthur Rimbaud"); he is given to self-destruction and self-reconstitution (*OPC*, 693), filth and sublimeness (*OPC*, 865)—a "betweenness" with respect to "the problem of his life" (*OPC*, 816) that attaches him firmly to his century, "pilgrim upon the roads/Both frozen stiff and well-baked" (*OPC*, 957, "À ma bien-aimée"). Curiously, the recognition of such division is a recognition of his integrity, which his entire work, from *Sagesse* on especially, struggles to lay bare. "J'ai dit à l'esprit vain . . ." affirms this rejection both of "impassiveness" and "ostentation" and describes a poetics of that "naïveté profonde" which demands letting go of so much that would mask one's "cracked" unity. Verlaine's understanding of the oneness of love's differences is crucial, for it confirms his sense of the "simplicity" of "tout ce qu'il fallait inéluctablement qu'il fût" ("everything he inevitably had to be" *PR*, 590). The broadly "confessional" character of much of his work, poetry and prose, may also be best understood in this overall optic of self-definition and above all, the definition of his accumulated selfness, its "innocence," its simple, unified livedness, the divinity of its unfoldedness—despite its creases and crumples.

Central to such self-understanding is Verlaine's logic of forgiveness. Verlaine always tends to rise over feelings of guilt, as in *Romances sans paroles*, published in 1873 when Verlaine was still in prison;

> Il faut, voyez-vous, nous pardonner les choses:
> De cette façon nous serons bien heureuses
>
> . . . .
>
> Soyons deux enfants, soyons deux jeunes filles
> Eprises de rien et de tout étonnées
>
> Qui s'en vont pâlir sous les chastes charmilles
> Sans même savoir qu'elles sont pardonnées.
> You must, you see, forgive us things:
> In this way we shall be happy
>
> . . . .
>
> Let's be two children, two young girls
> In love with nothing and amazed at all
> Running off pallid beneath chaste bowers
> Not even knowing of their forgiveness.
>
> (*OPC*, 193)

Innocence seems a possible given, an ontic datum, if we perceive all our gestures and words to be caught up in "a pure and broad movement" (*OPC*, 209).

Sagesse redresses this consciousness, though not nearly as much as we might think. "God alone is offended who alone forgives," Verlaine writes in poem 15, "but/One's brother is saddened, pained and hurt" (*OPC*, 255)—a poem intended for his ex-wife, (*OPC*, 1122), which ends: "Ô ma soeur, qui m'avez puni, pardonnez-moi!" ("Oh my sister that has punished me, forgive me!" *OPC*, 255). We may read here fine distinctions between notions of intrinsic guilt or innocence, inevitable hurt and divine forgiveness. *Sagesse* is bathed in the light of purifying and regenerative love, essentially beyond recrimination. "Who can, without trembling"—he asks in "Du fond du grabat . . ."—"judge upon earth?" (*OPC*, 275);

and, in "J'avais peiné . . ." ("I Had Struggled . . ."), a "Lady" named "Prayer" announces to him:

> "Je suis la douceur qui redresse,
> J'aime tous et n'accuse aucun,
> Mon nom, seul, se nomme promesse."

> "I am the gentleness that sets aright,
> I love all and accuse none,
> My name, alone, is named promise."
> (*OPC*, 243)

Sagesse recounts the spiritual and emotional self-recreation of Verlaine, who basks in the total clemency of a God (*OPC*, 381) he had ceased to "venerate" (*OPC*, 95). "Innocence, oh beautiful after untold Ignorance," he writes in *Amour* (*OPC*, 410–12, "Un conte"); and, in *Mes Prisons*, the intensity of feeling still reverberates in 1893: "Think about it: to feel innocent, to believe one is, at least to believe, and for good measure to know one is! *Innocent*, just think!" (*PR*, 352).

Of course, *Sagesse* and other collections remain aware of guilt. The logic of innocence is inescapably tied into such notions, and is profoundly Catholic, modern, and Western, to that extent. Verlaine thus continues to hope for Christian forgiveness, beyond the intrinsic innocence that divine love represents (*OPC*, 245); "un regret rouge et noir" ("a red and black regret") persists (*OPC*, 415). *Bonheur* still speaks of the great difficulty of forgiveness (*OPC*, 657, "L'Incroyable, l'unique horreur . . ." ["The Incredible, Simple Horror . . ."]), while recognizing that forgiveness is merely the self's decision to opt for that *abandon*, that *délaissement*, essential to his poetics of love (*OPC*, 658). The same volume senses that his "guilt" and "innocence" are karmic ("Obviously I am expiating a very old sin (Very old?) that my blood is at times shaken with," *OPC*, 668); and "Pénitence," from *Liturgies intimes* (*OPC*, 755), and "Craintes" ("Fears"), a posthumous text (*OPC*, 999–1000), deeply express the moral and spiritual pertinence of what he elsewhere calls "ma délictueuse et criminelle sorte de vie" ("my felonious and criminal kind of life," *PR*, 354).

But Verlaine's work also insists on the spiritual necessity for forgiveness and compassion before our fumbling, and curiously frank, gestures (*OPC*, 326). From prejudice we need to progress to peace, a shift requiring desire, consciousness, prayer, (self-)deter-mination (*OPC*, 432). Self-forgiveness is the point of origin of all further origination, or (self-)creation (*OPC*, 504, "À la manière de Paul Verlaine" ["In the manner of Paul Verlaine"]); only it can al-low the self to declare, "no remorse, no real regret, no disaster!" (*OPC*, 509). For to reach a sense of cosmic innocence entails an as-suming of the innocence of "nos innocents esprits" ("our innocent spirits," *OPC*, 521), a seizing of the virginal power of being—its realness and its virginity, its intrinsic spirituality, simultaneously. At the close of *Bonheur*, Verlaine speaks simply of "ma belle et ma chaste pensée" ("my beautiful, my chaste thought," *OPC*, 702): it is this force alone that can (re)found being in innocence and beauty. In practical terms, innocence requires an indulgence that is neither indifference nor weakness but is founded upon "great gentleness and blessed fine accord" (*OPC*, 686–87), "L'Indulgence qui n'est pas . . ." ("Indulgence That Is Not . . .")—upon love and conscious-ness of the power of love, and upon a simplicity of vision wherein innocence is, no matter what, always presumed. "Hein?" he writes in "À Charles Baudelaire"—"Hein? mourir simplement, nous, hommes de péché" ("Eh? just die, men of sin like us," *OPC*, 734). The confused "life" and "honor" of "our poor souls" is, curiously, a sign of their innocence ("Les Extrêmes Opinions" ["Extreme Opin-ions"], *OPC*, 852). If *le sublime* can be both "reef" and "haven," so too, in innocence, can *l'immonde* ("the filthy"; "J'ai beau faire . . ." ["In Vain Do I . . ."], *OPC*, 865–65, *Epigrammes*).

Forms: Constancy, Disarticulation, Horizon

Let us circle back, like many a Verlainean poem, to our beginnings. What, textually—prosodically, syntactically, lexically—are the im-plications of the "parallel" though imbricated stylistic modes of this poetic oeuvre? What are the practical manifestations of Verlaine's "Art poétique" (*OPC*, 326–27), with its insistence upon "musi-cality," "nuance," nonsatiricalness, moderation in rhyme, inel-oquence, "adventure," and "anti-literature"? Very compactly: 1. Verlaine's criterion of poetic "musicality" can be linked to his remarkable skills in manipulating what he called, speaking of Baudelaire, "the infinite complications of versification proper" (*PR*, 611); 2. this manipulation is somewhere between classical con-trol and a bold disarticulation, involving the *impair* and other tactics, which allows Verlaine to speak of ineloquence and adventure and achieve a kind of "strange and fantastic harmony" he can consider antiliterary ("Nocturne parisien" ["Parisian Nocturne"], *OPC*, 85); 3. literature remains, however, what Verlaine is consciously producing, but with an attitude of "capriciousness") (*OPC*, 74), "play" (*OPC*, 849), a music hall or *café-concert* style (*PR*, 432), *zutisme* (*OPC*, 159–67, *Album zutique* [*Damned Album*]), "invective" (*OPC*, 897–964), sheer naturalness (*OPC*, 683); 4. nonsatiricalness, the refusal of biting irony or sarcasm is, despite *Invectives* and a few other texts, a principle to which Verlaine adheres, preferring wit or mischievousness—he is, after all, the wittiest French poet of the past three centuries; 5. the questions of "nuance" and rhyme I shall deal with below: the former is essentially a matter of lexicon, semantic decentering and metaphor. In what follows, I shall deal mainly with the base elements of Verlaine's poetic *musique*—meter, stanza, composition, syntax, rhyme—and offer a few observations on lexical and metaphorical characteristics. In all areas we shall see that Verlaine's mastery, despite its frequent offhandedness, is remarkably "worked," as he likes to say, and equal to that of Lamartine, Baudelaire, and Hugo.

First, meter. An analysis of a spread of collections, from *Poèmes saturniens* of 1866 to *Chair*, printed a month after Verlaine's death in 1896, reveals many interesting details. The *Poèmes saturniens* contains twenty texts—more than half—written exclusively in alexandrine verse; two other poems combine *impair* and *pair* meter with the alexandrine (12/15, 12/8). Five poems opt for the 10-syllable meter throughout, two others deploying the 10/5 configuration. Only three poems are in conventional 8-syllable meter. The remaining five poems are structured rhythmically in what we, somewhat erroneously, judge to be typical Verlainean prosodies: 7-syllable; 4/3; 7/4; 5-syllable. *Romances sans paroles*, written largely during the Rimbaud "epoch," shows a greater range of metric device: of the twenty-three poems, only three are in alexandrine entirely, with two others opting for 12/7 and 12/6 combinations. The other eighteen poems show these metric patterns: two in 10-syllable line; five in 8-syllable line; one in 6-syllable line; two in 4-syllable line; one in 4/8 combination; three in 5-syllable *impair*; two in 7- and two in 9-syllable *impair*. If we skip over the middle years of Verlaine's production, his closing rhythmic habits are reflected in the following details: the twenty-five poems of *Liturgies intimes* include nine exclusively in alexandrine, with one other in 6/6/12 formation; seven in 8-syllable line; three in 7-syllable line; one in 9-syllable line; one in 10-syllable line; one has an 8/9/7 metric structure; and two, delightfully, enjoy the complications of a 9/11/13 rhythm.

Elégies is short, twelve poems, all in the classical alexandrine. *Dans les limbes* returns to prosodic variety, but with caution, giving: eight poems in alexandrine verse; seven in octosyllables; one in 10-syllable line; two in 7-syllable *impair*. Finally, *Chair* provides only two texts in alexandrine, with one other in 8/4 rhythm; nine in 8-syllable line; one in half-alexandrine 6-syllable line; two in 7- and one in 9-syllable *impair*. Metrically, then, Verlaine is more classically conscious than some anthologies would have us believe, but we should not forget the disarticulation—and harmonies—of the use of the *impair*, nor the remarkable suppleness he displays within *any* meter, via audacious enjambment, *coupe*, rhyme, and alliteration, which tend to press for a reordering of lines beyond metric limitation.

Secondly, stanzaic structure is a major mechanism of poetic production that tends to aerate and loosen any metric tightness which might otherwise prevail, while offering a semblance of structural and compositional solidity. Some rapid figures first: *Poèmes saturniens* contains twelve sonnets, plus a number of others in which sonnets are "buried" (e.g., "Nocturne parisien," *OPC*, 83–86: 6-28-42-12-14-4) or which are anti-sonnets of a sort (the 13-line "Crépuscule du soir mystique," *OPC*, 70, and the 15-line "Initium," *OPC*, 78); thirteen poems of varying length composed entirely of quatrains, plus three others of 16-line structure and others, like "Il Bacio" (*OPC*, 82), with a 4-4-8 composition; three poems using terza rima, sometimes with a 1-line flourish at the end, emphasizing Verlaine's predilection for effective or colorful closure; others still of different stanzaic or compositional structure, such as "Marco," with six 9-line stanzas, or the plain but striking 20-line "Le Rossignol."

Those other volumes examined for their metric structure, and adding in the early *Fêtes galantes*, reveal the overwhelming domination of short stanzaic form: 2-line up to a 6-line maximum, with occasional 1-line "stanzas," except for the rather more compositionally varied *Dans les limbes* (10 of 17 poems based on the quatrain, but also longer structures such as 18-, 30-, 24-line stanzas and apparently unusual combinations such as 12-7-1, 9-11, 17-1, giving in total more traditional blocks) and the *Elégies* (all longer structures, largely 60–80 lines, with some favoring of sonnet or quasi-sonnet forms within these structures: "À mon âge, je sais..."—5-13-16-2-8-10-44-15-2-13-12; "D'après ce que j'ai vu..." ["After What I've Seen..."], 30-13-14-1; "Incorrigible, toi..." ["You Incorrigible..."], 51-13-12-4). The quatrain, moreover, holds exclusive sway in more than half of the poems examined: *Romances sans paroles*, 14 of 22; *Fêtes galantes*, 12 of 22; *Liturgies intimes*, 11 of 24; *Dans les limbes*, 10 of 17; *Chair*, 7 of 16.

A careful scrutiny of the collections of the "middle" years does not affect the legitimacy of our conclusions: 1. Verlaine moves French poetry, beyond the sonnet, to further overt or implicit compactness, and in the direction of the various modern modes of the *art bref* of poets from Apollinaire and Reverdy to Char and Guillevic; 2. variety is evident, yet constancy prevails: if there is "adventure," there is also that "order" espoused by Parnassians and symbolists from Baudelaire and Gautier to Mallarmé and Laforgue. Disciplined form remains as an aesthetic emblem or fetish, finally channeling "authenticity" and "being oneself" into stable molds.

Thirdly, syntax, punctuation, and continuity: 1. Verlaine makes ample use of punctuation, the endless appositions, parentheses, accumulations that punctuation allows syntax to carry; 2. his syntax is sure and subtle, never subjected to those ellipses sprouting up in the later Mallarméan sonnets; 3. the longer poems or stanzaic groupings reveal a classical and audaciously modern elaboration of discourse: Racine or Lamartine, but with bold enjambments and *rejets, coupes,* displaced caesura, and all those mechanisms mentioned in 1. above; 4. the shorter poems often fuse stanzas into one supple global syntactic structure, at times witty, at other times solemn, or else magically lilting, conjuring all the effects not just of syntax, but of rhyme, alliteration, meter, and so on.

Fourthly, rhyme. Here, again, Verlaine excels, due to both his intrepidness and his quick yet sure sense of old and new harmonies. His practice with respect to the sonnet, and the quatrain in general, is enough to convince us. The quatrain, whether within the sonnet or without, employs the usual *abab* or *abba* combinations, but does not hesitate to opt for the *rime plate, aabb,* nor to go to the extremes of *aaaa/bbbb.* As for the tercet, we observe a practice surpassing that of Baudelaire, whose technical skills in sonnet-writing he regards as supreme. Over and above the half-dozen combinations identified in Baudelaire's tercets, the following seven rhyme schemes can be discovered: *efg/eeg, eff/efg, efg/efg, eef/egg, eef/efe, eee/fff, efe/fef.* Very occasionally only an assonance is consciously used; and, sometimes, the element unrhymed (*f* in *efg/eeg*) is not taken up in the quatrains, which, moreover, sometimes follow the tercets.

Let me rapidly note a few other niceties of Verlaine's rhyming manner, by which he clearly set great store ("Un mot sur la rime," *PR*, 696–701): the 3-line stanza is often set in Dantean terza rima, but rhymes, *riches* or *suffisantes*, can be contained within the stanza overflow without opting for the terza rima, and form many combinations, in fact. The same variety can be found in the reasonably common 5-line and 6-line stanzas; the 2-line stanzas Verlaine occasionally chooses, tend to elect the serene and litanical *aa/bb* scheme. The *rime plate* tends to be reserved for the longer, more "discursive" texts, but can be used to effect in many more intricate combinations. Verlaine likes to use alternating or imbricated rhymes close to each other, especially if he wishes to create a form in itself emblematizing meaning. Alternatively, the practice can be used less for symbolist lyricism than to generate witty and lively texts, differently "nuanced" and ambiguous.

Fifthly, lexicon and metaphor. Verlaine's vocabulary is wideranging, bold, sensitive to the enhancements of form. Certain poems or even collections possess particular lexical and semantic characteristics, others provide alternations—the whole in keeping with his "developed" poetics of "parallelism," authenticity, and a spontaneity founded upon "work." Verlaine's lexicon can extend to argot, the *zutique*, the scatological, but it always reveals itself poetically, and is subject to aesthetic constraints, not purely semantic ones. The same is true of Verlainean metaphor: it is never purely decorative, nor is its function strictly explanatory. Verlaine's metaphors and similes are not surrealist, nor are they either Rimbaldian, *voyantes*, or provocative à la Lautréamont. But they are original, whether delicate, solemn, or laughingly outrageous. A glance at some of the following poems will reveal these figurative characteristics: "Nevermore," from the *Poèmes saturniens* (*OPC*, 61), with its subtle personifications of autumn and sun, its delightful "les cheveux et la pensée au vent" ("hair and thought blown by the wind"); "Cythère" ("Cythera"), from *Fêtes galantes*

(*OPC*, 114), whose first 3-line stanza gracefully accumulates trope upon trope:

> Un pavillon à claires-voies
> Abrite doucement nos joies
> Qu'en éventent des rosiers amis;

> A latticed summer-house
> Gently shelters our joys
> That friendly roses catch wind of;

"Le Bruit des cabarets . . ." ("The Noise of Bars . . ."), from *La Bonne Chanson* (*OPC*, 152), with its omnibus become "hurricane," a wild grating metal monster "rolling its green and red eyes slowly"; "C'est la fête du blé . . ." ("It's Wheat Festival Time . . ."), the final poem of *Sagesse* (*OPC*, 291), whose second quatrain is brilliantly simple in its figurative production:

> L'or des pailles s'effondre au vol siffleur des faux
> Dont l'éclair plonge, et va luire, et se réverbère.
> La plaine, toute au loin couverte de travaux,
> Change de face à chaque instant, gaie et sévère;

> The straw gold crumbles at the whistling flight of scythes
> Whose flashing dips and gleams and reflects.
> The plains, far away covered with work,
> Change aspect by the moment, gay and severe;

and, finally, "Les Salons . . ." ("Salons"), from *Epigrammes* (*OPC*, 866), whose sparkling metaphorics fade into the stark reality of the poem's ending, with its allusion to art's trap of mere preciousness;

> Les Salons, où je ne vais plus
> M'ont toujours fait, pétards, fusées,
> Etrons de Suisse, soleils, flux
> Et reflux de mises osées,

> Traînes, pompons, rubans, volants,
> (Las! quoi! pas de décolletage?)
> L'effet de feux mirobolants
> D'artifice et d'art,—avantage

Verlaine

Précieux, mais où les talents?

The salons I no more frequent
Have always given me, bangers, flares,
Swiss cones, pinwheels, ebb and
Flow of daring placements,

Dress-trains, pompons, ribbons, flounces,
(Drat! What! no plunging necklines?)
The effect of wondrous works
Of fire and art—most fine

Advantage, but where's the talent?

Verlaine's art is, despite its grace and wit, predicated upon con-
summate control of formal and expressive means. Work and art
were synonymous for him to the end of his life. Madrigals, odes,
elegies, sonnets, he half-realized, however, were soon to become
things of the past. He himself toys, half-mockingly, with assonance,
while deeming rhyme to be central to poetry (see the section of
Chair entitled *Assonances galantes* [*Amorous Assonances*], *OPC*,
886–93) and holding free, blank verse to be inadequately equipped
to survive on poetic grounds ("Un mot sur la rime," *PR*, 696–701).
In the same essay, however, he recognizes the principles of liberty
and new possibility at stake, and senses the legitimacy of new
claims. Indeed, it is important to stress, too, in conclusion, the
significance of an almost entirely overlooked element of his oeuvre,
the publication, in 1886, of *Les Mémoires d'un veuf/Memoirs of a Wid-
ower*. Verlaine's tentative foray into the realm of *poème en prose*—his
allusion to Baudelaire's "Les Bons Chiens," from *Le Spleen de Paris*,
is explicit in his own "Chiens"/"Dogs"(*PR*, 68–69) and, although
some texts retain an initially hesitant *entrée en matière*, many others
are very fine prose poems answering all criteria that poets and
others have established for their evaluation. Let me close by merely
recommending the reading of "Mal'aria" (*PR*, 81–82), "Ma Fille"/
"My Daughter" (*PR*, 82), "Les Estampes"/"Prints" (*PR*, 90–93),
"L'Hystérique"/"Hysterical" (*PR*, 94), "Caprice" (*PR*, 118–19). Verlaine does not need them for "ce qu'on appelle la Gloire"/ "what
one calls Glory," as he says in "Littérature," from the posthumous
Invectives (*OPC*, 902–903), but they do show us a poet open upon the
future poetic options of the world that, in part, will come to reign.

· EIGHT ·

Rimbaud

Thirty-seven years after his birth in Charleville, on 20 October 1854, the man behind the myth we have come to know as Rimbaud died of gangrene poisoning and complications, in the presence of his sister, Isabelle, in the Hôpital de la Conception, Marseille. A precocious young pupil who skipped the *cinquième année* and an extraordinary Latinist, he was writing some of his most lasting work at the ages of fifteen and sixteen. Reading Rabelais and Hugo, straining under the limitations of family and province, Rimbaud soon broke loose in wild *vagabondages* as far as Belgium and Paris in the midst of the Franco-Prussian War. At sixteen he was already composing sociopolitical-cum-poetical "Manifestos" to his friends and mentors, Delahaye, Izambard, Demeny. Verlaine's invitation, upon receipt of sample poems, brought him quickly to Paris, to riotous and scandalous scenes with his mentor, but also to enlarged discussion and creation. The summer of 1872—Rimbaud is still only seventeen—took the pair to Belgium and England. Delahaye argued that *Les Illuminations* (*The Illuminations*) dates back to this period, despite Verlaine's placing of the work's composition in the 1873–1875 period. The year 1873 sees both poets—Verlaine is ten years Rimbaud's senior—quarreling back in London, then engaged in the fateful shooting scene in Brussels that sends Rimbaud back to mother, sister, and brother in Roche and the feverish completion of *Une saison en enfer* (*A Season in Hell*) and Verlaine to nearly two years of prison in Brussels and then Mons.

The following year Rimbaud again sets off for England, this time with Germain Nouveau. He teaches in London and Scotland, and seems to have renounced literature. The next few years find him exploring all means of nonpoetic self-renewal and -discovery: journeying to Germany, going on foot to Switzerland and Italy, returning to Charleville with illness, voraciously learning languages, joining only quickly to desert the Dutch colonial army, being robbed in Austria, further folding back upon Charleville with sorties into Sweden, Denmark, and, again, Italy (en route for Egypt), then, in 1878, to Hamburg, whence, on foot and in the snow, to Switzerland and Italy once more, and, this time, away to Cyprus. Illness again forces Rimbaud home, but in 1880 he returns to Cyprus and then moves on to Aden and Harrar, where he becomes a buyer-trader for Bardley's. He is the first known European to penetrate into the interior as far as Bubassa and Ogaden, and is outwitted in his gun-selling to the powerful King of Choa, Menelik. In 1891, a tumor developing in his knee forces him to seek medical help in Marseille. After an amputation and attempted rehabilitation in Roche, he returns to Marseille for further treatment, dying on 10 November of the same year.

"Fleur hâtive et absolue, sans avant ni après" ("Hasty and absolute flower, nothing before nothing afterward"), wrote Laforgue of the meteoric and inimitable Rimbaud. But if no model was ever truly followed nor offered, Rimbaud's work has had the profoundest of effects upon every generation of poets since the partial publication, in 1886, at the hands of Verlaine, of *Les Illuminations*. Breton both adulated and turned from it; Reverdy deemed it a personally determining threshold; Claudel remained in awe of it, while seeking to overdetermine and appropriate its powerful spiritual thrust. Char, who accords an unusually long text to Rimbaud, gives him corresponding praise: his work spells the end of poetry's banal genericness and offers itself to "a civilization not yet appeared." Today, poets such as Michel Deguy, André Frénaud (*Notre inhabileté fatale* [*Our Fatal Incapacity*]), Jacques Dupon (*Une apparence de soupirail* [*An Air Vent Appearance*]), and Yves Bonnefoy, in his superb *Rimbaud par lui-même* and many essays since, continue to meditate the pertinence of this child prodigy.

Sensation and Dream

Rimbaud was in all likelihood only ten years old when he wrote "Le Soleil était encore chaud . . ." ("The Sun Was Still Warm . . .") at the Institution Rossat in Charleville. It is his earliest known poetic piece, prophetically in prose (*OC*, 3–5). It is interesting not the least for its sure portrayal of the setting sun lighting up green leaves and wilting flowers, flicking the tops of huge pines, poplars, and ancient oaks as the evening breeze cools the simple, quick sleep of the poem's *je;* but no less for its recounting, in the second, broken sequence, of the self's dream of one of its other lives. "Sensation," from the *Poésies* (*Poems*) and dated 1870 (*OC*, 41) reveals, too, this joy within corporeal, sensory immediacy, and yet, also, the "dreaminess" of such primary experience—of vesperal blues, summer warmth, stinging wheat stalks, soft grass, freshening wind— which remains mental, spiritual. The opening verses of the exquisite "Soleil et chair" ("Sun and Flesh," *OC*, 46–51), also dating from 1870, may similarly plunge us into a visceral sense of the earth's splendor, but again nothing is perceived in flatly materialist terms.

All of Rimbaud's poetry manifests this chiasmal consciousness. On the one hand it roots itself in sensation, place, time, the physical: the station square of Charleville (*OC*, 59), an experience "on the train, 7 October 1870" (*OC*, 65), a visit "Au Cabaret-Vert, cinq heures du soir" ("At the Cabaret-Vert, 5 p.m.," *OC*, 66); on the other hand, sights, sounds, smells, and so on seem to escape their strictly physical rootedness: the crows of "Les Corbeaux" ("Crows," *OC*, 104) become a "delight," the wind of "La Rivière de Cassis" ("The Cassis River," *OC*, 126–27) is "salubrious," Nina's "raspberry and strawberry taste,/O flowered flesh,/Laughing at the keen wind kissing you" of "Les Réparties de Nina" ("Nina's Replies," *OC*, 56), the summer morning of "Aube" ("Dawn," *OC*, 194) with its forest path "empli de frais et blêmes éclats" ("filled with fresh and pallid brilliance"): everywhere slippage occurs between the sensory and the extrasensory, demonstrating the hybrid nature and affective origin of all physicality. The early "Roman" ("Novel"), from *Poésies* (*OC*, 62–63), hints at the "dreamed," fictional nature of the "real"; and the "splendeur de la chair! ô splendeur idéale!" ("splendor of flesh! oh ideal splendor!") of "Soleil et chair" is not so much an immersion in physiological ecstasy, as a consciousness of the correspondence between idea and matter, ideality and realisation, inside and outside. The corporeal is thus transcended at the same moment as the ideal becomes immanent. Does not the end of the poem—"the Gods, upon whose brow the Bullfinch nests,/—The Gods listen to Man and the infinite World!" (*OC*, 51)—succeed in articulating the equivalence of the microcosmic and the universal? And does not this stanza from "Les Réparties de Nina"—

> —Ta poitrine sur ma poitrine,
> Mêlant nos voix
> Lents, nous gagnerions la ravine,
> Puis les grands bois! . . .

> —Your breast upon my breast,
> Mingling our voices
> Slow, we would reach the ravine,
> Then the great woods!

—surpass the sensational, the physical?

For all the "indiscretion" and "brutality" that may be associated with Rimbaldian desire ("A la musique" ["To Music"], *OC*, 59–60), this desire remains subtle, seeking a higher expression, as in the "regret des bras épais et jeunes d'herbe pure" ("longing for thick, young arms of pure grass") of "Mémoire" ("Memory," *OC*, 122–23). Desire in Rimbaud, moreover, quickly leaves behind the sexual and the sensory. "Soleil et chair" shows desire as that inner force compelling Rimbaud to "fathom—and know, everything!" (*OC*, 49); "Vagabonds" reveals the poet soaring through and beyond familiar experience in search of "le lieu et la formule" ("the place and the formula," *OC*, 190); "Conte" ("Tale," *OC*, 179) concludes: "La musique savante manque à notre désir" ("Our desire falls short of the music of knowledge," *OC*, 179). Desire, perhaps by definition, is above all a sense of lacuna and possibility. It lacks focus to the extent that it is precariously founded upon a not-there, yet its emotional force is such that an inner sensing can rapidly focus realities either familiar or exotic, as "Le Bateau ivre" ("Drunken Boat") demonstrates (*OC*, 100–103). These realities may be good, bad, indifferent, or incomprehensible: "My hungers are bits of black air," Rimbaud writes in "Fêtes de la faim" ("Celebrations of Hunger"), "the ringing azure;/—My stomach tugging away./Unhappiness" (*OC*, 138).

Reality, sensory perception, desire, and dream are not conflicting realms of action and experience. Rimbaud, despite later misgivings, has a precocious sense of their convergence. Reincarnational dream blends easily into Rimbaud's first known poem, "Le Soleil était encore chaud . . ."; the first poem of *Poésies*, "Les Etrennes des orphelins" ("Orphans' New Year's Gifts," *OC*, 37–40), gives over a large place to dream: the children emerging from it, returning to it, the mother's "dream" shrouding her orphaned loved-ones, and so on. Although romanticized, this is still a powerful commitment to a real beyond the real, well prepared by Des-bordes-Valmore and Lamartine, Nerval and Verlaine, yet pushed beyond the confines of the dream proper, daydreaming, or Rousseauist *rêverie* to a more deliberate and psychically aggressive mode. In this mode, "splendid loves" may be dreamed into phantasmatic reality (*OC*, 69) or "green, snow-dazzled night" may be conjured up (*OC*, 101); there may be "crusades, voyages of discovery for which no account exists, republics without histories, stifled wars of religion, revolutions in mores, shifts of race and continent," as "Alchimie du verbe" ("Alchemy of the Logos") puts it (*OC*, 232). "A thousand dreams within me gently sting and burn," Rimbaud observes in "L'Oraison du soir" ("Evening Orison," *OC*, 72). And, although dream slips away from the willfully driven logic of desire, it is clear that they join to the extent of seeking uplifting and ideal (thought-)forms of being.

Ophelia thus dreams a "wild" reality of "Heaven! Love! Freedom!" ("Ophélie," *OC*, 51–52); the *rêve maternel* of "Les Etrennes des orphelins" (*OC*, 38) projects warmth, protection, perhaps the very vision that becomes the angelic, blissful dream of the children themselves at the poem's conclusion (*OC*, 39–40); and "Rêvé pour l'hiver" ("Dreamed for Winter," *OC*, 65) shows dream's purpose to be often simple, again a means of rerooting possibility in actuality. This simplicity of dream's purpose is, however, doubled with the same cosmic complexity implicit in Ophelia's "great visions" (*OC*, 52). "Les Soeurs de charité" ("Sisters of Charity," *OC*, 85–86) evokes those "vast ends, Dreams or immense/Strollings, through the nights of Truth" that tug at our existence, orienting our seeming blindness through the symbolic labyrinth of the human condition.

Dream may thus reaffirm distance, but it also reinstates meaning, the immediate psychical connection between what is, here and now—including "your hatreds, your fixed torpors, your lapses,/And your brutalities suffered yesteryear" (*OC*, 86) and all that is beyond. Dream may be momentarily felt to be *pure perte* ("pure loss"; "Comédie de la soif" ["Comedy of Thirst"], *OC*, 129), but more compelling is dream's clarifying, revelatory dimension: "les fleurs de rêve tintent, éclatent, éclairent" ("dream flowers tinkle, burst forth, enlighten," *OC*, 176). And there is no use in protesting that Rimbaud was drunk or drugged: he is acceding here to an alternative, illuminating state of consciousness. The *avertissement* ("Notice") to Rimbaud's *Les Déserts de l'amour* (*Deserts of Love, OC,* 169) renders clear the degree to which the "dreams to follow," in the text proper, carry with them "de douces considérations religieuses" ("sweet religious considerations") in the broadest sense of the term. Dream thus seems, for Rimbaud, to give or promise access to some greatly expanded sense of the Real, beyond the constraints imposed by the ego, yet ever in relation to them.

The opening section of "Veillées" ("Vigils"), from *Les Illuminations,* evokes something of this newly awakened consciousness that dream ushers in: "The air and the world not sought after. Life./— So, was this it?/—And dream freshens" (*OC,* 192). Dream's passage, "intense and rapid" (*OC,* 192), renders the distinctions between realities or psychical dimensions not so much dubious as hallucinatory, difficult to stabilize or hierarchize. Rimbaud's dream(ing) may be *termed* "evasion"—he himself uses such language in "Délires" ("Deliria," I, *OC,* 230) and "L'Impossible" (*OC,* 239)—but evasion clearly connotes expansion and not just an "adieu au monde dans d'espèces de romances" ("farewell to the world in kinds of romances," *OC,* 234). Dream may mean plunging into "les rêves les plus tristes" ("the saddest dreams") ("L'Alchimie du verbe," *OC,* 237); it may mean "monster loves and fantastic universes" (*OC,* 241, "L'Eclair" ["Lightning"]). But it can mean tenderness, passion, wonder, multiple otherness, profound transformation. And even the "sadness" of dream remains part of this new spaciousness of the real. Rimbaldian dream thus always implies deepening and extension—of self and other joined.

Problem, Revolt and Future

Before moving to an assessment of the Rimbaldian theory and practice he calls *voyance,* (*OC,* 270) I should like to refocus the kind of attention it is possible to give to the work of Rimbaud. If "Le Soleil était encore chaud . . ." opens on an idyllic, romantic note, by the time it is over we understand that many other dynamic forces are at work—social and psychological analysis, protest, irony, youthful disgust—and that Rimbaud will not be a pastoral or confidential poet, even though these elements will persist and grow.

There is no surprise in finding that for Rimbaud, as for all other poets of his century, a great sensitivity develops to existential problem, social and spiritual imperfection—to *le mal* and its resulting *malheur*. Such a sensitivity is clearly fostered by Rimbaud's readings of the great poets preceding him, but it is equally a visceral, instinctive sensitivity, making his perception of problem crucially distinct. Problem and its perception imply many things for Rimbaud. The "Bal des pendus" ("Dance of the Hanged," *OC*, 53–54) evokes the implicit devilishness of human action, in a tone ironic, somewhat detached. "Vénus anadyomène" ("Venus Anadyomene," *OC*, 55) offers a distanced perception of the beauty of horror, but it also hints at a further problem beyond the deformation of flesh: the reversibility of the horror-beauty equation. This does not just mean that the ugly, the imperfect are recuperable, but that aestheticism may be intrinsically suspect: beauty equals horror. Deep ethical and spiritual questions thus float up, vaguely perceptible below the poem's surface.

Problem can be that ennui inundating the postromantic and symbolist era (*OC*, 176, "Enfance"), or the incapacity and sense of fatality penetrating existence (*OC*, 187, "Ouvriers" ["Workers"]). Seen in this perspective, not only is "the world vicious" (*OC*, 135, "Age d'or" ["Golden Age"]), but it exiles *or* appropriates the observing-participating self, curses *or* cajoles him, rendering him that "Maudit suprême aux nuits sanglantes" ("Supreme accursed one, of bloody nights") Rimbaud evokes in "Le Juste restait droit . . ." ("The Just Remained Upright . . ."; *OC*, 94). If, as he will insist in "Mauvais sang" ("Bad Blood"), "je n'ai point fait le mal" ("I have not done evil," *OC*, 224), the self can reach a point obliging him to confess, "misfortune has been my good" (*OC*, 219). Not only may consciousness of problem abound, but it may be chosen, privileged, despite contradiction and destruction (*OC*, 219).

Rimbaud's perception of *le mal* and *le malheur*, however, may be differently angled and couched. The existential problems of fright, bewilderment, and poverty depicted in "Les Effarés" ("The Bewildered," *OC*, 60–61) are treated with evident tenderness. The appalling stupidities of war and political and religious abuse are made, in "Le Mal" ("Evil"), to contrast with the sacredness of creation. And, then again, as "Le Forgeron" ("Blacksmith") stresses, as Rimbaud mulls over the aftermath of the 1789 Revolution, the perception of "evil" is predicated upon its end, not its perverse beauty: "Oh splendid glowings of the ironworks," cry out the workers, plunged into misfortune, "no more evil,/None!" (*OC*, 45). Likewise "Mauvais sang" bids a *second* farewell, this time not to the world, but to Rimbaud's perception of what he might accomplish via his poetic action upon the world, which he trenchantly calls "chimères, idéals, erreurs" ("chimeras, ideals, errors," *OC*, 224).

Implicit in the "withdrawal" articulated in "Mauvais sang" and "Le Bateau ivre" is a mode of revolt and self-transformation that links up with his ideas of progress and future. Curiously, the earlier poetics of revolt—as in "Le Soleil était encore chaud . . ." and "Les Poètes de sept ans" ["Seven-year-old Poets"], *OC*, 77–78), dated *28 mai 1871*—can go from irony and buffoonery to disgust and even hatred, yet always "intelligence" is balanced by "obedience." Revolt, in short, is real but unrealized. "L'Orgie parisienne ou Paris se repeuple" ("Parisian Orgy or Paris Repopulated," *OC*, 81–83) emphasizes the need to let go of "cowardice" in order to accomplish a total revolution that implies a degree of "wildness" or "madness." Revolt, too, entails exposure and chastisement: "Voilà! voilà! bandits!" ("There they are! there! rogues!" *OC*, 83). Rimbaldian revolt of this kind may stem from personal and observed suffering. "I am he who suffers and has rebelled!" he exclaims in "Le Juste restait droit . . ."—where revolt is shown to be an essential mechanism of inquiry, protest, and potential modification. Such revolt is, therefore, not merely narcissistic, but seeks progress toward an end. The "atrocious solitudes" (*OC*, 86) from which spring revolt's critical energies—"Et le poète seul engueulait l'univers" ("And all alone the poet balled out the universe," *OC*, 107)—seek to incite joining, construction, creation. And Rimbaud's second farewell, or second withdrawal, as articulated in *Une saison en enfer* from beginning ("Jadis, si je me souviens bien . . ." ["Before, If I Remember Well . . ."], *OC*, 219) to end ("Adieu"), remains a revolution of the first order. Revolt redefines itself in the light of love, patience, divineness; the *adieu* of "Adieu" "hold[s] on to the ground gained" (*OC*, 244), while reviewing the means of attaining to "future" and "dawn."

"Le Forgeron," like many of Rimbaud's poems, makes crucial use of the future tense in projecting, out of the teeming imperfections of peasant, bourgeois, industrialized and anachronistically aristocratic France, a "victorious" time-space freed of its *grands ef-*

fets and its *grandes causes*, a "great moving dream of living simply, ardently" (*OC*, 45). Nothing seems to separate present and future. The human being, as Rimbaud writes in "Soleil et chair," "will return to life, free of all his Gods,/And as he is of the sky, he will scan the heavens" (*OC*, 48). What Rimbaud calls *l'Idéal* in the same poem will guide toward this "redemption," just as it manifests itself *as* future, *now* (*OC*, 48). The questions, the doubts, which are essentially repressed knowledge for Rimbaud, need only that self-liberation generated by revolt at the idea of our stunted finiteness, for that visceral "faith" in being to be restored. "Lanky mare, long, so long oppressed," Rimbaud claims, "shoots forth from her brow! She will know Why! . . . /Let her leap free, and Man shall have Faith!" (*OC*, 49). Such liberation seems at once feasible and unfeasible in Rimbaud's eyes. "Le Bateau ivre" returns us from a past of dazzling discovery, via the vacuous "present" of the poem, to yet another vision arisen of the flight of a "million birds, o future Vigor" (*OC*, 102). Future thus slips into a particular mode of itself: progress, which is a mode of being rendered linear, more plodding and dogged, more geared to a poetics of long struggle than instantly available transformation; "faith" is at once maintained and deferred. "The vast child Progress," as Rimbaud calls it in a fragment from the *Album zutique* (*Damned Album*, (*OC*, 113), thus engages in "our vengeful march" (*OC*, 124), "the rising up of new men and their on-the-march" (*OC*, 183), along what, in "Mystique," he terms "la ligne des orients, des progrès" ("the line of Orients, of progress," *OC*, 193). As "Démocratie" ("Democracy") insists (*OC*, 204), the motion is "true," but the logic of progress is one of postponement of unfulfilled desire. "Science, the new mobility!" Rimbaud can be reduced to exclaiming in "Mauvais sang"; "Progress. The world is marching. Why would it not be turning?" (*OC*, 221). Such a vision of the future reign of "l'*Esprit*" (*OC*, 221) may well maintain the essence of Rimbaud's hope, but there is no doubt that the bitterness and irony prevalent diminishes the impact of this vision. Just as, in the powerful and poignant "Angoisse" ("Anguish," *OC*, 196–97), we cannot but be struck by the immense tensions that have sprung up between Rimbaud's sense of possibility and his avowal of "la honte de notre inhabileté fatale" ("the shame of our fatal incapacity," *OC*, 196).

"Angoisse" remains, however, a splendid testimony to what transcends all reduction of Rimbaud's poetics to labored and plati-

tudinous progressiveness: the constant idea of creative (self-)trans-
formation, grounded in "love, strength—higher than all joys and
glories" despite the "demon" that threatens to crush his "youth"
(*OC*, 197). Such a future leaps far beyond past experience and its
memory, current physical experience and its limitations, and, as
"Jeunesse" ("Youth") from *Les Illuminations* makes clear, radically
modifies our conception of what is:

> Ta mémoire et tes sens ne seront que la nourriture de ton impulsion créa-
> trice. Quant au monde, quand tu sortiras, que sera-t-il devenu? En tous
> cas, rien des apparences actuelles.

> Your memory and your senses will be but the food of your creative im-
> pulse. As for the world, when you leave, what will have become of it? At
> all events, nothing of present appearances.
>
> (*OC*, 208)

The closing texts of *Une saison en enfer*, like the *future Vigueur* of "Le
Bateau ivre," point beyond *voyance* as textual or existential practice, to an ontology of new wisdom and new adoration. "Matin"
("Morning," *OC*, 242) is politically and spiritually inspired in a
way beyond the wild excess of pure anarchy and in a spirit of an
embrace of life at once transcendent and quotidian. "The song of
the heavens, the march of peoples!" he concludes, "Slaves, let us
not curse life" (*OC*, 242). In "Adieu" there is, on the one hand, a poetics of the "I, I who called myself magus or angel, freed from all
morals, [who] am brought back to earth, with a duty to seek out,
and rough reality to embrace! Peasant!". "But no friend's hand!"
Rimbaud cries out, "and where shall I draw my succor?" (*OC*, 243).
On the other hand, "Adieu" draws, in conclusion, upon Rimbaud's
power of spontaneous self-regeneration: "Recevons tous les influx
de vigueur et de tendresse réelle. Et à l'aurore, armés d'une ar-
dente patience, nous entrerons aux splendides villes.//Que par-
lais-je de main amie! . . . . il me sera loisible de *posséder la vérité
dans une âme et dans un corps*" ("Let us receive all influx of vigor and
real tenderness. And at dawn, armed with ardent patience, we
shall enter splendid cities.//Why was I speaking of a friend's
hand! . . . . . . I shall be free to *possess truth in a soul and in a body*"
(*OC*, 244). Exploitation of the self's resources can give to the "future" what the present does not seem to have, the power of a truth
filled with splendor.

Voyance

Rimbaud's letters of 13 and 15 May 1871, to Georges Izambard and Paul Demeny respectively, demonstrate eloquently the remarkably conscious nature of that poetic program of *voyance* for which he opts at the age of sixteen. "Il s'agit d'arriver à l'inconnu par le dérèglement de *tous les sens*" ("It's a matter of reaching the unknown via derangement of *all the senses*"), he writes to Izambard (*OC*, 268). "The poet," he goes on to say to Demeny, "becomes *a seer* via a long, vast and reasoned *derangement of all the senses*. All forms of love, suffering, madness; he seeks himself, he exhausts within himself all poisons, so as to keep only their quintessence" (*OC*, 270). The dangers to the self are again recognized, the plunge into "accursedness"; yet the chance of "supreme knowledge," and the feeling that *voyance* is an ultimate "cultivation of the soul" (*OC*, 270), sweep aside reservation and concern. Moreover, Rimbaud remains sensitive to a certain absoluteness attaching to private visionary experience that is beyond criticism: "et quand, affolé, il finirait par perdre l'intelligence de ses visions, il les a vues!" ("and even if, crazed, he ended up losing comprehension of his visions, he has seen them!" *OC*, 271). Seeing is experience, and transcends all explanation. The Demeny letter goes much further in historically situating *voyance*—in relation to the early Romantics, Lamartine, Hugo, and the Baudelaire generation of Gautier, Leconte de Lisle, and Banville, Baudelaire himself being "*a true God*" despite his aestheticism and formal oldness: "Les inventions d'inconnu réclament des formes nouvelles" ("Inventing unknownness demands new forms," *OC*, 272–73). It is hard not to see, however, the divergences between the work of these poets, including the much admired Verlaine, and Rimbaud's *Les Illuminations*, the purest poetic concretization of Rimbaud's theory of *voyance*.

The act of poetic seeing is many things. "Le Bateau ivre" suggests by quasi-anaphoric, quasi-paradigmatic association that seeing is an accomplishment of what others only "thought they saw" (*OC*, 101). Like the sadomasochistic prince-genius of "Conte," seeing seeks out "truth, the hour of essential desire and satisfaction" (*OC*, 178). *Voyance* can involve plunging into the surreally exotic, into exalting metamorphosis (*OC*, "Ce qu'on dit au poète à propos de fleurs" ["What Is Said to the Poet About Flowers"], *OC*, 95–100);

it can participate in the "processing of the fairylike" ("Ornières" ["Ruts"], *OC*, 188–89), of the magical, the alchemical; it can accede to dance and joy, the flashing, fragmented experience of multi-levelled being quite inadequately transcribed into "sentences" ("Phrases" ["Sentences"], *OC*, 185–86). "Voyelles" ("Vowels," *OC*, 103) points to the Baudelairian synaesthetic potential of seeing, its fusional capacity; just as the centrally significant "Vies" ("Lives," *OC*, 181–82) evokes our ability to realize with Rimbaud the extent to which one is "réellement d'outre-tombe" ("really from beyond the tomb"), to know from experience "the stupor that awaits you"—which is "something like the key to love" (*OC*, 181–82).

When Rimbaud states, at the conclusion of "Parade" "I alone have the key to this wild parade," he seems to be raising a fundamental question about the validity of his acts of *voyance*. In "Soir historique" ("Historic Evening," *OC*, 200–201), is the experience of harmonies "impossible" and yet heard to be swept aside as esoteric self-truth, outside sharing? Is the Rimbaud with the key merely one of those "master jugglers" that "Parade" describes, or merely the owner of a key to a private circus? Certainly, he can speak of "phantasmagories" ("Métropolitain," *OC*, 197) or conjure "seen" realities only to say immediately that "they don't exist" ("Barbare" ["Barbarian"], *OC*, 198). Or, again, his poetic *reportages* may be termed "délires" (*OC*, 228), "hallucinations" (*OC*, 234), in which, as Rimbaud argues in "Alchimie du verbe," the "simple hallucination" of *voyance* is compounded by the "hallucination of words," and mental disorder is merely deemed "sacred" (*OC*, 234). Self-doubt? Lucidness? Redefinition of his existential and spiritual program? Does he not write, in a *brouillon* of *Une saison en enfer:* "Now I can say that art is a foolishness" (*OC*, 251, "Bonr" ["Happiness"]). "Nuit de l'enfer" evokes the vast visions of "conversion" and "spiritual concert" seemingly realizable via *voyance*, while swinging all the way to a loss of "principles," lassitude, and near-despair. Yet, in its midst, the poem tellingly speaks of the logic of belief in the structure of the real ("Je me crois en enfer, donc j'y suis" ["I think I'm in hell, so I am"]); and, despite all, in "Fiez-vous donc à moi . . ." ("So trust me . . ."), Rimbaud plunges back into the full power of his *voyance*, into a guidance and a healing in which, "decidedly, we are out of the world" (*OC*, 226–28).

A number of points need to be retained with regard to the theory and practice of *voyance*. First, the latter does demand a preparedness to bid farewell to "current appearances" (*OC*, 208), conventional modes of seeing the real. Sensory limitations are understood as restrictions blocking access to other dimensions, equally valid, of the real: dream, meditation, clairvoyance, out-of-body experience, all psychic experience of (our) otherness. "Voices reconstituted," as Rimbaud writes in "Solde" ("Sale," *OC*, 208–209), "the fraternal awakening of all choral and orchestral energies and their instantaneous applications; the unique opportunity to free up our senses"—in an "infinite and wild surge toward invisible splendors, unsensed delights" (*OC*, 208–209). Secondly, *voyance* remains embedded in a paradoxical vision of more simple, physically knowable joy: the plainly "seen" country barns, carts, and June wheatfields of "Le Forgeron"; the "white visions" of children's dreams (*OC*, 38) or the *rêverie* in "Sensation." *Voyance*, in short, may be an altered state of consciousness, but it is nevertheless a part of our totally available consciousness. As "Being Beauteous" shows, seeing plugs us into a wider reality in which "the colors intrinsic to life deepen, dance about and move freely around the Vision, upon the worksite" (*OC*, 181).

Thirdly, despite those inevitable interruptions in seeing recounted in "Départ" ("Departure," *OC*, 183), *voyance* can willfully turn away from the "excessively seen," in a new "affective" mode (*OC*, 183), to achieve what, Rimbaud elsewhere calls "harmonic ecstasy" and "heroic discovery" (*OC*, 202). *Voyance* is, over and above affective and intellectual ambiguities, (self-)revelation, (self-)illumination, a discovery less of the mystical character of being than of the very *real* immensity of its psychical gestalt(s). "A chaque être" ("To every being"), Rimbaud writes in "Alchimie du verbe," "plusieurs *autres* vies me semblaient dues. Ce monsieur ne sait ce qu'il fait: il est un ange" ("several *other* lives seemed to me to be due. This man doesn't know what he's doing: he's an angel," *OC*, 237). Only in brilliantly lit flashes do we accede to a deeper, *inner* sense of our spiritual nature and purpose: "I saw that all beings are fated to be happy" (*OC*, 237, "Alchimie du verbe"). *Voyance* at its most attuned affective best, leaps beyond the struggling reversals of the logic of *le mal* of Vigny, of Baudelaire, Lamartine, beyond the progressive visions of Hugo, sees and senses the inner logic of love and happiness within each of us, despite "current appearances." Fourthly, *voyance*, in its very accession to the "fecundity of the spirit and [the] immensity of the universe" (*OC*, 206), stumbles back upon two sources of frustration: language and reason. The contradiction inherent in "noting the inexpressible" and "fixing vertigos" (*OC*, 233, "Alchimie du verbe") is painfully evident to the skeptic of *Une saison en enfer*. And the unimaginable psychic wealth of being does not fare well when brought under the limited and limiting scrutiny of reason. Not that Rimbaud, any more than the admiring surrealists, has much choice: reason, as his *lettre du voyant* to Paul Demeny originally maintained, is brought to bear upon the psychically and sensorily unsettled and unsettling. Reason seeks to understand, to enlarge itself. It may, as in *Une saison en enfer* especially, retreat into fear, doubt, rejection. But Rimbaud never loses sight of the difficulties in matching the rationally focused with the mental "fecundity" of *l'esprit*. "Notre pâle raison" ("Our pale reason"), he argues in "Soleil et chair," "nous cache l'infini!/Nous voulons regarder:—le Doute nous punit!" ("hides the infinite from us!/We want to see with our eyes:—Doubt punishes us!" *OC*, 49). When Rimbaud writes in "Mauvais sang" that "la raison m'est née. Le monde est bon. Je bénirai la vie" ("reason was born to me. The world is good. I shall bless life," *OC*, 224), the "reason" dominating this changed consciousness inherits its visionary buoyancy precisely from the illuminations of higher consciousness that *voyance* makes available. "Reason" is transformed; consciousness has been expanded; *voyance* does continue, in its more spiritually and ethically transparent form.

Fifthly, and lastly, if Rimbaud can maintain to Izambard, in his letter of 13 May 1871, that "it is false to say: I am thinking. One ought to say: I am being thought" (*OC*, 226), he espouses a position capable of varying interpretation, but in which being is defined from the outside. Rimbaud's statement in "Nuit de l'enfer," however, attributing being to belief—"I think I am in hell, therefore I am"—demonstrates that he also sees all forms of reason and *voyance* as involving belief and therefore choice, self-definition. The self may be in the process of being thought, but it is also thought itself. *Voyance* thus moves back and forth between a poetics of psychical receipt, passivity, openness, and a poetics of intervention, chosen belief, willed psychical creation. That such a tensional logic anticipates all the debates of cubism and surrealism, *l'absurde* and existentialism, structuralism and deconstruction, is less important in my view than the ultimate lesson of *voyance*: there is no contradiction between inside and outside, self and other, *je* and *autre*, thinking and being thought. We just need to think about it, and, as Rimbaud says, reason can be (re)"born" (*OC*, 224).

Lives: Childhood, Partiality, Simultaneity, Continuity

"Le Soleil était encore chaud ..." has already shown the young Rimbaud stepping eagerly into the otherness of (his) existence: "I dreamed ... I was born in Reims in the year 1503 ..." (*OC*, 3). "Alchimie du verbe" reports that "to each being, several *other* lives appeared due. ... Before several men, I chatted aloud with a moment of one of their other lives" (*OC*, 237). One cannot read Rimbaud intelligently and not take him in a substantially literal way. Of course, Rimbaud can question the very phenomenon of the existential otherness he, other-wise, proclaims. "Vite! est-il d'autres vies?" ("Quickly! are there other lives?") he queries in "Mauvais sang." Yet we have already seen a great deal of the *will* for otherness, the *perception* of otherness via *voyance,* the affirmation that the otherness seen *remains* despite loss of its conscious "intelligence." And "Nuit de l'enfer" and "Délires," which immediately follow "Mauvais sang," are clearly predicated upon the idea that "la vraie vie est absente" ("true life is absent," *OC*, 229), a "being-in-the-world" that *voyance,* consciousness of otherness in its innumerable forms, renders a "being-out-of-the-world," a "not-being-in-the-world" (*OC*, 227, 229). "Vies" hints at the feeling of "exile" that may spring from the consciousness of the "untold riches" of seen and enacted otherness; the sensation of being "really from beyond the grave" may carry with it concern and "atrocious skepticism" about Rimbaud's ontological exploration; but none of this takes away from the reality of existence's layered or multidimensional psychicalness (*OC*, 182). "Lives" are very much what is at issue in Rimbaud's conception, and perception, of life. This section shows the scope of the existential in Rimbaud, the *ampleur* of life as we temporally perceive it.

The child and childhood constitute a major theme in Rimbaud's poetry, and indeed his entire oeuvre is that of a prodigious teenager or child-poet—as Verlaine called him. What interests me here is Rimbaud's awareness of the nature of childhood. "Les Etrennes des orphelins" stresses innocence, pensiveness, attentiveness, availability to some "distant whispering" within and beyond them. Rimbaud does not gratuitously or cynically evoke the orphans' contact with angelic forces: it is their very "sensitivity" that renders possible such access to the Other. Rimbaud's work, in this sense, may be said to be a witting pursuit and fostering of the childlike within himself. Like those "children in mourning" of "Après le déluge," he peers through inner and outer windows upon "the marvelous images" (*OC*, 175).

Certainly, Rimbaud's poetry reveals many child personas. "Les Poètes de sept ans" sheds much innocence and knows exile; but dreams of freedom abound, and "visions crush his bewildered eye." Rimbaud('s child) is many children, a child acceding to its many others, "here below" and "beyond." If childhood can be confusion, as in "Les Poètes de sept ans" or "Les Chercheuses de poux" ("Women Looking for Lice," *OC*, 87), it is also a fusion of the fragments of being. "Enfance" (*OC*, 176–78), captures superbly this experiential multiplicity, in which the self is at once "saint," "savant," "pedestrian of the highway." And "Guerre" ("War," *OC*, 205), too, seems directly to conjure this multivocalness:

Enfant, certains ciels ont affiné mon optique: tous les caractères nuancèrent ma physionomie. Les phénomènes s'émurent.

Child, certain skies have sharpened my perception: all characters gave nuance to my countenance. Phenomena were deeply moved.

"Ah! that life of my childhood" Rimbaud reflects in "L'Impossible," for childhood is becoming, "progress" (*OC*, 113), disturbance, active *gêne* (*OC*, 141). "O *mon* Bien! O *mon* Beau . . . Cela commença sous les rires des enfants, cela finira par eux" ("Oh *my* Wealth! oh *my* Loveliness! It began beneath the laughter of children, it will end with it" (*OC*, 184, "Matinée d'ivresse" ["Morning of Intoxication"]).

Rimbaud's poetry is penetrated at once by the experience of temporality and uniqueness, and by that of eternity and nonfragmentation. Although we remain uncertain as to the attribution of titles to Rimbaud's principle collections, it is apt that *Poésies* and *Les Illuminations* evoke plurality, whereas *Une saison en enfer*—whose title is Rimbaud's—points to singularity, particularity: *one* season in the seasons of Rimbaud, just like the experience of Beauty as bitter, "*one* evening" in a "life [of] feasting" (*OC*, 219). "For you I pull out these few hideous pages from my diary of damnation," Rimbaud tells us at the threshold of *Une saison en enfer* (*OC*, 219). Such focusing upon the part, "these few . . . pages," allows for an experience of the full intensity of particular existential features. Particularity, giving full-blown life to the fragment, entails reversal, generating poetry and then a poetics of silence: *"Plus de mots"* ("No more words," *OC*, 223); a discourse of (self-)liberating movement—as in "Le Bateau ivre"—and then a discourse of self-fixity: "One does not leave" (*OC*, 222); a "farewell" to "people who die upon the seasons" in search of "divine clarity" ("Adieu") and then a reversed "farewell" to "ideals" ("Mauvais sang"). These reversals are seemingly endless: the world as vice, the world as goodness; the self as hiddenness, the self as revelation; experience as sophistry, experience as truth; and so on.

No wonder Rimbaud's poetry escapes our reductive, thematicizing grasp: contradiction and combination abound. The "whispering" of the children of "Les Etrennes des orphelins" is "sad and sweet"; "Les Réparties de Nina" shows the convergence of love and filth, poverty and illumination, just as spiritual delight and material shabbiness may be telescoped in "Les Effarés" or, in "Morts de quatre-vingt-douze" ("The Dead of Ninety-Two," *OC*, 63), human beings may be "ecstatic and great in torment." The parts conjure up a larger and potentially transcendent whole; the whole still has seemingly contradictory component parts. Rimbaud's vision here might be said to be metonymic, synedochic. His accumulations in "Enfance"—"Il y a. . . . Il ya a. . . ."; "Je suis. . . . Je suis. . . ."—push toward a cosmic vision of the "differences of sameness," as Michel Deguy would say. Existence is perceived as the dreamlike site of "des êtres de tous les caractères parmi toutes les apparences" ("beings of all types amid all appearances," *OC*, 193, "Veillées").

At the conclusion of "Qu'est-ce pour nous, mon coeur . . ." ("What, For Us, My Heart . . ." from *Derniers vers* (*OC*, 124), Rimbaud declares, in the midst of visions of cataclysmic transformation of "the old earth," *"Ce n'est rien: j'y suis; j'y suis toujours"* ("It's nothing; I'm in it; I'm still in it," *OC*, 124). Despite or within contradiction and reversal, Rimbaud's consciousness maintains a sense of what we might think of as buoyant ongoing rightness of participation. "Vis et laisse au feu/L'obscure infortune" ("Live and leave to the fire/Obscure calamity"), Rimbaud throws out as a response to the world's "viciousness" in "Age d'or." His "wolflike self-consumption" (*OC*, 139, "Le Loup criait ..." ["The Wolf Screamed ..."]) seems perfectly to fit with an acceptance of the ephemeralness of what constitutes him as a poet: "Que comprendre à ma parole?/Il fait qu'elle fuie et vole!//O saisons, ô chateaux!" ("What is there to be understood in my speech?/Made to flee and fly!//Oh seasons, oh castles!" *OC*, 140). Such self-parading, however, involves letting the self go to death, to nature's course—as described in "Bannières de mai" ("May Banners," *OC*, 131–32). This is not despairing self-abandonment, but a curious self-constitution: "We know how to give our life away in its entirety every day" ("Matinée d'ivresse"). If Rimbaud adds, "This is the time of ASSASSINS" (*OC*, 185), the deathly catharsis remains also an "intoxicating dawn." The wanderings or *vagabondages* (*OC*, 190) in which Rimbaud engaged are an appropriate metaphor for this going that is also an on-going, of which he speaks at the outset of *Une saison en enfer:* "You know neither where you are going nor why you are going, enter everywhere, be responsive to everything" ("Mauvais sang"). The "world [is] your fortune and your peril," Rimbaud writes in "Jeunesse," a now problematic, now ecstatically privileging experience of life as that teeming energy he calls "Faim, soif, cris, danse, danse, danse, danse!" ("Hunger, thirst, screams, dance, dance, dance, dance!", "Mauvais sang").

Divineness

"Soleil et chair" offers, once again, a sure entry into much that is central in Rimbaud's discourse of the divine. Fundamental is the sense of the godlike, loving soul of the earth (*OC*, 47), the fact that all is bathed in love "within God" (*OC*, 47). If love continues to be deemed "the great Faith," Rimbaud is already sensitive to a certain disappearance of divinity as humankind moves to usurp godliness (*OC*, 47). "The other God [of Catholicism] teaming us up to his cross" renders the path of divineness "bitter" (*OC*, 48), shifts us from the natural rhythms of earth-godliness and from a more natural intuition of our inner "celestialness" that remains "free of all [our] Gods" (*OC*, 48). Thought can, then, assume the confidence, the "Faith," in a divineness that earth's loving and "redemptive song" ceaselessly conveys (*OC*, 48–50). Our fabricated gods yield to "the Gods within whose brow the bullfinch makes its nest,/— The Gods listen to Man and the infinite World!" (*OC*, 51).

"Les Poètes de sept ans," however, pulls Rimbaud's discourse of the divine along crucially different lines: a distrust and even dislike of God—"l'autre Dieu" ("the other God") (*OC*, 48) of religion and dogma—and a love of mankind. "Les Pauvres à l'église" ("The Poor at Church," *OC*, 79–80) insists upon the irony of social and spiritual hierarchy and power in the context of a would-be divineness lost in habit, fear, gross contrasts with, "outside, the cold, hunger, carousing men" (*OC*, 79). Here, "faith" is "beggarly and stupefied" (*OC*, 79). "Les Premières Communions" ("First Communions," *OC*, 88–92) tops off this trilogy of satirical deconstructions of doctrinaire divinity, focusing upon the foolishness involved in "grasseyant les divins babillages" ("reading the divine prattle with thick accents"); the reduction of the Virgin to some bookish ghost; the sapping of "mystical soarings" through repetition, mediocre iconography, or what Rimbaud calls "the poverty of images" (*OC*, 90); the wretchedness of the intervention, within the mystical, of all those "filthy madmen/Whose divine work still distorts worlds" (*OC*, 91); the sad fact—for Rimbaud remains nostalgically sensitive to the beauty of Christian symbolism—that Christ constitutes an "eternal thief of energies" (*OC*, 92).

Thus is it that Rimbaud's poetry can generate a degree of critical dismantling of the divine that pushes his "atrocious skepticism" into direct refusal of "ma vieille part de gaieté divine" ("my old share of divine gaiety," *OC*, 182). Such skepticism leads only to madness. There yet remains, in Rimbaud, a "vigilance of soul" ("L'Eternité"), and never does he cease to search for a key to the divineness of our being. Poems like "Mystique" (*OC*, 193), "Aube," "Fleurs" ("Flowers," *OC*, 194–95) speak of recognition of "the goddess," of things "like a god," just as "La Rivière de Cassis" (*OC*, 126–27) speaks of "the voice of a hundred crows . . ., true/And good voice of angels' (*OC*, 126). Rimbaud's entire oeuvre, as he suggests in "Ce qu'on dit au poète à propos de fleurs" (*OC*, 95–100), is an act of "self-exaltation toward candors/More candid than Marys" (*OC*, 99). Two of the great, later poems of *Les Illuminations*, "Dévotion" ("Devotion," *OC*, 203) and "Génie" ("Genius," *OC*, 205–206), are pertinent here, for the first is a poem of (re)affirmation pointing to the discovery of that "very high clergy" needed to celebrate the divineness of all things; and the second evokes the genius of "love, a reinvented and perfect measure, an unforeseen and marvelous reason, and eternity" (*OC*, 205). Superstitions may be set aside, but the "promise" of love and "adoration" remains in this vision redolent of Catholic symbolism yet beyond all but its purest principle.

Une saison en enfer demonstrates that, with this sense of distilled and transcendent divineness, there continues that darker *hantise* of "hellishness" pervading the great poetic work of the entire century. "Mauvais sang" argues that this obsession is linked to a loss of evangelic confidence; to feeling cut off from "Christ's counsel"; to the temptation of clinging to any old "divine image"; to the self's foolishness after the intense experience of "mon abnégation, . . . ma charité merveilleuse" ("my abnegation, . . . my marvelous charitableness," *OC*, 222). "L'Impossible" presents a similar tension: "C'est cette minute d'éveil qui m'a donné la vision de la pureté!—Par l'esprit on va à Dieu!//Déchirante infortune!" ("This moment of awakenness gave me the vision of purity!—Through the spirit one goes to God!//Heart-rending misfortune!"; *OC*, 241). Much that is central to Rimbaud's sense of divineness elaborated from "Soleil et chair" onward suffers loss, then, indeed to the point where in the *brouillon* "Bonr" he declares: "Je hais maintenant les élans mystiques et les bizarreries de style" ("I now hate mystical upsurges and stylistic oddities," *OC*, 251). But this loss should not be thought of as more real or conclusive than what we find in "Adieu" or "Mauvais sang." The latter declares that "God makes my strength, and I praise God," though Rimbaud is quick to clarify: "I do not believe I am embarked upon a wedding with Jesus Christ as father-in-law.//I am not a prisoner of my reason. I did say: God" (*OC*, 224–25). Rimbaldian divineness eschews dogmatism, remaining "divine love alone," for he still craves "freedom in salvation." "Adieu" speaks of *la clarté divine* (*OC*, 242), though it does retain as fundamental the notion of "spiritual combat" (*OC*, 244). Divineness moves, in Rimbaud's work, between the pole of givenness and that of problematized future accomplishment, and there is no reason to privilege one place or moment of perception over another.

Love, Charity, Happiness

"The world thirsts for love," Rimbaud tells us in "Soleil et chair." "Amour, appel de vie et chanson d'action" ("Love, call to life and song of action"), he reaffirms in "Les Soeurs de charité" (*OC*, 86), linking love to language, song, and poetry itself. "Le Forgeron," however, suggests that, if love may become a revolutionary fervor, such fervor remains "something in one's heart like love." It completes reason and logic, giving depth to idea, felt possibility to pure theory. When Rimbaud exclaims in "Chanson de la plus haute tour" ("Song From the Highest Tower," *OC,* 132–33), "Ah! Que le temps vienne/Où les coeurs s'éprennent," ("Ah! May the time come when hearts are amorous") (r)evolutionary ideology slips into pure emotional aspiration, a cri de coeur. Such recourse to the visceral logic of emotion takes us right back to that nonintellectualized immediacy of Rimbaud's early poems. Love, in "Soleil et chair," is the giving and receiving of sun and earth, the root principle of a cooperative, non-Darwinian world. A synonymy of love and divineness is thus rapidly generated: "C'est la Rédemption! c'est l'amour! c'est l'amour" ("It's Redemption! it's love! it's love," *OC,* 50). Rimbaud's "ideal," which is shaken but never dislodged, is that of "infinite love" (*OC,* 49).

Such a love would seem to exceed the frontiers of Stendhal's four-pronged concept of *amour-passion, amour-goût,* physical love, and *amour de vanité,* being much more spiritualized, as Rimbaud hints in his albeit tendentious *Un coeur sous une soutane* (*A Heart Beneath a Cassock*): "I, moreover, had been born for love and for faith" (*OC,* 159). Certainly, love, as witness *Les Déserts de l'amour,* can experience loss of the Adored and the Adorable (*OC,* 172); and love can, as "Le Bateau ivre" proclaims, be "acrid" and render "torpid" (*OC,* 103). Love is, however, never reduced to pure cynicism or bitterness. *Les Illuminations* makes clear the degree to which "something like the key to love" lies at the heart of its poiesis (*OC,* 182, "Vies"). "Dévotion" confirms this logic of a love much closer to agape than to eros; and "Génie" deems love a "genial" sharing or equality, what "Mauvais sang" calls "divine love" (*OC,* 224).

"Charity," Rimbaud argues in "Jadis, si je me souviens bien . . . ," is the "key to the ancient feast" (*OC,* 219), thus seeming to equate love and charity. This is a charity, in its quintessential Christian form, greater than faith and hope but accompanying them, but also a charity or primal love knowing difference but not fostering division. "Mauvais sang" is not merely some vestige of Catholic regret ("*de profundis Domine,*" *OC,* 222), it is addressed as much to the self's "marvelous charity, here below, however!" (*OC,* 222), a charity felt to be somehow endangered. "Adieu" closes *Une saison en enfer* with a question that seems to have haunted Rimbaud since at least 1871, when he wrote "Les Soeurs de charité": "Am I deceived? Could charity be the sister of death for me?" (*OC*, 243). "Les Soeurs de charité" sketches out the story of heroic (male) youth turning from "the uglinesses of this world" toward some desired "sister of charity." This feminine force, however, is not woman herself, not physical love nor even love's "charming and grave Passion" (*OC*, 86). Rather is "charity" poetry and justice: these will be his twin "implacable Sisters," who will yet abandon him to his "atrocious solitudes" and to the final resort of charity or love as pure aspiration, "out of this world," continuing in "mysterious Death, o sister of charity" (*OC*, 86).

The essence of Rimbaldian charity does not change, only the conditions surrounding its accomplishment; and while Rimbaud bites deeply into "la réalité rugueuse" ("rugged reality," *OC*, 243, "Adieu"), he is ever ready to redefine the real from a psychic and spiritual perspective. Life and death are thus highly relative terms. Charity as sister of life or sister of death: charity remains a sister to Rimbaud, an integral part of that "magical study/Of happiness" which he deems central in "Ô saisons, ô chateaux" ("Oh seasons, oh castles," *OC*, 140). Rimbaldian love, charity and happiness step beyond the bounds of the conventionally received and perceived. "Mauvais sang" makes clear his refusal of "established happiness, domestic or not" (*OC*, 225). Like the acts of charity and love, the state of happiness lies on both sides of a line separating life and death, "real" and "ideal": "sisterhood" and "fraternity" are notions that transcend strict physicality. The experience of happiness in "Sensation" is compared to being "heureux comme avec une femme"/"happy as with a woman" (*OC*, 41). "I had glimpsed conversion to good and happiness—salvation," he writes in "Nuit de l'enfer"—a happiness wherein emotion and ethics merge, and "hellishness" is understood to be a merely passing "season."

Old and New Forms

My final analysis of poetic form and mode may be usefully framed by two assessments Rimbaud himself provides. On the one hand, his letter of 15 May 1871 to Paul Demeny argues that, although Baudelaire may be deemed "the first seer, the king of poets, *a true*

God," his poetic form remains "shabby" (*OC*, 273). "Inventing un-knownness," he insists, "demands new forms" (*OC*, 273): a revolution in sensibility and thinking must be accompanied by transformation at the formal level. On the other hand, the second part of "Délires" declares that "poetic old-fashionedness had a good share in my alchemy of the logos" (*OC*, 234). Of course, Rimbaud is not referring here to earlier poems such as "Les Etrennes des orphelins," whose composition (December 1869) predates his consciousness of the radical expressive options available to him; the poem's use of conventional alexandrine meter, *rimes plates*, a narrative mode, standard dramatic divisions à la Vigny will continue to be stylistically pertinent well into Rimbaud's career. The remaining pages will look at meter, stanzaic form, rhyme, vocabulary, overall tone and mode; address the notion of *illumination;* assess the form of the prose poetry, consider it as "theater" and as *roman (romance)*; wrestle with the concept of poetry as illusion and truth.

First, meter: *Poésies* is dominated by the alexandrine, with even the texts of the so-called *bribes* ("fragments"), *Les Stupra (The Stupra)* and *Album zutique*, espousing this form in sixteen of twenty-two cases. Of the nineteen poems of *Derniers vers* and *Fêtes de la patience (Celebrations of Patience)*, however, only two choose the alexandrine: the *impair* molds the latter "collection" (2×11 syllables, 1×7, 4×5, 3 mixtures of *impair* and *pair*), and in the former, two of the seven texts opt again for the 11-syllable structure, three others for mixed metric orchestration. Only one poem, "Vieux de la vieille" ("Old Woman's Old Man," *OC*, 116), elects free verse, Rimbaud clearly preferring to shortcut directly to the prose poem, after various Verlainean experiments with poems of 1 or 2 syllables in the "Conneries" ("Bloody Absurdities") of *Album zutique* (*OC*, 114–15). None of this is to say that 8- and 10-syllable meters are eluded, the former playing an important role in the first group of forty-four poems in *Poésies* (7 of 44), balancing the alexandrine's presence (31 of 44); the second, 10-syllable line popping up twice in the *impair* environment of the twelve *Fêtes de la patience*. Various other stylistic features may be critical in coloring and giving texture to meter, so that the 10-syllable "Bruxelles" becomes a relatively audacious poem via enjambment, ellipsis, enigmatic allusion, rapid-fire evocation, pure sonority, and general impishness of tone and turn of phrase.

Secondly, poem and stanza structure: *Poésies* demonstrates considerable variation, though all within existing guidelines. Thus, "Les Etrennes des orphelins" and "Le Forgeron" offer conventionally splayed-out dramatic-narrative structure with, respectively, stanzaic organization, in lines per stanza, of 9-26-28-20-28 and 13-13-30-21-23-31-23-16-8; one is not far from Lamartine or Vigny in this respect. *Poésies* generally, however, is structurally governed by the traditional quatrain, rather than this earlier more ample stanzaic and textual form. Not taking into account the fifteen sonnets of the first forty-four poems and the three sonnets of *Les Stupra*—all of which display that classic 4-4-3-3 stanzaic structure so dear to Baudelaire and Verlaine—the quatrain dominates throughout, to a lesser degree in the more boisterous texts of the *Album zutique*, but manifestly in *Derniers vers* and *Fêtes de la patience*. The number of quatrains can go as high as forty, with "Le Bateau ivre" at twenty-five and "Les Réparties de Nina" at twenty-nine, but tend to be in the mid-to-lower range, Rimbaud never being long-winded. For example, the first forty-four poems give one single quatrain, one of two quatrains, one of three, one of five, three of eight and nine, one of ten, two of eleven, one of twelve, one of sixteen, one of nineteen, plus the longer examples quoted; *Derniers vers* gives one each of four, five, seven and ten quatrains; *Fêtes de la patience* one each of two, three and seven, with two of five and six. And the quatrain may combine with other stanzaic forms, as in "Les Premières Communions," with eight × 6-line, followed by twenty-two quatrains; or "Comédie de la soif" ("Comedy of Thirst," *OC*, 127–30), with three × 8-line, two quatrains, one 8-line, two × 6-line, three × 5-line, two quatrains. Other stanzaic structures may be used, but are rare: "Les Effarés," with its twelve 3-line (non–terza rima) structure; "Accroupissements" (*OC*, 76–7), seven 5-line stanzas; "Le Coeur du pitre" (*OC*, 80–81), three 8-line stanzas; "Les Corbeaux" (*OC*, 104), four 6-line stanzas; "L'Angelot maudit" ("Accursed Cherub," *OC*, 117–18), seven 2-line stanzas; and so on. With constancy and consciousness of the relative charm of *la vieillerie poétique*, Rimbaud achieves inflection and change within harmony, and aspires to that punchy succinctness admired in Baudelaire and Verlaine.

Thirdly, rhyme: here, quantitatively, Rimbaud's *Poésies* breaks no new ground. The *rimes plates* of Vigny's modern myths or Hugo's massive "legendary" or visionary works may appear; the quatrain dictates its implacable *rimes croisées* or *rimes embrassées;* other stanzaic forms largely follow tradition. Very rare even are those Verlainean audacities such as the *abaaabab* structure employed in "Le Coeur du pitre." Rich and weak rhymes may come and go, and it is perhaps in the use of bold enjambment, marked lexical dash, and general semantic punchiness that Rimbaud's use of rhyme attains to its greatest power. Assonance is nearly disregarded (see "Jeune ménage" ["Young Household"], *OC,* 136), and free verse makes but one scant appearance before the leap into prose poetry. Fourthly, Rimbaud's lexicon: though not Hugolian, it remains considerable and, especially in certain verse forms, seems to provide an outlet for revolutionary poetic energy. The Jarry- or Ubu-like *saperlipopettouilles* and *saperpouillottes* of "Le Soleil était encore chaud . . ." foreshadow the youthful lexical invention running through *Poésies:* neologisms and deformations, exoticism and innuendo, use of proper names and capitalization. This is partly in line with the lexical adventurousness of Laforgue, Verlaine, Banville; partly intrinsic and adolescent genius; partly French poetic tradition going back to St. Amant and even Villon. In Rimbaud, however, the desire for lexical rampage is quickly assuaged; he remains a poet of great classicism, always clear and pertinent no matter what the impulsiveness pressing upon his language.

Fifthly, a few observations on tone and mode: irony and simple gaiety, satire and ease, may coincide, as in "Au Cabaret-Vert," where form mimics this "tension." "Oraison du soir" also generates deep personal truth and irony within the confines of a sonnet at once stylistically complex and simple. Part of the power of *Poésies*—and of the prose poems, too—comes from Rimbaud's sense of aesthetic orchestration, harmony, closure. Yet does the inclusion of *bribes* and *brouillons* in *Poésies* give the poems naturalness and impulsiveness. Thus does the *etc.* . . . at the close of "Age d'or" mock the very closure it accomplishes and invite us to think beyond and step *out.* Rimbaud's conventional mode is matched by a mode of "fancifulness"—"Ma bohème" is simultaneously a *fantaisie,* for example (*OC,* 69). And, again, the alternation and range of tone in Rimbaud does not simply take us from, say, "Les Poètes de sept ans" to the *connerie* of the *Album zutique,* "Cocher ivre" ("Drunk Coachman," *OC,* 115), for within the *Album zutique* itself tone, purpose, and mode may vary so greatly as to give us "L'Humanité chaussait le vaste enfant Progrès" ("Humanity Outfitted the Vast Child Progress," *OC*, 113). "Que comprendre à ma parole?" ("What can be understood in my speech?") Rimbaud asks in "Ô saisons, ô châteaux!" (*OC*, 140), "il fait qu'elle fuie et vole!" ("it is all flight and fugue"): poetic language and mode as movement, or what "Mauvais sang" calls dance: "Faim, soif, cris, danse, danse, danse, danse!"

Sixthly, poetic mode as mental painting: *illumination* as poetry's "colored plates." Even in *Poésies* Rimbaud is taken at times by a certain type of visual representation. "Le Buffet" ("Sideboard," *OC*, 68–69) would seem to offer a kind of poetic *nature morte*, just as "L'Eclatante Victoire de Sarrebrück" ("The Dazzling Victory of Sarrebrück," *OC*, 68) is related to a "brilliantly colored Belgian engraving selling for 35 centimes in Charleroi" (*OC*, 68). These two poems of 1870 either describe an anonymous, perhaps naive piece of art or else evoke a scene in largely objective descriptive terms. *Les Illuminations* are mainly to be seen metaphorically as landscapes. Such a "reinvented," "enchanted," and "alchemical" poetic mode (*OC*, 232–33) may seem to correspond insufficiently to known mental landscapes, but accession to the unknowns of self and other remains the central conceptual axis along which his work travels. At once esoteric and available, Rimbaud's *illuminations* are "studies" (*OC*, 233), in every sense of the word. Choosing the verb to express the "inexpressible," the "fixing" they offer is necessarily relative (*OC*, 222).

Seventhly, some brief observations on the prose poem to which Rimbaud may be said to *return* after "Le Soleil était encore chaud . . .": 1. the syntax of Rimbaud's *Les Illuminations* is very largely as sure, as coherent as that of any surrealist poem or text; 2. fragmentation can occur, however, and paratactic structures can result, giving an architectural or sculpted quality to poems like "Veillées" or "Barbare" (*OC*, 198); 3. at other times, and frequently throughout *Les Illuminations*, the sentence ("Phrases," *OC*, 185) tends to establish an independence of function and semantic impact despite its insertion within the continuity of paragraph or overall text; 4. there is often in Rimbaud's prose poems, despite his tendency to denigrate anything that could be described as pure aesthetic play, an impulse to recognize them as "studies" or "colored plates" and thus to grant them the kind of closure found in "Les Ponts"; 5. the sudden appearance of free verse poems in the middle of *Les Illuminations*—"Marine,"

"Mouvement"—shows Rimbaud to be indifferent to the formal or aesthetic innovation implicit in his prose poem inventions, and yet alert to form per se; 6. while the titles of the poems of *Les Illuminations* are not inherently esoteric, they do often possess a simple enigmaticalness, as if straining to convey the maximum within the minimum. "Bottom" (*OC*, 202) and "H" (*OC*, 202–203) are excellent examples, but even titles such as "Antique," "Fleurs," "Promontoire" ("Promontory," *OC*, 199) reveal their unsettling force when reread in the context of the poems; 7. Rimbaud's conception of the poem as *roman/ce:* already he termed "novel" one of his *Poésies* (*OC*, 62), no doubt as a provocation anticipating his remarks a year later to Paul Demeny about the silliness of so many poets' "rhymed prose" (*OC*, 269). But if poetry is not merely telling stories in verse, both *Poésies* and *Les Illuminations* constitute "tales" of a kind (*OC*, 178, "Conte") and *d'espèces de romances* (*OC*, 234, "Délires"). If *Les Illuminations* are *romans, contes, romances,* they are so as anti-novels and anti-songs of the self's others; 8. these tensions result in Rimbaud's feeling, as expressed in "Alchimie du verbe," that not only are his psychic experiences "hallucinations," but so too are the very words he uses in *Les Illuminations,* "magic" thus becoming sophistical, fallacious. A poetics of new poetic form and mode as locus of illuminated truth flips, via a crisis of confidence, into a poetics of illusion and deception. Poetry and experience are questioned by the revamped poetry and experience of *Une saison en enfer.* The *"truth in a soul and in a body"* of which "Adieu" speaks (*OC*, 244) recedes from the presence of *voyance* to a future locus of possession. But the self-doubt of "Alchimie du verbe" is but a *feeling* about world and word among other feelings. It is not a dénouement, the end achievement of a poetic purpose. The new forms of Rimbaud's *voyance* remain, and, as his letter of 15 May 1871 to Paul Demeny makes clear they are not just forms, passing though they inevitably are.

· NINE ·

Lautréamont

Very little is known of the life of the young poet Isidore-Lucien Ducasse, who has come to be known by his pseudonym, Lautréamont. He has left us with a handful of letters, his (in)famous *Chants de Maldoror* (*Songs of Maldoror*), printed but never put on sale in his lifetime, and the equally puzzling *Poésies* (*Poems*), published a few months before his utterly enigmatic and seemingly desperately solitary death in his Paris rooms on 24 November 1870. Born in Montevideo on 4 April 1846, he is in principle of the generation of Mallarmé and Verlaine, though his discovery belongs to the end of the century and even the surrealist period. There is an 1874 edition, but that of Genonceaux in 1890, with its perceptive and situating preface, really marks Lautréamont's appearance upon the literary scene. Lautréamont came to Paris at the age of fourteen, after continuing disputes with a father sensitive only to his son's academic successes. Boarding at the Lycée impérial in Tarbes and studying later at Pau, Lautréamont possessed an intelligence that often led to distinction, though somewhat decreasingly, as Philippe Soupault's fine 1946 preface argues. The year 1869 finds Lautréamont living in Paris, having already published at his own expense, but anonymously, the *Chant premier* ("First Song") of *Les Chants de Maldoror*. His life, from all accounts, was lonely, given to walks, reading, and writing rather than to café exchanges and socializing. The 1869 edition, with Lacroix and Verbroeckhoven, was suspended immediately prior to sale, due to concerns of potential prosecution. Several changes of Paris address in the last year of his life remain unexplained, as mysterious as his demise.

Great modern critics and writers have pored over Lautréamont's slim but unforgettable oeuvre: Maurice Blanchot, Gaston Bachelard, and so on. As Roger Caillois has said, there is, despite our at times anxious astonishment reading Lautréamont, simply a sense of his striking "power of communion." The surrealists recognized this quickly, embracing its strangeness, ambivalence, and irony. Breton, Soupault, Aragon, Eluard all have credited Lautréamont with a revolutionary incisiveness. Gide regarded him as "le maître des écluses pour la littérature de demain" ("the sluice-master for tomorrow's literature"). Little wonder, then, that writers like Marcelin Pleynet and Philippe Sollers have been drawn to Lautréamont's swarming honeycomb. Julien Gracq calls him "ce dynamiteur archangélique" ("that archangelic dynamiter"), and Camus is fascinated by what he deems to be the "total revolt" articulated by this "metaphysical dandy." If the ethical orientation of Lautréamont's work can thus be neglected or misperceived, certainly Le Clézio's observation stands pertinent, that Lautréamont offers a classical case of the exploration of the real via the dialectical fusion of dream and lucidity. And Char rightly gives particular weight to *Poésies*, as does Reverdy to what he perceives as the exemplary "tragic" dimension of *Les Chants de Maldoror*.

Reading

Throughout *Les Chants de Maldoror* Lautréamont offers us an intense critique of the act of reading. And he does this, moreover, having already distanced himself from his writing by assuming a pseudonym—an act that reconstitutes the writer as reader of the self('s text). The critique of reading is thus an autocriticism, an exploration of self's alterity focused back upon the self. Reading is a penetration into the labyrinth of the other, as Lautréamont stresses from the outset of the *Chants de Maldoror* (*OC*, 123). It thus can be dangerous in its potential self-alienation. Ideally, some balance should be maintained between apprehension, *défiance*, and "une logique rigoureuse et une tension d'esprit" ("rigorous logic and mental tension"). When Lautréamont evokes that slippage of reader to "monster" (*OC*, 124), he no doubt cautions against both extremes of reading: the monstrousness of deeming oneself sharply apart from the textual horrors that can proliferate, as well as the monstrousness of one's utter absorption by a vampiric textuality. Satire cannot disengage the reader, as if (s)he were beyond the existence so intensely allegorized; but nor is satire predicated upon impotent surrender to the duplicities evoked in Baudelaire's

"Au lecteur" and pushed beyond Lautréamont's poetics by Jarry's fin de siècle pursuit of our "ignoble double."

In effect, *Les Chants de Maldoror* offers us persistent and subtle guidance in our reading of its complexity. The reader needs to be "attached/torn free," as Michel Deguy writes of the poet: at once involved, com-passionate, and yet objective, detached (*OC*, 136). This intimate removal is prescribed at the close of the *Chant premier*, where Lautréamont asks for suspension of severity of judgement, to allow for a recognition of the strange power working through the textuality (*OC*, 160). Moreover, the reader must understand that literature is a dramatization of "la timide personnalité de mon opinion" ("the timid personality of my opinion," *OC*, 261). The satire read is thus, once again, a satire of the self. Clarity of perception is required in reading this particular poetic fiction, for its "truth" could easily escape us. "I warn whomsoever may read me," Lautréamont writes in the *Chant quatrième* ("Fourth Song"), "to be careful not to come to some vague, and even more so false, idea of the literary beauties I pluck off like so many leaves, in the excessively rapid development of my sentences" (*OC*, 275). The "singularity" of the ideas exposed should not be lost, we are told— the opening pages of the *Chant cinquième* ("Fifth Song") are instructive (*OC*, 285–87)—simply because their mode of expression may be found bizarre, bizarrely beautiful.

Purpose, in short, takes precedence over stylistic flamboyance. The reader needs to recognize the fundamentally *poetic* nature of Lautréamont's unfolding "intelligence" (*OC*, 286): poiesis as creation, transformation, (r)evolution. And is not the *Chants de Maldoror.* followed by the *Poésies*? And does Lautréamont not warn the reader, upon the threshold of the *Chant sixième* ("Sixth Song"), of the *incompleteness* of his mission at this point—a mission that cannot be equated with the "inopportune . . . exclamations" of *un élève de quatrième* (*OC*, 321)? "Prudence" and precaution are urged upon the reader, as at the beginning of the *Chant cinquième*, for these seem to be precisely the qualities required to generate the maximum of sym-pathy for a text whose satire, whose deep moral purpose, can only be fully sensed in reciprocity—no matter how "cadaverous" the other's reasoning may be (*OC*, 287). Reading Lautréamont must thus avoid the dangers of being vampirized by the other; and the temptation to reproach the other for unleashing "d'amères accusations contre l'humanité dont je suis un des membres (cette seule remarque me donnerait raison!) et contre la Providence" ("bitter accusations against humanity one of whose members I am [this remark alone would prove me right!] and against Providence," *OC*, 323). If reproaches or "attacks" are to be envisaged, Lautréamont suggests the reader orient them toward form. But his argument that in *Poésies* "feelings are the most incomplete form of reasoning that can be imagined" (*OC*, 374) is as applicable to the *writing* of *Les Chants de Maldoror* as to its reading. Writing is merely the place of the self's theatricalization of "the timid personality of my opinion." Lautréamont persists in demanding a readership privileging purpose over form (*OC*, 286), sensing, as he does in the *Poésies*, that Bonnefidian superiority of the "philosophy of poetry" over poetry itself (*OC*, 384).

Literature and Its Likeness

From the opening page of *Les Chants de Maldoror*, literature is characterized as swamp, poison, desolation and "bitter fruit" (*OC*, 123). Its "painting of the delights of cruelty" (*OC*, 125) constitutes a portrayal whose very fabric soaks up the horrors it recounts, projecting them out like so many "mortal emanations [that, in turn] will suck up [the reader's] soul like water sugar" (*OC*, 123). The satire of human cruelty thus becomes such an intense enactment that it risks "swamping," "poisoning," and "desolating" the reader in literature's "troubling" sweep (*OC*, 135), in its "frightening" and "hideous" movement (*OC*, 141). Of course, Lautréamont sees literature also as "song," "creation," and "philosophy of poetry" (*OC*, 384). It is a "lamp" (*OC*, 195), an illumination clarifying "holy anger" (*OC*, 195). Yet it remains a "présence inopportune" ("inopportune presence," *OC*, 196), a "chant impie [aux mines explosibles]" ("impious song [with explosive mines]," *OC*, 219), an "act and a place" of danger, given its study of "the real and inexplicable contradictions that inhabit the lobes of the human brain" (*OC*, 255).

The post-Stendhalian mirror that Lautréamont holds up to the real may appear to deform, but its task is simple, however disturbing its images. "Le rire, le mal" ("Laughter, evil"), he writes in the *Chant quatrième*, "l'orgueil, la folie, paraîtront, tour à tour, entre la sensibilité et l'amour de la justice, et serviront d'exemple à la stupéfaction humaine: chacun s'y reconnaîtra, non pas tel qu'il devrait être, mais tel qu'il est" ("pride, madness, will appear, one af-

ter the other, between sensitivity and love of justice, and will serve
as an example to human amazement: each will recognize himself in
them, not such as he ought to be, but as he is," *OC*, 257). The six
chants are not all of a piece, but are parts of that "fleuve majestueux
et fertile" ("majestic and fertile river") that poetry is for the
Lautréamont of *Poésies* (*OC*, 361). From a literature of and as satire,
Lautréamont seems poised to shift to a literature beyond satire, to a
"poetry [that] is to be found everywhere that the stupidly mocking
smile of duck-faced man is not" (*OC*, 326). Literature as "perni-
cious overthrowing" (*OC*, 353), the closing section of the *Chant sixième* tells us, gives way to a poetry not felt to be "outside the
ordinary march of nature" (*OC*, 353). The "abrogation" of literature
that *Poésies* evokes (*OC*, 369) thus coexists with literature as an act
of self-transformation and hope (*OC*, 369). Lautréamont's conception of literature hinges upon the latter's continuity, the delicate
equilibrium it can bring about between its intrinsic *malheur*, its
satire of *malheur*, and its capacity for generating a consciousness of
"two-sidedness" (*OC*, 371). Literature may delve into existential
and ontological problem, but it remains a place for the transformation of problem, for the snatching of "beauty" from "death" (*OC*,
371). It is thus, again, a place of philosophic action (*OC*, 372), "freedom to do good," of "practical truth" (*OC*, 377). To allow literature
to remain at the level of pure struggle against *le mal* is to risk making occult its capacity for transcendence of *le mal* (*OC*, 388). "Il
n'existe pas deux genres de poésies; il n'en est qu'une" ("There are
not two kinds of poetry; there is only one," *OC*, 361). Literature or
poetry is, once more, flowing and "fertile" (*OC*, 361). The *Poésies*
and *Les Chants de Maldoror* are this fluviality, this becoming fertility
despite their alleged differences.

It is not then surprising that *Les Chants de Maldoror* is inspired by
principles of metaphoricity and likeness; and, not dissimilarly, the
logic of reading Lautréamont follows the author's conception of his
writing as constant analogical and differential slippage. This, in
turn, makes us realize to what degree *Les Chants de Maldoror* and
Poésies bring us face to face with fundamental modern issues of
naming and unnameableness, representation and imagination,
presence and absence. To conceive of literature as merely a mode
of enacting questions of likeness and dissemblance, truth and
fiction, is to appreciate the profound relativity of literature. The
comme that swarms throughout Lautréamont's work strives both to

reconcile and join and constitutes a clear confession of problematized and ambivalent, multiple and changing perception. No page is thus anything but merely passing. "Où est passé ce chant . . . On ne le sait pas au juste" ("Where has the song gone to . . . One doesn't know exactly") (*OC*, 161). Likeness, or writing the world and one's perception of it as constantly mutating metaphor, can only unfold, then fade, intrinsically partial. "C'est un homme ou une pierre ou un arbre qui va commençer le quatrième chant" ("A man or a stone or a tree is going to start off the fourth song") (*OC*, 250); Mervyn is as "beautiful . . . as the fortuitous encounter upon a dissecting-table of a sewing machine and an umbrella" (*OC*, 327). Identify, definition, likeness are caught in the tensions of metaphor and metonymy. For Lautréamont, the logic of "likeness," of literature reduced to an endless series of *comme*, implies the separation and unity of *chant* and *chant*, *Les Chants de Maldoror* and *Poésies*. It represents a vision of literature as non-fixity, as metamorphosis, as images coming together and flowing apart, projected, undecidable.

Satire, Morality, Truth

Les Chants de Maldoror offers us a text of exemplary satire. Lautréamont, via the antiheroic Maldoror, rails against the stupidity and degradation of humanity, and founded his work upon what has been seen; it is a writing of *choses vues* ("seen things," *OC*, 126), in the great realist tradition of Balzac, Flaubert, and, ultimately, Maupassant and Zola. Lautréamont's attack upon "la stupide comédie" (*OC*, 140), our "sickness" and "madness" (*OC*, 159), lends paradoxical power and dignity to the "songs" of the oddly heroic renegade, Maldoror. And does he not rail against self-complacent wickedness (*OC*, 194), injustices that stimulate a seemingly worthy dream of "holy" and "severe mathematics" (*OC*, 190, 194), betrayal of friendship (*OC*, 128), and the abandonment of the Creator, resisted to the end by Maldoror's—and Lautréamont's—"verve épouvantable" ("dreadful zest," *OC*, 167)? Observation thus leads to defiance (*OC*, 217), which presents new possibilities. The "provable" nature of the accusations (*OC*, 223), their nonimaginary source (*OC*, 291), seems to be a traditional basis for ethical clarification and social transformation. "Pourquoi rouvrir, à une page quelconque, avec un empressement blasphématoire, l'in-folio des misères humaines" ("Why reopen, at any old page, with blasphemous haste, the folio of human wretchedness"), Lautréamont asks in the *Chant sixième*. The quick answer appears adequate to a reading of *Les Chants de Maldoror* as pure satire: "Rien n'est d'un enseignement plus fécond" ("Nothing is more richly instructive," *OC*, 342).

Before proceeding to an assessment of Lautréamont's ethics in *Les Chants de Maldoror*, it is important to note a number of other factors: 1. when Lautréamont's toad evokes the "infernal greatness" of Maldoror, the tensions of a Baudelairean satanism and a Hugolian recuperation of evil by good, remain manifest (*OC*, 159); 2. the toad questions skepticism within the larger discourse of Maldoror's embrace and perverted transcendence of skepticism (*OC*, 159); 3. similar tensions may be observed in the "contrast" between Maldoror's "violent" and poisonous "tongue" (*langue; OC*, 198) and his singing of the "moral grandeur" of the ocean, "immense comme la réflexion du philosophe, comme l'amour de la femme, comme la beauté divine de l'oiseau, comme les méditations du poète" ("vast like the philosopher's reflection, like woman's love, like the bird's divine beauty, like the poet's meditations," *OC*, 141); 4. Maldoror's action is seen as a chosen perseverance in *le mal*, despite the glimpsed vision of a gentleness of soul (*OC*, 198): Maldoror's satire is thus wittingly turned against himself; his "transcendence" is desperate, but chosen; 5. kindness, goodness, may be unlocatable (*OC*, 202), but they are in the mind and language of Maldoror, and underpin every criterion of his *démarche*; 6. what Lautréamont terms *la conscience*—at once consciousness and conscience—is the most powerful mechanism of self-knowledge (*OC*, 214–15), although the "tortures" it may occasion create the tensions of self-evasion and guilt; 7. the text of *Les Chants de Maldoror* pushes aggressiveness to its limits in a kind of negative idealization, a bittersweet exaltation of *le mal* and *le mal d'aurore*; 8. those "inépuisables caricatures du beau" ("inexhaustible caricatures of the beautiful") that we are in the eyes of the Maldoror/Lautréamont (*OC*, 273), once again portray the divided nature of a discourse caught between satiric laceration and a haunting nostalgia of the ethical aesthetic; 9. similarly, the "preface of the renegade" does have a future that it only hints at itself due to its parodic status (*OC*, 323); 10. the *Chants de Maldoror* may be at once a blossoming and a defoliation of monstrousness and cruelty, but *Poésies* offers us the writer as a "tamer" of "monsters" (*OC*, 366–67).

Les Chants de Maldoror, despite its parodic mode, generates a satire predicated upon perceived ethics and felt truth. Lautréamont's work is, nevertheless, far from simplistically didactic. That someone—but is it the narrator, Lautréamont, Ducasse, or Maldoror?—is the "energetic defender [of morals]" "in these incandescent pages" (*OC,* 161) is made to be both clear and unclear. Evidence is easily adduced to support conflicting theses. *Les Chants de Maldoror* is made into a locus of conflict, and hence of self-questioning and self-discovery.

A number of important factors pertaining to Lautréamont's ethical stance may be stressed at this point. First, revolt may be perceived as an ethics of refusal, self-sufficient outrage that can slip into a self-parodying perpetration of outrage: this is the oft-admired antiheroism of Maldoror himself. Secondly, Lautréamont's "poésie de la révolte" ("poetry of revolt"), as he calls it in his letter of 21 February 1870 to Verbroeckhoven (*OC,* 399), may be seen as an ironic demonstration of *le mal* leading to *le bien* (*OC,* 398). Satire as pure social and psychological critique, however, would also seem to have its purpose, and indeed belongs to an ancient French tradition best exemplified by La Bruyère and La Rochefoucault. Thirdly, Lautréamont is not insensitive to the dangers of "une morale étroite" ("a narrow moral lesson") (*OC,* 362). An ethical stance, then, does not mean moral stasis. Fourthly, *Poésies* seek to make clear the dangers of sadness and doubt for they lead to *le mal:* existential problem, moral degradation (*OC,* 370). A certain mode of questioning is inherently vitiating; another, clarifying, liberating, ethically wise.

Finally, Lautréamont's ethics founds itself upon freedom—"nous sommes libres de faire le bien" ("we are free to do good"), he writes in *Poésies* (*OC,* 377)—in order to oppose the "nothingness" (*OC,* 377) of the drift of mind or the sterility of the choice of *le mal.* Poetry has, thus, moral "utility" (*OC,* 378); it can be action *for,* and *in, le bien.* Lautréamont is a poet of remedy, a healer of the very wound that *Les Chants de Maldoror* seems to have gouged. If Maldoror appears to have "vaincu l'*Espérance*" ("conquered *Hope*") in order to plunge headlong into "la carrière du mal" ("the career of evil," *OC,* 234), Lautréamont realizes that his ethics cannot usefully come to rest upon a mere rejection of such anti-action or melancholy. Literature needs to go beyond an ethics of suffering and stoicism to an ethics of love of what is positive and possible (*OC,* 384). *Les Chants de Mal-*

doror seeks originality *and* ethical innovation, as Lautréamont points out to his publisher, Verbroeckhoven, in October 1869, both in their exaggeration of *le mal* and in their search for remedy beyond.

A question of truth remains, however. Can morality be stabilized; is it not movement, action, and therefore beyond what we may think of as truth? For Lautréamont, we may emphasize three perspectives. First, satire would seem to be predicated upon distinction, a "painting" or portrayal (*OC*, 125) that knows, and reveals what it knows. The revelations and confessions of Maldoror/ narrator/Lautréamont may be exaggerated, but they are "true" (*OC*, 125). The text of *Les Chants de Maldoror* is unambiguous in its laying bare of being: "O être humain! te voilà nu comme un ver, en présence de mon glaive de diamant!" ("Oh human being! there you are, naked as a worm, before my diamond sword!"; *OC*, 162); its task involves the tearing away of "masks" and "sublime untruths" with which we deceive ourselves (*OC*, 161–62).

Second, while truth may seem to offer some "supreme" reign over the real (*OC*, 184), it can be plagued with its "fugitives apparitions" ("fleeting appearances" *OC*, 261), its error-inducing "partiality" (*OC*, 285). Truth can be thus shown to be linked to *mores* as social relativity. Lautréamont displays a certain residual conviction in humanity's collective sense of truth: "L'homme est certain de ne pas se tromper" ("Man is sure not to be mistaken," *OC*, 388). There is, here, an almost Hugolian faith in truth's progression and emerging absoluteness. And this is part of our third perspective. Lautréamont, despite the recognition of falsehood, can say; "Tout est le contraire de songe, de mesonge" ("All is the opposite of dream and lie," *OC*, 393). Truth's relativity does not affect its status, its meaning. "Il y a" ("there is"), Lautréamont writes at the end of *Poésies*, "plus de vérité que d'erreurs, plus de bonnes qualités que de mauvaises, plus de plaisirs que de peines" ("more truth than error, more good qualities than bad, more pleasures than pains," *OC*, 394). Truth is choosable, available to our freedom. The greater "truth" in life and literature is predicated upon consolation and kindness (*OC*, 387).

Hatred and Love

Les Chants de Maldoror argues, at once seriously and satirically, that what Lautréamont calls "human charity" is merely "a vain word one no longer finds even in the dictionary of poetry" (*OC*, 169). As the six cantos unfold, so too does the full sense of what André Frénaud terms the "unacceptability" of the self, the impossibility of human friendship and love (*OC*, 128). But does not Maldoror himself speak of the gravedigger of *Chant premier* as possessing "les restes en lambeaux d'une charité détruite" ("the tattered remainders of a destroyed charity," *OC*, 154)? And does not Lautréamont suggest that hatred is a degraded, perverted love, stemming from frustration (*OC*, 147)? There are, indeed, various passages that point to hatred as consciously avoiding the "generosity" of love, and maintaining the sentiment that *"they* don't love me!" (*OC*, 172). The *Chant deuxième* also shows hatred to be an affective blockage, rooted in self-definition as "monster," and quickly giving way to an *amour-propre* that imposes solitude (*OC*, 178). In this way, hatred, murder, refusal are presented as simple habits (*OC*, 208), appalling yet modifiable, anti-loves "resolving" to reveal themselves in anti-relationships (*OC*, 220). And, as *Poésies* makes clear, hatred is intimately linked to fear. Maldoror's own hatred is even called into question and redefined as a "fear of [the Creator's] hatred" (*OC*, 201). Fear, terror, are regarded as simply inadequate modes (*OC*, 387), just as the "courage to suffer, injustice" is a perversion of a "love of justice" (*OC*, 384). Is it outrageous to see in the narrator's "fear" before the "sentence" of death weighing upon him—not just a premonition of Ducasse's mysterious early demise, but a deep fear rooted in the ambivalences of his writing of *Les Chants de Maldoror*?

If choice is available, so inevitably is reversal. If hatred is degradation of love, love is always spectrally present in the discourse of hatred. Love itself—Maldoror's of the shark, or the pederasts (*OC*, 210–11, 302–303)—can rapidly slip to the ironies of violence and hatred. That reversal is always available is shown in Maldoror's rape of the adolescent in the *Chant troisième* ("Third Song"), where such hatred of the other is met, not with the anticipated hatred, but with compassion (*OC*, 231). "La fraternité n'est pas un mythe" ("Fraternity is not a myth"), Lautréamont writes in *Poésies* (*OC*, 374). The human being can choose to be the "sister of the angel" (*OC*, 377). To do this, however, requires going beyond pity to exaltation (*OC*, 387). A poetics of compassion would thus seem to remain embedded in a vision of fear, defensiveness, melancholy, suffering. As such, it liberates insufficiently, tending rather to tie us to existential problem than to allow us to think and feel beyond or through it. Thus Lautréamont says, "l'amour n'est pas le bonheur" ("love is not happiness" *OC*, 380).

Happiness demands stepping beyond the conceivable distortions and misappropriations of love, as in Lautréamont's statement that "the love of a woman is incompatible with the love of humanity" (*OC*, 375) or his enigmatic assertion that "l'amour ne se confond pas avec la poésie" ("love is not to be confused with poetry," *OC*, 387). Poetry is both superior and inferior—superior inasmuch as it can rise above the deformations and overly personal characterization and focusing of love; inferior because life necessarily "exceeds the sign," as Bonnefoy has put it; because poetry can merely *point* to the glory of love-as-universality; because love itself is exceeded by a higher ambition within the poetic act, that of pointing through love to happiness. Such a high purpose, Lautréamont argues (*OC*, 381), far from building itself upon a logic of angelic fall leading to human "elevation," requires a recuperation of the angelic within us. Happiness is a remembering of such a mode of being and an opting for its creation.

Freedom, Imagination and Reality

At the beginning of *Les Chants de Maldoror*, Maldoror evokes the "innateness" of a "cruelty that it has not depended upon me to erase" (*OC*, 143). Lautréamont's entire oeuvre strives to demonstrate the simple unworkability of such a position, though his principal creation would seem to maintain its nobility and desperate dignity. Thus is *le mal* seen to be given and received beyond our volition (*OC*, 143). Impossibility, impotence, imprisonment weigh down upon us psychologically and morally, and the self and its meaning are defined from the outside (*OC*, 169). "Le chasse-neige implacable de la fatalité" ("The implacable snowplough of fatality," *OC*, 172) sweeps all before it in some quasi-naturalistic model of behavioristic determinism become, literally, monstrous in its proportions. In this perspective, the Creator, the All-Powerful, the Eternal, as Lautréamont varyingly writes, usurps self-determination and is judged responsible for the self's being (*OC*, 184). Maldoror may be prepared to assume himself, but his will and capacity for self-assumption are constantly eroded by the spying and transgression of "the Celestial Bandit" (*OC*, 296–97). Freedom seems thus to be at best relative, locked into a very masculine struggle for "master[y] of the universe" (*OC*, 340), and ultimately illusory, caught up in the mechanisms of fate and destiny we only think we can control. Worse, God's intentionality is dubious, smacking now of moral indifference or sheer "madness" (*OC*, 134, 158), now of outright terrorism (*OC*, 183), "injustice" (*OC*, 194), or drunkenness (*OC*, 235). In this way Lautréamont points to Maldoror's duplicitous and no-loss attitude: his would-be satanic *complainte* bemoans *both* his lack of freedom to be thoroughly satanic and thus shed all trace of divinity, *and* his domination by an unjust and insane Creator who, prevents him from assuming the power of divine justice and wisdom that God cannot maintain.

Lautréamont's discourse upon the divine in *Les Chants de Maldoror* is deliberately complex. If the God-Satan struggle persists (*OC*, 147), the freedom or power implicit in divinity would nevertheless seem to penetrate all being(s), by virtue of what Maldoror calls "l'étincelle divine qui est en nous" ("the divine spark within us," *OC*, 129). Creation in a larger sense may be exterior to us (*OC*, 127), but in a vital smaller sense it is interior. God can barely be an evasion, as Maldoror suggests in the *Chant deuxième* (*OC*, 174), or, if this is so, it would indeed be an evasion of our own divinity. Lautréamont constantly points—like Hugo in *La Fin de Satan*—to the intrinsic angelicism of Maldoror (*OC*, 348), to a divinity that haunts him in many forms, like those noble "missionaries" that so astonish him in the *Chant deuxième* (*OC*, 198).

We may read the celebrated passage of the Celestial Bandit's invasion of Maldoror's "sleeping" consciousness (*OC*, 296–97) less as a discourse on freedom than as a powerful satire on our desire to insist upon the separateness of rationality and dream; on our fear of communion and love not only with otherness but with the otherness of the self. *Poésies* makes no bones about what remained an unresolved issue in *Les Chants de Maldoror*: the real transcends the physical world, the immortality of the soul is felt and affirmed (*OC*, 152, 371), along with a divine "wisdom" and "absolute goodness" (*OC*, 371–72) in which we presumably share, "the divine spark." To doubt the full mystery of the real, and thus deny our freedom to believe in its mystery, is futile and presumptuous (*OC*, 372).

Les Chants de Maldoror already articulates, via its insistent discourse of doubt and denial, a poetics that goes well beyond mere "reception" of life imposed to an acknowledgement of power and choice within the self; non-suicide may be a rock-bottom act of hope, but it is a residue (*OC*, 226). God may seem to cancel "autonomy" (*OC*, 297), but self-definition as revolt and refusal, even as irritation, is already an assumption of that power of divine (self-) creation Maldoror could not deny within himself. Such an assumption may not activate our power of love, kindness, and happiness, as the *Poésies* encourages, but it remains a strong residual reminder of our (divine) self-creative potential. Maldoror's perseverance may be in and for *le mal* (*OC*, 178–9), his perception of Mervyn's "will" for convergence may be thought sadistic (*OC*, 350), but everything points to an existential logic of freedom of action.

Poésies, in fact, predicates itself completely upon a poetics of possibility. The past can be refuted, the real can be recast, "remade," as Ponge will say: "will" and "proclamation" only are required (*OC*, 365). Being and reality are matters of acceptance and refusal, "action [qui] me fait souvenir de ma force que j'oublie à toute heure" ("an action [which] makes me remember my strength that I constantly forget," *OC*, 377; cf. *OC*, 371). The "free[dom] to do good" is, however, not twinned with a freedom to do evil (*OC*, 377). Freedom is absolute, yet its propensity would center all action around a logic of love, good, and happiness, making *le mal* "unacceptable" (*OC*, 375). "Je n'accepte pas le mal. L'homme est parfait. L'âme ne tombe pas. Le progrès existe. Le bien est irréductible" ("I do not accept evil. Man is perfect. The soul does not fall. Progress exists. Good is irreducible," *OC*, 375). To understand Lautréamont is above all not to betray the simple strength of such articulations.

To see the real, for Lautréamont, a seer as great and as lucid as Rimbaud, is to open oneself to the fullness of one's being. "La raison, le sentiment se conseillent, se suppléent" ("Reason and feeling counsel each other, stand in for each other"), Lautréamont writes in *Poésies*, "quiconque ne connaît qu'un des deux, en renonçant à l'autre, se prive de la totalité des secours qui nous ont été accordés pour nous conduire" ("whoever knows but one of them, renouncing the other, deprives himself of the totality of help granted us to guide us," *OC*, 382). By the same token, however, this ethical model for being is based upon the need to alert ourselves to the continuum of consciousness and the continuum of emotion. The real can only be sensed in its fullness if we *commit* ourselves to its fullness: doubt then can lead to hope, *malheur* to *bonheur*, blockage to freedom, fear to gentleness. Here, the imagination is crucial in Lautréamont's eyes. *Poésies* demonstrates the (self-)recreative power of the imagination, its ability to project a real of astonishing mental and spiritual dimensions in the face of heavy odds. It is our *belief* in the structures of our imagination that gives rise to the real; an imagination that senses this partiality, can also attain to "impartial[ity]," fullness (*OC*, 380). The real of any individual originates within: "il [/elle] n'a pas d'autre lumière que celle qui se trouve dans sa nature" ("he[/she] has no other light than that found within his[/her] nature"), Lautréamont writes near the close of *Poésies* (*OC*, 389). Far from being *surdéterminé/e*, each person is a locus of option, "divinely sparked" freedom, a locus imagining the real s/he wills.

Desire, Despair and Self-Destruction

Les Chants de Maldoror endeavors to demonstrate that a poetics of *le mal* depends upon choice, willed and projected imagination. Lautréamont can speak of the "hypnotic" quality of Maldoror's "cretinizing" discourse (*OC*, 353)—a discourse that can "make a pact with prostitution" (*OC*, 31), choose to "attack" humanity and the "Creator" (*OC*, 170, 322), decide to "live with sickness and immobility" (*OC*, 265), though a discourse, too, centered upon some "soif insatiable de l'infini" ("insatiable thirst for the infinite") (*OC*, 134), a sense of the "opinionated" nature of itself (*OC*, 261). If *Poésies* offers a clarifying expression of Lautréamont's literary purpose and existential desire—"before [the] filthy charnel-houses [of impotence, blasphemy, asphyxia, stifling, rage] . . . , it is time to finally react against what shocks and bows us down so sovereignly" (*OC*, 363)—so, too, do tactic and desire shine forth through Lautréamont's conscious organization of *Les Chants de Maldoror* in its relation to what is to follow (*OC*, 322, 324).

The *Chants de Maldoror* often articulates a symbolist desire for "mathematical" purity, Baudelairean "elevation," *angélisme* (*OC*, 190–91). Desire aspires to the consolation of some eternal, self-contained conceptual system such as algebra might afford: "O mathématiques saintes, puissiez-vous, par votre commerce perpétuel, consoler le reste de mes jours de la méchanceté de l'homme et de l'injustice du Grand-Tout!" ("Oh holy mathematics, may you, through your perpetual commerce, console my remaining days for the wickedness of man and the injustice of All-That-Is!"; *OC*, 194). Such desire, seemingly noble, seemingly pure, remains nevertheless to be read as an anti-desire, a desire predicated upon Mallarméan horror, Laforguean lunacy, Rimbaldian revolt. Desire may soar, but in shedding its telluric purpose, becomes existentially irrelevant: "ne jugeant rien sur la terre capable de le contenter, et aspirant plus haut" ("judging nothing on earth able to satisfy him, and aspiring higher," *OC*, 212). Similarly, metaphor—"that rhetorical figure [which] renders many more services to human aspirations to the infinite than those who are steeped in prejudice or false ideas strive usually to imagine": (*OC*, 278)—while seeming to offer access to the "infinite," may well cloud our real spiritual, ethical purpose and desire as immanent beings. There is no doubt that such an awareness remains central to an understanding of Lautréamont's poetics of metaphor in *Les Chants de Maldoror*. If desire is to be transcendent, it must, à la Rimbaud, ultimately practice itself here below, in the plane of incarnation's lessons.

Maldoror's history is that of a conscious, willed "defeat [of] *Hope*" and a resultant assumption of (self-created) "evil" or existential problem (*OC*, 234). Elevation there may be, but it is now "un vol élevé, sans espérance et sans remords" ("a flight raised high, without hope, without remorse" (*OC*, 219), "un désespoir qui m'enivre comme le vin" ("a despair intoxicating me like wine," *OC*, 135). Such despair stems from existential fatigue, a loss of calm consciousness of available option (*OC*, 177, 213). "Avec ma voix et ma solennité des grands jours" ("With my voice and solemnness for great occasions"), Lautréamont writes at a critical point in the first part of *Poésies*, "je te rappelle dans mes foyers déserts, glorieux espoir" ("I call you back to my deserted hearths, glorious hope," *OC*, 368). The reader is given specific anti-Dantesque instructions to "abandon all despair" upon his poetic entry (*OC*, 374), an order Lautréamont the poet has just chosen himself to obey. Despair, he argues, "feeding with predetermination upon its phantasmagoria, leads ... the writer to the mass abrogation of social and divine laws, and to practical and theoretical mischievousness" (*OC*, 369).

If *Les Chants de Maldoror* sings the desperateness of *le mal*, it is clear from his correspondence that Lautréamont appreciates both the dangers of its logic and pseudo-mimetic literary practice, and the advantage of taking this risk. On the latter point he will explain to Verbroeckhoven that "j'ai un peu exagéré le diapason pour faire

Lautréamont

du nouveau dans le sens de cette littérature *sublime* qui ne chante le désespoir que pour *opprimer* le lecteur, et lui faire *désirer le bien* comme remède" ("I somewhat exaggerated the pitch to strike a new note in the direction of that *sublime* literature singing despair merely to *oppress* the reader and have him *desire good* by way of remedy," *OC*, 398, letter of 23 October 1869; my italics). On the former point, a later letter renders explicit Lautréamont's switch from the (self-)risk of mimetic parodic despair to the clarity of the song of hope, even though his need remains "to attack the doubt of the century (melancholies, sadnesses, pains, despairs, . . .)" *OC*, 400). *Poésies* clearly both shifts to a mode of hope and maintains the satire of *Les Chants de Maldoror*. Work to come—but never written, as far as we know, for *Poésies* only partially fulfills this mandate—"corrects" Hugo, Musset, Byron, Baudelaire "in the direction of hope" (*OC*, 400). The *Chants de Maldoror* should be read, however, as doubt's "homage paid to hope" (*OC*, 380).

That the risk taken by Lautréamont was real to Ducasse, I should like briefly to emphasize. Writing for Lautréamont was at once a vigorous and dangerous adventure. The narrator of *Les Chants de Maldoror* is unambiguous as to the perils of self-cretinization and self-destruction his "imaginary" tale implies: "Vous avez reconnu" ("You have recognised"), he asserts to the reader in the *Chant cinquième*, "le héros imaginaire qui, depuis un long temps, brise par la pression de son individualité ma malheureuse intelligence" ("the imaginary hero who long has been breaking via the pressure of his individuality my unfortunate intelligence," *OC*, 328). And, toward the close of the *Chant cinquième*, is not the prospect of imminent death evoked to "explain" the quasi-inexplicable character of the barely completed work at hand (*OC*, 308)? *Les Chants de Maldoror* is riddled with allusions to self-destruction, the desire for death, the bliss of death, the possibility or probability of death (*OC*, 142, 313, 353, etc.). And it is rife with a sense of enacted expiation, guilt, shame, and fear (*OC*, 129, 339). Lautréamont's poetic oeuvre, taken as a whole, may sketch out a tense and urgent poetics of ethical and spiritual survival. *Les Chants de Maldoror*, however, brings its author/narrator to an extreme point of immersion in that very problem he seeks to remedy. The death so frequently alluded to is no doubt an ironic self-referential jest as the text itself nears its narratorial end. But it evokes, too, the intensity of Maldoror's experience of impasse and self-hatred. Inevitably, the reader is led to ponder the poignant convergence of fiction and reality in that most obscure disappearance of the author whose *Poésies* do not succeed in "saving" him from the (self-)destructive turmoil of *Les Chants de Maldoror.*

Reversal and Continuity

The epigraph to *Poésies* seems to be fairly explicit and programmatic: "Je remplace la mélancolie par le courage, le doute par la certitude, le désespoir par l'espoir ..." ("I am replacing melancholy with courage, doubt with certainty, despair with hope," *OC*, 361). In many ways it would make of *Poésies* a work, founded upon a poetics, of reversal, substitution, radical (self-)change. Lautréamont "denies" the human past as a vale of tears, as a constant unfolding of *le mal* wept over, preferring to "proclaim" positive thinking, feeling and (self-)creation (*OC*, 365). The "clarity" of the clarifying reversal of *Poésies* is surely, he argues, at their close, at least as pertinent as ambivalence (*OC*, 395)!

In effect, however, the two parts of the *Poésies* revolt "positively" against the "negative" revolt articulated in *Les Chants de Maldoror*. They offer a "positive" or "clear" denial of a "negative" or "vague," ambivalent denial (*OC*, 395). As such, they recuperate the essence of *Les Chants de Maldoror*—"change method," as Lautréamont puts it to his banker, Darasse (*OC*, 401, letter of 12 March 1870)—but without changing purpose. "I do not wish to be stigmatised by the designation of *poseur*," Lautréamont writes at the outset of the *Poésies* (*OC*, 361). Reversal, in effect, speaks of a gamut of possibles, a range of states, visions, anti-visions. If *Les Chants de Maldoror* seems to privilege "the real and inexplicable contradictions that inhabit the lobes of the human brain," then the book can also *already* point to the desirability of an open mind—the possibility less of "struggling against *le mal*, [which] is to do it too much honor" (*OC*, 388) than of extending consciousness to its *other* extreme, of the feasibility of willed action, poetic or other.

Lautréamont "retracts" nothing in his "reversal": the "replacement" of *Poésies* is part of a larger process of continuous elaboration of one's unity and becoming. The poetry, with its ethics, of *Les Chants de Maldoror* and *Poésies*, is the "majestic and fertile" flow of the same "river" (*OC*, 361). "There are not two kinds of poetry," he affirms, thereby recuperating not only his own *Chants de Maldoror* but also all those severely criticized poetic tactics of Baudelaire, Hugo, Lamartine, Musset, and others, "there is but one" (*OC*, 361). In the singing of despair, "it is thus always *le bien* that one is singing, finally, only via a more philosophical and less naive method than the earlier school [of Hugo and others]." Such is Lautréamont's expression of the continuity of high poetic endeavor, both individual and collective (*OC*, 398). "Je n'ai pas besoin" ("I do not need"), Lautréamont tells us in *Poésies*, "de m'occuper de ce que je ferai plus tard. Je devais faire ce que je fais. Je n'ai pas besoin de découvrir quelles choses je découvrirai plus tard. Dans la nouvelle science, chaque chose vient à son tour, telle est son excellence" ("to busy myself with what I shall do later. I was destined to do what I am doing. I do not need to discover what things I shall discover later. In the new science, each thing comes in its turn, such is its excellence," *OC*, 388). Lautréamont's *scienza nuova* is predicated upon a vitality *now* (*OC*, 371, 375). Continuity and progress demand an intense attachment to maximum feasibility now, but this attachment permits neither a hardening of the past's arteries nor an idealization, a dreamy departure into the future from life now.

The reversal or reclaiming of one's ethical continuity that *Poésies* articulates, constitutes for Lautréamont a gesture going beyond revolt and stoicism. "Suffering is a weakness," he can thus provocatively write, "when one can stop it and do something better" (*OC*, 368). Hope is our real courage, whereas "the poetic meanings of the century," tending to look at the "puerile wrong side of things," "are merely hideous sophisms" (*OC*, 401). The "replacement of doubt by certainty" (*OC*, 361) may evoke for the reader ideas of improbable and unjustified commitment, but Lautréamont's incitement to abandon doubt is essentially a plea to remember our emotional and imaginative totality. There are, he maintains, simply "better things to do." Doubt, on this unbroken scale of human (self-)creativity, is the "beginning of despair," a "fatal slope" (*OC*, 370), whose effects can be reversed, however, because doubt always constitutes a largely unrecognized, "homage to hope" (*OC*, 380).

The Naive and the Profound: Questions of Style

"M'emparant d'un style que quelques-uns trouveront naïf (quand il est si profond), je le ferai servir à interpréter des idées qui, malheureusement, ne paraîtront peut-être pas grandioses" ("Seizing hold of a style some will find naive [when it is so profound], I shall use it to interpret ideas that, unfortunately, will perhaps not appear grandiose," *OC*, 325). Thus speaks Lautréamont, in the *Chant sixième*, of his chosen stylistic mode. The remaining pages of this chapter will look at the various elements of Lautréamont's style and form. First, let me stress the sweeping embrace of this style, with its visionary accumulation upon accumulation. Its lexicon is rich, though never technical nor given to neologism; its syntax is complex yet controlled and cogent: one thinks of the creative prose of Breton or Reverdy, both admirers of Lautréamont, rather than of Gide or Proust. However, all these comparisons underscore the pertinence of a style that, simultaneously, can give itself to self-caricature, excess, and play. Secondly, all of Lautréamont's work is prose poetry, a writing once again hybrid, tensional in its mode, endeavoring to do, as Michel Deguy says, "at least two things at the same time." While it is unlikely that Lautréamont had read any of the great, innovative *poèmes en prose* of his century—Baudelaire, Mallarmé, Rimbaud, even Verlaine—it is clearly within this framework that we read *Les Chants de Maldoror* and *Poésies*. With Baudelaire, whose work is generally recognized in *Poésies*, real affinity exists. We may find the same dualities at play, the "satanic" fascination and the desire for transcendence. And we see, too, an ambivalent control that seems to risk settling for Baudelairean aestheticism and the elevations of the imaginary.

But Lautréamont goes further in self-reflexive self-subversion, and the vastness of this poeticized prose adventure far exceeds the exquisite miniatures of *Le Spleen de Paris*. It is, moreover, in this latter regard that Lautréamont also bids adieu to Mallarmé, for the poet of *Les Chants de Maldoror* finally shows in *Poésies* a clean pair of heels to any trace of dalliance with high aesthetic refinement. His awareness of rhetorical power is always marked by a deep personal intensity that *Poésies* makes fully evident. The *Illuminations*, especially, but also *Une saison en enfer* make Rimbaud a poet more blatantly committed to the unconscious than Lautréamont ever felt the need to be. Certainly, the author of *Les Chants de Maldoror* gives himself great imaginative freedom of rein; but he is perhaps less purely *voyant*. Lautréamont's *Poésies* read like some of Rimbaud's disavowals; but Lautréamont seems to have understood the continuity and fullness of his poetic logic from the very outset. Rim-

baud's self-consciousness and purposiveness seem to have been there, full-blown, in the first words of *Chant premier.*
A number of other important factors remain to be teased out: 3. the "gothic" mode of *Les Chants de Maldoror,* which Lautréamont is conscious of having chosen (*OC,* 128, 146), involves a false naïveté allowing for the full exposure of "vampirism," "satanism," and so on, but in the context both of their parody and satire, and of their ambivalent transcendence. The "gothic" *Chants de Maldoror* pushes us into the trap of our own (self-)doubts and (self-)fears, but in the hope that we will reemerge through the "profundity" of our consciousness thereof; 4. the divisions and asterisked subdivisions of *Les Chants de Maldoror* with its often noncontextualized narrative perspectives and scenes (*OC,* 250–52), the frequent parentheses that open up, the primitive lists that roll on (*OC,* 366–67), the frequent fragmentation and discontinuity of the *Poésies*—these and other factors can give the impression of a poetry rawly structured, incoherent, absurdly kaleidoscopic, a kind of *poésie brute* not unlike the work of a Dubuffet or a Wölfli. However, much in Lautréamont points to a conscious stylistic and structural mastery worthy of Baudelaire or Hugo: the individual sentence structure is sophisticated; the overall orchestration of *Les Chants de Maldoror* seems to be based upon a principle of "synthesis" followed by "analysis"; the divisions and subdivisions themselves suggest a refusal of pure creative *dérive* and a deliberate multiplication—as with the lists and parentheses—of optics. Even the disorienting noncontextualization of many passages serves the purpose of intensifying attention and reader participation. The very notion of *chant* evokes the surging forth, visceral and psychic, of rhythms from within. Such rhythms, in *Poésies* and *Les Chants de Maldoror,* constitute a convergence, to which modern poets such as Reverdy, Michaux, and Dupin are particularly alert, of spontaneity and *justesse.* In this way do disparates attain to coherence and meaning; 5. irony is a major stylistic, even structural, tactic in Lautréamont's work: it gives to many convoluted passages of *Les Chants de Maldoror* their idiosyncratic, tongue-in-cheek quality (*OC,* 253, 261, 268, 270), their provocative caricatural tone; and it combines exquisitely with Lautréamont's self-conscious use of rhetoric. Ironic use of pure rhetoric—"Il est temps de quitter ces souvenirs glorieux, qui ne laissent, après leur suite, que la pâle voie lactée des regrets éternels" ("It is time to say farewell to these glorious memories, that

leave behind them but the pale milky way of eternal regret," *OC*, 274)—can simultaneously poeticize and depoeticize: to the extent that rhetoric is perceived to be sophistry, potentially leading away from the powerful purposes *Poésies* espouses. Such hyperbole could be compared with Lautréamont's excessive use of exclamation: a double mark allowing perception to move in at least two directions simultaneously, and thus speak at once of reversal and continuity; 6. Lautréamont's use of metaphor, or more usually simile, may be clearly related to the foregoing. The bursts and processions of images—as Baudelaire and Reverdy preferred to call them—can almost take over certain passages of *Les Chants de Maldoror*. Their force, their surreal outrageousness are well designed to attract the favor of Breton: in them lies a profundity synonymous with their very wildness.

Four more fundamental elements need to be commented upon: 7. intertextuality; 8. the style of the *comédie dramatique* ("dramatic comedy"); 9. apostrophe; and 10. autobiography. The question of intertextuality has given rise to much commentary, especially with regard to *Poésies*, manifestly pastiched or mock-pastiched—just as Stendhal's epigraphs to each chapter of *Le Rouge et le Noir* are often ill-attributed. The *Poésies* are more blatant in elaborating (upon) those multiple *renvois*, echoes, and allusions that people the mind and oeuvre of Lautréamont, giving it its layered discourse, and its connection to Byron, Milton, Southey, Musset, Baudelaire (*OC*, 398), to Hugo, Lamartine (*OC*, 400), to Corneille, Racine, Voltaire, Rousseau (*OC*, 401), and to many others. The *Chants de Maldoror* becomes what Barthes calls "une chambre d'échos" ("an echo chamber"), where language, ideas rejoice in their *épaisseur sémantique* ("semantic density"), as Ponge writes, though in Lautréamont not for the sheer fun of the play but rather for that deeper "happiness" (*OC*, 387) that could come about if we might let go of doubt and despair in order to "create good" (*OC*, 377); 8. *Les Chants de Maldoror* Lautréamont deems to be a kind of *comédie dramatique* (*OC*, 253): its mode, both of style and consciousness, hovers between reason and (mock-)*folie*, seriousness and the grotesque, truth and farce (*OC*, 253–54). On the one hand, there is his idea of literature as "theorem," with its consequent "proofs" (*OC*, 323); on the other, literature tends to work/write against concision, tight geometrical sense, giving itself to impulse, apparent rambling, expansiveness, which is then—via some illusion—reined in (*OC*, 261–62, 352). But, of course, there are never really two hands in Lautréamont, any more than in Rimbaud: their oeuvres may be "two-sided," but they are continuous, instantaneous. On 9. the question of apostrophe, suffice it to say here that *Les Chants de Maldoror* opts, from the outset, for a style and a form both implicating and confronting the reader, initially evoked as a third person, thereafter broadly apostrophized, engaged in a powerfully unidimensional (non-)dialogue. Such somewhat Baudelairean apostrophe exceeds the illusions of omniscience, yet enjoins association, utter complicity, via the sweet-talking of *tutoiement*. It thus quickly becomes an address of temptation and yet of challenge, a pseudo-dialogue full of sophistry, teasing, and assault. For the narrator-hero to address the reader is to place the latter at the crossroads of choosable affinity and identification, and possible distanciation. To apostrophize is to intensify, to personalize, to realize the discourse at hand; to give presence to language, to transform potential play, interiority, intertextuality, into action, thought, feeling within us as readers. It "dramatizes" poiesis within us, ensures (self-)creation's "seriousness," its being "about things."

The final and tenth element of this brief analysis is centered upon the idea of Lautréamont's poetry as "autobiography." Certainly, *Les Chants de Maldoror* and *Poésies* taken together may be viewed as confession, at once real and parodic, intensely individualized yet allegorized by the movement generated between the narrative *je* and the apostrophized *tu*. *Les Chants de Maldoror* elects a mode theatricalizing phantasm and permitting the exorcism of fears, doubts, despairs. Such a release of the "designs of life" (*biography*) may induce ambivalence in our response to (anti-)heroic "self-story," as Deguy calls it. But the aesthetic and ethical trap opened by autobiography, narcissism, self-indulgence, self-pity, is compensated by a profoundly lucid and ironic self-consciousness that allows Lautréamont's texts to deconstruct much of what they seem to construct. It is this particular mode of "autobiography," caught between privacy and exchange, that makes *Les Chants de Maldoror* and *Poésies* truly "instructive poems" (*OC*, 324).

· TEN ·

Laforgue

Brought up in Tarbes in a family of eleven children, Laforgue, like Lautréamont and later Supervielle, was born in Montevideo—fourteen years after Lautréamont, however, and nearly six after Rimbaud—on 16 August 1860. Coming later to Paris, where he attended the Lycée Fontanes (Condorcet), well known to Mallarmé, these years were marked by the death of his mother, and by his improbable failing of the *baccalauréat*. His late youth was given to reading poetry, philosophy, and scientific writings and this was a time, too, of frequenting Left Bank literary cafés, striking up friendships with critics and poets such as Paul Bourget, Gustave Kahn, Charles Cros, and following Taine's courses on aesthetics. He also became at this time the private secretary to the director of the *Gazette des Beaux-Arts*, Charles Ephrussi, but in 1881, at the age of twenty-one, he elected to become "reader" to the Empress of Germany, moving with her from Koblenz to Berlin, from Hamburg to Baden-Baden. Laforgue's *Complaintes* (*Laments*) were largely composed at this time, and his writings on art and interest in music similarly developed. The poems of *L'Imitation de Notre-Dame la Lune* (*Imitation of Our Lady the Moon*—finally published in the same year as *Les Complaintes* (1885), and within two years of his death from tuberculosis—and the *Moralités légendaires* (*Legendary Moralities*) come shortly afterward, the latter, however, along with his *Derniers vers* (*Last Verse*), appearing only posthumously thanks to the efforts of friends. The last year or so of his life is lit up by his meeting, and subsequent marriage, with the equally frail Englishwoman Leah Lee. Married on 31 December in England, Laforgue catches a "cold" on the return to Paris that, aggravated, leads to his death on 20 August 1887. Leah Lee returns to England only to follow him to the grave on 6 June 1888. They were both just twenty-seven. Laforgue's volume *Des Fleurs de Bonne Volonté* (*Flowers of Good Will*) bears witness to some of these vicissitudes.

Laforgue's literary impact is at once significant and subtle, and extends well into the international scene. T. S. Eliot speaks of the effect of both a blatantly modern ironic yet lyrical sensibility, and a formal alertness at the level of rhythm and lexicon. A "furtif nourricier" ("furtive foster-father"), his "compatriot" Jules Supervielle calls him. And, indeed, his discreet poetic nourishment has gone to poets as diverse as Apollinaire and Jarry, Michaux and the Oulipo group, Frénaud and Yves Bonnefoy, who has recently devoted an entire lecture series at the Collège de France to the *Moralités légendaires* alone.

Lament: From *Ennui* to Anguish

All except two of the poems of *Les Complaintes*, published in July 1885, take up in their title the notion of *complainte*, a term that traditionally designates popular songs of essentially tragic or spiritual lament. Laforgue, without thus deforming this existing practice, appropriates it with originality and deep personal urgency. Lament, for him, leaps beyond pure song or lyrical wailing to a fervent exclamatory yet argued discourse wavering between deposition and "placet" or request for existential favor and justice (*PC*, 37), between recognition and exposure of presence's ennui, suffering, and imperfections, and mock, yet authentic, prayer (*PC*, 38), desire for "propitiation" (*PC*, 35), intercession, and stellar or lunar intervention (*PC*, 44). Lament thus entails a profound and grating expression of the experience of the "sunday-ness" of life (*PC*, 52), its "exilescent" (*PC*, 122) and repetitious strain despite the illusory shifts of seasonal and epochal color; and, yet, in addition, a nostalgia and vague angelicism that both reach toward the ideas of love, communion, reciprocity. Lament moves thus between "poverty" ("Complainte du pauvre jeune homme," *PC*, 106–108), and "wisdom" ("Complainte du sage de Paris" ["Lament of the Paris Sage"], *PC*, 126–29), despair and residual élan. It may turn in upon itself even, as in "Complainte des complaintes" ("Lament of Laments," *PC*, 130), for it is always the song of intrinsic impotence.

That Baudelairean "tradition," extending through Verlaine and Mallarmé, of ennui, *spleen, taedium vitae* veritably ravages the work of Laforgue. The "dailiness" of existence (*PC*, 86), its dull *ritournelles* ("ritornelles," *PC*, 46), even its more excited dances (*PC*, 44), partake of a *fadeur*, even a sickly "idiocy" (*PC*, 50), that are at once monotonous, barren, and yet curiously prolix (*PC*, 71). "Seul et tout à ses aises, l'Ennui" ("Alone and utterly at ease, Ennui") seems to be infinite in its manifestations (*PC*, 103, 113); "native" to the self ("Je m'ennuie, natal! je m'ennuie" ["I'm Bored, Native, I'm Bored"], *PC*, 218), yet inherent in things. "Spleen came to me from everything," Laforgue writes in "Arabesques de malheur" ("Misfortune's Arabesques") from *Des Fleurs de Bonne Volonté* (*PC*, 269); it is synonymous with that *Mal* of "Impassible en ses lois . . ." ("Impassive in its Laws," *PC*, 393). Is not "En deuil d'un Moi-le-Magnifique" ("Mourning for an I-the-Magnificent") the opening line of the dedicatory text of *Les Complaintes*, "À Paul Bourget" ("To Paul Bourget," *PC*, 29)? Is it not pregnant with a "rage" and an existential "nausea" ("Enfer" ["Hell"], *PC*, 460, and "Bouffée de printemps" ["Whiff of Spring"], *PC*, 406) that, while compensated by wit and affective resilience, only find their equal in Baudelaire and Rimbaud?

Laforguean lament is thus frequently ferocious, beyond artifice: a poetic expression distinct from romantic fervor in its biting raunchiness, its increasingly disarticulated, strident antiheroism. Lament finds itself placed at the center of the poet's conflicting senses of destiny and meaninglessness. The twin epigraphs to *Les Complaintes* ironically point to this double disempowerment: "Au petit bonheur de la fatalité//*Much ado about Nothing*" ("Haphazard Fate," *PC*, 27). And, of course, lament-as-poetry is steeped in this contradiction and this irony. Seemingly intervention, it yet begs for intervention. Seemingly self-possessed and self-expressing, it realizes the self's lack of grip upon its own being ("Dimanches" ["Sundays"], *PC*, 284–86). Seemingly creating self's "fate," it yet is caught both in fateful externality, "le Destin ce farceur" ("Destiny this joker," *PC*, 459) and an anarchy of the relative, a feeling that "this scandalous low-world/Is merely one of the thousand casts of the dice//Of the interplay [of] Idea and Love," as Laforgue puts it in "Pierrots" (*PC*, 145–49).

It should thus not surprise us to find that Laforguean lament proposes an endless discourse upon despair, fear, anguish. The discourse is at once visceral and emotional, intellectual and spiritual, and stems from the impotence and intransitivity of those paths that *can* lead to meaning: the paths of body, heart, mind, and soul. Solitude, suffering, fear, "blasphemy," doubt, ennui, "remorse": these are some of the many forces underpinning the relentless Laforguean discourse at hand. "I want," he concludes "Oh! je sais qu'en ce siècle . . ." ("Oh! I know that in this Century . . ."; *PC*, 390–91), "to be drunk, beyond truce and measure, with despair's delights" (*PC*, 391). This discourse of despair, however, for all its sardonic turning against its known narcissism, produces a lament of unforgettable authenticity, "oozing long white tears" ("Complainte des blackboulés," *PC*, 79–80), living amid "the great Sob of things" ("Devant la grande rosace en vitrail, à Notre-Dame de Paris" ["Before the Great Stained Glass Rose, at Notre-Dame de Paris"], *PC*, 345–46). In the words of "Complainte sur certains temps déplacés ("Lament upon Certain Displaced Times," *PC*, 101–102):

> Le couchant de sang est taché
> Comme un tablier de boucher;
> Oh! qui veut aussi m'écorcher!
>
> The blood setting is stained
> Like a butcher's apron;
> Oh! trying to skin me alive too!
> (*PC*, 101)

Far from all gratuitousness, yet plunged into the quotidian—"My great anguishes metaphysic" ("Complainte d'une convalescence en mai" ["Lament of a May Convalescence"], *PC*, 124–25), "have assumed the state of chagrins domestic" (*PC*, 125)—his endless *complainte* is the discourse of despairing desire traversing presence. As such it elaborates a poetics of great compassion and tenderness. "On les voit chaque jour . . ." ("We See Them Every Day . . ."; *PC*, 387) offers wonderful testimony to this, cutting through the usual, abundant ironies directed toward "ce néant trop tout" ("this nothingness too everything"), as he calls life in "Complainte du temps et de sa commère l'espace" ("Lament of Time and Its Crony Space," *PC*, 113–14), showing that Laforguean lament remains a discourse of love.

Lunacies

In 1885, the same year that *Les Complaintes* were published, Laforgue brought out, in November, his *Imitation de Notre-Dame la Lune* (*Imitation of Our Lady The Moon*). The volume's liminal text,

"Un mot au soleil pour commencer" ("A Word to the Sun to Begin With," *PC*, 135–36), focuses upon the "friendliness" of the moon (epigraph, *PC*, 133), but elects the moon as emblem and object of worship only as an anti-gesture. Its pallor and its essence, its remoteness and its coldness are symbols of an inner world of experienced emotions. To choose the moon, over the sun, and indeed the earth itself, is to choose a symbol of the self's "orphanlike" nature (*PC*, 135), of the self's anguished and ironic self-consolation via art and symbol, a symbol of "inorganic aggregatedness" (*PC*, 135) rather than livingness. But the entire collection renders clear the knowing and pointed paradox thus entailed. "Clair de lune" ("Moonlight," *PC*, 140), for example, underscores the "blindness" of lunatical anti-existence, its "fatal," sterile, even "suicidal" character. To opt for such a logic of "lunacy" is to recognize the absences that riddle the self's sense of presence; and to elect a symbolics that both mimics them and, (self-)mockingly, aesthetically exceeds them. "Climat, faune et flore de la Lune" ("The Moon's Climate, Fauna and Flora," *PC*, 141–43) demonstrates well this double and contradictory tactic. On the one hand, "lunacy" affords oblivion, "sans comment ni pourquoi" ("without how nor why," *PC*, 142), beyond disintegration and birth alike—a kind of desert wherein pain and rawness are lost in the "fixity" of the moon's "Immaculate Conception" (*PC*, 141). On the other hand, Laforgue's disgust with such "stagnancy," such self-mirroring deathliness, is finally admitted. The "nothingness" (*PC*, 165) of lunacy or lunatical anti-nature, its "distress" (*PC*, 163), its "frightening" character (*PC*, 165) are seen to be part of some "rumination of finality" (*PC*, 142). Certainly the "lunacy" of art may (seem to) offer solution, "consolation" (*PC*, 157), a kind of aesthetico-spiritual *dandysme* (*PC*, 146) that would spectrally fill the existential gap:

> Je ne suis qu'un viveur lunaire
> Qui fait des ronds dans les bassins,
> Et cela, sans autre dessein
> Que devenir un légendaire.

> I am but a lunar hedonist
> Making circles upon the pools,
> And that, without other design
> Than becoming a legend of my time.
> (*PC*, 160)

Such an optic may appear to be one of idle playfulness, of innocuousness before ubiquitous "vice" (*PC*, 162); but lunacy also implies contradiction, a "sterility" (*PC*, 167) that explains Laforgue's cri de coeur in "Etats" ("States")—"Ah! ce soir, j'ai le coeur mal, le coeur à la Lune" ("Ah! tonight my heart is ill, my heart is lunar," *PC*, 166). At the point where lunacy risks congealing as madness, however, Laforgue seems capable of tilting his poem, so that the equation or equivalence runs back to its less vitally menacing pole. It is here that Laforgue's humor reaffirms its significance: shifting and unstable though it may be in its tone, humor tends to divert emotion, guarding it from the abyss of lunatical madness. True, the humor of *Les Complaintes, L'Imitation de Notre-Dame la Lune*, and other volumes can grate. And equally true is Laforgue's consciousness of the limitations of humor, the danger of its "killing Love," the "vanity" of its discourse. "Complainte du vent qui s'ennuie la nuit" ("Lament of the Weary Wind at Night," *PC*, 89–90) concludes with a powerful expression of this concern and the posthumous "Pour le livre d'amour" ("For the Book of Love") could not be more explicit:

> J'ai craché sur l'amour et j'ai tué la chair!
> Fou d'orgueil, je me suis roidi contre la vie!
> Et seul sur cette Terre à l'Instinct asservie
> Je défiais l'Instinct avec un rire amer.
>
> I have spat upon love and killed flesh!
> Pride-crazed, I have stiffened against life!
> And alone on the Earth enslaved by Instinct
> Instinct I defied with a bitter laugh.
>
> (*PC*, 337)

And yet, if humor fronts onto bitterness, "mortal mockery" (*PC*, 195), even what Laforgue calls "Excuse macabre" ("Macabre Excuse," *PC*, 315), it can be lighter, offer witty linguistic acrobatics, simpler fun and play ("Jeux" ["Games"], *PC*, 175), or a smile of gentleness. The gamut is considerable and can unfold within the same poem. If it is true that genius, as Laforgue suggests in "Epicuréisme" ("Epicureanism," *PC*, 319–20), is "the clown . . . /Sobbing and smiling, but with bitter smile" (*PC*, 319), it is equally true that humor's smile implies a tenderness and a resistance that can break free of intransitive revolt and implicit affective violence. Numerous poems reveal this striving via nervously equilibrated flashes of humor that, while marked by the feeling that life and art are but a "Farce éphémère" ("passing Joke," *PC,* 329), render subtly manifest the hope and love of Laforgue's quizzical *démarche.*

Laforguean "lunacies" embrace a clear-cut thematics of death and suicide. *Les Complaintes* swarms with images of night, autumn, and winter, innocent in the abstract, but quickly assimilated to discourses of abandonment and abdication ("Complainte du pauvre chevalier-errant" ["Lament of the Poor Knight Errant"], *PC,* 73–74), the world's hostility and the death of love ("Complainte du vent qui s'ennuie la nuit," *PC,* 89–90), the routine of mortality ("Grande complainte de la ville de Paris" ["Great Lament of the City of Paris"], *PC,* 117). Poems such as "Complainte—litanies de mon sacré-coeur" ("Lament—My Sacred Heart Litanies," *PC,* 120–21), "Complainte des débats mélancoliques et littéraires" ("Lament of Melancholy and Literary Debate," *PC,* 122–23), and "Complainte d'une convalescence en mai" pour out feelings of death's utter obsessiveness (*PC,* 124), of the self perceived as "the terrestrial History-hearse/Dragged to nothingness by instinct and chance" (*PC,* 120). Little wonder that the final poem of *Les Complaintes* is titled "Complainte—épitaphe" ("Lament—Epitaph," *PC,* 131), (one thinks of André Frénaud, and, of course, the Mallarméan influence) or that "Clair de lune" can equate sterility and suicide, and beg for a self-effacing immersion in lunar light: "May I wash my hands therein of life!" (*PC,* 140). Such "self-scalping" may take the Romantic but upbeat form of self-exile in some exotic "Far-West," as Laforgue puts it in "Albums," from *Des Fleurs de Bonne Volonté,* and there is no doubt that Laforgue's poetics of suicide is linked, as with Baudelaire and Mallarmé, to a desperate desire for self-renewal. One of the many "Dimanches" of the *Derniers vers* ("C'est l'automne, l'automne..." ["It's Autumn, Autumn..."], *PC,* 287–89), while dreaming of a final farewell to the ennui(s) of existence, seeks a departure in togetherness and love; and, even in a poem such as "Simple agonie" ("Simply Dying," *PC,* 293–95), where Laforgue argues the case for utter obliteration—

> Que nul n'intercède,
> Ce ne sera jamais assez,
> Il n'y a qu'un remède,
> C'est de tout casser.

Laforgue

Let no one intercede,
It never will be enough,
There's only one remedy,
Breaking everything up.
(*PC*, 294)

—even here destruction remains predicated upon ideality, frustrated vision, an uprising of self's deep aspiration dulled to nihilism. The posthumous poems are increasingly written under the sign, and with the presentiment, of death. "Not one day when, coward I am, I think not of death," he writes, in the moving "Citerne tarie" ("Cistern Gone Dry," *PC*, 464). The obsession with mortality, passingness, becomes absolute; the lunar, lunatical symbolism gives way to a sense of impotence and impasse where the resilience of *dandysme*, of playfulness grows faint. "The Hugos and Caesars—a bit of ash in the wind," he muses in "Excuse macabre" (*PC*, 315), a poem dedicated to Shakespeare's Hamlet. The soul may continue to fascinate as an eternal infinite, but "Les Têtes de morts" ("Faces of the Dead") haunt and compel equally (*PC*, 331), as they will his contemporaries Manet, Michelet, and Maupassant. At best, in these largely late poems, life may be deemed "both splendid and macabre" ("Rosace en vitrail" ["Stained Glass Rose"], *PC*, 343–44). At worst Laforguean lunaticalness can, as with Mallarmé, hold everything to be nothing, life itself reduced to deathliness, "rien qu'un Cercueil perdu qui flotte dans la Nuit" ("Nothing but a lost Coffin floating in the Night"), as he writes in "Rêve" ("Dream," *PC*, 454). As a poem or fragment such as the posthumous "O gouffre, aspire-moi! . . ." suggests, however, the suicidal impulse can be merged with an intuition of cosmic union wherein, once more, the reversibility of ontic equations is highlighted: nothingness, self-annihilation, becomes recovery of some divine undividedness:

O gouffre aspire-moi! Néant, repos divin . . .
Assis sur le fumier des siècles, seul j'écoute
Les heures de mes nuits s'écouler goutte à goutte
O père laisse-moi me fondre dans ton sein.

Oh chasm suck me in! Nothingness, divine repose . . .
Sitting on the dunghill of centuries, alone I hear
The hours of my nights drip-drip away
Oh father let me melt within your bosom.

The posthumous "La Chanson des morts" (again written earlier, in 1878) may seem characteristically cynical in its textual response to the question posed by its epigraph—"Qui vous dit que la mort n'est pas une autre vie?" ("Who tells you death is not another life?")—but the epigraph itself cannot but leave us with the firm sense that the logic of self-destruction and death-wish remains interlocked with a logic of otherness, of spiritual ideality, of self-transformation beyond the aesthetic and symbolic niceties of Notre-Dame la Lune.

Presence and Nothingness

Jules Laforgue's experience of presence is undeniably caught up in, on the one hand, the feelings of ennui, exile, and so on that underpin his conception of *complainte*, and, on the other hand, the symbolism of lunaticalness that, while seeming to effect some release, permits an ironic half-consolatory embrace of presence itself. Life, as Laforgue readily admits, is only too "quotidian" (*PC*, 86), a daily, necessarily assumed affair. "Le cru, quotidien, et trop voyant Présent" ("the raw, daily and too garish Now"), he calls it in "Mettons le doigt sur la plaie" ("Let's Put Our Finger on the Wound"), from *Des Fleurs de Bonne Volonté* (*PC*, 196): an excessive affair, for all its sterility, a being too visibly "there," all too eternally "now"— "no more centuries!" he exclaims in the posthumous "Suis-je" ("Am I," *PC*, 418–19), "it's forever today." Moreover, if such *présence* is experienced as existential difficulty, even anguish, there is a degree to which, as with Baudelaire, Laforgue embraces its full logic in recognizing the need to go beyond pure ideality toward the simple presence of "human exchange" ("Pétition," *PC*, 291). Such a perception strips ideality of its hygiene, and plunges it *back* into the possible "dailiness" of human love. One could readily quote passages from "Ô géraniums diaphanes..." ("Oh Diaphanous Geraniums") from *Derniers vers* (*PC*, 305) or, again, from "Apothéose" ("Apotheosis," *PC*, 399–400), where the self's "heart" may be hurt, bruised, yet remains alive, streaming with love. Or one might adduce similar evidence of Laforgue's *choosing* of presence from other posthumous texts such as "Prière suprême" (*PC*, 417), with its singing of the self's *crying out now*, before eternity, in solemnity and near death; or "La mémoire d'une chatte naine que j'avais" ("Memory of a Dwarf Cat I Had," *PC*, 410), where a simple, passing presence is celebrated, a presence beyond high fancy or intellectualism, yet "deep," meaningful. Laforgue's poetics, however, is sorely tempted by a persistent, near-obsessive discourse upon nothingness that threatens to undermine the fragile giving of the self to the logic, and the hope, of *présence*. Time can be deemed *nul*, just as eternity is *nulle* ("Préludes autobiographiques" ["Autobiographical Preludes"], *PC*, 31). When Laforgue exclaims and questions, in "Complainte des voix sous le figuier boudhique" ("Lament of Voices Beneath the Buddha Tree," *PC*, 40–43), "Life or Nothingness! Ah! what a discipline!/ Why between these two factories is there no Eden?" (*PC*, 42), it is clear that a tight, ironic equivalence is felt to exist between life and nothingness, both having withdrawn beyond the edenic realm of fullness. "This nothingness too everything," he writes, switching the optic of equivalence: life equals nothingness becomes nothingness equals everything. This does not mean that Laforgue cannot appeal to *something*, the unconscious, for example, in the latter poem, or the pure notion of Eden, as in the previous text; nor does it mean that death cannot assume proportions of nothingness that life cannot match. The obsession of "the no more ever, the true nothingness of nights" (*PC*, 124, "Complainte d'une convalescence en mai") is an eloquent reminder of this: death's nothingness can, in such instances, contrast with life's warmth, its sweet simplicities, its coziness and its freshness ("Guitare" ["Guitar"], III, *PC*, 322), a contrast seemingly giving the lie to the *présence*/nothingness equation. Most frequent, however, is the explicit articulation of this equation, the expression of a feeling that, "between two nothings," human existence is merely a Pascalian "day of wretchedness" ("Sonnet pour éventail," *PC*, 330); that there is literally "nothing to be done upon Earth" (*PC*, 208, "Dimanches").

Various qualifying points need to be taken into account: 1. the reversibility of the *présence*/nothingness equation, touched upon above: if nothingness is presence, it attains to a kind of anti-fullness, a variegated deployment of its forms, however negatively perceived; 2. *présence* can be viewed in contrast to death's nothingness, as shown above, a logic clearly growing out of reversibility, yet pushing it further: nothingness = *présence* = something = pain *and* positive experience; 3. the sense of life's nullity gives rise, as with all Romantic and symbolist poetics, to a countermovement, away from *le mal*, horror, spleen, via desire, aspiration, will; such a movement from nothingness can manifest itself (a) *in* presence (as love, compassion, etc.) or (b) *against* presence (as art, poetry, aesthetic transcendence) or (c) *outside* presence (as metaphysical postulation and intuition). Poems such as "Complainte du temps et de sa commère l'espace" provide ample evidence of these various (and mixed) modes. The latter ends upon the following note:

> Nuls à tout, sauf aux rares mystiques éclairs
> Des Elus, nous restons les deux miroirs d'éther
> Réfléchissant, jusqu'à la mort de ces Mystères,
> Leurs Nuits que l'Amour distrait de fleurs éphémères.

> Null to all, but the rare mystic flashes
> Of the Chosen, we remain two ether mirrors
> Reflecting, till the death of these Mysteries,
> Their Nights that Love distracts with passing flowers.

(PC, 114)

The Laforguean tactic of worshipping the moon's nothingness contains all of these elements (a, b, c) and may be best read as an anti-gesture, made out of despair, a turning toward an at least self-created, pure artificial nothingness (of poetry and its invented symbolisms).

Nobody is deceived, least of all Laforgue himself. The ironies of, say, "Litanies des derniers quartiers de la Lune" ("Litanies from the Moon's Last Quarters"), from *L'Imitation de Notre-Dame la Lune* (*PC*, 176), remain abundant, and contrast with those moments when a consciousness of an otherness is elaborated. Thus is it, on the one hand, that the "soulness" of our being can be deemed to be everything (*PC*, 331, "Les Têtes de morts"); that the "little" we comprehend and accredit can be thrust ironically before the "All which is inexorably shut off from us," though intuited (*PC*, 409, "Triste, triste" ["Sad, sad"]); that, despite the terrible tensions of our being and our sense of nothingness, Laforgue compulsively blurts out, at the end of "L'Angoisse sincère" ("Sincere Anguish," *PC*, 424–26):

> Quelqu'un sait! quelqu'un voit! et du fond de l'abîme
> Il doit prendre en pitié l'angoisse de mes nuits.

> Someone knows! someone watches! and from the deep abyss
> He must take pity upon the anguish of my nights.

(PC, 426)

Thus is it, too, on the other hand, that Laforgue can deem nothingness itself to be the locus of such transcendence. "Nothingness, divine repose . . .," Laforgue writes in the posthumous "Ô gouffre, aspire-moi! . . ." ("Oh chasm, suck me in! . . ."; *PC*, 396); and, in the powerful "Suis-je?" he concludes that "nothing exists but Brahman, it is all, everything is it": the ultimate equation of being and nothingness. "Divinity" and unity may be projected *out* of nothingness, or they may be projected *into* nothingness. The end result is the same in Laforgue's poetics: if presence is relative, so too is nothingness, so much so that the latter's irreality is reduced to the status of pure symbol.

While it is true, then, that Laforgue's work repeatedly focuses on factors of passingness and loss, non-(self-)possession and consequent self-disbelief, it is equally true that his poetics, like André Frénaud's today, is centered on compensatory and equilibrating notions of self's persistence ("Et c'est bien dans ce sens, moi, qu'au lieu de me taire,/Je persiste à narrer mes petites affaires" ["And it's in that sense that instead of keeping quiet,/I persist in recounting my affairs quite trite"], *PC*, 223) and self's remaining within a context of general effacement ("Plus d'heures, plus d'humains, et solitaire, morne,//Je reste là, perdu dans l'horizon lointain" ["No more hours, no more humans, and solitary, glum,//There I stay, lost in the distant horizon"], *PC*, 348). "All shimmers and then passes," Laforgue writes in "Soir de carnaval" ("Carnival Night," *PC*, 353). A "banal Destiny" perhaps (*PC*, 353), but one that is all there is. Laforgue can often stress the *errance* of existence that can give the impression of being caught *neither* here *nor* there, but between the points of being's real emergence. Yet he knows, too, that such errancy is meaningful: "Nobles et touchantes divagations sous la lune" ("Noble and touching ramblings beneath the moon," *PC*, 172).

Metaphysics, Question, Vanity

"Je vague, à jamais Innocent" ("I roam, forever Innocent"), Laforgue declares in "A Paul Bourget," "par les blancs parcs ésoteriques/De L'Armide Métaphysique" ("through the white esoteric gardens/Of Metaphysical Armida," *PC*, 29). Thus does he underscore the profoundly contemplative nature of his poetic practice, the intrinsically psychical dimension of an errant quest that centers itself upon the physical only to meditate its meaning. Thus, too, does he underscore the fundamental innocence of his being as it plunges into its own otherness, the "beyondness" of its meta-*présence*. The liminal poems of *Les Complaintes* immediately following "A Paul Bourget"—"Préludes autobiographiques" (*PC*, 30–34), "Complainte-placet de Faust fils" ["Lament-Petition of Faust Son"], *PC*, 37), "Complainte des voix sous le figuier boudhique" (*PC*, 40–43)—waste no time in establishing the program of this metaphysical inquiry. "Seul, pur, songeur" ("Alone, pure, dreaming," *PC*, 30), the poet/narrator delves into the very reality of presence; the availability or otherwise of "something," "somebody," "nobody" (*PC*, 31); questions of continuity with or without transcendent possibility; desire and search; time, eternity, and nothingness; vanity and purpose; knowledge and the unconscious; self and absoluteness; imagination's "ferment" (*PC*, 37) and *taedium vitae*; choice and blindness; and so on. Thus is the heart's "accursedness" simultaneously its "sacredness" in Laforgue's "Complainte d'un certain dimanche," and, in the same poem, twittering sparrows are glimpsed suddenly, despite depression, as transmogrified souls, forms whose being is infinitely steeped in what is beyond form. "Complainte des pubertés difficiles" ("Lament of Difficult Puberties") similarly leaps beyond a discourse of idle, disenchanted depiction of social fact to the deeply sensed transformation love represents and mysteriously, contradictorily, promises (*PC*, 57). "Complainte de l'ange incurable" ("Lament of the Incurable Angel," *PC*, 67–68) shakes off the clinging frustrations of sensuality's *hic et nunc* and exclaims the inherent nostalgia for an angelicism beyond art, truth, or even godliness—a yearning, à la Baudelaire, for what Laforgue calls, in *Le Concile féerique* (*PC*, 179–89), those "unknown galas/In Sidereal/Annals."

The "soulness" of existence may be treated with irony, but it remains equally real and felt, a mode of self-analysis cutting through the rawly finite to the meta-finite, the in-finite. As Laforgue argues in "Impossibilité de l'infini en hosties" ("Impossibility of the Infinite in Hosts"), from *Des Fleurs de Bonne Volonté* (*PC*, 228), this does not mean that the meta-physical is located in some elsewhere, for it is simply there, "at our doors! at our windows!" Poems like the posthumous "Médiocrité" ("Mediocrity," *PC*, 335) may convey a more remote and desperate sense of the non-finiteness of all that is, the latter poem opening as follows:

Laforgue

Dans l'Infini criblé d'éternelles splendeurs,
Perdu comme un atome, inconnu, solitaire,
Pour quelques jours comptés, un bloc appelé Terre
Vole avec sa vermine aux vastes profondeurs

In the Infinite riddled with eternal splendors,
Lost like an atom, unknown and alone,
For a few allotted days a lump called Earth
Flies with its vermin in the vast depths.

But it is equally true that an intense alertness remains to the "splendors," the "depths," the immense mystery of the physical. "L'Angoisse sincère" and "Litanies nocturnes" ("Nocturnal Litanies," *PC,* 429–32), also posthumously published, may become snarled up in doubt, plain rational ignorance, and fear, yet crucial to their appreciation is Laforgue's intuitive sense of the orchestrated magnificence of some transcendent principle within all being. At such moments, the feeling of the chaos of physics yields to the impulse of the dazzling "glory" and "evidence" (*PC,* 429) of some metaphysics at work. "Suis-je?" pushes inquiry into being to the point of vertigo, but while anchored in the preciousness of the self's consciousness, it succeeds in postulating a metaphysics of Brahmanic unity involving the perpetual transmutation of separates in some universal super-physics.

With characteristic wit, Laforgue points to the intersecting of the quotidian and the metaphysical, when he speaks, in the "Complainte d'une convalescence en mai," of "mes grandes angoisses métaphysiques/[Qui] sont passées à l'état de chargrins domestiques" ("my great metaphysical anguishings/[that] have become mere domestic chagrins"). For the logic of *meta* is clearly always linked to the logic of a here and now. In Laforgue this translates into an endless tussle between alienation and purpose—and a tussle that articulates itself most commonly both via antithetical expletive and exclamation, and via a vigorous questioning seemingly more tense and anguished than that, say, of Lamartine. Laforguean questioning addresses itself, for the most part, to the *why* of existence. It wrestles with the why of love, of all self-other relations, as in "Complainte des complaintes," or it can ask for the logic of poetic action, of *complainte,* itself. Suffering and imperfection are understandable targets (*PC,* 160); though the question *why* can center equally upon feelings of exile and feelings of belonging.

Seeing himself as "le Grand Chancelier de l'Analyse" ("The Grand Chancellor of Analysis," *PC*, 287), "perdu dans le pourquoi des choses de la Terre" ("lost in the why of the things of the Earth," *PC*, 414), Laforgue seems to be immersed in that relative ignorance that a Philippe Jaccottet of today at once deplores and resists. Ignorance, however, offers Laforgue a curious proof of ontic meaning, despite extreme and testing emotion. "And I still question," he writes in the posthumous "Curiosités déplacées" ("Out of Place Inquisitiveness," *PC*, 351), "wild with anguish and doubt!/For at least there is an Enigma! I wait! and wait!" Perhaps such a residual, impulsive logic stems from those occasional resurgent memories of "innocence and love," purity, gentleness, and belief that he recounts in "Veillée d'avril" ("April Vigil," *PC*, 414). Remembrance counters ignorance and rekindles affective fires out of context, yet with the urgency of all *actes de présence*. At such moments the *why* is diluted to a *how*, as in "Dimanches" ("Je m'ennuie, natal! . . ."), from *Des Fleurs de Bonne Volonté*: "Comment lui dire: '"Je vous aime'?" ("How can I tell her 'I love you'?"), he asks, "je me connais si peu moi-même" ("I hardly know myself," *PC*, 218).

Such confidence is largely only glimpsed, however, and not only does questioning return, but it can be overtaken by stoic resignation—"Suffer, love, wait still and [. . .] dance/Without even asking the universal Why" (*PC*, 427, "Résignation")—or by a disgust stemming from impotence. "Que me fait de tenir la formule de Tout?" ("What does it matter to me to hold the formula for Everything?"), he asks in "Berceuse" ("Lullaby"), yielding to a project of existential futility that threatens to swamp all effervescence. "Vanity, vanity, vanity, I tell you," he can, in effect, exclaim from the beginning of *Les Complaintes* (*PC*, 32, "Préludes autobiographiques"). Our "soarings" can thus be deemed "vain" (*PC*, 73, "Complainte du pauvre chevalier-errant"); events as seemingly life-bringing as a rainfall are futile (*PC*, 215, "Dimanches" ["Le ciel pleut sans but . . ."/"The sky rains aimlessly . . ."]); all celebration is held to be tragic vanity (*PC*, 353, "Soir de carnaval"); the "masterpieces" of the world—happiness, art, woman—crumble to irrelevance despite their divinity (*PC*, 41), leaving the "self stooped over beneath the What's the Point," as Laforgue puts it in "Petites misères d'automne" ("Small Autumnal Wretchednesses,") from *Des Fleurs de Bonne Volonté* (*PC*, 251).

Let me stress, moreover, the degree to which the logic of vanity is an assumed and exteriorized project of mind and heart. Laforgue is quite explicit, in fact. "Shrug your shoulders at everything," he advises in "Pierrots" (*PC*, 149), *feeling* the futility of self's intervention in an existential round *felt* to be meaningless, purely—and poorly—theatrical. The need is there, he argues, to "live without aim" (*PC*, 129, "Complainte du sage de Paris"), to change purpose into anti-purpose, to consciously project a non-project. Loss of confidence, a feeling of "le mal de tout, sans but" ("the general, aimless evil," *PC*, 325), constitutes a shift of belief, an exchange of one belief-system or project for another. "What henceforth does this world of misery matter to me!" Laforgue cries out in the posthumous "Lassitude"; "I shall weep over it, but struggle, what's the point?/If it is, in futile, nameless ash,/To scatter, one day, throughout nature" (*PC*, 415). Vanity can be transformed, Laforgue can become what he in fact calls himself, in "Complainte des complaintes," "Sisyphe [. . .] par persuasion" ("Sisyphus [. . .] by persuasion"): resistant, persistent, self-convinced despite the eternally recurring question "WHY!—Why!" (*PC*, 130). But, so frequently, the mind orients him in other directions, toward other feelings.

Intuitions and Possibles

There is a perspective, however, in which we may view Laforguean questioning less as a sign of (senti)mental closure than of openness, minimal as it may be. Like Baudelaire's *plaie*, Laforgue's sense of vanity can be the ground of a curious series of possibilities half-denied, half-present. To some extent what is at stake here is the openmindedness of all thought, the latter's capacity both for embedding itself within its rigidifying patterns and for sensing its *others*, its endless *possibles*, via a shedding of "habits and programs" that limit and constrain (*PC*, 173, "Nobles et touchantes divagations sous la Lune" ["Noble and Touching Ramblings beneath the Moon"]).

That there is a "Source of the Possible" (*PC*, 114, "Complainte du temps et de sa commère l'espace") is less important than the evident reality of the *notion* of the possible in Laforgue. Possibility comes less from the outside than from the inside. Laforgue's impression of his genius, for example—"Le coeur me piaffe de génie/Eperdûment pourtant, mon Dieu!" ("My heart prances with genius/Yet bewilderedly, my God!"), he exclaims in "Complainte des débats mélancoliques et littéraires" (*PC*, 122–23)—clearly arises as an intuition of originality, of origin, within himself. The possible may be deemed almost "inconceivable," as Laforgue hints in "Dialogue avant le lever de la Lune" ("Dialogue Before Moonrise," *PC*, 161–62), but this is clearly a case of the mind giving itself mixed messages. It is in this optic that the moon becomes a (mental) place both of potential and irony, possibility and pure fiction. "Sois l'Ambulance" ("Be the Ambulance"), he entreats the moon, "de nos croyances!//Sois l'édredon/Du Grand-Pardon!" ("of our beliefs!//Be the eiderdown/Of All-Forgivingness!"; *PC*, 138). Similarly, earth itself, our daily experience thereof, Laforgue clearly understands to be a potential deriving from us, from our consciousness, "une simple légende/Contée au Possible par l'Idéal" ("a simple legend/Told to the Possible by the Ideal," *PC*, 222). "To be able to do nothing! O Rage!" (*PC*, 452) is a terrible acknowledgement of the dismantlement of self's project of genial accomplishment, both artistic and existential; yet, in "Marche funèbre pour la mort de la Terre" ("Funeral March for the Earth's Death," *PC*, 338–40), while this dismantlement continues, the poem of the vast human "epic" is riddled with the "yets," the "remembrances," the "magnificences," and the "surges" that remain pertinent to Laforgue's (anti-)vision. For, if blockage and effacement are really felt, it is equally true "qu'on peut tout!" ("that we can do anything!"), that all is feasible, as Laforgue insists in the posthumous fragment "Les Spleens exceptionnels" ("Exceptional Spleens," *PC*, 480). "Who, then, is stopping me," he questions, "before these black opiums whose rancor stultifies."

While it could be maintained that the nature of the possibility intuited in lines such as those of "Les Spleens exceptionnels" is ambiguous, a close reading of any Laforguean text reveals the extent to which all possibles are deemed intrinsically liberating while at the same time often overshadowed by (self-created) notions of self-delusion, self-indulgence (*PC*, 145). The feasibility of hope (*PC*, 420) can thus be held to be a self-administered "opium"; music, too, is a drugging of the senses (*PC*, 460); poetry, love, truth, the unconscious, and all other possibles, can be caught up in a logic of impotence, incapability, despite the remarkable power of positive intuition they may harbor and generate. In effect, the intuition of possibility, whatever form it may take, requires that it be supported, as in Bonnefoy's poetics of being, by desire, will, conscious belief—but by forces not constantly eroded by counterbeliefs, such as those represented by irony, skepticism, even a certain nihilism.

Laforgue's desire for transcendence may thus be strong, as he exclaims, "Ah! des ailes/A jamais!" ("Ah! wings/forever!"; *PC*, 68, "Complainte de l'ange incurable"), but preceding negative assertions ("Ni Dieu, ni l'art, ni ma Soeur Fidèle" ["Neither God, nor art, nor my Faithful Sister"]) undercut the power of desire and will. Similarly, in "Complainte de Lord Pierrot," Laforgue may will himself beyond the "universe," feel even "less and less localized," but his very goal is paradoxically characterized as an "adopt[ion of] *impossible* life" (my emphasis). Laforguian *angélisme* thus seems to involve a desire at once real, urgent and yet predicated upon the "inconceivable" (*PC*, 214), the "unfinishable" (*PC*, 210), the "edenic" (*PC*, 285), the music played "beyond the granted keyboards," the remaining need for "mirrors happier than language." In "Dimanches" ("C'est l'automne, l'automne . . ."), Laforgue goes so far as to say:

> Il ne s'agit pas de conquêtes, avec moi,
> Mais d'au-delà!

> It's not a matter of conquests, with me,
> But of beyonds!
>
> (*PC*, 289)

If we look at Laforgue's conception of truth, such tensions are again manifest. It is quickly posited as an intuited possible and an object of desire, yet equally quickly felt to be absent (*PC*, 39, 65) or relative, associated with a "beyondness" yet subsumed within some "Beyond more certain than Truth!" (*PC*, 68). It does not take much to have him slip toward the belief that "all is a day-dream" (*PC*, 364), though he can understand the degree to which the dream of everything does indeed belong to the self. "Je suis le coeur de tout" ("I am the heart of all"), he writes in "Hypertrophie" ("Hypertrophy," *PC*, 359): truth may be relative, intensely personal, but it remains the truth. Truth remains as a guide, but its apparent nonabsoluteness—its subjectivity—frustrates and blocks access to the assumption of its deep logic. "Complainte du sage de Paris" articulates such implications and even comes close to penetrating the enigma when Laforgue declares that "tout est écrit et vrai, rien n'est contre-nature" ("Everything is written and true, nothing is counter to nature," *PC*, 127). Truth, here, would be a possible always realizable, always unconsciously realized, the truth of all that is, the truth of all presence, all (senti)mental unfoldment, the truth of self, as Laforgue perhaps unwittingly hints in "Pierrots" ("Scène courte mais typique" ["Short But Typical Scene"])—"mon âme . . ./Est au fond distinguée et franche comme une herbe" ("my soul . . ./Is basically distinguished and open like grass," *PC*, 151)— as well as the truth of being after self, beyond self's death, the truth not just of what Laforgue feels as the individual's unconscious (*PC*, 128), but of some collective unconscious drifting beyond the self (*PC*, 270).

Laforgue's conception and intuition of the possibility of truth may be read with further profit in the light of his persistent discourse upon "mystery." Here, too, the focus may commonly be upon the ancient sadness that attaches to it (*PC*, 96, "Complainte du soir des comices agricoles" ["Lament of the Agricultural Show Night"]), or upon the absurd hiatus between our apparent buoyancy and the unwittingness that remains and can lead to anguished and frenzied questioning. "Manger, rire, chanter— pourtant tout est mystère" ("Eat, laugh, sing—yet all is mystery"), he laments in the posthumous "Noël résigné" ("Resigned Christmas," *PC*, 465). Such a focus of attention can shift, however, both subtly and significantly. The mystery of being may be "Très-Sourd" ("Most Deaf," *PC*, 118), but it is indubitably there; the heartbreak of "la vieille énigme" ("the old enigma") felt today, may yield, *still* today, to the felt reminiscence of the self's soul opening like a "naive flower" (*PC*, 475, "Aux rayons consolants . . ." ["To Consoling Rays . . ."]); "the sober and vesperal weekly mystery/Of sanitary statistics/In the papers" (*PC*, 281, "L'Hiver qui vient" ["Winter Coming"]) may be part of those "small mysteries" (*PC*, 164) that so often preoccupy and depress Laforgue, yet it speaks also of infinite ontic depth; the poor beggar's "belief in the Enigma" still contrasts poignantly, in Laforgue's mind, with the contemporary willful denial of the "silent Gods": "You are not!" (*PC*, 421, "L'Espérance" ["Hope"]). The intuition of the actuality of mystery may spark off a resignation to the discrepancy between the immensity of cosmic enigma and the self's capacity of absorption and penetration. Mystery's perceived and felt actuality implies both knowledge and ignorance, but the latter, unlike Hugo's ignorance, cannot maintain its joyousness, its sense of positive participation in dazzling greatness. The enigma of being Laforgue knows to be possibility and nourishment (*PC*, 114, "Complainte du temps et de sa commère l'espace"), yet he remains incapable of assuming it within him as a leavening agent, the source of his *own* possibility.

Like Philippe Jaccottet today, Laforgue not infrequently turns to the metaphor of "festiveness," of *fête* or celebration, in articulating his poetics of the possible. Many poems evoke the merriment of the social round, its dancing, drinking, chatting rhythms, at once balletic and theatrical, artful and unreal. Such *fêtes* constitute in themselves a significant part of that "triste et vieux Mystère" ("sad and old Mystery," *PC*, 96) that Laforgue laments, and seem paradoxical, contradictory in the face of the larger sweep of cosmic enigma that besets his consciousness. The contrast gives rise to an irony feeding upon felt incongruity, yet we should not overlook two residual paradoxes: 1. an ongoing consciousness of the continuing possibility of the deep meaning and possibility of the metaphor of *fête*; 2. the fact that there is an essential assimilation of banal and great mystery, which tends to function negatively for Laforgue, giving to the cosmos the same festive frivolity of mundane event. "At fêtes here-below I have always sobbed," he affirms in "Soir de carnaval" (*PC*, 353); and, in "Noël sceptique" ("Skeptical Christmas," *PC*, 327), he can declare his deep affective and social marginality:

> Je suis le paria de la famille humaine,
> À qui le vent apporte en son sale réduit
> La poignante rumeur d'une fête lointaine.

> I am the pariah of the human family,
> To whom in his filthy nook the wind brings
> The poignant rumblings of some distant celebration.

Interestingly, Laforgue is clearly aware of his alienation and of a moving quality attaching to that very seeming banality from which he is cut off. If his irony would point to a sharp criticism of human festivity, his consciousness remains undeniably attuned to the deep potential of the apparently trivial interlacements of being that society's mechanisms may generate. He is far from blind to the irony of his own ironies, in fact. For, if felt to be justified upon one level, they risk severing all possible link to what, in "Fantaisie" (*PC*, 341–42), he will call "the Feast of love." Such thought structures, continually projected upon that cutting edge of deep, even at times bitter irony, affect all of Laforgue's metaphors of possibility; and *fête*, for all its becoming atemporal, "Fête éternelle" ("Eternal Feast," *PC*, 145, "Lassitude"), a possible of infinite dimensions and truly real for the imagination—*fête*, then, remains enmeshed in factors of distance, blockage, nonattainment. The universe may be moving towards some apotheosis, as "Prière suprême" hints, yet it will be a "Fête lointaine où nous ne serons pas" ("distant Feast at which we shall not be."

And so the metaphors and mental structures of intuited possibility unfold. I shall close this section by offering some compacted sense of Laforgue's perception of two haunting possibles, god(liness) and the unconscious. With respect to the first: 1. Laforgue's sense of god(liness) hovers between possibility as external and as internal; 2. the fact that God or god(liness) needs to be "remade" (*PC*, "Locutions des pierrots" ["Pierrots' Expressions"]) tends to stretch Laforgue's poetics of the divine between a feeling of irretrievable loss and a continuing need for "prayer without pretension" (*PC*, 214, "Petite prière sans prétention" ["Short Unpretentious Prayer"]); 3. similarly, the "other world" may be deemed "nonsense," but it remains embedded in the consciousness ("La Cigarette," *PC*, 333); 4. such tensions prevent Laforgue neither from seeing the human become priest/ess, nor from summoning forth the still felt and posited omniscience he lacks: "Show yourself, appear,/God, eternal witness" ("Eclair de gouffre" ["Chasm Lightening"], *PC*, 349); 5. Laforgue's possible, intermittent "atheism" remains not only haunted by ghosts of the divine, but involves in itself a switch of belief, a *theism* that is at once refusal and new acceptance ("Intarissablement" ["endlessly"], *PC*, 350); 6. all sense of god(liness) hesitates between what, in "Lassitude," he calls "my divine dream" and "chimera": we are close here not just to a sense of truth and possibility as impoverished solipsism, but also to the notion of the self as a true and stunning projector of the real *as* "divine dream"; 7. Laforgue's affirmation of god(liness), as in the closing stanza of "L'Angoisse sincère," or the third stanza of "Trop tard" ("Too Late," *PC*, 457–58), is principally counterbalanced by that sense of "le Mal, le Doute et la Souffrance" ("Evil, Doubt and Suffering") that plagues the century's poets, from Vigny to Lautréamont, in one form or another; 8. some possible resolution may be said to emerge from Laforgue's Buddhist distinction between "Brahm [et] apparence" ("Brahmin and appearance"), as he puts it at the end of "Litanies nocturnes" (*PC*, 429–32); 9. it would be possible to explore further the implications of the posthumous poem-fragment "Pourtant!—S'il y avait . . ." ("Yet—If There Were . . ."; *PC*, 478), which stresses the possible intrinsic goodness of all that is, and those of Laforgue's above-mentioned logic of (self-)creation, as expressed in the paradoxically titled "Hypertrophie."

The second of our two final Laforguean possibles, the unconscious, sketches out a logic predicated in large measure on the elements I can only point to here: 1. when Laforgue says, in the "Préludes autobiographiques" of *Les Complaintes* (*PC*, 30–34), "moi, ma trêve, confiant,/Je la veux cuver au sein de l'INCONSCIENT" ("my truce, confidently,/I want to ferment in the bosom of the UNCONSCIOUS"), he is deploying a typically double, ironic discourse, which on the one hand genuinely turns to the unconscious as a realm of untapped (self-)knowledge, while on the other it argues for a retreat from life (*ma trêve*) into oblivion and unconsciousness: the poem acts, then, as an opening onto both the gravity *and* the tense lucidity underpinning Laforgue's work; 2. the following poem, "Complainte propitiatoire à l'inconscient" ("Propitiatory Lament to the Unconscious," *PC*, 35–36), articulates less ambivalently a poetics of instinctual, visceral spirituality, feeling that conscious thought itself—which, however, remains the vehicle of his oeuvre—is nothing more than "original leprosy, insane drunkenness,//Raft of Evil and Exile": the very consciousness that has identified problem is deemed unable to solve it; 3. the unconscious is, however, thought capable of "shuffling cards, dictionaries, sexes" (*PC*, 83, "Complainte de Lord Pierrot"), of redefining our being, our existential facts and the linguistic networks and grills we lay over them; 4. as "Complainte du temps et de sa commère l'espace" suggests, the unconscious is thus a potential means of affective resolution and a way out of "ce néant trop tout" (*PC*, 113); 5. it is, thus, perhaps not surprising that Laforgue's poetics of the unconscious, while striving to take itself seriously, to explore its "strata of instincts, potential paradises,//Nights of heredities and limbos of latencies//... So as to see..." (*PC,* 127, "Complainte du sage de Paris"), can also quickly slip into an irony no doubt *stemming* from such idealization; the continuation of the same poem is exemplary in this regard, the unconscious dropping to the status of "la grande Nounou où nous nous aimerions/À la grâce des divines sélections" ("the great Nanny in which we would love one another/By the grace of divine selections," *PC,* 128); 6. art, however, despite the fierce persistence of conscious ironies, the "self-agitation" of its gesture, remains "led" by the unconscious in some way not easy to define ("La Lune est stérile" ["The Moon is Sterile"], *PC,* 167–68)—"pointilleux mais emballé,/Inconscient mais esthète" ("fastidious but madly keen,/Unconscious but an aesthete"), as he wrote in the earlier "Complainte des formalités nuptiales" ("Lament of Nuptial Formalities," *PC,* 75–78); 7. one of the most significant features of the unconscious is the ontic buoyancy Laforgue somehow knows it implies: it is that very force of which he has need in doubt and anguish, for he feels its intrinsic message, as he writes at the close of "Nobles et touchantes divagations sous la Lune," to be: "n'aie pas peur" ("Do not be afraid," *PC,* 174). As other poems such as the posthumous "Pour le livre d'amour" (*PC,* 337) imply, fear is at loggerheads with love, and access to the deeper realms of our being can replace fear with that confidence given to, and by, love.

Love

There can be no doubt whatsoever that the meaning and logic of love is at the very center of Laforgue's life, his work, his overall poetics. Love, for him, is the "only categorical imperative," affecting mind, soul and body (*PC,* 172, "Nobles et touchantes divagations sous la Lune"), as centrally pertinent as that paradoxical disregard of it, of which he speaks in "Pour le livre d'amour" (*PC,* 337). Childhood understood this well, he reflects in "Lassitude": a time when "ce trésor d'amour ... était tout pour moi,/Ma force, mon recours, mon but, mon espérance" ("the treasure of love ... was all for me,/My strength, my recourse, my goal, my hope." That much of Laforgue's poetry is, indeed, a lament for the loss of hope and for the establishment of a reign of impotent desire and reciprocal self-other misunderstanding is at once true, and yet, only partially so. Certainly Laforgue seems quick to place himself under a sign of incontrovertible paradox, far from the supreme clarity of Marceline Desbordes-Valmore, when he quotes Sainte-Beuve in the epigraph to "Complainte d'un certain dimanche": "Elle ne concevait pas qu'aimer fût l'ennemi d'aimer" ("she did not conceive loving to be the enemy of loving" *PC*, 52). Certainly he can feel unloved, uncompensated by genius ("Complainte des pubertés difficiles," *PC*, 57); caught in a relational structure of ephemeralness or noncoincidence of intent (*PC*, 76, "Complainte de l'ange incurable"; *PC*, 359, 401, "Hypertrophie," "Désolation"); implacably alienated, apart, "alone, without love, without glory! And the fear of death!" (*PC*, 441, "Les Après-midi d'automne" ["Autumn Afternoons"]). Desire, however, though seemingly intransitive, remains persistent, love's logic urgent and unceasing. In pre-surrealist fashion dream supplants reality, brushing aside the "old compromises" (*PC*, 84) as well as the absurdities of some donjuanesque chase (*PC*, 146), conjuring the fiction of the other giving herself to the self—"Ah! qu'une, d'elle-même, un beau soir sût venir/Ne voyant que boire à mes lèvres, ou mourir!" ("Ah! that one, freely, one fine evening might come,/Seeing but a quenchment at my lips, or death!"; *PC*, 84, "Complainte de Lord Pierrot"). Much of Laforgue's poetry, in fact, may be described as monologues upon self-other relations, or actual dialogues, or evocations of scenes and encounters, real and dreamed, largely abortive in intimate if not broadly social terms.

Love's elusiveness may be attributed, in Laforguean perspective, to many factors. Of course, there is the other's—the woman's: Laforgue's discourse of love is highly focused and rarely speaks of deep friendship, adoration of flowers or pebbles or landscapes, planetary or cosmic emotion—plain and legitimate refusal of the self. "Ni vous, ni votre art, monsieur" ("Neither you, nor your art, sir"), as Laforgue says with typical wit in "Complainte des blackboulés" ("Blackballees' Lament," *PC*, 79). But the self, too, assists in the creation of the relational structures it, at times, too quickly ascribes to the other. Laforgue, ultimately, is deeply aware of this: he knows that humor and irony, his, are "traps" that "perhaps will . . . /Kill Love!" (*PC*, 90, "Complainte du vent qui s'ennuie la nuit"); he knows that art and literature are stopgap measures, in a sense diversions, that his central ambition is or should be love ("Esthétique" ["Aesthetics"], *PC*, 205–206), that art risks "offering every kiss a carapace of emptiness," whereas his true *complainte* seeks to leap outside of itself. "Aimer, être aimé!" ("To love and be loved!"; "Complainte-litanies de mon sacré-coeur," *PC*, 120–21); he knows, too that not only art, but "Spleen [and] Pain" are desperate and self-defeating consolations ("Excuse mélancolique," *PC*, 428), readily "drying up . . . your ocean of love" ("Désolation," *PC*, 401–402). The logic of love is, in fact, so sensitively perceived, that Laforgue's work, while often centered upon problem as externality, as located in the other, can at times catalog with the utmost clarity all that impedes or disallows the very thing that he knows he most needs.

Thus, the fear of the body is felt and assumed as problem (*PC*, 91). "Elément non-moi!"/"Non-me element!" he jokingly, but pointedly exclaims in "Signalement" ("Description," *PC*, 272–73). Thus, he realizes how men do not take seriously enough the women they know, though he senses, too, the reciprocal nature of the relational structure (*PC*, 148). "Bookish" misogyny may temper many encounters and possibilities (*PC*, 30, "Préludes autobiographiques"), and, although (dis)belief, fear and criticism may be mutual (*PC*, 151, "Pierrots," "Il me faut vos yeux . . ." ["I Need Your Eyes . . ."]), this contradiction of love's intent Laforgue does not neglect. The very relativity of love's discourse that he feels about and within him, and which is thus in part generated and maintained by the self, leads to a *vivotement* or "ticking over" rather than to true life, as he suggests in "Etats," from *L'Imitation de Notre-Dame la Lune* (*PC*, 166). The "arrangements," the compromises, the theater of such relativity, however, while bemoaned, are also assumed and, even, sung; they may not be resolved, transformed, deemed transformable, but they do become *Les Complaintes* and his other textualizations.

Relativity, in effect, Laforgue can only accept as *complainte:* his high desire is absolute affinity, intimacy, reciprocal belonging and possession. "Sisters, mothers," he laments in his aptly titled "Maniaque" ("Maniacal," *PC*, 197), "widows, Antigones,/Lovers! but never my Wife." Various poems such as "Arabesques de malheur" (*PC*, 269) affirm this conception of ideal, absolute shared love; all else is "factitious,/It's fake. That's justice/To my mind, that's how I love" (*PC*, 269). Love can thus become synonymous with folly or "madness," a disregard for all that is exterior to love (*PC*, 269); but it demands, too, that reciprocal confession, understanding, and "astonishment" which "spleen" can so pathetically subvert (*PC*, 86, 269). The feeling of the self's exile from the fullness of presence can mean that Laforgue may choose to project love out of the *hic et nunc*. "Ailleurs" ("Elsewhere"), he writes in "Dimanches" ("Mon sort est orphelin . . ." ["My fate is orphaned . . ."]), from *Des Fleurs de Bonne Volonté*, "loin de ce savant siècle batailleur . . . /C'est là que je m'créerai un petit intérieur,/Avec Une dont, comme de Moi, Tout n'a que faire" ("far from this battling learned century . . . / There I'll make m'self a little foyer,/With One with whom, as with me, Everything has nothing to do," *PC*, 247). However, such ideality has nothing exotic or hygienic about it. It is neither Romantic nor Mallarméan in its fundamental character. In this sense, as "Pétition" contends, ideality in Laforgue's discourse of love seeks to transcend itself—to attain to "simply[,] human exchanges" that possess that capacity to be "simply[,] infinite exchanges/At the end of days/Harvested in full and joint embrace" (*PC*, 291). Laforgue may come close to bogging himself down in a sense of his own unlovedness ("Who ever loved me? I get stuck/On this impotent refrain," he writes near the close of *Les Complaintes*, *PC*, 122); but, equally, in the same volume already, he knows of the ubiquitous logic of love, of the generation, in which he is involved, of some at once individual and cosmic "air divin, et qui veut que tout s'aime" ("divine air, wanting everything to be love," *PC*, 118). His principal impulse in the generation and propagation of this latter melodious will, however, goes to love as private affinity: his "Ève, sans trêve" ("truceless Eve") is a particular woman, truth in a body and soul now, as Rimbaud might have said, a woman who just might "adopt Man as equal!" ("Pétition," *PC*, 291).

Poetry: Immolation and Immorality, Mirroring and Uniqueness

Laforgue's "Complainte d'un autre dimanche" terminates as follows:

Ah! qu'est-ce que je fais, ici, dans cette chambre!
Des vers. Et puis, après? ô sordide limace!
Quoi! la vie est unique, et toi, sous ce scaphandre,
Tu te racontes sans fin, et tu te ressasses!
Seras-tu donc toujours un qui garde la chambre?

Ce fut un bien au vent d'octobre paysage . . .

Ah! what am I doing here, in this room!
Rhyming. And so what? oh sordid slug!
Life is unique and, beneath this diving-suit,
You're telling your endlessly sifted tale!
Will you always then keep to your room?

It was a very October-windy landscape . . .

Poetry as (self-en)closure, as self-burial, as some eremitic sordidness, a "self-story," as Michel Deguy would say, that plunges the poet into futile self-repetition and self-limitation rather than some vibrant symbiosis with the world. And even if, as the last line shows, some such contact does remain, Laforgue's conception of poetry seems deeply linked to a problematics of "interiority" ("Intérieur," *PC*, 318) and self-immolation. "Martyres, croix de l'Art, formules, fugues douces" ("Martyrs, Art Crosses, formulas, sweet flights"), he writes in "Préludes autobiographiques" (*PC*, 31). Indeed, although a poem such as "La Lune est stérile" argues that "Art is all, by the divine right of Unconsciousness;/*Après lui, le deluge!*" many poems stress what even this poem, and its title, convey, namely the "immorality" or "amorality" of poetry, its retreat into inner purity, its "abdication" (*PC*, 74) from ethical concern and commitment. Given, however, Laforgue's paradoxical fascination with and immersion in presence, it is not surprising that poetry is held to be a Sisyphian task (*PC*, 130), a *démarche* caught between resignation and persistence (*PC*, 149), "refrain impuissant" ("impotent refrain," *PC*, 122) but at least refrain.

Laforgue's conception of poetry can, indeed, fall under a seemingly relentless barrage of irony, criticism, and deconstruction. Writing poetry thus builds itself into existence, yet predicates itself upon decomposition—"Eponge définitivenent pourrie" ("Definitively Rotten Sponge") is the title of an unpublished fragment (*PC*, 480)—and self-annulment. As such, poetry's logic is arguably not understood (*PC*, 130) and denied as futile (*PC*, 135). "Books in which man put futile victories," he writes in "Marche funèbre pour la mort de la Terre" (*PC*, 338–40), where those contradictions of art become blatant, as in "Certes, ce siècle est grand! . . . ." ("Certainly, This Is a Great Century . . ."; *PC*, 388–89), in a context of negative belief, purposelessness, superfluity. Art and poetry can thus slip quickly from any idolatry they may enjoy and fall prey to that sense of self-annihilation Laforgue projects into the very activities he otherwise prizes. "Néant, la Mecque/Des bibliothèques" ("Nothingness, the Mecca/Of libraries"), he grimacingly notes at the end of *L'Imitation de Notre-Dame la Lune* (*PC*, 176), shifting worship and design to make room for his sentiments of emptiness and sheer dusty temporality, sentiments no doubt linked to his perception of the intransitivity, the "sterility," the sadly bloodless "ecstasy" of *l'art pour l'art* ("La Lune est stérile"). Aesthetic "aim" (*PC*, 167) thus becomes an anti-aim, ontologically. Laforgue's very vision is undercut, radically devalued. Baudelaire's poetic flowers become "sheafs . . . of a late Me," as he writes in "Complainte des complaintes" (*PC*, 130), those blossomings of absence that a Bernard Noël or a Jacques Dupin can speak of today, in their gestures of poetic deconstruction. Poetry, in this perspective, deteriorates, as with a Philippe Jaccottet, into "lie"; and the ideality of poetry, in itself a "nonsense," is insufficient to stay up this lie, as Laforgue suggests in "Dialogue avant le lever de la Lune" (*PC*, 161–62), adding:

> Mais, tout est conteste; les livres
> S'accouchent, s'entretuent sans lois!

> But, all is dispute; books are born
> And slaughter one another lawlessly!

Poetry is converted into non-proof, the anarchy of their simultaneity, their canceling-out of each other, the feeling of their intrinsic mortality.

None of this means that Laforgue fails to appreciate the "nobility" and the pathos that can attach to what he calls his "Nobles et touchantes divagations sous la Lune" (*PC*, 172). Such wandering and wild digressions are, after all, his chosen mode of expressing the self's shifting authenticity, and of offering it "to GUSTAVE KAHN and also to the memory of little Salammbo, priestess of Tanit," as the *dédicace* to *L'Imitation de Notre-Dame la Lune* shows (*PC*, 134). An offering to a mythical lunar goddess, one might say; but a purpose addressed, too, to life, even though emblematized by symbolist aestheticism à la Gustave Kahn. Yet poetry and art give rise, implacably, to disappointment in Laforgue's mind. As "Complainte des bons ménages" ("Lament of Good Households," *PC,* 82) wittily demonstrates, they "dupe" the man, the non-aesthete in him; they are "sans poitrine," bosomless, a love one cannot "have constantly on one's hands," for it is too bloodless, too ascetic, too conventlike an experience. "Making literature," Laforgue maintains in the liminal "Avertissement" to *Des Fleurs de Bonne Volonté* (*PC,* 193), is thus synonymous with that *vivotement,* that half-life he deems at the very root of his problems. Those "sentences, colored baubles,/Clots of remembrances," of which he speaks in "Dimanches" ("J'aime, j'aime . . ." ["I love, I love . . ."], *PC,* 257–58), are the production of what Laforgue thinks of as a poetics of quick self-portrayal (*PC,* 200, "Aquarelle en cinq minutes" ["Watercolor in Five Minutes"]), borrowed language and thought, and sheer clowning (*PC,* 205–206, "Esthétique").

It is no wonder, then, that love's logic can sweep over that of poetry and art. Not only, in a sense, does love underpin Laforgue's creative act, but it ideally would subvert and usurp it. "Rien, partout . . . /Ne vaut deux sous de jupe,/Deux sous d'yeux" ("Nothing, everywhere . . . /Is worth a ha'p'orth of skirt,/A ha'p'orth of eyes," he writes at the end of his "Petites misères d'octobre," from *Des Fleurs de Bonne Volonté* (*PC,* 224–25); and "Fifre" ("Fife Player") from the same volume (*PC,* 239), opens after a searing epigraph from *Hamlet,* upon a tone of high but ironic pathos:

> Me ferais des blessures!
> Et ma Littérature
> Fermerait boutique.
>
> Would do myself injuries!
> And my Literature
> Would shut up shop.

In the final analysis, Laforgue's conception of poetry seeks to override disappointment, futility, and a sense of sacrifice of the self in some amoral aesthetic void. The posthumous "Apothéose" (*PC,* 328) shows a poet accepting the chilling but simple dignity of the poetic act as an ephemeral mirroring, enigmatic yet linked to some instinctual knowing and willful meditation—a mirroring of being via that improbable little knot of words that is a "sonnet." Even the "self-crucifying" poem "Simple agonie" seeks, beyond the sense of poetry's "pariah" self-rehearsal, a firm feeling of its own paradoxically already intuited purpose:

> Oh! que
> Devinant l'instant le plus seul de la nature,
> Ma mélodie, toute et unique, monte,
> Dans le soir et redouble, et fasse tout ce qu'elle peut
> Et dise la chose qu'est la chose,
> Et retombe et reprenne
>
> . . . .
>
> Selon la tâche qui lui incombe

> Oh! that
> Sensing the loneliest moment of nature,
> My melody, all and sole, may rise up,
> In the evening, gathering itself, doing all it can
> Saying the thing that the thing is,
> Subsiding and resuming
>
> . . . .
>
> After the task befallen it.

Poetry is seen as some great singing of existence, à la Lamartine or à la Guillevic; as some gesture of total self-giving; as an exquisite expression of the self's particularity; as a crucial and persistent, wave-like effort of repossibilization; as a saying of the real; as an assumption of felt duty, of that "task of hope," which Bonnefoy evokes at the close of his *Ce qui fut sans lumière*—and no matter how much that Frénaldian "non-hope" may seem to gnaw away at our "possibles."

Modes and Forms

Laforgue's work may be seen as inspired, but by no means bound, by three principal modes. On the one hand it is punchy, resilient, tongue-in-cheek, ironic; yet it retains an aesthetic aspiration bordering upon an asceticism of which that recurrent lunar sterility is a powerful emblem. And yet, again, it would do the greatest disservice to Laforgue's brief but intense meteoric flight, were we not to recognize the degree to which a great passion, an immense, struggling attachment to the deep ethicalness and spirituality of our earthly passage, fires and fuels an oeuvre far from idly witty or aesthetically withdrawn. Laforgue is driven at once by certain fundamental Verlainean, Mallarméan, and Rimbaldian modes, to the extent that irreverent (self-)deconstruction, pure symbolist ideality, and the most powerfully self-searching modern neo-lyricism mark the *Complaintes* and other collections. But it is precisely because Laforgue's poetry *fuses* modes that it can be said neither that symbolist (self-)evacuation toward the deployment of its "signifiances idéales" prevails; nor that scoffing, parodic nimblewittedness dominates; nor again that sheer affective or moral, philosophical urgency sweeps away other tendencies. Parnassianism can thus be brushed aside by Laforgue's "Klop, klip, klop, klop, klip, klop," as in the "Derniers soupirs d'un Parnassien" ("A Parnassian's Last Sighs," *PC*, 407). The abundant sculpted posthumous sonnets and other forms may border upon a mode à la Leconte de Lisle or à la Gautier, yet they reek of a quite unesoteric lyricism and a mode that may be described as the poetic equivalent of naturalism's Maupassant or even its Henri Becque—the biting pessimism, the text as some satirical but "exilescent and stepmotherish tune" (*PC*, 122). Such modes, at once tonal and formal, take us beyond naturalistic theater, and lie somewhere between Vigny's conception of poetic "drama," Mallarmé's *Igitur*, Maeterlinck's *Pelléas et Mélisande*, and even Jarry's 1897 *Ubu roi*. But, then again, such Laforguean proclivities are often pure *interiors* (*PC*, 384, "Intérieur"), expressionist (self-)portrayals like so many Van Gogh or Gauguin landscapes, whose mode is one of existential interiority but whose form refuses that tombal, textual interiorness, where nothing "authorial" is "expressed." There again, the ironic or implicit intertextuality of a poem such as the posthumous "Soleil couchant" ("Sunset," *PC*, 385) or "L'Hiver qui vient" points up the degree to which private states are perceived by Laforgue in relation—to Lamartine, Hugo, Verlaine, Rimbaud. His mode is thus never pure, never monochromatic; his self-reflexiveness is symbiotic, open upon texts, conscious of contiguity and mosaic. His poem can thus be *complainte* or *litanie*, song, popular ballad or "air" or "madrigal" (*PC*, 106, 109, 111, 440), just as he can range from the "cosmic" mode, to the "dilettantish" mode of the *pierrot*, to "autobiographical" manner. The astonishing thing in Laforgue's work is that the shifts occur within a line or two, and indeed modes may be simultaneous.

In the space that remains I shall offer a necessarily compact assessment of the equally fascinating array of formal features that underpin these shifting or fused modes in Laforgue's poetry: 1. meter stays centered upon the alexandrine, but even where the latter reigns supreme, as in "Complainte du temps et sa commère l'espace" (*PC*, 113–14), it is undercut or profoundly modified by the audacious "deconstructions" of enjambment, vocabulary, and tone. This, moreover, is true in the alexandrine's combination with other meters such as 12-8 and 12-9, as in more supple structures, like the 12-3-12-8-8 or 12-8-4-3 orchestrations of "Complainte du soir des comices agricoles" or the opening of *Le Concile féerique*, respectively (*PC*, 95, 181). A remarkable metric range is deployed outside the dominant alexandrine convention, going from the variation on the 10-syllable line of the "Complainte du pauvre chevalier-errant" (*PC*, 73–74), 10-10-10-7-3-14, through the framed idiosyncratic central flourish, 8-8-8-8-1-3-8-8-8-8, of "Complainte du pauvre jeune homme" (*PC*, 106–108), or the 7-3-7-7-7 *impair* modulations of a poem such as "Stérilités" ("Sterilities," *PC*, 169), to the post-Verlainean practice of "Le Mystère des trois cors" ("Mystery of the Three Horns," *PC*, 282–83), with its slippage from 5-syllable lines to 5-5-7-3 rhythm and on to free verse forms fluidly melded with recognizable metric patterns. A poem like "Dimanches" ("Ils enseignent" ["They Teach"], *PC*, 274), without transgressing Verlainean usage, certainly demonstrates the extreme metric jauntiness to which Laforgue is given: 3-11-3-11// 5-6//3 (×16)//6-6-6-6. As Laforgue's epigraph puts it, "Jacques Motley's the only wear" (*PC*, 274); 2. rhyme continues to play a major role and can be bold, semantically dissonant, at once a vehicle for brashness and exploration, and their formal generator—just like surrealist associative techniques. Every poem has its gems, often in abundance; 3. stanzaic structure, too, commonly avoids the predictability to be found in the century's poetry all the way to Mallarmé and Rimbaud, even Verlaine. Certainly the sonnet can have its moment, though most are posthumous and thus consciously excluded from the consciously shaped collections. Certainly the quatrain can recur with regularity and yet metric variation. But 2-line, 3-line, 5-line, 6-line and 7-line stanzas are common, as well as simple combinations thereof and sudden extensions or occasional swaths of longer stanzas, as in the "Préludes autobiographiques," at once reminiscent of Lamartine or Vigny, yet so distant; 4. in conformity with Laforgue's growing sense of the futility of what he calls in "Derniers soupirs d'un Parnassien," a "rebellious meter" (*PC*, 407), free verse becomes an expressive tool felt to be increasingly powerful as his mastery of it develops. Poems such as "L'Hiver qui vient" or "Dimanches" ("Bref, j'allais . . ."), from *Derniers vers* (*PC*, 279–81), demonstrate the delight Laforgue can take in this new form that his symbolist contemporaries embraced with similar relish. Indeed, all the *Derniers vers* opt for free verse forms, while continuing to exploit contrasts with resurgent "unfree" components, adherence to the quickly obtained impacts of rhyme, and a rough metric constancy or range that does not, as yet, extend to the more liberal *verset* of Claudel or Saint-John Perse; 5. although Laforgue does not follow the example of Baudelaire's *Le Spleen de Paris* or Mallarmé's *Poèmes en prose* and does not seem to have read anything of Rimbaud other than the *Poésies*, he does have his one moment wherein poetry and prose fuse their optics and purposes: the "Grande complainte de la ville de Paris" (*PC*, 115–17), a *prose blanche* ("white prose"), as he calls it, exquisitely dense, compacted into staccato, parataxic fragments—a great poem of modernity's bursting, but difficult lyricism, far from Vigny's "Paris" or even Apollinaire's "Zone"; 6. Laforgue's poetic vocabulary, like Hugo's, is remarkably extensive and thus, despite the relative slimness of his final output, tends to push out the limits of consciousness and the latter's resulting thematics. Laforgue's lexicon, however, is more provocative, more raucous in its intentions. Neologisms abound, distortions, compoundings, hyphenations, phonemic ellipses, or compactions; witty, extravagant juxtaposition, incongruousness forced into sharp or simple droll contiguity—these are features that heighten Laforgue's lexical dexterity and give it both poignant and impish originality; 7. Laforguean metaphor acquires much of its force from this lexical suppleness and, also, from the will for audacity that can mark his rhymes. The metaphors of *Les Complaintes* or *Derniers vers*, for example, may be synaesthetic, because they push relationships beyond conventional perception, but they are less aesthetically caressed than Baudelaire's without ever plunging into either the *voyance* of Rimbaud or the sheer phantasmagoric drift of the surrealists. They are, moreover, slipping frequently into metonymy, assuming the many faces of figuration. They are constant in their teeming self-transformation, as especially when given over to a consciousness reveling in its

> gisements d'instincts, virtuels paradis,
> Nuits des hérédités et limbes des latences!
> Actif? passif? ô pelouses des Défaillances,
> Tamis de pores! Et les bas-fonds sous-marins,
> Infini sans foyer, forêt vierge à tous crins!

> strata of instincts, potential paradises,
> Nights of heredities and limbos of latencies!
> Active? passive? oh lawns of Lapses,
> Sieves of pores! And the underwater depths,
> Infinity without focus, virgin forest out and out!

Poems like this "Complainte du sage de Paris" (*PC*, 126–29) simply unravel trope after trope, metaphor after metaphor; 8. a similar propensity is seen in Laforgue's bent for the swift accumulation of the poem's elements. The last poem alluded to is, again, a good example, as are the "Préludes autobiographiques" (*PC*, 30–34) and "Grande complainte de la ville de Paris." But, in large measure, this poetry is breathlessly, telescopically rhythmed; its perceptions swarm and multiply, rather than easing themselves into some extended melody or some gently teased-out meaning; 9. the subtitles and especially the epigraphs that play an important role in certain poems, and particularly in *Des Fleurs de Bonne Volonté*, can both deepen the modal qualities of the text and set up a rich intertextual play that, often, as with the Shakespearean quotations, provide a psychological and philosophical coherence and intensity echoed, further, in his *Moralités légendaires* (*Legendary Moralities*); 10. the noticeable, though not frequent, parentheses Laforgue opens up in certain poems such as "Complainte du temps et de sa commère l'espace" or the posthumous "Au lieu de songer à se créer une position" ("Instead of Thinking of Making a Position for Oneself," *PC*, 316–17), have the effect of multiplying and complicating poetic voice. In that, they function rhythmically and semantically like those so common rushes of accumulating fragments of perception and reflection, or, again, in a manner not dissimilar from that achieved in the ubiquitous quick-fire dialogues Laforgue likes to incorporate into his poetry; 11. although rare poems can be found in which punctuation may be held to an unusual minimum, as in the first stanza of the posthumous "J'écoute dans la nuit..., " Laforgue prefers to adhere to a finely articulated formulation of his shifting meanings. In this, he clearly opts not to embrace the late hermetic and esoteric manner of Mallarmé; and aesthetic "interiority" is compensated by a desire for self-expressive discourse, a more immediate communicative impulse toward the other; 12. the exclamations that rarely leave Laforgue's poems tend, equally, to demonstrate this latter point.

They may be the sign of a certain level of evocative impotence, but at the same time they illustrate the lyrical intensity and the mental, affective urgency that attach to a poetry never truly seeking aesthetic refuge and repose to the detriment of what concerns him most: ontic, existential resolution. His poems are means, not ends; places of struggle, passage, and presence, rather than networks of pure transcendence; 13. the *points de suspension* that regularly recur similarly *open* the poem to what it is not, rather than locking it into the purely *textual* polysemy that, in the 1880s, invited Laforgue's acquiescence. They break the hold of pure aestheticism and pure textual interiority, as they do in Bonnefoy's *Dans le leurre du seuil*. The white space that bathes Mallarmé's *Un coup de dés* or, today, Guillevic's tiny *quanta*, but to which Laforgue remains relatively indifferent, could be seen as producing the opposite effect upon the reading mind; 14. finally, to follow Laforgue into the "bottom drawer" of his creation—the numerous variants, the considerable body of unpublished material, and the *brouillons*—is to realize the degree to which mortality, uncertainty, and multiple intention explode the nicely shaped limits of achieved form. The latter is thus always balanced by the unfinishedness, the streaming desire of creativity. Forms are rendered evanescent, relative; they revert to places of *passage,* from the "ends" one might have wished to make them. The *brouillon* points to the degree to which all forms are mere scraps in the workshop of our brief presence.

· Ends and Rebeginnings: A Conclusion ·

The collective accomplishments of the great French poets of the nineteenth century are vast. Their endless fascinations have continued to demand rereading, reinterpretation, and this often in the light of discoveries of new source materials and the publication of new editions. If the twentieth century has thus understood the absolute pertinence of the work of Desbordes-Valmore, Baudelaire, Rimbaud, Mallarmé, and all those poets with whom this book has wrestled, it has also understood the relativity of our perception of them. This has been a great gain, for it has allowed us to perceive the deeply meaningful "undecidability" of meaning itself, the added wisdom of the founding mothers and fathers of our modern poetic tradition, and the openness that can lie within each of us if we choose to remain available to it.

The poets of nineteenth-century France have induced within us a deep, if still mistrustful sense of the complexity of selfhood. They have pushed us to perceive the possible beauties and horrors, the simplicities and the difficulties of the reciprocal and shifting symbolisms of self and world, self and other, self and word. If the nineteenth century never stopped struggling with *le mal*, with questions of doubt, pain, loss, death, and alienation, what strikes us nevertheless is the sheer psychological and ethico-spiritual intensity of the poetic *démarches* of every poet examined, from Marceline Desbordes-Valmore and Lamartine to Lautréamont and Laforgue. The aesthetic may have great significance for all such poets, and the cases of Baudelaire and Mallarmé are merely exemplary in this regard. But there is not a single great poet of this century whose essential focus is not upon root ontological considerations. Desbordes-Valmore's entire work is centered upon the power and the monolithic simplicity of love. Lamartine's poetry never ceases to thread the harmonies of telluric attachment and mystical intuition. Vigny's life purpose weds private ethical contemplation to a vision of collective intellectual and spiritual transformation. Baudelaire's ironies may cut deep, but they are ultimately the sign of a compassion and a spiritual desire and will that render his poetry existentially compelling. And so on, down to Lautréamont's

complex, ambiguous tussle with the ethical, psychological, and ontological issues that haunted his *Chants de Maldoror* and *Poésies;*
and, finally, Laforgue's intricate mosaic of aesthetic, affective, and
spiritual urgencies. All of these poets know the trials of personal
option, will, and self-definition, the tensions and hesitations of the
self's assumption of something beyond its banal, strictly rational-
ized and culturally constrained modes. Their work, seen individually and collectively, proposes not fixed equations, nor definitive
solutions. It is always becoming, moving, not anchored in a logic of
closure. One needs only to read Baudelaire's *Fusées* and *Mon coeur
mis à nu* to explode the myth of the pure aesthete or the satanic
dandy; or, in the case of Mallarmé, ponder the relationship between *Vers de circonstance* or *Le tombeau d'Anatole* and *Igitur* or *Un
coup de dés;* or, again, reread Hugo not just in the light of *La Fin de
Satan* or *Dieu,* but from the angle of the latter's countless probing
fragments. No pretty *méli-mélo* for this century; what counts is visceral ontological intensity, combativeness, quest.

The poetry and indeed the entire literature of the twentieth century have been profoundly affected by the poets I have just reread.
No neatly tidied ends, then; just continuings, rebeginnings, revi-
sions of still changing poetic oeuvres. Dada's debt may be largely
owed to a consciousness emerging from the ruins wrought by the
First World War, but its roots may be found in the soil of *Les Fleurs
du Mal* and in Lautréamont's devastations. Jarry, Beckett, Ionesco,
and others raise their minimalisms upon the ironies and stoicisms
that people the poetic universes of Vigny, Laforgue, even Hugo. It
is in the great romantics and symbolists that many surrealists, poets and artists, see the nascent fervors that inspire their own in-
quiries into the mysteries and paradoxes of "the real functioning of
the mind"; and cubist painters and poets (Apollinaire, Reverdy,
Jacob, Cendrars) see in Baudelaire and Mallarmé their rigorously
aestheticizing precursors. Mallarmé's impact upon Valéry is legend, as is Rimbaud's upon Claudel. And is not Michel Deguy a
subtle commentator, of Verlaine, Rimbaud, Baudelaire; has not
René Char written powerfully of Hugo and Rimbaud; is Yves
Bonnefoy not the greatest contemporary reader of Baudelaire and
the symbolists?

For the great questions that Desbordes-Valmore and Lamartine
pursue, persist at the heart of the major poets and thinkers of our
time: the tensions of meaning and form, tellurism and aestheticism,

of what Bonnefoy terms *la présence et l'image;* the legitimate claims of (self-)inquiry, (self-)interrogation, based upon observed or experienced suffering, and the claims of confidence, consent, (self-)love; the taut relation between satire, accusation, exposure, on the one hand, and forgiveness and compassion, on the other; the fundamental question of dialectical, oppositional thinking and expression, as opposed to thought, language, and (anti)structure that might transcend the *fêlures* of our numberless differences and separations; the logic of metaphor, *correspondance, affinités secrètes,* in the debate of unity within distinction; the nature of consciousness and the status of nature, seemingly external phenomena, in relation to the psyche; questions of mortality and infinity; the conception of the feminine; fatality and choice, impotence and (self-)(re) creation. The list can be greatly extended, but we recognize ourselves easily within such swirling foci.

To read, today, the work of Francis Ponge or Andrée Chedid, Philippe Jaccottet or Marie-Claire Bancquart, André Frénaud or Anne Teyssiéras, Jacques Dupin or Denise Le Dantec, is to feel, rumbling between the lines of their texts, the endlessly rebegun processes of poetry so exemplarily lived and pursued by the great poets of the nineteenth century, themselves caught up in their own rebeginnings of Racine, St-Amant, Chénier, their own *fuite en avant* beyond all concluding. If questions of syllables and rhythm and form fascinate—and well into the richly diverse prose poetry of Baudelaire and Mallarmé, Rimbaud and Lautréamont—the counting is of the heart, speaking of the urgency of poetry's "task of hope," as Bonnefoy writes, its mission of spiritual, affective, and ethical (re)creation. Such a mission seeks not repose, nor self-satisfaction, but a "place" beyond poetry itself, and, indeed, an "act" beyond place.

· Selected Bibliography ·

Adam, Antoine. *Verlaine*. Paris: Hatier, 1965.

Adatte, Emmanuel. *Les Fleurs du Mal et Le Spleen de Paris*. Paris: Corti, 1986.

Albouy, Pierre. *La Création mythologigue chez Victor Hugo*. Paris: Corti, 1968.

Ambrière, Francis. *Le Siècle des Valmore*. 2 vols. Paris: Seuil, 1987.

Apollinaire, Guillaume. *Oeuvres poétiques*. Paris: Gallimard, Pléiade, 1959.

Aragon, Louis. *Hugo, poète réaliste*. Paris: Edns. Sociales, 1952.

Aranjo, Norman. *In Search of Eden: Lamartine's Symbols of Despair and Deliverance*. Brockline-Leyden: Classical Folia Edns., 1976.

Aurevilly, Jules Barbey d'. *Victor Hugo*. Paris: Editions d'Aujourd'hui, 1985.

Austin, Lloyd. *L'Univers poétique de Baudelaire*. Paris: Mercure de France, 1956.

———. *Poetic Principles and Practice*. Cambridge: Cambridge University Press, 1987.

Bachelard, Gaston. *Lautréamont*. Trans. Robert Dupree. Dallas: Dallas Institute Publications, 1986.

Balakian, Anna. *Literary Origins of Surrealism*. New York: King's Crown Press, 1947.

Baldensperger, F. *Alfred de Vigny. Contribution à sa biographie intellectuelle*. Paris: Hachette, 1912.

Banville, Théodore. *Oeuvres*. Genève: Slatkine, 1972.

Barlow, Michel. *Poésies. Verlaine*. Paris: Hatier, 1982.

Barrère, Jean-Bertrand. *La Fantaisie de Victor Hugo*. Paris: Klincksieck, 1972–1973. 3 vols. (Paris: Corti, 1949–60).

———. *Hugo, l'homme et l'oeuvre*. Paris: Hatier, 1952.

———. *Victor Hugo*. Paris: Desclée de Brouwer, 1965.

Bartfeld, Fernande. *Vigny: Moïse*. Paris: Lettres Modernes, 1967.

———. *Vigny et la figure de Moïse*. Paris: Lettres Modernes, 1968.

Barthes, Roland. *Le Degré zéro de l'écriture, suivi de Nouveaux essais critiques*. Paris: Seuil, 1972.

Bassan, Fernande. *Alfred de Vigny et la Comédie-Française*. Paris: Jean-Michel Place, 1984.

Baudelaire, Charles. *Oeuvres complètes*. Paris: Gallimard, Pléiade, 1961. (*OC*).

Baudouin, Charles. *Psychanalyse de Victor Hugo*. Paris: A. Colin, 1972. (Edns. du Mont-Blanc, 1943).

Béguin, Albert. *Poésie de la présence*. Neuchâtel: A la Baconnière, 1957.

———. *L'Ame romantique et le rêve*. Paris: Corti, 1939.

Bellet, Roger. *Mallarmé. L'encre et le ciel*. Seyssel: Champ Vallon, 1987.

Benjamin, Walter. *Charles Baudelaire: A Lyric Poet in the Era of High Capitalism*. London: NLB, 1973.

Bibliography

Bertocci, Angelo Philip. *From Symbolism to Baudelaire*. Carbondale: Southern Illinois University Press, 1964.

Bertrand, Aloysius. *Gaspard de la nuit*. Paris: Flammarion, 1972.

Bertrand, Louis. *Lamartine*. Paris: Fayard, 1940.

Bersani, Leo. *Baudelaire and Freud*. Los Angeles: University of California Press, 1977.

_____. *The Death of Stéphane Mallarmé*. Cambridge: Cambridge University Press, 1982.

Birkett, Mary Ellen. *Lamartine and the Poetics of Landscape*. Lexington: French Forum, 1982.

Bishop, Lloyd. *The Romantic Hero and His Heirs in French Literature*. New York: Peter Lang, 1984.

Bishop, Michael. *The Contemporary Poetry of France*. Amsterdam/Atlanta, GA: Rodopi, 1985.

_____. *Michel Deguy*. Amsterdam/Atlanta, GA: Rodopi, 1988.

_____. *René Char. Les Dernières Années*. Amsterdam/Atlanta, GA: Rodopi, 1990.

_____. *Philippe Jaccottet*. Wolfville, Nova Scotia: Edns. du Grand Pré, 1993.

Blanchot, Maurice. *L'Espace littéraire*. Paris: Gallimard, 1955.

_____. *L'Entretien infini*. Paris: Gallimard, 1969.

_____. *L'Amitié*. Paris: Gallimard, 1971.

Bonnefoy, Yves. *Rimbaud par lui-même*. Paris: Seuil, 1961.

_____. *Le Nuage rouge*. Paris: Mercure de France, 1977.

_____. *Entretiens sur la poésie*. Paris: Mercure de France, 1990.

Bonneville, Georges. *Les Fleurs du Mal de Baudelaire. Analyse critique*. Paris: Hatier, 1972.

Bornecque, Jacques-Henry. *Les Poèmes Saturniens de Paul Verlaine*. Paris: Nizet, 1967.

_____. *Vigny par lui-même*. Paris: Seuil, 1967.

Bouché, Claude, ed. *Lautréamont, du lieu commun à la parodie*. Paris: Larousse, 1974.

Bowie, Malcolm. *Henri Michaux. A Study of His Literary Works*. Oxford: Oxford University Press, 1973.

_____. *Mallarmé and the Art of Being Difficult*. Cambridge: Cambridge University Press, 1978.

_____, with Alison Fairlie and Alison Finch, eds. *Baudelaire, Mallarmé, Valéry*. Cambridge: Cambridge University Press, 1982.

Bowman, Frank Paul. *French Romanticism*. Baltimore: Johns Hopkins University Press, 1990.

Braillard, Georges. *Jacques Dupin*. Paris: Seghers, 1974.

Breton, André. *Manifestes du surréalisme*. Paris: Gallimard, 1985.

_____. *Oeuvres complètes*. Paris: Gallimard, Pléiade, 1988.

Brombert, Victor. *La Prison romantique*. Paris: Corti, 1978.

_____. *Victor Hugo and the Visionary Novel*. Harvard University Press, 1984.

Broome, Peter, and Graham Chesters. *The Appreciation of Modern French Poetry 1850–1950*. Cambridge: Cambridge University Press, 1976.

_____. *André Frénaud*. Amsterdam/Atlanta, GA: Rodopi, 1986.

Bibliography

Brunfaut, Marie. *Jules Laforque, les Ysaye et leur temps*. Brussels: Brepols, 1961.

Caradec, François. *Isidore Ducasse, comte de Lautréamont*. Paris: Gallimard, 1975.

Cardinal, Roger, and Robert Stuart Short. *Surrealism: Permanent Revelation*. London: Studio Vista, 1970.

———, ed. *Sensibility and Creation*. London: Croom Helm, 1977.

Carré, Jean-Marie. *Lettres de la vie littéraire d'Arthur Rimbaud (1870–1875)*. Paris: Gallimard, 1931.

Carter, A. E. *Verlaine: A Study in Parallels*. University of Toronto Press, 1969.

———. *Paul Verlaine*. Boston: Twayne, 1971.

Castex, Pierre-Georges. *Vigny*. Paris: Hatier, 1957.

———, et al. *Relire Les Destinées d'Alfred de Vigny*. Paris: S.E.D.E.S., 1980.

Caws, Mary Ann. *A Metapoetics of the Passage*. University Press of New England, 1981.

Cellier, Léon. *Autour des Contemplations: George Sand et Victor Hugo*. Paris: Lettres Modernes, 1962.

———. *Verlaine et la Commune*. Ottawa: Edns. de l'Univ. d'Ottawa, 1973.

Chadwick, C. *Verlaine*. London: Athione, 1973.

Char, René. *Oeuvres complètes*. Paris: Gallimard, Pléiade, 1983.

Chaussivert, J.-S. *L'Art verlainien dans La Bonne Chanson*. Paris: Nizet, 1973.

Chérix, Robert-Benoit. *Commentaire des Fleurs du Mal*. Genève: Cailler, 1949.

Chesters, Graham. *Some Function of Sound Repetition in Les Fleurs du Mal*. Hull: University of Hull, 1975.

———. *Baudelaire and the Poetics of Craft*. Cambridge: Cambridge University Press, 1988.

Citoleux, Marc. *Alfred de Vigny, persistances classiques et affinités étrangères*. Geneva: Slatkine, 1977.

Clancier, Georges-Emmanuel. *De Rimbaud au surréalisme*. Paris: Seghers, 1959.

Claudel, Paul. *Oeuvre Poétique*. Paris: Gallimard, Pléiade, 1957.

———. *Oeuvres en prose*. Paris: Gallimard, Pléiade, 1965.

Clauzel, Raymond. *Sagesse et Paul Verlaine*. Paris: Malfrère, 1928.

Clément, Catherine. *Vies et légendes de Jacques Lacan*. Paris: Le Livre de Poche, 1985.

Clement, N. H. *Romanticism in France*. New York: Kraus, 1966.

Clerget, Fernand. *Paul Verlaine et ses contemporains*. Geneva: Slatkine Reprints, 1980. (Bibliothèque de l'Association, 1897.)

Cogman, Peter. *Hugo. Les Contemplations*. London: Grant and Cutler, 1984.

Cohn, Robert Greer. *L'Oeuvre de Mallarmé: 'Un coup de dés'*. Paris: Les Lettres, 1951.

———. *Mallarmé's Masterwork*. Hague-Paris: Mouton, 1966.

———. *Toward the Poems of Mallarmé*. Los Angeles: University of California Press, 1980.

———. *Mallarmé. Igitur*. Los Angeles: University of California Press, 1981.

Collie, Michael. *Laforgue*. London: Oliver and Boyd, 1963.

Bibliography

_____ and J. M. L'Heureux, eds. *Jules Laforgue: Derniers Vers*. Toronto: University of Toronto Press, 1965.

_____. *Jules Laforgue*. London: Athlone Press, 1977.

Corbière, Tristan. See Cros, Charles.

Cornell, Kenneth. *The Symbolist Movement*. Yale University Press, 1951.

Cornille, Jean-Louis. *Rimbaud nègre de Dieu*. Lille: Presses Universitaires de Lille, 1989.

Coulon, Marcel. *Verlaine, poète saturnien*. Paris: Grasset, 1929.

Cros, Charles, and Tristan Corbière. *Oeuvres complètes*. Paris: Gallimard, Pléiade, 1970.

Davies, Gardner. *Vers une explication rationnelle du 'Coup de dés'*. Paris: Corti, 1953.

_____. *Mallarmé et la 'couche suffisante d'intelligibilité'*. Paris: Corti, 1988.

Décaudin, Michel. *La Crise des valeurs symbolistes*. Toulouse: Privat, 1960.

Deguy, Michel. *Choses de la poésie et affaire culturelle*. Paris: Hachette, 1986.

_____. *La Poésie n'est pas seule*. Paris: Seuil, 1987.

_____. *Arrêts fréquents*. Paris: Métailié, 1990.

Derrida, Jacques. *Positions*. Paris: Minuit, 1972.

_____. *Dissemination*. Trans. Barbara Johnson. University of Chicago Press, 1981.

_____. *Margins of Philosophy*. Trans. Alan Bass. University of Chicago Press, 1982.

Desbordes-Valmore, Marceline. *Oeuvres poétiques*. 2 vols. P.U. de Grenoble, 1973.

_____. *Poésies*. Paris: Gallimard, Coll. Poésie, 1983. (*P*)

Dillman, Karin. *The Subject in Rimbaud from Self to "Je"*. New York: Peter Lang, 1984.

Doolittle, James. *Alfred de Vigny*. Boston: Twayne, 1967.

Ducasse, Isidore: see Lautréamont.

Dupin, Jacques. *Dehors*. Paris: Gallimard, 1975.

Durand-Dessert, Liliane. *La Guerre sainte. Lautréamont et Isidore Ducasse*. 2 vols. P.U. de Nancy, 1988.

Eaubonne, Françoise d'. *Verlaine et Rimbaud ou la fausse évasion*. Paris: Albin Michel, 1960.

Eigeldinger, Marc. *Le Platonisme de Baudelaire*. Neuchâtel: A la Baconnière, 1951.

_____. *Alfred de Vigny*. Paris: Seghers, 1965.

_____. *Poésie et métamorphoses*. Neuchâtel: A la Baconnière, 1973.

_____. *Lumières du mythe*. Paris: Presses Universitaires de France, 1983.

Emmanuel, Pierre. *Baudelaire*. Brussels: Desclée de Brouwer, 1967.

Fairlie, Alison. *Baudelaire: Les Fleurs du Mal*. New York: Barron, 1960.

Fongaro, Antoine. *Matériaux pour lire Rimbaud*. Presses Universitaires du Mirail-Toulouse, 1990.

Fortescue, William. *Alphonse de Lamartine. A Political Biography*. London: Croom Helm, 1983.

Fowlie, Wallace. *Lautréamont*. Boston: Twayne, 1973.

_____. *Poem and Symbol*. Philadelphia: Pennsylvania State University Press, 1990.

Bibliography

Frénaud, André. *Notre inhabileté fatale.* Paris: Gallimard, 1979.

———. *Haeres.* Paris: Gallimard, 1982.

Fumet, Stanislas. *Notre Baudelaire.* Paris: Plon, 1926.

Galand, René. *Baudelaire. Poétiques et poésie.* Paris: Nizet, 1969.

Gateau, Jean-Charles. *Abécédaire critique.* Genève: Droz, 1987.

Gautier, Théophile. *Espana and Emaux et camées.* Oxford: University Press, 1908.

Gely, Claude. *Victor Hugo, poéte de l'intimité.* Paris: Nizet, 1969.

George, A. J. *Lamartine and Romantic Unanimism.* New York: AMS Press, 1966.

Gibson, Robert. *Modern French Poets on Poetry.* Cambridge: Cambridge University Press, 1961.

Gill, Austin. *The Early Mallarmé.* 2 vols. Oxford: Oxford University Press, 1986.

Grant, Elliott. *The Career of Victor Hugo.* Harvard University Press, 1945.

Greene, Robert. *Six French Poets of our Time.* Princeton University Press, 1979.

Greimas, A. J., ed. *Essais de sémiotique poétique.* Paris: Larousse, 1972.

Greenberg, Wendy Nicholas. *The Power of Rhetoric. Hugo's Metaphor and Poetics.* New York: Peter Lang, 1985.

Guichard, Léon. *Jules Laforgue et ses poésies.* Paris: Nizet, 1977.

Guillemin, Henri. *Lamartine.* Paris: Seuil, 1987.

Guillevic, Eugène. *Vivre en poésie.* Paris: Stock, 1980.

———. *Choses parlées.* Seyssel: Champ Vallon, 1982.

Guyaux, André, ed. *Arthur Rimbaud: Illuminations.* Boudry: A la Baconnière, 1985.

Hackett, C. A. *Rimbaud l'enfant.* Paris: Corti. 1947.

———. *Rimbaud.* London: Bowes and Bowes, 1957.

———. *Rimbaud. A Critical Introduction.* Cambridge: Cambridge University Press, 1981.

Hanson, Laurence and Elisabeth. *Verlaine: Fool of God.* Random House, 1957.

Henry, Freeman. *Le Message humaniste des Fleurs du Mal.* Paris: Nizet, 1984.

Higgins, Ian. *Francis Ponge.* London: Athlone, 1979.

Hiddleston, J. A. *Poems: Jules Laforgue.* Oxford: Blackwell, 1975.

———. *Baudelaire et Le Spleen de Paris.* Oxford University Press, 1987.

Houston, John Porter. *The Design of Rimbaud's Poetry.* Westport, CT: Greenwood Press, 1977.

Hugo, Victor. *Les Châtiments.* Paris: Le Livre de Poche, 1964. (*LCH*)

———. *Les Orientales, suivi de Les Feuilles d'automne.* Paris: Le Livre de Poche, 1964. (*LO,FA*)

———. *Odes et ballades.* Paris: Le Livre de Poche, 1964. (*OB*)

———. *Les Contemplations.* Paris: Le Livre de Poche, 1965. (*C*)

———. *La Légende des siècles.* 2 vols. Paris: Garnier-Flammarion, 1967. (*LS1, LS2*)

———. *Poésie. III.* (*Poèmes de jeunesse, Nouveaux châtiments, La Fin de Satan, Dieu, Toute la lyre, Dernière gerbe, Océan*). Paris: Seuil, 1971. (*FS,D,O*)

Bibliography

_____. *Poésie*. I. Paris: Seuil, 1972. (*Les Chants du crépuscule, Les Voix intérieures, Les Rayons et les ombres*, etc.) (*CC, VI, RO*)
_____. *Oeuvres poétiques*. Vol. III. (*Les Chansons des rues et des bois, L'Année terrible, L'Art d'être grand-père*.) Paris: Gallimard, Pléiade, 1974. (*CR, AT, AGP*)
Huysmans, J.-K. *A rebours*. Paris: Fasquelle, 1955.
Ionesco, Eugène. *Hugoliade*. Paris: Gallimard, 1982.
Ireson, J. C. *Lamartine: A Revaluation*. Hull: University of Hull, 1969.
Jaccottet, Philippe. *L'Entretien des muses*. Paris: Gallimard, 1968.
Jasenas, Eliane. *Marceline Desbordes-Valmore devant la critique*. Geneva: Droz, 1962.
_____. *Le Poétique: Desbordes-Valmore et Nerval*. Paris: Delarge, 1975.
Jean, Georges. *La Poésie*. Paris: Seuil, 1966.
Jensen, Kjell Olaf. *Le Gnosticisme dans les grandes épopées de Victor Hugo*. Paris: Pensée Universelle, 1977.
Johnson, Barbara. *Défigurations du language poétique*. Paris: Flammarion, 1979.
Jones, P. Mansell. *The Background of Modern French Poetry*. Cambridge: Cambridge University Press, 1968.
Kahn, Gustave. *Symbolistes et décadents*. Paris: Vanier, 1902.
Kaplan, Edward. *Baudelaire's Prose Poems*. Atlanta: University of Georgia Press, 1990.
Kempf, Roger. *Dandies, Baudelaire et cie*. Paris: Seuil, 1977.
Knapp, Bettina. *Music, Archetype and the Writer*. Philadelphia: Pennsylvania State University Press, 1986.
Kristeva, Julia. *La Révolution du langage poétique*. Paris: Seuil, 1974.
La Charité, Virginia. *The Dynamics of Space. Mallarmé's Un coup de dés jamais n'abolira le hasard*. Lexington: French Forum, 1987.
Laforgue, Jules. *Lettres à un ami*. Paris: Mercure de France, 1941.
_____. *Pages de la guêpe*, ed. J. L. Debauve. Paris: Nizet, 1969.
_____. *Poésies complètes*. Paris: Le Livre de Poche, 1970. (*PC*)
_____. *Mélanges posthumes*. Genève: Slatkine, 1979.
_____. *Textes de critique d'art*. Ed. Mireille Dottin. P.U. de Lille, 1988.
Lamartine, Alphonse de. *Oeuvres poétiques complètes*. Paris: Gallimard, Pléiade, 1963. (*OPC*)
Lautréamont. *Oeuvres complètes*. Paris: Corti, 1969. (*OC*)
Lauvrière, Emile. *Alfred de Vigny, sa vie et son oeuvre*. Paris: Grasset, 1945.
Lawler, James R. *The Language of French Symbolism*. Princeton University Press, 1969.
Leakey, F. W. *Baudelaire and Nature*. Manchester: Manchester University Press, 1969.
Le Clézio, J. M. G. et al. *Sur Lautréamont*. Paris: Edns. Complexes, 1987.
Leconte de Lisle, Charles. *Oeuvres*. 3 vols. Paris: Belles Lettres, 1877.
Leuwers, Daniel. *Introduction à la poésie moderne et contemporaine*. Paris: Bordas, 1990.
Little, Roger. *Saint-John Perse*. London: Athlone, 1973.
_____. *Rimbaud: Illuminations*. London: Grant and Cutler, 1983.

Bibliography

Lloyd, Rosemary. *Baudelaire et Hoffmann. Affinités et influences.* Cambridge: Cambridge University Press, 1979.

MacInnes, John. *The Comical as Textual Practice in Les Fleurs du Mal.* Gainsville: University Press of Florida, 1988.

MacLean, Marie. *Narrative as Performance. The Baudelairian Experiment.* London: Routledge, 1988.

Majewski, Henry F. *Paradigm and Parody.* Charlottesville: University Press of Virginia, 1989.

Mallarmé, Stéphane. *Oeuvres complètes.* Paris: Gallimard, Pléiade, 1945. (*OC*)

——. *Pour un tombeau d'Anatole.* Ed. Jean-Pierre Richard. Paris: Seuil, 1961.

Marchal, Bertrand. *Lecture de Mallarmé.* Paris: Corti, 1985.

——. *La Religion de Mallarmé.* Paris: Corti, 1988.

Martino, Pierre. *Verlaine.* Nantes: Boivin, 1944.

Mathias, Paul. *La Beauté dans Les Fleurs du Mal.* P.U. de Grenoble, 1977.

Michaux, Henri. *Passages.* Paris: Gallimard, 1963.

Montal, Robert. *Lautréamont.* Paris: Editions Universitaires, 1973.

Moreau, Pierre. *Les Destinées de Vigny.* Paris: SFELT, 1946.

——. *Le Romantisme.* Paris: Del Duca, Edns. Mondiales, 1957.

Morice, Louis. *Verlaine. Le Drame religieux.* Paris: Beauchesne. 1946.

Mossop, D. J. *Baudelaire's Tragic Hero. A Study of the Architecture of Les Fleurs du Mal.* Oxford University Press, 1961.

——. *Pure Poetry.* Oxford University Press, 1971.

Murphy, Steve. *Le Premier Rimbaud ou l'apprentissage de la subversion.* P.U. de Lyon, 1990.

——. *Rimbaud et la ménagerie impériale.* P.U. de Lyon, 1991.

Musset, Alfred de. *Premières Poésies. Poésies nouvelles.* Paris: Le Livre de Poche, 1966.

Mutigny, Jean de, *Victor Hugo et le spiritisme.* Paris: Nathan, 1981.

Naughton, John. *The Poetics of Yves Bonnefoy.* University of Chicago Press, 1984.

Nerval, Gérard de. *Les Filles du feu. Les Chimères.* Paris: Garnier-Flammarion, 1965.

Noël, Bernard. *Le Sens la sensure.* Brussels: Talus d'Approche, 1985.

Nojgaard, Morten. *Elévation et expansion. Les deux dimensions de Baudelaire.* Odense University Press, 1973.

Noulet, Emilie. *L'Oeuvre poétique de Stéphane Mallarmé.* Genève: Droz, 1940.

Pachet, Pierre. *Le Premier Venu. Essai sur la politique baudelairienne.* Paris: Denoël, 1976.

Péguy, Charles. *Victor Marie, comte Hugo.* Paris: Gallimard, 1934.

Perrone-Moisés, Leyla. *Les Chants de Maldoror de Lautréamont, Poésies de Ducasse.* Paris: Hachette, 1975.

Perse, Saint-John. *Oeuvres complètes.* Paris: Gallimard, Pléiade, 1972.

Petitfils, Pierre. *Rimbaud.* University Press of Virginia, 1987.

Peyre, Henri. Preface to *Poems of Jules Laforgue.* Trans. Patricia Terry. University of California Press, 1958.

Bibliography

————. *Qu'est-ce que le symbolisme?* Paris: Presses Universitaires de France, 1974.

————. *Rimbaud vu par Verlaine.* Paris: Nizet, 1975.

Pichois, Claude. *Baudelaire, études et témoignages.* Neuchâtel: A la Baconnière, 1967.

Pierrot, Jean. *The Decadent Imagination 1880–1900.* University of Chicago Press, 1981.

Pierssens, Michel. *L'Ethique à Maldoror.* Presses universitaires de Lille, 1984.

Ponge, Francis. *Méthodes.* Paris: Gallimard, 1961.

————. *Le Parti pris des choses, suivi de Proêmes.* Paris: Gallimard, Coll. Poésie, 1967.

Poulet, Georges. *Trois essais de mythologie romantique.* Paris: Corti, 1985.

Prévost, Jean. *Baudelaire.* Paris: Mercure de France, 1964.

Quesnel, Michel. *Baudelaire solaire et clandestin.* Paris: Presses Universitaires de France, 1987.

Ramsay, Warren. *Jules Laforgue and the Ironic Inheritance.* Oxford: Oxford University Press, 1953.

————. *Jules Laforgue. Essays on a Poet's Life and work.* Carbondale: Southern Illinois University Press, 1969.

Raymond, Marcel. *De Baudelaire au surréalisme.* Paris: Corti, 1963.

————. *Romantisme et rêverie.* Paris: Corti, 1978.

Reverdy, Pierre. *Note éternelle du présent.* Paris: Flammarion, 1973.

————. *Cette émotion appelée poésie.* Paris: Flammarion, 1974.

Richard, Noel. *Le Mouvement décadent.* Paris: Nizet, 1968.

Richard, Jean-Pierre. *Poésie et profondeur.* Paris: Seuil, 1955.

————. *L'Univers imaginaire de Mallarmé.* Paris: Seuil, 1961.

————. *Onze études sur la poésie moderne.* Paris: Seuil, 1964.

Richardson, Joanna. *Verlaine.* New York: Weidenfeld and Nicholson, 1971.

Richter, Mario. *La crise du logos et la quête du mythe.* Neuchâtel: A la Baconnière, 1976.

Rimbaud, Arthur. *Oeuvres complètes.* Paris: Gallimard, Pléiade, 1963. (*OC*)

Roche, Denis. *Dépôts de savoir & de technique.* Paris: Seuil, 1980.

Rossard, J. *Pudeur et romantisme.* Paris: Nizet, 1982.

Roubaud, Jacques. *Autobiographie, chapitre dix.* Paris: Gallimard, 1977.

Roy, Claude. *Les Soleils du romantisme.* Paris: Gallimard, 1974.

Rudwin, Maximilien. *Satan et le satanisme dans l'oeuvre de Victor Hugo.* Paris: Les Belles Lettres, 1926.

Saint-Gérand, Jacques Philippe, ed. *Vigny. Oeuvres poétiques.* Paris: Garnier-Flammarion, 1978.

Saurat, Denis. *Victor Hugo et les dieux du peuple.* Paris: Edns. du Vieux Colombier, 1948.

Scherer, Jacques. *Le 'Livre' de Mallarmé.* Paris: Gallimard, 1957.

Scott, Clive. *A Question of Syllables.* Cambridge: Cambridge University Press, 1986.

Soulié-Lapeyre, Paule. *Le Vague et l'aigu dans la perception verlainienne.* Paris: Belles Lettres, 1969.

Bibliography

Stamelman, Richard. *Lost Beyond Telling*. Ithaca: Cornell University Press, 1990.

St. Aubyn, F. C. *Arthur Rimbaud*. Boston: Twayne, 1975.

Steinmetz, Jean-Luc. *Le Champ d'écoute*. Neuchâtel: A la Baconnière, 1985.

———. *La Poésie et ses raisons*. Paris: Corti, 1990.

Stephen, Philip. *Paul Verlaine and the Decadence. 1882–90*. Manchester University Press, 1974.

Sungolowsky, Joseph. *Alfred de Vigny et le dix-huitième siècle*. Paris: Nizet, 1968.

Swinburne, Algernon Charles. *A Study of Victor Hugo*. London: Chatto and Windus, 1886. (Fulcroft, 1976)

Symons, Arthur. *The Symbolist Movement in Literature*. New York: Haskell House, 1971.

Taylor-Horrex, Susan. *Verlaine. Fêtes galantes and Romances sans paroles*. London: Grant and Cutler, 1989.

Tetel, Marcel, ed. *Symbolism and Modern Literature*. Durham: Duke University Press, 1978.

Thomas, Jean Jacques. *La Langue la poésie*. Presses universitaires de Lille, 1989.

Toesca, Maurice. *Lamartine ou l'amour de la vie*. Paris: A. Michel, 1969.

Underwood, V. P. *Verlaine et l'Angleterre*. Paris: Nizet, 1956.

Vadé, Yves. *L'Enchantement littéraire*. Paris: Gallimard, 1990.

Valéry, Paul. *Poésies*. Paris: Gallimard. Coll. Poésie, 1974.

Verlaine, Paul. *Oeuvres poétiques complètes*. Paris: Gallimard. Pléiade, 1962.

———. *Oeuvres en prose complètes*. Paris: Gallimard. Pléiade, 1972. (*PR*) (*OPC*)

Verstraëte, Daniel. *Rimbaud*. Paris: CERF, 1980.

Viallaneix, Paul. *Vigny par lui-même*. Paris: Seuil, 1964.

Viatte, Auguste. *Victor Hugo et les illuminés de son temps*. La Ferté-Milon: Edns. de l'Arbre, 1942.

Vier, Jacques. *Histoire, substance et poésie des Fleurs du Mal*. Paris: Lettres Modernes, 1959.

Vigny, Alfred de. *Oeuvres complètes*. I. Paris: Gallimard, Pléiade, 1986. (*OC, I*)

———. *Lettres d'un dernier amour*, ed. V. L. Saulnier. Geneva: Droz, 1952.

———. *Journal d'un poète*. Paris: Edns. d'Aujourd'hui, 1981.

———. *Oeuvres complètes*. II. Paris: Gallimard, Pléiade, 1948. (*OC*, II)

Ward, Patricia. *The Medievalism of Victor Hugo*. Philadelphia: Pennsylvania University Press, 1975.

Weinberg, Bernard. *The Limits of Symbolism*. University of Chicago Press, 1966.

Winspur, Steven. *Bernard Noël*. Amsterdam/Atlanta, GA: Rodopi, 1991.

———. "Ethics, Change and Lautréamont." *L'Esprit Créateur* (Summer 1987): 82–91.

Wren, Keith. *Vigny. Les Destinées*. London: Grant and Cutler, 1985.

Zayed, Georges. *La Formation littéraire de Verlaine*. Paris: Nizet, 1970.

Zimmermann, Eléonore M. *Magies de Verlaine*. Paris: Corti, 1967.

Zweig, Paul. *Lautréamont ou les violences du Narcisse*. Paris: Lettres Modernes, 1967.

· Index ·

Index

Index

Index

Index

Index

Index

Index

· *About the Author* ·

Michael Bishop is Professor of Modern French Literature and Culture at Dalhousie University. He has published extensively in the modern field and especially the area of contemporary poetry, and edits the *Collection Monographigue Rodopi en Littérature Française Contemporaire*, as well as the new *Chiasma* series in modern French interdisciplinary studies. His major publications include *Pierre Reverdy: A Bibliography* (1977), *The Language of Poetry: Crisis and Solution*, ed. (1980), *The Contemporary Poetry of France* (1985), *Michel Deguy* (1988), *René Char. Les Derniéres Années* (1990), *Philippe Jaccottet* (1993) and he has edited various special issues of *Dalhousie French Studies*: *La Poesie québécoise depuis 1975, Simone de Beauvior et les féminismes contemporains* and *De Duras et Robbe-Grillet á Cixous et Deguy*. He is currently preparing books on contemporary French women's poetry, André du Bouchet, and modern poetry since surrealism.

NL 2/19